CASTLEREAGH

By
IONE LEIGH

COLLINS
ST JAMES'S PLACE, LONDON
1951

PRINTED IN GREAT BRITAIN
COLLINS CLEAR-TYPE PRESS : LONDON AND GLASGOW

ACKNOWLEDGMENTS

I AM much indebted to the late Marquess of Londonderry and the Marchioness Dowager for their kindness in placing at my disposal so unreservedly the Londonderry Papers at Mount Stewart and Londonderry House and in the Archives at Newtownards, and for allowing me to use unpublished material. The letters are for the most part undated, but I have included extracts in the text where they seemed relevant. I wish to express my gratitude also to the Marquess Camden for allowing me to see certain of the Camden Papers, and to Dr. Montgomery Hyde for permitting me to use various documents in his possession. The quotations from Mrs. Arbuthnot are taken from *The Journal of Mrs. Arbuthnot, 1820-1832*, by kind permission of Messrs. Macmillan.

The portraits of Metternich and Csar Alexander are reproduced by gracious permission of His Majesty the King. For those of Emily, Viscountess Castlereagh, Castlereagh as a young man and Charles Stewart I am indebted to the Marchioness Dowager of Londonderry; for the portrait of Princess Lieven I am grateful to the Director of the Tate Gallery, and for the remainder to the Director of the National Portrait Gallery.

CONTENTS

ILLUSTRATIONS

" And what shall I say of Lord Castlereagh, that spouter without beginning—middle, or end—who has not an idea in his head, nor a word to say for himself—who carries the House of Commons by his manner alone—who bows and smiles assent and dissent—who makes a dangling proposition of his person—and is himself a drooping figure of speech—what shall I say of this inanimate automaton? Nothing! For what can be said of him?"

WILLIAM HAZLITT: *On the Present State of Parliamentary Eloquence*, 1820

" From the point where we stand now, nothing is visible but the splendid outlines of the courage, the patience, and the faultless sagacity which contributed so much to liberate Europe and to save England in the crisis of her fate."

Essays by the Marquess of Salisbury, 1861-1864

CHAPTER I

I

THERE exists no more melancholy example of the disillusionment that success and fulfilled ambitions bring in their train than the life of Castlereagh. He climbed to the greatest heights. He was largely responsible for the downfall of Napoleon ; at the peace settlement he placed England in the forefront of the nations; he became the arbiter of Europe; royal sovereigns courted him; but these things brought him hatred and calumny—and destroyed him.

He has come down to us in the pages of history as a cold, lifeless automaton, as a cruel, efficient machine, as a heartless, malignant fiend; but searching through the few personal letters that remain to us, the love letters to his wife, the affectionate correspondence with his brother, Charles, the mention of him by his friends and by his enemies, and all the evidence that we can gather concerning him, there emerges gradually a human being, gentle, kindly, cultivated, a nature affectionate, constant, tender; and all the vituperation and abuse seem to be entirely the work of political enemies.

Castlereagh had the grand manner. In an age of exaggerated extravagance his tastes were simple, his dress was simple, he had exquisite style. Even in the days of his triumph, at the Congress of Vienna, when he suddenly appeared among the envoys in their splendid uniforms and decorations wearing his ordinary dress-coat, with only the Star of the Garter gleaming on his breast, Talleyrand was forced to exclaim: " *Ma foi, c'est distingué.*"

He was distinguished; he was all that was elegant and courtly; and he was handsome. With soft brown hair, steady, observant blue eyes, a sensitive mouth beautifully moulded, and a noble carriage, he was a graceful, attractive figure. And no one dreamed, when war broke out between England and France, with Pitt standing securely at the helm, that the strength, perseverance and wise statesmanship of this fastidous young Irishman would bring about the ultimate defeat of Napoleon; nor did anyone surmise that before he was thirty, he would crush rebellion in Ireland with an iron hand, and bring into effect a measure which would call down on his head forever the bitter curses and the undying hatred of his countrymen.

It was Castlereagh who brought about the Union of Great Britain and Ireland, and for this statesmanlike attempt to solve a problem which is still unsolved, he was never forgiven. From the passing of the Act of Union until his dying day he was persecuted with a fury which must have made his life intolerable, and which did not cease even when he was laid in the grave. " Ireland will never forget the statesman of the legislative union," runs the inscription on Castlereagh's tomb in the Abbey.

Ireland never did forget it. She surrounded his name with calumnies, though none of them bear examination. She denounced him for his cruelties, although the cruelties he is alleged to have practised during the Irish Rebellion even Lord Brougham, his political enemy and sternest critic, declares to be entirely unfounded. " Far from partaking in these atrocities," Brougham states, " he uniformly and strenuously set his face against them." He thought him a man of cold temperament and determined character, but not of a cruel disposition. " And to him more than perhaps anyone else," Brougham asserts, " was owing the termination of the system stained with blood." [1]

But he had the Irish against him, and they make passionate enemies. He had the Whigs against him, and they wrote the histories. He had the poets against him, and their inflamed imaginations were responsible for all the cant phrases remembered by those who never stopped to examine their truth.

He was a poor speaker, and could not, like Canning, make his impress upon the pages of history with a single phrase; yet when he entered the Cabinet, his grave common sense, his unobtrusive ability, his perfect integrity, won for him more confidence than all the brilliance

[1] Brougham's Historical Sketches of Statesmen of the Reign of George III.

of his famous rival. In spite of the paucity of his phrases, Brougham, who took a delight in collecting all the slips he made, declares that the gallantry with which he would stand up to the most brilliant debaters, made him upon the whole "rather a favourite with the audience whose patience he was taxing mercilessly." "Nor can anyone have forgotten," he observes, "the kind of pride that mantled on the fronts of the Tory phalanx, when their chosen leader stood forth, and presenting the graces of his eminently patrician figure, flung open his coat, displayed an azure ribbon traversing a snow-white chest, and declared his high satisfaction that he could now meet the charges against him face to face, and repel with indignation all that his adversaries were bold and rash enough to advance."[1]

Strangely, after all the malignant attacks on him, come the words of his most bitter opponent, the great Irish patriot, Grattan, who, as he lay dying, said to his son: "Don't be hard on Castlereagh. I beg you not to attack him, for he too loves Ireland. The Union is passed, the business between me and him is over, and it is for the interest of Ireland that Lord Castlereagh should be minister."

That he saved Ireland from French domination and from the horrors of civil war, that he gave her a peace and tranquillity she had not known for six hundred years, these things were forgotten. The Irish fastened on him an odium that blackened his memory all down the years, and from which his reputation has only of late years been rescued.

When the long war with Napoleon was over and Castlereagh returned from the Congress of Vienna, where he had settled the affairs of Europe with such distinction, the House of Commons to a man rose and cheered him. But the people soon forgot that he had pulled them through the war, that he had defeated the tyrant, and brought them through the dark years to victory. It was not his fate to retire with his laurels still upon him; he remained in office through the darker years that followed. After any great struggle the peace years are more difficult to bear than the war years. The heroics are over, the glory is passed, but the privations continue. A wave of crime that had to be stemmed swept over the country. Murder, robbery, rioting had to be put down, law and order restored. Castlereagh was blamed for the severity with which this was done, and before long an English mob too was shouting for his blood. Shelley was writing:

[1] Brougham's Historical Sketches of Statesmen of the Reign of George III.

" I met Murder on the way,
   He had a mask like Castlereagh,
   Very smooth he looked yet grim,
   Seven bloodhounds followed him."

Byron, not to be outdone, joined in hot pursuit:

   Cold-blooded, smooth-faced, placid miscreant,
   Dabbling its sleek young hands in Erin's gore.

Castlereagh faced the outcry cool and unruffled. Outwardly he turned to stone, but within him suppressed emotions wrought on his mind, till, in a fit of despair and depression, brought on by years of endless toil and the ingratitude which was its reward, aided perhaps by some psychological disturbance which hastened the disintegration of his reason, he sought release from the black nightmare that his life had become.

In the life of Castlereagh, so lonely and tragic, so disciplined, so strong and purposeful, we have the history of England during a struggle which offers so close a parallel to our own times, that all the agony of a past world is discernible through the sad experience of our own.

2

Castlereagh was a year old when the sad fate that was to pursue him through life struck its first blow. His mother died. She had been all that was gracious and lovely, and her death was the first shadow to fall on him. All through the years he wore her miniature and a plait of her hair in a locket round his neck ; when he died it was found on him, with the word " Irreparable " written across it.

His father, Robert Stewart, had married Lady Sarah Seymour Conway in 1766. She was an English girl, charming and accomplished, the daughter of the Marquess of Hertford, Lord Lieutenant of Ireland. Her future seemed bright enough on her wedding day, when she stood before the altar in the Chapel Royal of Dublin Castle, and took Robert Stewart as her husband. It seemed to augur well for them both when, preferring the gaiety of the capital to sober Newtownards where the Stewarts lived, they settled down at 28 Henry Street, Dublin, in a house belonging to Alexander Stewart, the bridegroom's father. But their married life was to be a short and tragic one. Within two years, at the age of twenty, Lady Sarah was the mother of a child, Alexander, who died when he was barely a year old. In the very month that he died, weighed down with sorrow, she gave birth to another son, who was called Robert after his father, and who became known to the world as Viscount Castlereagh; but his fame she was never to know, for a year later, being again in childbirth, she died at the age of twenty-two with her third child unborn.

Robert was born on 18 June 1769, a year which marked the birth of two other great men, the Duke of Wellington and Napoleon Buonaparte ; curiously enough, he was to be responsible for the rise of the one and for the downfall of the other.

After his mother's death he was dispatched to Newtownards to stay with his grandfather, while his father remained in Dublin, plunging into politics in an effort to forget the dark tragedy which had suddenly overwhelmed him. In these early years Robert saw his father at rare intervals, and had to content himself with his grandfather, who was a pleasant enough person, engaged most of the time in airing Ireland's bitter wrongs or in building houses at Newtownards.

A shrewd businessman, he had bought the whole district of Newtownards and of Comber,[1] and had built there a Market House and a Market Square, long rows of houses which grew continually, and a house for himself facing the Market Cross.

It was to this house, in a sleepy little village, that Robert came, and his earliest days were passed in an atmosphere that was domestic and comfortable. Alexander Stewart, his grandfather, was apparently the founder of the family fortunes. He had been born at Ballylawn in Donegal, a district granted to the family by James I, with whom they claimed kinship, but he had moved from Ballylawn as soon as he was old enough to be apprenticed, and had established himself in crooked business in Belfast, where he prospered apace. Succeeding

---

[1] The name Castlereagh derives from the baronies of Castlereagh, or Castell-rioughe, and Ards, in which were situated the manors of Newtownards and Comber. These estates included the demesne land of Mount Pleasant, which, renamed Mount Stewart, became the family seat of the Londonderrys.

to the Ballylawn estate, he moved to London, where he did the shrewdest stroke of business of his life ; he met a cousin, Mary Cowan, who had no pretensions to looks, but who had a tempting fortune, acquired by her father when he was Governor of Bombay; Alexander married her, and it was her fortune he was laying out in real estate in Northern Ireland.

Alexander had gentle manners, a benign countenance, and political ambitions; at one time he succeeded in getting into the Irish House of Commons, but he did not stay there long. His methods were questioned, he was accused of bribery and corruption, and was unseated two months later.

When Robert was six his solitary childhood was interrupted, for his father married a second time. Again his choice was an English-woman. Again it was commendable, for he married the Honourable Frances Pratt, the eldest daughter of Lord Camden, who had become famous as Chief Justice Pratt, and as Lord Chancellor of England. She was a woman of great charm, beauty, and intelligence, but not the least of her attributes was the powerful political connections she brought her husband. It was to Alexander's house that the bride came when she left England. The bridegroom was happy, finding new perfections in her daily, and was delighted to see how soon she won the love and confidence of his son, Robert.

Alexander received her with great cordiality, and she remained under his roof until they moved to another house in Newtownards which was bought with " all the gentleman's stock of furniture." She was of an easy disposition, expressed herself pleased with the house, and agreed that it was all very convenient. Her father, Lord Camden, missed his dear " Fanny," who had been a friend and a companion to him as well as a daughter, and wrote to his new son-in-law that she left a chasm that nothing could fill.

A month or two after the bride arrived at Newtownards a strange episode occurred. She seems to have been visited by some queer affliction, and arrived home one day quite naked. This was strange enough, but her behaviour was apparently stranger; she was put to bed, and Dr. Haliday, who was called in, pronounced her " light-headed." The malady however, passed off after an interval, and does not seem to have recurred, but she was kept in retirement as much as possible after the incident.

Her father, Lord Camden, paid a visit to the Stewarts at New-townards before the year was out. He was full of forebodings regarding the American Colonies, which we were then in process of losing, and talked with some concern about the line George III and his Government were taking. In his lighter moments he conversed with young Robert, whom he found highly interesting. They became firm friends and after he left, Robert engaged in a correspondence with him, inquiring apparently "in a very pretty letter" how to make a magic-lantern.

When he was eight it was decided that he should go to school. Camden, who was greatly interested in "his friend, little Robert," was consulted on the subject, and replied: "Whether a private or public education is best has long been an undecided controversy ; but I am sure an education at home is the very worst, and I speak after great experience and observation. Robert is a charming boy, and has excellent natural parts, but if he grows up under your roof, he will be utterly spoiled."

With a father who was always in Dublin, concerned with Parliamentary matters, or else "roaring and toasting" at the Down Hunt, a stepmother who was kindly and sympathetic, but who was ever in a state of bearing a child, or recovering from the effort—for in that age of fecundity she was blessed with eleven—with spinster aunts adoring him, and grandfather Stewart indulging him, school seemed a very necessary step. But he was not a strong child, and it was thought better to keep him in Ireland than send him to Eton.

His father had now been returned for County Down in the Whig interest. He was living at this time in Dublin with his friend Lord Charlemont, the great Irish patriot, who spurred him on night and day; he was also deeply engaged with Grattan, whose extreme views and whose influence Fanny feared. She found Grattan a respectable man, but violent, and wished her husband was "less an Irishman." She loved England, and all that England stood for, and she feared greatly that Alexander was a rebel, and that all the family hated England.

The desire for independence was increasing every hour in Ireland, and it filled her with concern. Her husband she found reasonable and liberal enough in most matters, but in politics no rock was ever so immovable. It did no good to argue with him, for when she ventured

C.   17   B

her comments on political questions he would laugh and bid her look
to her nursery. But he wrote to her twice a week from Dublin, filling
his letters with accounts of debates and Cabinets at Charlemont's,
which seemed to occupy him completely. She was afraid that her
father might be influenced by her husband's views, and wrote to
Camden that she hoped he would stand up in defence of England to
the last; she did not want him to be accused of partiality to Ireland.

3

In this atmosphere of Irish polemics and English sympathies Robert
grew up, and it is not surprising that his loyalties were divided: for
these divided loyalties were implicit in his parentage and environment.
All the years of his childhood and early youth were spent in Ireland,
where his family had been settled for so many years, but though he
was Irish by birth, on his mother's side he was English, while his
ancestors were Scottish. Out of this tangled skein the threads of his
character were woven; the solid virtues of the Englishman and the
Scot were added to the charm and quick intelligence of the Irishman,
and his love and respect for England lay as deep in his heart as his
affection for Ireland.

He was now on his way to the Royal School of Armagh in the charge
of a tutor, but he wrote home from school that he was "still a true
American," his interests at the age of eight being entirely with the
Revolutionists. Ambition already stirred him, for writing about his
studies, he remarks : "No boy shall get above me."

After a year or two at Armagh the tutor who had been sent with
him fell ill, and a young divinity student, John Cleland, whose
acquaintance Robert had made at Newtownards, was appointed in his
place. The Rev. John Cleland's connection with the Stewart family
was to last throughout the whole of Robert's life. Writing of him
in later years, Cleland describes him at the age of ten, when he was
committed to his care, as a "sickly, enfeebled child, and wasted in his
left arm by an Issue long previously applied." "He had been under
a Regimen of medicine," he continues, "and it was for the care of
his health I was selected to take charge of him. And thus rearing him
from his childhood, and such a state of weakness and debility, naturally

excited in me an affection and attachment which could not otherwise have been effected." [1]

In 1781 Robert's grandfather, Alexander Stewart, died, and his father inherited an estate about four miles distant from Newtownards, on the shores of Lough Strangford. It was richly planted with trees, and abounded in bays, creeks and islets, but there was as yet no house, and the family lived in four stone and slate cabins on the sea shore, while "Mount Stewart" was being built. Robert was twelve, and must have found it exciting to be living in a cabin on the edge of the sea. He could go sailing and fishing. He could go for long rambles along the beach and listen to the birds. He could lie in his cabin stretched out on his bed reading, or watch the mists lifting over the Mourne Mountains far away in the distance.

He left the Royal School of Armagh, and continued his studies under the Rev. Mr. Storrock, who lived in the neighbouring village of Portaferry. Mr. Storrock must have found him rather a handful in those days. On one occasion he horrified him by blowing up the remains of an old church. It was the ancient church of Ballyphilip which he and a school-fellow disposed of in this summary fashion. [2]

Camden was soon over on another visit, and Robert heard Irish politics discussed with the usual vehemence. Camden's sympathies with Ireland were growing, his visits to the Stewarts having resulted in his modifying his views a good deal. The Irish had many grievances, not the least of which was the fact that all Bills passed by the Irish Parliament had to receive the approval of the British Privy Council, while Bills passed by the British Parliament were binding on Ireland. Encouraged by the progress of the American Colonists the Irish had started an agitation for legislative independence. It was 1782; England was seriously occupied with America; she was at war with France and Spain, who were helping America in her struggle for independence. When Ireland appealed for troops to repel a rumoured French invasion, she had been told by the British Government to deal with the menace

[1] Londonderry Papers. Unpublished.

[2] Annals of the Parish of Portaferry. (Diocese of Down and Connor. Ancient and Modern. Vol. I.) In these Annals, the Church is described as being "so close and firmly cemented that it does not appear to admit water" which suggests that it was an old pagan temple converted into a church. Owing to the fact that they did not admit water, these buildings never decayed, and but for Castlereagh's boyish frolic the ancient church of Ballyphilip would probably still be in existence.

as best she could. In this way the Volunteers had been formed, with the result that Ireland's demand for independence was now backed by eighty thousand men under arms. When Camden returned to England he supported Ireland's claim. "The present demand from the Parliament of Ireland," he declared, "only echoes the voice of a brave, a generous, and an *armed* people; and I dread what might ensue if its justice, or expediency, is questioned."

Wise counsels prevailed, due chiefly to Britain's precarious situation, Ireland's claims were conceded, and a new Independent Parliament was formed in Dublin. "Ireland is now a nation," Grattan cried.

Towards the end of 1784, Camden, who had resigned his seat as Lord Chancellor twelve years before, took office again. The Stewart family received a letter from him saying: "I ought likewise in common decency to write to you now, if it was only to inform you that I am this week to be declared President of the Council. The papers say I am to be an Earl." He was not very enthusiastic about entering the Cabinet. "The pleasantest circumstances in opposition, and for which I always loved it," he wrote, "is that it has no secrets and requires no hypocrisy, whereas a minister never pulls off his mask, nor opens his mouth."

Robert's father hastened to send his congratulations. He was delighted with the new Honours, for he was ambitious to become a peer himself, and Camden had promised to use all his influence on his behalf. That same year, unfortunately, he lost his seat in the Irish Parliament, but far from abandoning his political pursuits he became one of the leading spirits in the Volunteer movement. He raised a regiment in County Down called the Ards Independents. They agitated in Dublin for parliamentary reform, but did not get it. Although the Irish had gained their legislative independence they still suffered from grievous disabilities. Pitt who, at the age of twenty-four, had just become Prime Minister, wished to placate them, but he had to proceed cautiously. He brought forward a measure to remove the duties on imports from Ireland to England, and after a great deal of opposition in the House, and much vexation, for all the English manufacturers were against it, the Bill with certain amendments was ultimately passed. But it was received with such little enthusiasm in the Irish Parliament, whose members were irritated by the amendments and thought it degrading to be dependent on the

British Government for the regulation of their commerce, that it was never put into operation.

Camden, who had supported it with all his might, began to feel disillusioned with Ireland. At the end of 1785 he was writing: " I sometimes think of Ireland, but never with pleasure, for though we in England have taken the utmost pains to court her goodwill, we receive no return but distrust, jealousy, and almost defiance . . . they have not the least affection for the sister kingdom, which they ofttimes mention with scorn and anger, and scarce ever with civility."

4

In spite of these views, in 1786 he was again in Ireland. Robert was now seventeen, and his grandfather found him a delightful companion. They had great arguments, and he thought Robert an excellent debater. He was also a good listener, and enjoyed Camden's conversation, and his knowledge of affairs. They were both musical, and Robert, who was a fine 'cellist, played for him gladly. But a serious accident occurred while Camden was at Mount Stewart, which distressed him deeply. Robert, who spent a great deal of his time on the lough, had set out for a sail one day with Henry Storrock, his tutor's son. It was a fine morning, and they were sailing along in bright sunshine, when a squall of great violence, such as frequently comes down on this part of the coast, suddenly hit the boat. She heeled over on her side, and " overset." The boys were three miles from the shore and in the greatest danger. Storrock could not swim at all, and Robert knew very little of the art, yet he managed to keep himself and young Storrock afloat on the water for over an hour. Storrock's father and Mr. Cleland were looking out of the window of the Temple, a small octagonal building in the grounds, when suddenly they missed the vessel. The two reverend gentlemen flew down to the beach, and put off in an open boat to the rescue. They were only just in time. When they reached the boys, Storrock was completely unconscious, and Robert had lost the power of his limbs, and almost his sight, from the coldness of the water.

At Mount Stewart the episode is inscribed on a picture of the lough put there by Robert's father. It ends with the words: "Let not these particulars of a deliverance almost miraculous pass without just emotions of gratitude to the Almighty Preserver, and let it teach a due reliance on his Providence in the greatest of dangers."

For a while the water did not attract Robert as much as before, but he soon got over his unfortunate adventure, and was again to be seen sailing up the lake, steering amidst its hundred islands. Often he would land on an island, kindle a fire under the trees, and cook the widgeon or rabbit he had shot, or the fish he had caught. Sometimes he would sleep under the awning of the boat, and return home in the early morning.

5

It was a happy carefree existence that Robert lived in these days ; the world was not treating him as ill as it was to do in later years; but the easy flow of his life was soon to be interrupted, for Camden, interested as ever in his future, advised his father to send him up to Cambridge. The thought of a university career had already entered Robert's mind, for though he loved hunting and shooting and sailing, and all the sports of manhood, he had a mind that subjected itself to pitiless self-examination, and he had already come to the conclusion that he was sadly ignorant. And so, in the autumn of 1786, he left the salt breezes of Mount Stewart and the blue mists of the Mourne Mountains, and all the beauty of the Irish countryside. He took leave of his step-mother and her brood, which by that time numbered eight, and accompanied by his father he set out for England.

Before term started he paid a visit to Lord Hertford, who was delighted with his " grandson Stewart," and described him to Horace Walpole as a " prodigy." He invited him to visit Sudbourne Hall again at Christmas, an invitation which Robert's father accepted for him. Robert had been hoping to visit Lord Camden in the holidays, but this intention, as he informed Camden's daughter, Lady Elizabeth Pratt, was " entirely knocked up." Apart from his affection for the old statesman, he had formed a very deep attachment for Camden's eldest daughter. She was many years his senior, but he loved her with an adoration that a young man will often conceive for a woman of mature years. On his very first day at St. John's, the 28 October 1786, he was writing to her:

" MY DEAREST LADY ELIZABETH,

Being now compleatly settled at St. John's, and become a house-keeper, I sit down, this being the first night I ever spent in my own house, to thank you for your letter and neckcloths. . . . I am sorry to tell you, my Dr Lady Elizabeth, my intended visit to Camden place at Christmas is entirely knock'd up, my intention was to have gone and spent the first part of the vacation with my grand-father and afterwards to have gone on to you, but my father thinks it necessary I should remain at college in the Holydays, only as Lord Hertford made it a point that I should visit him at Christmas I am to go there for a week, so that all our schemes are at an end. I am sorry for it but it can't be help'd. I have a great deal to tell you, which shall be the subject of a future letter; altho' I am not to see you, pray don't forget me, but place me the 18th in your list of correspondents.

ever yours affecly.

R. STEWART "[1]

He lived a quiet life at Cambridge in spite of all the temptations it offered. Although his health had improved greatly since he had lived at Mount Stewart, he was never very robust, and even had he had the inclination, he would not have had the stamina to enter too heartily into the social life of the university. This was not altogether a disadvantage, for Cambridge in those days was the seat not so much of learning, as of debauchery, gambling, duelling, drinking, and excesses of all kinds. Robert was never a drinking man, and though the tall pale youth with his courteous manner and grave blue eyes excited attention, and he received invitations to many a festive meeting, he preferred to stay in his rooms reading, rather than drink himself under the table with the noblest. He did not shun pleasure; but gambling, drinking, and eating were never his idea of pleasure. He was also bent on passing his examinations.

" Of late," wrote Wordsworth, who was at St. John's too at this period, " hath beer also contributed not a little to produce plucks.

[1] Londonderry Papers.

For indeed beer is a good thing for making the mind heavy and loaded." He must have agreed with Wordsworth, for he took to drinking lemonade in great excess, and applied himself to his studies. In the first terminal examinations he did not do very well, but though men of rank were not expected to study hard, Robert, when he found that study was necessary to his academic reputation, laboured in mathematics and classics " like a poor man whose industry was his only fortune." [1]

He missed his dear friend, Lady Elizabeth, and wrote to her constantly. She had been on many visits to Mount Stewart, and they had played duets together, and had long and intimate conversations which still lingered in his memory. He had never enjoyed talking to anyone as completely as he enjoyed his talks with her; he confided in her all his ambitions and all his disappointments, all his hopes and all his fears. He was now planning again to see her in the holidays, but his father decided against a visit to the Camdens on account of Robert's health. Writing to Lady Elizabeth, Robert said: " You are good enough to say that you regret my absence. Be assured that I feel the separation most sensibly. The time I have been with you has been some of the happiest of my life and I would willingly purchase a repetition of it, at the price of bad health." [2]

He was suffering from an inflamed throat and a slight temperature at this time and, prescribing his own treatment as he loved doing, he put himself on a vegetable diet " to allow nature to recover its tranquillity under the lighter pressure of vegetable sustenance." He found his health improved under this system, and his temperature went down.

It is interesting to find him prescribing for himself a vegetarian diet in an age when doctors seemed to prescribe bleeding for every ailment.

He was to spend the summer in Ireland, and when term was over he made eager preparations for his journey home. His trunk burst several times before his servant Joe was finished with the packing, but eventually he got off. On the way he remembered a debt which he had left unpaid, and conscientiously enclosed a bank note in a letter to Lady Elizabeth asking her to settle it for him. The devil, he wrote

---

[1] Londonderry Papers. Camden to Robert Stewart, Castlereagh's father.

[2] Londonderry Papers.

to her, must surely have reminded him of it, to make him go to Ireland as poor as possible. He enjoyed the journey home. His carriage and four horses rolled along the countryside in the summer sunshine and he was enchanted with the scenery. He was travelling with a college friend, and they lingered on in Wales because they could not force themselves to leave so much beauty. They amused themselves listening to bards by the roadside, and rolling great stones down immense precipices. Robert was hoping to find a letter awaiting him at Holyhead from Lady Elizabeth, but he was disappointed.

At 11 o'clock at night, with a storm blowing up and rain pouring down, he was rowed out to the packet boat which was to take him to Dublin. Wet to the skin, he went to bed immediately he got on board, but was as sick as possible before they even set sail, remaining in that miserable state for eighteen hours. He wrote to Lady Elizabeth from Henry Street, Dublin, saying: " We arrived at the quay about ten, from whence we proceeded, with as many things as the customs house harpies would permit, to the first Irish hotel I ever made trial of, and trust that I shall not again have occasion to revisit it. . . . Yesterday we dined at Lord Moira's, cordial and kind to the greatest degree, Lady Granard I believe I should fall in love with, if it was lawful." [1]

He was happy to get to Mount Stewart, and to be idle for a while. He went riding round the estate with his father. He went sailing down the lough again, shooting again. According to Dr. Felton Reede, who claims to have known the family intimately for thirteen years, he " did not always confine his shots towards the feathered race." [2] Apparently he wooed and won a fair maid under the protection of Lord Charles Fitzgerald, whom he was in the habit of visiting on his excursions, and he was duly requested to give an account of his attentions. Declining to do so he was called out. The meeting took place on a small, rocky island near the harbour of Ardglass, and a couple of shots discharged without effect ended the affair. The moment the duel was over he set out to join his father at a shooting party. They had a good day, and were sitting over their wine in the evening, when an express arrived with news of the duel.

[1] Londonderry Papers.

[2] Felton Reede, *Private Life of Lord Castlereagh*, reprinted in *Observer*, 18 August 1822.

Astonished and dismayed, his father called on Robert to explain. Robert coolly replied that he had a vague recollection of the matter, but as it had happened in the early morning the particulars were already erased from his mind.

In the autumn he was back at St. John's, but though his health was again troublesome, and he went through the term strenuously dieting, he managed to come first in the first class, during what proved to be his last examinations; for Camden, who had become alarmed at his recurring symptoms, persuaded him now to come to town and get medical attention. He feared some constitutional weakness, and was relieved to find from the doctor's diagnosis that the trouble was " no more than the usual consequences of a young man's indiscretion." [1]

For a few months Robert stayed with Camden and they enjoyed each other's society more than ever. Camden's conversation always gave Robert the greatest pleasure, and improved his mind, he felt, " more than any intercourse with books could have done." " Stupidity itself," he declared, " must steal something from hence." [2]

When he left Camden, and returned to Mount Stewart, the question of a career arose. It had long been in his father's mind that politics was the sphere for Robert, but Robert did not find himself particularly fitted to take an active part in politics, for he was not in sympathy with any of the parties in Ireland. He thought long and deeply about the subject, for if he were to make politics his career, he must eventually attach himself to some party. But he could come to no conclusion. The more he considered the Irish parties the more his apprehensions increased. He knew that he would come to no decision until his feelings were composed, but his mind was in a complete turmoil. An attachment to a party, as he informed Lady Elizabeth, was " the only means by which a disposition that required some degree of encouragement" could advance; but he was so decidedly opposed to the principles of all the Irish parties that even were he to act with any of them, he felt that he would only wish them to fail.

"The service of Government here," he wrote to Lady Elizabeth, " is too irksome even to make it desirable to be employed, therefore I

[1] Camden to Robert Stewart, Castlereagh's father. Londonderry Papers.
[2] Robert Stewart to Lady Elizabeth Pratt. Londonderry Papers.

shall continue for some time in my present state of inactivity—possibly grow sick of it—and return to philosophy, a pursuit which, I am convinced, is infinitely more productive of happiness to the person engaged in it."

He had thoughts of going to London for a while, but Camden, whose advice he sought, was not encouraging. "Would you come to London and plunge at once into all the profligacy and dissipation of this vile metropolis," he wrote back, "or would your father be easily brought to give his consent to such a change?" And he advised him to return to St. John's for another year or two. But Camden had once said to him: "You may study books at Cambridge, but you must come into the great world to study men." Robert preferred to take the latter advice, and to leave academic honours to others.

He never returned to Cambridge. He spent his time on the lake again, he joined his father's regiment of Volunteers, he paid another visit to the Camdens. He loved Camden's quiet courtesy, his easy kindness, his gracious manner; he admired the cultivated and polished atmosphere of his home; and he was overjoyed to see Lady Elizabeth again, to be playing duets with her, and having long and intimate conversations that never seemed to end.

In the evenings he did the round of parties and assemblies with Lord Bayham, Camden's son. Lord Bayham was a Junior Lord of the Admiralty. He was a modish young man who spent most of his time lounging in the windows of Brooks's or Almack's, riding in the park or driving his smart phaeton at break-neck speed, to the terror of all pedestrians. At one time Camden had feared that his son thought only of cutting a figure, and that he had little regard for the state of the country. But he was now twenty-nine, and married, and had sobered a good deal. Robert at the age of nineteen admired him greatly; he went to hear him speak in the House of Commons when he supported Pitt over the Regency question. The year 1788 was an anxious year for England, for the King, who had been seriously ill, was now declared insane, and the Prince of Wales, debauched, reckless, irresponsible, was to become Regent. Pitt was determined to limit the Prince's powers, for he was not only a man of deplorable habits, he was also the unofficial Leader of the Whigs, the rallying point for all those who criticised the Government and jeered at the King.

Fortunately, before the Prince could take over the reins of Government the King recovered, and Pitt's Ministry was saved.

While he was in London, Robert went to the House frequently and listened to many of the debates. He followed the trial of Warren Hastings, which had just begun, and Camden was interested to see how he pursued the evidence with the same concentration that he gave to everything that engaged his attention. In Camden's opinion Robert had a mind that would adapt itself to any sphere of life that he might be placed in ; his talents were universal. " He was equally formed," he thought, " either for public or private life, though he would naturally be impelled rather to the éclat of the former station than the obscurity of the other. He had a fine head for reasoning, and a fluent elocution." He could write both prose and verse with ease; he could play the 'cello as well as any. He could speak in public. He could be, in fact, whatever he chose—" a philosopher if he pleased, or a mechanic "—he was fit for anything. The only thing now wanting, he felt, was " to direct his pursuits to some great and noble end," to which, after the irregular flights of youth were abated, his own judgment and ambition would naturally lead him. His discretion for his years seemed remarkable. Apart from his talents, he possessed " those qualities which make men beloved in private life—humanity, good nature, liberality." [1] Such a person the shrewd, discerning Lord Chancellor of England found Robert at the age of nineteen, and he did his best to direct him towards a public career. Many were the discussions they had together, and on most subjects they agreed; only when it came to Ireland was there discord.

To Lady Elizabeth, Robert once wrote: " I have written to Lord C. I should have done so before, but it seldom is in my power to say anything on Irish Politicks, in which we are perfectly agreed, and I had rather risk an opposite discussion in conversation, than on paper." [2]

For the moment, however, his feelings had found a new outlet in a boyish passion for Mrs. Jordan, the beautiful Irish actress who charmed crowds nightly at Drury Lane. She was twenty-six, had one child by her first marriage in Ireland, four children by Sir Richard Ford, and was to have ten more by the King's son, H.R.H. The Duke of Clarence, whose mistress she became two years later.

[1] Camden Papers.   [2] Londonderry Papers.

Robert never missed a night of her acting and, according to Camden, he saw "The Romp" and "Richard Coeur de Lion" twenty times. But his passion was interrupted by a sore throat, which started up a temperature, and kept him indoors. Confined to the house, he gave himself up almost entirely to music, finding solace and comfort in his 'cello. To Lady Elizabeth it must have been a joy to have him at her side again, unburdening his heart to her, enchanting her by a hundred small graces, sharing with her the sweetness of intimacy, talking of his future, of his aspirations, finding in her warm sympathy some healing for the unrest in his soul. He possessed so many proofs of her regard; they added, as he once wrote to her, additional charms to the sentiment which united them.[1]

He was still undecided as to his future career, still distracted about parties and politics. In England he admired Mr. Pitt, and all that his grandfather, Camden, stood for. "I have the highest opinion and confidence in Mr. Pitt as a Minister," he wrote to Camden, "I have also a strong prejudice and persuasion of the virtue of an administration into which you enter." Like his grandfather he was for the British Empire and constitutional liberty; and yet in Ireland he was opposed to the British Government's policy, his leanings being towards the Whigs. It is little wonder that his mind was disturbed and distressed and that he thought the pursuit of philosophy and music a far happier state than the pursuit of politics. But he was to be swept into the political arena, whether he wished it or not, for when he returned home, Ireland was getting ready for her General Election : his father, who had in this year, 1789, been created a Baron,[2] being unable as a Peer to stand again for County Down, suggested that his son, now the Hon. Robert Stewart, should stand in his stead. Intelligence, ambition, noble birth, influential connections, dignity and discretion had already marked him out for a public career, and at the age of twenty he overcame his qualms, and stood for Parliament as an Independent member, backed, as his father had been before him, by the Whigs and Dissenters.

It cost him a great deal of trouble to get into the Irish Parliament; it cost him physical strain and agony of mind. It also cost him over

[1] Londonderry Papers.

[2] He chose as his title "Baron of Londonderry," Londonderry being the county where the original family estates were situated.

£60,000,[1] for he was opposing Lord Downshire, who was almost a reigning prince, and who had hitherto controlled both seats in County Down. But the very canvass, and the plunging into such a scene as an Irish Election with its noise and riot and tumult, its clamour and its flow of abuse, gave him a fair insight into the tempers and dispositions of men, revealing to him how far he could trust them, teaching him how to meet calumny.

His father, in his intense desire for his son's success, mortgaged his home and his property to the hilt in order to raise the funds required, and Mount Stewart remained unfinished for many years.[2]

6

Robert hardly knew what had tempted him to engage with so much eagerness in the contest he had just fought, but as he entered the Irish House of Commons he was greatly moved; he felt a proud satisfaction at being a member of that august body whose task it was to govern Ireland.

Seated under that grand and solemn dome he could see about him the most gifted men of the day, the ablest orators, the most elegant courtiers; and with these he was now associated. He was just twenty-one. He had fought the election at the age of twenty, and had

[1] This sum has been questioned by some authorities, but I discovered the actual mortgage sheet for that amount in the Archives of Lord Londonderry's Estate Office at Newtownards, proving the expenditure.

[2] It has been asserted that the house was never finished during the lifetime of either himself or his eldest son and that he lived in confined quarters for the remainder of his life, but this can hardly be the fact since there exists in the Archives of Lord Londonderry's Estate Office at Newtownards an inventory left by Castlereagh's father in 1821, according to which the house contained six reception-rooms and twelve bedrooms at the time of his death. This can hardly be termed " confined quarters." The statement is probably due to a note which has been added to the Castlereagh Correspondence published by Castlereagh's half-brother Charles, according to which Castlereagh's father lived the remainder of his life in " *an old barn* with a few rooms added." The Inventory is pretty conclusive evidence of the fallacy of this statement, and suggests that the note was added at some later date in error.

only been allowed to take his seat because he had turned twenty-one before the House met.

Hitherto his life had been comfortable and easy; now the gravest responsibilities rested on him; and his mind was burdened by the fact that he had not yet come to any decision as to the line he meant to pursue. The true aim of statesmanship is the prosperity of the State, and he was convinced that the prosperity of Ireland was linked with that of England; but he came of a family which had always acted in opposition to the British Government; he also owed it to his electors to vote with the Opposition. He was greatly attached to Mr. Pitt, yet he was " thrown into a situation where he was precluded from affording him that support which his feelings inclined him to give."

He was under no illusions about the Irish House of Commons. It was a corrupt House, the majority of whose members were either in the pay of the Crown or servile followers of great landowners. It was a Protestant House, for the Catholics, who represented three-fourths of the population of Ireland, were not allowed to vote or to sit in Parliament. In such a circle of legislators Robert was ill at ease, and listening to the impassioned speeches of his countrymen he felt afraid for Ireland. He found himself between contending forces of the greatest intensity, among religious extremists whom he could neither understand nor bring himself to support, for though he was Protestant it seemed to him the inalienable right of all men to think and worship as they wished; though he was Protestant he always favoured Catholic Emancipation. Writing to Lord Bayham on the subject he said: " Education it is our object to impose on them— their priests will ever resist instruction which must weaken their control. Intermarriage it is impossible to prevent, and equally harsh and unnecessary to forbid. Allowing them to have apprentices is an act of justice. The bar alone weakens the system of self-defence, which we, the minority are obliged to adopt." [1]

He was strongly in favour of concessions to the Catholics, and yet at this time he was against the franchise, an important concession which they were soon to obtain.

Seeking advice from Camden, whose wisdom had guided him throughout his life, he received a letter from the old Lord Chancellor suggesting that he should for the time being reserve his opinions and

[1] Londonderry Papers.

proceed with caution; it was not necessary for him to give decided views, except on questions where he was pledged, but although he was Independent, as everyone knew, there might be no harm in his professing himself a friend of the Pitt administration. Robert followed his advice, and when he rose to make his maiden speech he praised the honesty of Pitt's intentions, words which did not fall pleasantly on Opposition ears; and if there were some like Dr. Drennan who found him " a most promising young man, one of the handsomest in the House, and perhaps one day to be the most able," [1] there were others who eyed with suspicion a man who voted with the Opposition, and at the same time mentioned Pitt with sympathy and admiration. Political difficulties were already gathering round his head, demanding from him courage, patience and judgment; but these qualities he had never lacked.

7

When the House was up, instead of spending his time in Dublin with the other members, drinking five days a week, he returned to Mount Stewart and spent the time quietly at home. While he was there a curious adventure befell him. He had been out shooting all day, and the pursuit of game had taken him so far that he had lost his way. Night descended, a storm blew up, and being far from home and uncertain how to get back, he presented himself at the nearest house. Sending in his card, he asked for shelter for the night. The hospitality of the Irish country gentry is proverbial, and he was warmly received, his host inviting him to join in the festivities that were proceeding, promising him good shooting if he would prolong his visit for a few days, though he regretted that the house was so full that he could not make him as comfortable as he could have wished. Robert thanked him for his courtesy, and joined the party. Later in the evening, when he was retiring for the night, the butler conducted him to a large room, which looked as though it had not been in use for some time, but there was a blazing peat fire in the grate and a couch made up for him to sleep on, and being very tired after a long day, he stretched himself on the couch and was soon asleep.

[1] Drennan Letters.

In the middle of the night he woke suddenly, startled by a light that seemed to come from the chimney. The fire was out, and yet there was a light shining right across the room. He sat up in bed sharply, and was startled to see on the hearth a beautiful naked boy with a dazzling radiance about him. The boy looked at him earnestly for a moment, then the vision faded and all was darkness again. For the moment he was stunned, but he soon recovered himself and decided that his host or some of the visitors had been either amusing themselves at his expense, or trying to frighten him. The thought of this annoyed him so much that the next morning at breakfast he maintained an icy reserve, and announced his intention of departing immediately. His host remonstrated with him, reminding him of his promise to join the shooting party, but Robert coldly excused himself. As his host pressed for an explanation, he told him of his nocturnal adventure, observing that in his opinion practical jokes were quite unwarrantable with strangers. His host in deep concern summoned the butler and asked him where Captain Stewart had slept the night. The butler replied that he had slept in the " Boy's Room," as it had been the only one vacant. It was a room which he had been forbidden to use under any pretext, for it was haunted by the " radiant boy ";[1] and there was a tradition in the family that to whomsoever the "radiant boy " appeared there would come great prosperity, followed by a violent death.

The story of the " radiant boy " is well known in Cumbrian lore, and there are reports of his having appeared in other houses in Ireland. Sir Walter Scott, to whom Robert once related his experience, told Lady Holland in after years that only two men had told him they had actually seen a ghost, and both had put an end to themselves.[2]

8

At the age of twenty-one Robert was going through the emotional experiences common enough to youth. Although there was about him a kind of shy reserve which made him easier in the society of

[1] *Haunted Houses* by C. G. Harper, 22 December 1824.

[2] Lady Holland's Letters to her Son (1821-45).

men, he was not unattracted by women. At eighteen he had been ready to fall in love with Lady Granard, "if it was lawful." His passion for Mrs. Jordan had taken him to the play twenty times, though there is no evidence to prove that he ever got any nearer to the adored one. Dr. Felton Reede,[1] who asserts that "his Lordship was very gallant and always partial to female society," divulges an *affaire* with Nelly Stoal, who was apparently a maidservant living with her father in a small farmhouse on the farther side of the Stewart estate.

According to Reede, her naïve charm attracted Robert and, sailing on the water daily as was his custom, he found it a simple matter to visit her and gain her affections. She was pretty and petite, and was often to be seen in a white frock and coral beads walking demurely beside him. In his small boat rigged as a cutter, they made many excursions together amid the islands of the lake.

Soon he was building a little cottage on one of the rocks projecting out to sea, for a child was born to them, Reede asserts, to whom Robert was entirely devoted ; and there with Nelly and his infant son, his books and a serving boy, he took up his residence.

He did not pay many visits to Mount Stewart at this period, and his father began to grow uneasy about him, but his friends would often visit him in his remote little cottage. There was dancing on the green, picnics, music, and conversation ; life was simple, and he was content. In the beauty and perfect peace of these surroundings he lived an idyllic life.

But a life of idle pleasure would never satisfy for long a youth of Robert's temperament, spurred as he was by ambition and conscious of his abilities. It was 1791, and the world was moving to a crisis. Everywhere about him men were exulting in the French Revolution. Freedom had come to an oppressed people. But Robert's cool mind questioned everything. Who knew whether it were indeed liberty for the people, or a new tyranny of the people? Who knew where it would end? Who knew to what shores it might spread? In Ireland the mob was as inflammable as the rabble of Paris, the people as downtrodden; they were only too ready to follow the lead which France was giving; already they were aflame with revolutionary ideas. As in Paris, so in Dublin, it was a time when depravity and luxury

[1] *Private Life of The Marquess of Londonderry*, by Felton Reede.

ruled the great, and hunger ruled the poor; for in contrast to the fashionable quarters, where the English Viceroys and their suites were housed in splendour, there was the Dublin of the slums, mean, wretched, neglected, displaying its open sores. Half the inhabitants were in rags, many of them without shoes and stockings; the polish and elegance of the privileged classes could not hide the dirt and squalor that scarred the face of Dublin. Added to the poverty were the religious disabilities and all the abuses which a nation living in subordination to a corrupt government must necessarily suffer. It was the material that revolutions feed upon.

Robert was only too aware of the distress that prevailed in his country. The way it was governed he had never liked, but he preferred even the Irish Government to a revolution.[1] With the French doctrines gaining ground he felt that there was more necessity than ever for its amendment, for the people were beginning to clamour. The Catholics were calling for emancipation, the Protestants for complete independence. He feared that the Catholics might ally themselves with the discontented Protestants, and then what tumult would arise?

He hoped Ireland would escape the distresses that France was doomed to suffer; he still believed she could only escape with the help of Great Britain ; but it was a bad thing, he felt, " that the connection between the two countries must be preserved by abuse, and that they must be contented to live in subordination and corruption." [2] " Let us for God's sake have a liberal settlement," he wrote to Camden, " it will, I am persuaded, unite more cordially the two countries, will deprive a vindictive opposition of their ground of attack, and attach to government many men who now wish them well, but cannot act with them as a party on constitutional points." [3]

When the House met, he was in his place, voting again with the Opposition, for he was more than ever opposed to England's government of Ireland. The Lord-Lieutenant was deeply dissatisfied with his attitude, and before long a letter was dispatched to Whitehall with the Lord-Lieutenant's complaints and a suggestion that the grievance should be carried to Lord Camden, " who ought to be responsible for this gentleman's conduct." Grenville, the Home Secretary, replied

[1] *Charlemont Correspondence.* Letter from Robert Stewart to Camden.
[2] *Charlemont Correspondence.*
[3] Londonderry Papers.

that he had " the strongest assurances from Mr. Stewart's connections
of his real desire to give support where he can do it consistently with
the engagements to which his contest forced him." Grenville wrote
also to the Chief Secretary, Major Hobart, suggesting that he " might
contribute to fix him in the right way." Major Hobart's reply was
not reassuring. " I should have felt a real pleasure," he said, " in
contributing to fix in the right way a young man certainly of talents
and of very pleasing manners, but let the representation of his conduct
be what it may, take my word for it he is a decided enemy of the
King's Government in Ireland; and perhaps a more dangerous one
from the circumstances of his English political connections being such
as to warrant his professing himself a warm friend of Mr. Pitt's
administration in England."

Robert, in spite of his discretion, was getting into trouble all
round. The Lord-Lieutenant was complaining to Whitehall because
he always voted *with* the Opposition. Dr. Drennan, his former
admirer, was finding him " a half-blooded fellow " and the " meanest
of the human race " because on occasion, he voted *against* the
Opposition. He now received a communication from the secretary
of the Northern Whig Club, of which he was a member. The
Northern Whig Club was also dissatisfied with him, finding his
propensities " quite too English." Robert himself had long been
dissatisfied with the Northern Whig Club, finding its principles far
too revolutionary.

Replying to the secretary he made his position very clear. " I
have observed the temper," he wrote, " and the turn of mind of this
country long enough to discover one truth, that if we wish to preserve
internal harmony and external respectability, above all it is our object
to remain connected with Great Britain."

" Where is the successor to Great Britain? " he asked, " if we
detach ourselves from her? Is it France? That pile of ruins! That
melancholy example of misapplied philosophy, of political experiment
and popular delirium! Are we prepared to tear asunder the ties of
interest, affection, blood, constitution, everything nearest to our hearts
and dearest to our senses which unite us to Britain? "[1]

And yet, in spite of these sentiments, he was still voting against
the Government. The Chief Secretary complained again of such

[1] Londonderry Papers.

ungrateful behaviour in " the son of a Peer who had been so recently honoured." But Robert was not one of those who could be bought, and he continued to vote with the Opposition at every division.

9

The disturbing rumours which came from France exercised his mind a great deal, and during the year 1791 he decided he would go to Paris and find out for himself what was happening. When he set foot on the Continent, he heard, as he wrote Lady Elizabeth Pratt, that there was " scarcely a dissenting voice in France. Nay I am told," he continued, " in the provinces they openly profess their wishes for a republican government, think the King a useless expense, and wish to get rid of him."

He stayed for a while at Spa, where a small society of refugees had found a brief haven of refuge. It was an exclusive circle of French aristocrats, who were still living under the shadow of the Revolution, but living with charm and gaiety and elegance. Robert enjoyed their picnics and their drives; he enjoyed their free and unembarrassed conversation. But when they talked proudly of their return to power, it must have surprised him to find that their pride had not been softened by misfortune, that they took no account of the changed conditions that were beginning to prevail, and that they expected to return to France without giving up one degree of all that they had previously possessed, that even in exile and seclusion they carried their pride with them.

The Spa waters, he wrote to Lady Elizabeth, did him a great deal of good, but he soon tired of " the indolence they impose," and left Spa for Paris. When he arrived he called on Madame de Staël, to whom he had a letter of recommendation, but though she received him very cordially, and asked him to sup with her once a week, he found her enormously ugly, and feared he had not sufficient French to appreciate her for her wit. His knowledge of French was actually quite serviceable, but it always embarrassed him to speak the language, and in Madame de Staël's presence he felt a greater coward about it than ever. He noticed that she distrusted her husband, whom he rather liked, and that her admirer was a " bishop with two club feet." [1] The

[1] Londonderry Papers.

bishop was probably Talleyrand, known at that time as the Bishop d'Autun. He had been lame from childhood, but seemed nevertheless, in an age of scandal, to have created quite a stir, counting Madame de Staël amongst his many conquests. It is surprising that his name meant so little to Robert at the time that he does not even mention it; he was to make a greater impression on him in later years.

While at Paris, Robert went to Court, and saw the King and Queen, whose tragic end was so soon to come. The beautiful Marie Antoinette seemed in very good spirits, and nobody had any suspicion that their Majesties were on the eve of that sad flight from the capital, which was to end in their arrest. The contrast between their court and ours amused him; his audience did not last two minutes, he wrote to Lady Elizabeth, and he was not spoken to. " Visitors never are upon the whole," he added, " it is better than making such a torment of it as we do."

He also attended some of the sessions of the National Assembly, and saw history in the making. Robert was not carried away with the French Revolution like so many Englishmen of his day. He did not rank it as the noblest work of human integrity and human wisdom. He had a cool intellect, and took a long view. It seemed to him that once the over-heated minds of the French people had calmed down and their delirium abated, they would be disappointed in the blessings they expected from their new Government, but he discovered, in what they had done, much to approve as well as much to condemn.

" I feel as strongly as any man," he observed, " that an essential change was necessary for the happiness and for the dignity of a great people, long sunk in a state of degradation. I lament that those in whose hands the fate of their country devolved aimed at accomplishing so much more than could be effected at once without introducing confusion."

He applauded the aspirations of the people which had led to so unparalleled a change, but he could not approve the principles of the revolutionary leaders. He was convinced they were unsafe. " I trust," he said, " that no country in which I have either stake or affection will follow their example."

But his country was already following their example. Earl Camden, writing to him, observed, " I am afraid your Kingdom has caught the spirit of the National Assembly. You will remember a famous epitaph of a man who killed himself with physick. 'I was well. I wanted to be better. I took physick and died.' I wish your countrymen would make the application."

When Robert returned home he found his country in as great a ferment as the Continent. Even the Northern Whig Club, of which he was still a member, had been celebrating the anniversary of the fall of the Bastille, the Volunteer Companies marching through the streets with banners flying and drums beating, followed by the members of the Whig Club wearing the green cockade.

It seemed to Robert that the government under which Ireland suffered would no longer be endured, and he feared that unless a change were effected England would lose Ireland altogether. The Irish were beginning to show undisguised hostility towards Great Britain and expressing the utmost contempt for the British. Robert saw the storm clouds gathering and felt that the coming tempest was being met by the English with nothing but ignorance and incapacity. He feared the lengths to which a distracted and turbulent people might go; he knew how difficult it would be to lead them back to order once the spark of rebellion had been fired.

New demands were being hurled at the Government, a new outcry arose, and at length the English Parliament began to wake to the fact that there was an Irish question. Though Pitt rejected the Irish demands as extreme, he felt it necessary to pass a measure freeing the Catholics from the worst penalties under which they suffered.

In 1793 they were given the franchise and certain other civil rights; but though they were allowed to vote for Members of Parliament, they were still disqualified from holding a seat. Three-fourths of the population, which was Catholic, was still to be represented by a Protestant Parliament—a Parliament which did not even represent the Protestants, for the members were chosen by a few landowners who controlled the elections. Nor did it alleviate matters that Parliament had no control over the executive government, which was exercised by the Lord-Lieutenant, who was an Englishman, appointed by, and responsible to, the English Ministry. As Grattan said, Ireland was governed by "responsible officers who were not resident, and resident officers who were not responsible."

Reviewing the position Robert wrote to his grandfather, saying: "Depend upon it, my dear Lord C, you must change your system with respect to Ireland; there is no alternative now her independence is admitted but to govern her by reason, or unite her to Great Britain by force. A middle path will not do. . . . Give Ireland such a government as your own. When she abuses it, depend upon it you will find a union a much more practicable measure; but as to continuing the present system, depend upon it, it is no longer possible. . . . It would require less force to unite the two kingdoms than to govern as heretofore."[1] The question of a Union he was broaching at a time when scarce anyone in Ireland would have been found brave enough even to mention it in a whisper. Pitt, however, had long had the question of Union in his mind, but he was occupied at the moment with more pressing problems; he was striving to prevent England from being drawn into a war which was ultimately forced upon her.

10

From across the channel uneasy reports continued to arrive: the King and Queen of France had been put under restraint; Austria and Prussia were arming. France believed that she could keep England neutral, and with England neutral, she could manage the rest of Europe. Pitt's attitude strengthened her in this conviction, for Pitt was affecting a complete ignorance of what was happening in France; he was even discontinuing armaments, and was trying to lull the nation into a feeling of security, maintaining in the face of everything his attitude of absolute neutrality. It is not surprising that in April 1792, Chauvelin, the French Ambassador at the Court of St. James, was instructed to secure not only the neutrality of England but, if possible, her friendship and alliance.

In the first efforts of the French nation England had exulted. "How much," Fox had cried, " is this the greatest event that ever happened in the world, and how much the best."

In 1791, Thomas Paine published *The Rights of Man*, and political societies were formed for the rights of humanity. The influence of Paine was spreading through the towns and weaving districts, and Pitt was growing alarmed. But when, in April 1792, France invaded

[1] Londonderry Papers. Dated Dublin, 26 Jan. Probably 1793.

Belgium, he did not move: he only demanded that Holland should remain untouched.

In this same month, Robert undertook another journey to the Continent. With France and Austria at war, however, he took the precaution of staying in England for a few weeks in order to see what course events would take.

The reports of the early engagements between the French rabble and the Austrian troops were not alarming. At Lille the French had fled at the first sight of an Austrian sentry; they had run off and murdered their General. At Verdun the French Commandant had committed suicide, and the fortress had surrendered. By the autumn the Austrians were marching on Paris.

There seemed no reason why Robert should postpone his journey any longer, and in September 1792, he proceeded to Brussels, writing to Lady Elizabeth that he intended staying till December when she would be finished with Bath. But he did not stay till December, for the situation suddenly reversed. Dumouriez, the French General, barred the Paris road at Valmy, outwitted the Austrian commander, and completely routed his armies. The cannonade of Valmy, Goethe declared, announced the birth of a new era.

It did not surprise Robert " that Frenchmen should fight with spirit, all men will do it, when their passions are brought into action," but he was amazed that " undisciplined recruits," of which the French army was principally composed, " should be capable of resisting the first troops in Europe in pitched battle," [1] that an army of 100,000 of the finest soldiers should flee in disorder before the untrained boys and ragamuffins that France had sent against them. The Austrians and Prussians had disgraced themselves entirely, and were now engaged in throwing the blame on each other, while twenty thousand French emigrés, who had fought by their side, were returning to the Low Countries to starve.

The emigrés bore their misfortune with more fortitude than Robert could have imagined, recollecting the gay, heedless charming circle he had met at Spa. Robert did not go on to Paris, as he had intended, for the city was now in the hands of the mob. In September of this same year, 1792, they had broken into the prisons and massacred

[1] Londonderry Papers. Letter to Lady Elizabeth Pratt. Dated " Mt. Stewart, 23." Probably written in 1793.

41

the prisoners, which shocked British public opinion to the core. They had then, by the Decree of November 19, offered their assistance to all nations revolting against their rulers, which shocked even the British Government ; but Pitt did not move.

Robert watched events with growing concern—the Austrians and their allies were falling back, the French advancing—and when, in November, a French victory at Jemappes laid the whole of Belgium open to the enemy, he departed for home. All the English left Brussels; for although England was not at war with France, the situation was delicate. In August, when the King was taken prisoner, the British Ambassador had been recalled from Paris, and diplomatic relations broken off.

II

When Robert returned to England he found the Government and the Court as casual as ever. In spite of the thunder clouds rolling towards the shores of Great Britain life was going on in the same easy way. The Prince of Wales was still engrossed in his love affairs. Having quarrelled with his mistress, Mrs. Fitzherbert, a fat but charming woman of forty, with a set of not very good false teeth, he was now flirting with Lady Jersey, who had reached the dangerous age of grandmotherhood.

The poor King in spite of lucid intervals was mad as the winds, which was not to be wondered at, considering his unfortunate family.

The Prime Minister, who for the past year had been asserting, in a mood of sublime but exaggerated confidence, that " unquestionably there never was a time in the history of this country when, from the situation of Europe, we may more reasonably expect fifteen years of peace," was busily engaged in cutting down the army and dismembering the navy. In Parliament there was only one voice raised in warning; but vainly did Edmund Burke, the old statesman and orator, urge the Government to send help to Austria and Prussia before it was too late.

Burke was perhaps the only politician in England who from the first had eyed the events in France with doubt and misgiving. Though he had always been on the side of humanity, justice and liberty, he was perhaps the only one who discerned the difference between liberty and licence. But Burke, like Robert, was an Irishman, and knew only too well the psychology of violent mobs, and to what excess they could be driven by unscrupulous leaders.

The dandies at White's laughed at his large spectacles, his ill-fitting brown coat and bob-wig, his brogue that reminded them of " whisky and potatoes," but his " Reflections on the French Revolution " had already influenced public opinion. Liberty meant chiefly security of life, property, and opinion, he preached ; and he roused the attention of the English political classes to the dangers of the French Revolution, as Paine roused the passion of the weavers and carpenters for its ideals.

As the year 1792 drew to a close, many statesmen began to share Burke's apprehensions. Fox, however, remained faithful to his early convictions, and passionately proclaimed that the Revolution was essentially just, and should not be condemned for its errors, or even its crimes.

The Prime Minister, with great composure, averted his gaze, ignoring the French Revolution as though there were nothing more stirring taking place in the world than his budget, with its new tax on maidservants, and its excise on tobacco. His desire was for everything to be cheap and pleasant, for trade to prosper, and bad harvests to be abolished. Determined to avoid war with France, he expressed his conviction that she was too occupied with her internal affairs to be in a position to interfere with England for long years to come. With superb indifference he continued his peace policy in the face of all provocation.

Even a month before war was forced upon the nation, in a stormy parliamentary session he was still refusing to present an ultimatum to France. Burke rose in all his strength, and declared that war with France was necessary for the security of English liberties, for the well-being of Europe, and for the happiness of mankind. Already, he cried, the infection was spreading to these shores.

Sneers of derision greeted the announcement. Glaring at the offenders he drew from his coat a concealed dagger, and flung it on to the floor of the House. That dagger, he said, had been made in Birmingham. Three thousand of them, he happened to know, had recently been ordered by a disaffected Englishman. It was a characteristic weapon. It was an instrument of assassination.

Sheridan, the boon companion of the Prince of Wales, spoilt the dagger effect entirely by asking where the fork was.

"It is my object," Burke continued, "to keep the French infection from this country, their principles from our minds, their daggers from our hearts. I vote for the Bill, because I consider it the means of saving my life, and all our lives, from the hands of assassins. When they smile I see blood trickling down their faces; I see their insidious purposes; I see that the object of all their cajolery is—blood."

There were a few guffaws. There were suggestions of panic-mongering. Sheridan accused Burke of having lost his taste, of having become the slave of pantomimic gestures and contemptible conjuring tricks, filling his pockets with knives in order to lend point to his impassioned orations.

The Prime Minister remained unmoved. France had already annexed Savoy, Nice, the Austrian Netherlands, the Rhine Provinces, Belgium, even Antwerp—that pistol pointing at the heart of England. Pitt's only reply had been to send weak protests that were ignored. Few Ministries would have remained passive in the face of so much provocation. After their occupation of Belgium the French declared the Scheldt open and, encouraged further by Pitt's attitude, began preparing an invasion of Holland, in spite of the Treaty of 1788, which compelled England to go to the help of Holland if attacked. Still Pitt did not move; he merely registered another protest.

Even as late as December 1792 he had an interview with Maret, afterwards the trusted servant of Napoleon, in which he expressed a sincere desire to avoid a war which would be fatal to the repose and to the prosperity of the two nations. The only question which really disturbed him was the invasion of Holland. Maret assured him that instructions had been sent to Dumouriez to be circumspect in his conduct towards the Dutch and to make no attack either on the sovereignty or the privileges or the independence of that people. The next day, however, Maret apparently declared: "Peace is out of the question. We have 300,000 men in arms. We must make them march as far as their legs will carry them, or they will return and cut our throats."

The resumption of diplomatic relations, which had been broken off in August when our Ambassador was recalled, was pressed on the

Government by the Opposition; but events were moving rapidly towards war.

On the last day of December Pitt took a sterner tone with Chauvelin, the French Ambassador, informing him that the Decree of November 19 encouraged disorder and revolt in all countries, even in those which were neutral, that his Government would also never see with indifference that France should make herself sovereign of the Low Countries or general arbiter of the rights and liberties of Europe. If France were really desirous of maintaining peace and friendship with England she must renounce her views of aggression and aggrandisement and confine herself in her former territory without insulting other Governments, without disturbing their tranquillity, or violating their rights.

Three weeks later, on 23 January 1793, there came news which sent a shudder through the whole of England and a cry of horror and indignation. Louis Capet, King of France, had been executed. The following day Chauvelin was bidden to leave the Kingdom. William Cowper, who had felt a lifting of the heart in the first year of the Revolution, was now saying: " I will tell you what the French have done. They have made me weep for a King of France, which I never thought to do, and they have made me sick of the very name of liberty, which I never thought to be." [1]

The whole nation went into mourning. The curtain was rung down at all the playhouses. And when George III drove out of his palace his carriage was surrounded by angry mobs demanding war.

The King was now quite as impatient as his people with the cool, impassive attitude of the Prime Minister, who continued as ever to assert that war might still be averted. But now at the eleventh hour Pitt took the precaution of calling out the Militia, and even brought himself to the point of giving orders for warships to be put in commission. Darkness was closing round that solitary and stubborn figure and the war clouds that had long been gathering were breaking over his head.

As soon as Chauvelin reached Paris and reported his dismissal, France declared war on Holland and Great Britain. Pitt blandly announced that we were going to war to secure the

[1] Correspondence of Cowper—letter to Wm. Hayley, 29 Jan. 1793, quoted by Brown : *French Revolution in English History*.

Dutch in their possession of the Scheldt, which the French had now declared open to navigation against all Treaty obligations.

" A war for the Scheldt," exclaimed Burke. " A war for a Chamber-pot." The war was a crusade, he cried, upon which England must embark in order to repair an outrage against the moral order of Europe. " France is out of itself," he declared. " The master of the house is expelled, and the robbers are in possession."

It was the first day of February 1793. It marked the opening of a war which, in spite of Pitt's forecast that it would be over by Christmas, lasted for over twenty years. It was the beginning for England of a life and death struggle, during which the odds were generally against her, and her very existence was at stake. It was the end of the eighteenth century.

With its glitter of beautiful women, of witty and accomplished men, with its highly privileged society of culture and elegance, its intellectual movement for the perfection of human reason, and its profound enthusiasms of the heart, the eighteenth century was dying. It had enjoyed its last golden fling.

The old society, gallantry, wit and elegance were to be swept away, making room for the solid Victorianism which was to follow, for the cold, frugal, orderly way of life, which was no doubt a necessary astringent, but surely a chilling one. For what the new era gave in strength and virility hardly compensated for the richness and beauty it took away. The man who did not exist in the eighteenth century, said Talleyrand, did not know " *la douceur de vie.*"

Robert, who was destined to play so great a part in this changing world, had all the elegance, the tradition, the grace and breeding of the era which was passing. But his life was to be filled with unremitting toil, his fate was to be mingled with the creation of Empire and the doom of peoples, and all the glitter and gaiety of the eighteenth century were to pass over his head.

CHAPTER II

I

IN IRELAND Robert pondered over the situation. A letter had arrived for him from Bayham, Lord Camden's son. The French had laid an embargo on all British ships, he wrote, and the Navy was manning as fast as possible. It was War.

Lord Edward Fitzgerald, who had recently returned from Paris bringing with him a French wife,[1] had been informed by French Ministers that if war broke out between England and France, a landing in Ireland would be made. If there were a landing in Ireland, many Irishmen, Robert feared, would go over to the enemy. The Government was persuaded that the United Irishmen, a Society which had been formed in 1791, were sending emissaries to France. Lord Edward Fitzgerald himself was under suspicion. He was a charming person, young, ardent and enterprising; he was a patriot, who loved his country deeply; but he had just been dismissed from the army on account of his violent opinions, and had ruined a fine military career.

Robert did not doubt that there would be trouble; there might be civil war; for the Irish could never see salvation for themselves without broken heads. They hated England with the greatest bitterness and could never understand that Ireland was bound to rise or fall with Great Britain.

The fact of war seemed to crystallise all Robert's opinions; he felt now that his first duty was to give Pitt all the support he could, that he must direct his efforts first and foremost towards saving his country from France.

[1] Pamela, believed to be the daughter of Madame de Genlis by Philippe (Egalité), Duke of Orleans.

The January session of the Irish Parliament had opened a few days before the news arrived. He summoned his carriage and went down to the House. War was an ugly business, and none knew that better than Mr. Pitt, who had striven so hard to avoid it. But the French Revolution was like a contagious disease, the whole world was becoming infected by it. As Robert's coach passed slowly into College Green, where the Irish Parliament met, he scanned the crowds that had gathered there to see the members dismount. How ready they were to take their vengeance on any member of whom they chose to disapprove, how eagerly they would tear *him* to pieces if he incurred their displeasure; but he had not as yet incurred their displeasure, and he passed on unmolested.

Dressed as ever with extravagant simplicity, he looked extremely handsome as he entered the House. His hair was cut below the ears, framing the clear-cut features, the firm chin, the grave blue eyes. Dr. Drennan, watching him from the gallery, could not forbear the remark that he was " a proud aristocrat under the garb of great mildness and complaisance." But Dr. Drennan was one of the founders of the United Irishmen, and Robert's growing moderation and discretion did not please him. Nor was he pleased with Robert's frivolous reply to him, when, setting up in Dublin as a general practitioner and accoucheur, he had solicited the young member's patronage. Robert had answered that he did not know how to further his interests as an accoucheur, but was however his humble servant. It was a neat reply, and should have amused Dr. Drennan, but he never forgot it; it deterred him in later years from writing a similar letter to Fox, who would be capable, he felt, of replying in the same vein.

The House seemed strangely excited, Robert noticed, as he took in the scene. The Lord-Lieutenant had issued a proclamation disbanding the Volunteers, who might have become a menace to England in those distracting days, and an address of thanks was being moved to him for his action. There was a heated discussion, and Robert, rising to support the Government, passionately denounced the French Convention, which had gone to the length of executing its King. " Robert Stewart will be the shadow of Burke against France," said Drennan.[1]

[1] Drennan Letters.

Robert had hardly sat down again when a tall, dark young man jumped up. " I give my most hearty disapprobation of that address," he exclaimed, "for I do think that the Lord-Lieutenant and the majority of this House are the worst subjects the King has."

It was Lord Edward Fitzgerald. A general uproar ensued, the galleries were cleared, and the young man was required to apologise at the bar of the House. He refused to do so, but on the following day, after a good deal of pressure, he was persuaded to make some kind of apology. The utmost he would consent to say, however, was that he was sorry he did not understand the rules of the House. Being a brother of the Duke of Leinster and a nephew of the Duke of Richmond, being also an extremely popular member, his apology was accepted and he was allowed to resume his seat. His rash temper, however, soon got him into more serious difficulties, and his young life was to end most tragically a few years later.

For the moment his turbulence served to awaken the Government to the seriousness of the position in the country, where conspirators were meeting daily, planning to break off all connection with England, and to help France in an invasion of Ireland.

The possibility of such an invasion was not overlooked by the British Government. Pitt sensed the danger, but his first step, the conscription of a Militia in Ireland, threw the Irish into an even greater ferment. Though it was fiercely resisted Robert gave the Militia Bill his support. Being an unpopular measure in the north of Ireland, he wished, as he wrote to Camden, " to bear his full share of any odium that might attend it." Pitt had chosen the wrong moment, he thought, for an experiment which might be " hazardous at so critical a period," but once it was established he was the first to admit that it had succeeded, and hoped that " the full benefit would be drawn from so fortunate an effect." [1]

He was one of the first to apply for a commission, and in April 1793 he was gazetted "Lieutenant-Colonel of the Londonderry Militia." The announcement brought him a letter from his grandfather, reproaching him for entering into a " rash, and what my cold blood would call an inconsiderate engagement, which might have been avoided without any imputation of deserting the public."

Londonderry Papers.

2

Before the session was over Robert was in camp. Route marches and musketry practice, the enrolment and training of recruits were now the order of the day. But these activities did not keep his mind from dwelling on the dangers that surrounded Britain. News had come in of the retreat from Dunkirk, and had left him gloomy and apprehensive. It was Britain's first engagement, and it was not an auspicious opening to any campaign. The wretched remnant of the ten thousand men who had followed the Duke of York to the Netherlands in the summer of 1793, thinned by disease, maimed and half-starved, were retreating. Dunkirk had been a failure, our Prussian and Austrian allies were falling back again towards the Rhine, and men were singing:

> " Oh the rare old Duke of York,
> He had ten thousand men,
> He marched them up to the top of the hill,
> And he marched them down again.
>
> And when they were up, they were up,
> And when they were down, they were down,
> And when they were only half-way up
> They were neither up nor down."

Incompetent generalship was at the root of the evil; it had always been the bane of England. The men fought well enough, but the generals could not utilise their courage; and to place the lives of ten thousand men in the hands of one of the King's deplorable sons was nothing less than criminal. The Duke of York's main qualification for his position seemed to have been his capacity for drinking six bottles of claret at a sitting.

There was a story current that during the attack he had been entertaining the pretty and vivacious Lady Elizabeth Webster,[1] who had just returned from Dunkirk. She had been sitting alone with the

[1] She was later to become the famous Lady Holland.

Duke in his tent after dinner, she relates in her memoirs, unaware that an attack was imminent, and was surprised to hear suddenly a pattering noise like rain upon the canvas of the tent. She was more surprised when a messenger arrived out of breath to inform the Duke that the outposts were fighting, and had been driven in, and that a general attack might be expected. The news had filled her with terror, and the Duke was quite angry at the messenger's indiscretion in causing her alarm. He informed the messenger that he knew perfectly well what was happening, and had, out of consideration for his guest, concealed the news from her. Attacks apparently were incidental compared with the entertainment of fair ladies.

Lady Elizabeth was in a panic, " and fairly clung to the Duke for comfort." Whenever an officer entered, and whispered some information to him, and he gave an order, she was in " such a state of tremor " that he said nothing should be done but openly, and thenceforward gave his orders aloud, so that she might hear distinctly. He began to inveigh against the Duke of Richmond for not sending the Ordnance, and against the Artillery officers at Ostend, who had a habit of sending the carriages down the canal in one vessel and the cannon in another so that they never arrived together. His language of censure was unqualified. But he remained the soul of gallantry and asked his fair companion to choose the watchword. As she was too terrified to think of anything, he gave " Elizabeth and Success."

To prevent her hearing every volley that was fired, he ordered his band to strike up, and it played till some hours after midnight, when he sent her home with an escort of light dragoons. None too soon, apparently, for " no mobbed fox was ever more put to it to make his escape than we were," wrote Major Calvert, one of the Duke's officers. The Duke of York himself escaped by galloping in front of his two escort squadrons of dragoons in a chase over hedge and dyke, the Star of the Garter gleaming on his breast. He had abandoned his guns and most of his stores, had been chased out of Flanders, and was now being pursued ignominiously across Holland.

It was a strange way of conducting a siege, but the English were a strange people; they never prepared for war, they never took it seriously, and they never doubted the result. All their preparations were haphazard. Even now there was no plan, there was no concentration of policy or of forces. The Cabinet were still continuing with their stately deliberations, still employing their antiquated methods, still engaging the enemy with their text-book technique.

The war would be over by Christmas, Pitt had said. He was now beset by the fear that French agents were busy everywhere, that secret clubs and societies were striving to establish revolutionary principles in England. It had started him off on a burst of panic legislation. "And this man," Macaulay tells us, "whose name, if he had been so fortunate as to die in 1792, would have been associated with peace, with freedom, with philanthropy, with temperate reform, with mild and constitutional administration, lived to associate his name with arbitrary government, with harsh laws, harshly executed, with alien bills, with gagging bills, with suspensions of the Habeas Corpus Act, with cruel punishments inflicted on some political agitators, with unjustifiable prosecutions instigated against others and with the most costly and most sanguinary wars of modern times."

There was evidence enough of French agents in England, in Scotland, and in Ireland. Even as far off as India they were infecting the native Princes with their theories. But Pitt was exaggerating the danger; he had introduced Bills restricting the liberty of public meeting, the freedom of the press; he had extended the powers of the Statute of Treasons. He was at a loss to deal with the position. Pitt was a man of very extraordinary abilities, but he was a Peace Minister. What England needed was a *War* Minister, one who would develop all the resources of the country, and bend every effort towards the crushing of an enemy whose strength was an ever growing menace.

A few months later, as the year 1793 came to a close, news reached Robert of the surrender of Toulon. He took up his pen and wrote to his grandfather: "The only thing, my dear lord, which really dispirits me in this unprecedented struggle of order against anarchy, is the unfortunate facility with which France recruits her army as fast as the sword exterminates it. . . . A few days transform their raga-muffins into troops, which are not contemptible, even when opposed to the best soldiers in Europe. . . . A defeat is soon repaired, and its effects counteracted by the endless fortifications which protect their frontiers. In short, my dear lord, I do not like a retreat to which we have been driven, because I know it produces a mechanical effect on our enemy and gives them a most formidable confidence in themselves. The present moment seems so critical that I cannot be at rest. The tranquillity of Europe is at stake and we contend with an opponent whose strength we have no means of measuring. . . . What may be the result is beyond my perception."[1]

Robert was no believer in peace by Christmas. "Their mode of carrying on war is so new and so alarming," he informs Camden, "that were their attention not distracted by internal dissension, I should tremble lest they might set a force in action which nothing could withstand."[2]

3

Robert spent his leave at Mount Stewart, and enjoyed being amongst his family again. By this time children were growing up all about him, there being no fewer than eleven of them ranging from one year old to sixteen. Charles, the eldest of his brothers, or rather half-brothers, was Robert's favourite, and a friendship grew up between them that lasted throughout their lives, and was never troubled by the shadow of a quarrel. Charles, who was to enter the army, was guided always by the judgment and foresight of Robert, who extended to him an affection and a protection which not only helped him to climb to power, but which rescued him from many a tight corner, for Charles's escapades were legion. He was as tactless and as vain as his brother was wise and discreet.

Most of his leave Robert spent cutting down fir trees, putting up a tent which commanded a view of the sea and the distant hills, and joining the children in dog and duck parties. "Wells has made a very clever arbour for the children, where we had this evening a true dog and duck party of syllabub, curds and cream," he wrote to his aunt, Lady Elizabeth.[3] But his happy humour was suddenly dispelled by news that Earl Camden, who had been ill for some time past, was rapidly sinking. He had a great affection and respect for his grandfather, or more properly speaking, for his stepmother's father, and the news disturbed him profoundly. A snuff-box arrived for him containing a small lock of white hair, with a note inside. It read: " A

[1] Londonderry Papers. Letter undated, but probably written in December 1793.
[2] *Idem*
[3] *Idem.*

poor memento to remind you after I am gone of the constant love I ever bore you, since I can't help claiming you (if my vanity can be excused in taking to myself one of much nobler descent) as one of my own children."

Camden had always taken so great an interest in his career. When on his advice he had gone to Cambridge, his grandfather had said: " It will teach you to respect England and to love Ireland, for I wish both countries united by as strong a tie as your family and mine." To unite England and Ireland. If only that could be accomplished. One day it might be, but Camden would never see it.

When he had wished to leave Cambridge, the Earl, who had discouraged the idea, emphasising the advantages of a university education, had said to him: " I would not trouble you with these observations, if I did not wish to have you produced into the world of men with better accomplishments than other men of fashion as they are called. Your natural talents are excellent. Cultivation will make you perfect." But politics had claimed him, and he had cut short his university career in spite of his grandfather's admonition.

His father had nearly ruined himself to get him into Parliament, so much had he believed in him. His grandfather believed in him too. Taking a sudden decision he departed for London to pay his last respects to the dying.

It was an anxious journey, and he arrived to find his grandfather in a sad condition. He had just been brought back from Brighthelm-stone, where the Brighton waters had failed to cure him, and he sat "helpless in his chair, dosing from morning till night and never attempting to utter a syllable." [1]

But after a while, as Robert sat beside him, he began to take notice of his grandson's arrival, and showed the pleasure it gave him. Robert lingered on in London. In the daytime he sat with the old man, in the evenings he did the usual round of Assemblies with Lord Bayham, the Earl's son.

Robert declared he had not brought a very full wardrobe with him, but when he presented himself in the evening, his cocked hat under his arm, his attire was faultless, and Bayham congratulated him on his air of distinction. Bayham, ten years Robert's senior, was

[1] Haliday to Charlemont. Charlemont MSS.

rather short in stature, and had a tendency to corpulence, but his simple unaffected manner, his good-humoured round face, and his absence of genius made him an easy and pleasant companion. Robert thought he had " an exceptionally good head for business if he would only waste it a little more." The two of them were good company, and were welcomed at all the fashionable assemblies.

At one of these Robert met Lady Amelia Hobart. She was the niece of his commanding officer, Mr. Thomas Connolly, and the daughter of the Earl of Buckinghamshire, who had once been Lord-Lieutenant of Ireland. Lady Emily, as she was generally called, a gay, vivacious girl of twenty-two, made a deep impression on Robert. To judge from Lawrence's portrait of her, which was exhibited at the Royal Academy under the title of " A Lady of Quality," his attraction to her is not surprising. The portrait shows a beautiful girl, slim and graceful, with grey eyes and fair hair, dressed in a white frock with a blue sash tied at the waist. She may have been petulant, capricious, and indiscreet, as many of her contemporaries found her, she may have been the " fine, comely, good-natured, romping piece of flesh " that Haliday, the Stewart's family doctor, dubbed her, but Robert fell deeply in love with the fair Emily, and throughout his life his affection for her never seemed to waver.

It must have given the old Earl satisfaction to hear that Robert had formed an attachment for one of noble birth and no mean fortune, and the romance may have added a little interest to his darkening days.

4

Lady Emily was not without suitors, and Robert must have been a little disconcerted when she showed him a letter from Prince Philip Lichtenstein proposing for her hand. The letter was quite delightful, but Robert was not amused. It was written in French, and addressed to the Earl of Ancrum, the husband of Emily's sister. " In all the countries which I have visited," Prince Philip wrote, " I have never met a woman who has made on me so profound an impression as Lady Amelia Hobart. Your sister-in-law to an angelic face unites, as everybody is assured, so many lovable qualities that it would be strange if I were the only one who was sensible of them. I am resolved to undertake everything to make myself worthy of her; without your generous assistance, however, I feel I shall not succeed. With the exception of my face, which is certainly not very distinguished, and which is only too often a badge of introduction among ladies, there exists no advantage of rank, of birth, of illustrious alliances that I am not able to offer her as much as anyone in the world. As to the immense fortune of our family it is too well known to talk about. It is true I am the youngest of three brothers, but all the same I have at the moment an income of two thousand louis and it looks as though in a few years I shall have nearly five thousand. I beg you to inform Lady Emily's mother of my intentions and to speak in my favour, to tell her I shall employ all the moments of my life to render her daughter happy, and be assured of my eternal gratitude.

"Many of your compatriots would find in my being a foreigner a motive for exclusion, but I have too much faith in you to believe that you would share an objection so barbarous and unjust.

"The most serious objection would be an aversion for me or an inclination for another—these would cause me much pain but would not diminish my tender respect for her." [1]

The letter had its effect on Robert, for he proposed soon after, and was accepted. Lady Emily's family was delighted at the news. "You know I suppose how very much my uncle and aunt approve and admire your choice," wrote her cousin Harriet, "they are very well acquainted with Mr. Stewart and like him as much as you know he deserves."

Robert's love for Emily Hobart was to last till the end of his days. His letters to her are full of devotion, and prove how much warmth of feeling and sensitiveness lay hidden beneath his cloak of reserve.

"But above all," he writes to her, "tell me you love me, on that my existence depends, and I can never grow tired of hearing it."

In the midst of all the joy he felt Robert was deeply moved by his grandfather's condition, for there was no more hope for him. On 13 April 1794, before the wedding could take place, he had passed away. Overwhelmed with grief, Robert turned to Emily for comfort.

"Your heart," he wrote to her, "is too much alive not to feel for me at this moment; you have left me, as far as I am myself concerned, nothing to wish for: you have given repose to all my disquietudes

[1] Londonderry Papers.

and opened prospects of happiness which give me a new interest in life . . . for God's sake, dearest Lady Emily, continue to love me, and let me some day or other have the gratification to think that since you knew me your happiness has not diminished."

In the spring of 1794, while Robert was still in London, the borough of Tregony in Cornwall lost one of its members; the seat was in the gift of the Treasury, and Pitt was pleased to offer him the vacancy. Haliday, writing to Charlemont on 24 May, declared that the Prime Minister had " extended this munificence in the noblest manner—unsolicited and even unasked." [1]

Cornwall was the principal stronghold of the Government; it returned in all forty-four members, only one less than the whole of Scotland, sending up a solid phalanx of Crown supporters to Westminster. So that Robert, who lost no time in accepting the offer, was to come into Parliament under the patronage as it were of the Prime Minister. It was a step which alienated many of his friends in Ireland, who had long viewed with disfavour his leanings towards England, but it was consistent with the policy he had always expressed, that if Ireland was to preserve internal harmony and external respectability it was necessary above all to remain connected with Great Britain.

He set out immediately on a flying visit to Cornwall to make the acquaintance of his new constituents. Before leaving he transmitted a gift to Emily, with a graceful note.

" MY DEAR LADY EMILY,

My father commissions me to ask a favour for him, that you will accept the necklace and bracelet which my servant carries, and wear them as a very trifling mark of his regard.

Ever your most affectionate,

R. STEWART "

He also sent her a locket containing a portrait of himself painted by Cosway. It shows him at the age of twenty-five with powdered hair. A year or two later he was sending her some plaited strands to go inside the locket. Brown and soft and shining the hair

[1] *Charlemont Correspondence.*

lies behind the glass at the back of the locket, and is still to be seen
at Mount Stewart.

Robert stayed at Tregony only sufficiently long to entertain the
electors, and hastened back. Dining with Emily that evening he
confessed the perturbation in his mind at the thought of taking his
seat in that proud assembly he had always longed to join.

He was under no illusions about his powers of oratory, and he
was now to take his place among men whose oratory was unsurpassed
in any age. To take his stand opposite such giants as Fox and Sheridan
would need courage indeed, but courage was a quality which Robert
Stewart had never lacked. He had been in the Irish House of Commons
now for four years, and he comforted himself with the thought that
even though he were no orator, he had always stood his ground. He
had spoken before Grattan and Ponsonby, and had always been listened
to with respect.

Another matter that occupied his mind was the opinion of his
friends and colleagues in Ireland, and of his constituents at Down.
They would say, no doubt, that he was deserting them. But it was
no desertion. For of one thing he was certain; he would serve
Ireland as faithfully from Westminster as he had ever served her from
College Green, and who knew, he might render her even greater
service yet.

Robert found his duties at Westminster full of interest. It was
May 1794. The House of Commons was seething with excitement,
for the founder of an organisation called the London Correspondence
Society had just been arrested on a charge of high treason, documents
having been seized in his office proving a conspiracy to dethrone the
monarch and set up a republic in England similar to that of France.
Panic ruled the House, and a Bill to suspend the Habeas Corpus Act
was rushed through all its stages at a single sitting. The measure was
violently opposed by Fox. Robert watched with interest the great
Whig orator. Long nights at the gaming table, a life of unparalleled
dissipation had left their mark on that furrowed countenance with its
sallow hue, its puffy heavy-lidded eyes, its coarse heavy features; but
once he was on his feet, his bold stormy utterances, his supreme
humanity, his negation of cant and humbug, his large bountiful
sympathy fascinated the House and bore everyone away with him.

And yet it seemed to Robert that when Pitt rose, with his cool logic, his cold destructive criticism, Fox's fires burnt low, and all but flickered out. Pitt won the day, and although the Opposition forced no less than eleven divisions, the bill to suspend Habeas Corpus was passed by a large majority.

During the session Robert listened to debates on many subjects —debates on the policy of bringing the war to an end, debates thanking the managers of the impeachment of Warren Hastings, whose trial he had heard begun in 1788 when he was a boy of nineteen, and which was still dragging on. Burke and Sheridan were still fulminating against the wretched victim, Burke using all his eloquence to secure a conviction. Robert listened to his impressive flights of oratory. " It is not that culprit who is upon trial, it is the House of Commons that is upon its trial; it is the House of Lords that is upon its trial; *it is the British nation* that is upon its trial, before all other nations, before the present generation and before a long, long posterity." Not till the following year, 1795, did the Lords finally pronounce Hastings acquitted.

Robert took no part in the debate. He was not anxious to force a maiden speech on the House. He was content to bide his time. But listening to the discussions on bringing the war to an end his heart sank. It was no time, he felt, to be talking of peace, for the French were everywhere triumphant.

5

The war was in its second year. Commenting on the news, Burke cried: " Now they are bad, now good—up and down, and with them our poor hearts up and down also. Such mortals we are, depending for our happiness or misery on the last Gazette."

After Dunkirk, the French had continued driving back the allies; they had driven them out of Belgium and across Holland, in a bitter and ignominious retreat. Already they were making their wild boast that they would " dictate peace on the ruins of the Tower of London, and expose to the world the weakness of Britain's corrupting wealth."

Our only safeguard was the King's Navy, but hard on the news that the great naval arsenal of Toulon and thirty ships of the line had passed into the hands of the British Fleet had come the depressing report that Toulon had been evacuated. Pitt had failed to send Hood troops to hold the town, and Toulon had been re-taken by a young Corsican soldier, whose name was Napoleon Buonaparte.

The evacuation of Toulon with every gun firing on the blazing city from the surrounding heights was a worse picture than Dunkirk. Fifteen thousand refugees, wretched and despairing, trailed into England. And yet, a week later, Pitt was confidently asserting that there was " still a very good chance of all proving right in that quarter." Things proved far from right. Pitt tried a diversion in the West Indies, but at San Domingo the troops were decimated by yellow fever in a useless campaign where everything seemed doomed to failure.

The old King, hovering on the verge of insanity, seemed more sane, and certainly more shrewd, than his ministers. "The misfortune of our situation is," he observed, "that we have too many objects to attend to, and our force consequently must be too weak at each place."

In the Cabinet there was nothing but vacillation and hesitation. There was no decision, no initiative, no definite policy, no systematic plan.

Pitt and his jovial Home Secretary, Henry Dundas, improvised according to the needs of the hour, and when an emergency arose, rushed inadequate forces to whatever point the French chose to attack. The enemy was always left the initiative, and we remained inactive waiting for their move. "He who stays in his entrenchments is beaten," said Napoleon Buonaparte.

Henry Dundas, on whom Pitt relied when baffled by his own inexperience in the art of war, was a genial, bustling Scot, who, as Pitt would say, "had a turn for facilitating business." He had an enviable facility too with the bottle, but he had no turn for facilitating warfare. He was Pitt's boon companion, and the wits exercised their genius in lampooning the pair of them, and devising epigrams to delight the dinner-table. Some of them give an amusing picture of the leaders of the country.

PITT: " I can't see the Speaker, Hal, can you?
DUNDAS: Not see the Speaker? Damme, I see two."
PITT: " Europe's true balance must not be overthrown.
DUNDAS: Damn Europe's balance: try to keep your own."

The casual attitude of the Government was not very effective in the face of the violence of the enemy. In France, the rabble, urged on by savage leaders, many of them swayed by sadistic passions, were completely ruthless. They had destroyed their monarchy; they had desecrated their Church. In November 1793 they had held, in Notre Dame, a Feast of Reason during which a whore was elevated at the High Altar amid bacchanalian orgies.

"They make up in madness and numbers what they want in discipline,"[1] Robert had written to his grandfather towards the close of 1793. Pitt tried an attempt on Corsica, but again inadequate forces were dispatched. In spite of this, however, a young naval captain decided to attack, and in July 1794 Calvi fell, though it cost Nelson his right eye, and all but his life.

A black cloud of despair hung over the country. But suddenly, on the " Glorious First of June " 1794, there came news that Lord Howe, the old sea-dog, searching the Atlantic for an American grain convoy destined for hungry France, had met with the French Navy at the mouth of the Channel. Though he was unable to intercept the American convoy, he completely defeated the French fleet, taking six ships of war, and sinking another.

The King went down to meet the fleet: every window in London was illumined; the country went mad with excitement.

[1] Londonderry Papers.

CHAPTER III

I

IN THE midst of the national rejoicings, on 9 June 1794 the Honourable Robert Stewart and Lady Emily Hobart were married. They settled down at No. 3 Cleveland Square, a pleasant house overlooking St. James's Park, but as soon as the House rose for the summer recess Robert took his bride and set off for Mount Stewart. Interrupting their journey to spend a deferred honeymoon in the Lake District, they continued on their way to Ireland. We can imagine the joy in Robert's heart as he drove up with his wife to the gates of Mount Stewart, and pointed out to her the grey stone house standing solitary on the sea shore. His father and stepmother were on the steps waiting anxiously to welcome them, and were soon extending the same courtesy and affection to their son's wife as they had always reserved for their son. Robert was pleased to find that Emily was a success with his parents, and that she enjoyed the quiet atmosphere of Mount Stewart, but he was a little afraid lest her English reserve should make her appear inattentive to all the visitors who flocked to see them.

There was news about his brother Charles, who had now embarked on a military career. He had been wounded in action, and Robert was deeply moved when he heard of the boy's courage. He was only nineteen, and was already proving himself an intrepid soldier. Describing the incident to Lady Elizabeth Pratt, Robert wrote: " My dearest friend, the delightful detail of Charles's heroism reached Mount Stewart before us. The recital drew tears from me, and I really feel proud of having such a brother. How fortunate he has been (if so melancholy an event can justify such an expression) by one act to show his character to the world, and to establish it forever." [1]

[1] Londonderry Papers. Undated, but probably written during Lady Emily's first visit to Mt. Stewart, 1794.

Robert was not to remain long at Mount Stewart, for in a few days he was recalled to his regiment which was stationed at Drogheda. Emily, who accompanied her husband, did not mind the change. She found the officers good company, and Robert was proud to see how much she was admired. He would have preferred to have been with her at Mount Stewart, but he was kept too busy at headquarters to get away. Not that he disliked a military life; he found the business of the regiment quite absorbing. It was a little community to manage, the progress of which he found interesting to observe; and when his commanding officer gave over the management of the band to him he was delighted. Soon he had the little boys, as he said, " making the most horrible noises on the different instruments." He grew so enthusiastic over the band, that when his regiment was sent to Belfast, which was only a few miles from his home, he decided to take the band with him to Mount Stewart. In the regiment, he wrote to Lady Elizabeth, there was no one who cared for music, " the major excepted, and his taste is limited to five tunes which he makes them play like Uncle Toby for as many hours whilst he is getting drunk—the boys are almost worn out and Geisler (their master) broken-hearted."[1]

As Lady Elizabeth was staying at Mount Stewart, he was already engaging her services. " I am persuaded," he tells her, " if you will hear them play a little every day, and encourage them to aim at something like taste, that they will improve fast and add much to our parties at the Temple or on the water—I wish Charles could spare us a farmer who can play the clarinet as we have lost two lately." He was full of the band, and thought that his tent pitched in front of the house would make an excellent practice room for the men; it would also be " a capital addition to a breakfast at the Temple " to have them playing on the bank. The " Temple of the Winds " was some little way from the house, overlooking the sea. It was used in the summer evenings for parties, and during the day for rest or contemplation.

Robert's musical activities were a great relaxation to him, but he was soon to be deprived of them, for on 25 September 1794 Pitt wrote to him, asking for his assistance at Westminster at the opening of the coming session.

It was not in any way a convenient time for him to be setting out

[1] Camden Papers. Unpublished.

for London, for Lady Emily had been in poor health, grievously fatigued apparently by all the dances she had been attending, and would not be fit to accompany him. But Pitt's call had to be answered; he had very grave reasons, Robert knew, for gathering round him all the support he could muster. It was not only the war with its series of masterly retreats that was disturbing him, it was also the Irish trouble, for he had got himself hopelessly entangled in an ugly struggle with Lord Fitzwilliam, whom he had recently appointed Lord-Lieutenant of Ireland.

Fitzwilliam was popular in Ireland, for he was an ardent champion of the Catholic cause, and Pitt had intended a gesture of conciliation when he sent him out, but he had not expected Emancipation Bills, nor the dismissal of all his faithful supporters. He could not risk an open quarrel with Fitzwilliam, which would only result in stirring up the Irish, nor could he risk a quarrel with his own supporters, especially at such a time, when England was in the direst danger. He had made a blunder, Robert felt, and was about to make another. He was going to recall Fitzwilliam.

Emily was dispatched to Mount Stewart, and Robert departed for England. Apart from leaving his wife, he was also to be deprived of the pleasure of seeing Lady Elizabeth, who was waiting for him at Mount Stewart.

" My dearest friend," he wrote to her, " I have sensibly been led to postpone writing, first from the inclination I felt to name the very day on which we should meet, and latterly from the disinclination one feels completely to abdicate what we desire in our hearts. It is scarcely worth while to enumerate the reasons which have at last decided me to give up the pleasure of seeing you . . . the fact is my summer has been sacrificed, that I might have the fairer claim to command the autumn, never dreaming that any thing would carry me from hence till Spring. The meeting of the English Parliament before Xmas oversets all this, and deprives me of the scheme I had most at heart, for however you may think I prefer a Military life, believe me when I assure you, that no place, nor any other society, has half the charms for me that Mount Stewart has at this moment, in which creed if you are a sceptick, you do not confide in an assurance from me as you did.

" It is a great disappointment to me to lose our Musical studies,

64

EMILY, VISCOUNTESS CASTLEREAGH
By T. Lawrence

but it is a still greater to lose the confidential intercourse we should have had, which is delightful to me, and never enjoy'd with any one so completely as with you."

Robert's friends in Ireland were not very pleased at his deserting Ireland for Mr. Pitt. They felt that it was Lord Fitzwilliam who needed support, not the Prime Minister. Dr. Haliday suggested to Robert the delicacy and difficulty of the situation in which he was involving himself. But Robert assured him of Pitt's integrity, and tried to convince him that Pitt's one desire was to see Ireland happily settled. " He is Pittized with a vengeance which he candidly owns," wrote Haliday to Charlemont. " He turned the tables on me, wanting to proselyte me, which was surely not worth his pains."

Lord Charlemont feared for Robert's political salvation, and yet could not help at the same time " loving the amiable reprobate," who must, he felt, " regain his lustre, obscured as it is for the moment by accidental clouds." [1]

2

It was a long and wearisome journey to London; for though the sea passage was a matter of but six hours, travelling across the English countryside took six days. The weather was cold, the roads bad, and the horses slithered along, floundering and stumbling as they dragged the carriage through the thick mud. To make things worse a clammy creeping mist accompanied him on the way. Joe, his servant, was well known on the road, and his importance was so firmly established that he was feasted at every stage; and Robert was regaled, at each change of horses, by alternate fumes of porter and punch. It was too cold to open a window and ventilate the carriage, so he had to endure the atmosphere as best he could.

Crossing in solitude the same country which he had a few months previously traversed with his bride, Robert felt her absence the more keenly, and eased his mind by continually dispatching letters to her. At the end of a long day he would arrive at an inn completely exhausted, but always before retiring to bed, he wrote a letter to Emily.

[1] Charlemont MSS.

"I cannot retire to rest, Dearest dear wife, though a good deal fatigued," he wrote, "without sending you my blessing. Every stage that removes me farther from you adds to my regret and makes the time which is to elapse before I again cross the Channel seem of intolerable duration. Perhaps the noise and bustle of London may dissipate the anxiety of separation which reflection uninterrupted dwells on with real pain. My day now passes without event. I roll on from daybreak till long after the light is gone, and except for the relief of reading, I have nothing to divert my thoughts from the loss I have sustained. God Almighty protect you, Dearest of friends.

Ever your most devoted

ROBERT"

His health was still troublesome, and on the journey he began a curious régime, which seemed to suit his constitution extremely well. He "supped upon his tea," as he wrote Emily, "and breakfasted upon his supper," taking a meal of cold meat and madeira at seven in the morning, tea and toast for lunch, mutton chops and potatoes—"for the last of which I have taken a passion"—about tea-time, and his tea a little before retiring to bed. He felt unusually well on this diet, finding it far more comfortable to go to bed without a loaded stomach. "Tell Lady Elizabeth," he writes, "I have begun my meat breakfasts. I laid a foundation of roast fowl and madeira this morning with a super-structure of tea and toast. Nothing could answer better."

His thoughts full of Emily, he took the route over the Cumberland mountains, in order to avoid going by the Lakes where they had so recently spent their honeymoon, and he wrote, reminding her of Langholm where they had slept so comfortably and of the little bed-chamber at Keswick. "Would to God the moment was arrived when you should be confined as formerly and encircled by those arms which seem of no use at present but to prepare the morning post which is to attend at your breakfast."

By daylight he was up and setting out again on his cold, miserable, creeping journey; it seemed an endless time of roadside inns, beery breaths, and rumbling wheels, before he arrived at last in London. Entering his house he made a quick change, took his tea and toast, and set out for Putney.

When he reached Pitt's house he found the Prime Minister suffering from a bad attack of gout. His long, angular figure seemed thinner than ever, and his flushed face showed traces of pain and fatigue. To Robert's great surprise he was informed on arrival that his attendance would not after all be required.

He listened courteously to Pitt's apologies for any unnecessary inconvenience he might have been caused. It had been impossible to let him know, as he had only decided at the last moment, that in view of his health and increasing difficulties in the Cabinet, it would not be expedient to reassemble Parliament on 25 November as arranged. He was deeply grateful to him for having come so readily at his call, but now that Parliament was not to meet for some time, he would like him to return to Ireland where his presence and support would be so very important.

Robert took his leave ceremoniously; he must have been bitterly chagrined at his wasted journey and the unnecessary absence from Emily, but as he made his courtly bow, his face was impassive, and gave not the slightest clue to his feelings.

He knew only too well how much uneasiness Lord Fitzwilliam was causing Pitt, and how much trouble Pitt was having with his Cabinet over Ireland. Through a series of misunderstandings Fitzwilliam seemed to be fanning the flames of conspiracy all over the country. It was possible to think with the new Lord-Lieutenant that the complete removal of all the remaining restrictions on the Irish Catholics would be a wise and proper measure; but, wise or unwise in itself, there were a thousand reasons for wishing to avoid the discussion of it in time of ferment and danger. He was not surprised to hear later that Pitt had decided to recall Fitzwilliam, though he knew how much resentment this act would rouse. The recall of Fitzwilliam was a political calamity, and would only poison the relations between England and Ireland further; but Pitt was by this time too involved to do anything but extricate himself as best he could from the web in which he was entangled.

Robert was back again in Ireland before the Lord-Lieutenant left. The day of Fitzwilliam's departure was observed in Ireland as a day of national mourning. All shops were closed, and his coach was drawn down to the waterside by a silent body of citizens. The people were in a state of sullen indignation, full of gloomy forebodings, and in no mood to welcome Fitzwilliam's successor, who came, they felt, to resist all concessions and to enslave them further.

3

It was Robert's uncle, Bayham, now Lord Camden, who was sent out to Ireland to replace Fitzwilliam as Lord-Lieutenant, and Robert was in the Viceregal party when it proceeded to Dublin Castle for the ceremony of swearing in. Although the crowds beside the route seemed to Camden quiet enough as the procession made its way along, Robert, who knew the temper of the people, expected trouble. He had had some experience of Irish mobs, and as he surveyed the sullen faces from the window of the carriage, he felt that their silence was ominous.

The procession as usual was a very splendid one, but the guards on horseback, the principal Officers of the Household with their wands, the pages in their liveries, the grooms of the chamber, the footmen, the streets lined with soldiers, were a sight that must have been unendurable to a country on which it was forced.

As the procession was returning from the Castle ceremony, an angry murmur began to rise and swell through the crowd. At first it was like the low growl of distant thunder, but suddenly it burst, and the crowd made a rush at the Chancellor's coach.

The coachman lashed his horses to a gallop and succeeded in forcing his way through; he did not, however, evade the strategy of the crowd, for a great number of the insurgents darted off down a turning, and taking a short-cut, reached the house first. As the coach drew up at the gates some heavy stones were flung through the window, one of which struck Fitzgibbon (afterwards Earl of Clare) on the forehead. The riot spread. Windows were broken, a few heads too, and eventually the military were called out to restore order.

"I really pity poor Lady Londonderry," wrote Charlemont to Haliday. "Her delicate feelings must undoubtedly be sorely hurt even by the promotion of her brother at so unlucky and critical a period." [1]

Such was the state of affairs in Ireland when Camden was called

[1] Charlemont to Haliday, 2 April 1795. *Charlemont Correspondence II.*

to the office of Lord-Lieutenant. The Catholics had been roused to an unparalleled pitch of fury by the hopes which Fitzwilliam's administration had held out to them, and which the Government had frustrated. Disorderly scenes now broke out all over the country. News of disaffection and unrest began to pour in from every quarter. There were nightly meetings of large bodies of armed men, officers of the law were murdered, the country was on the verge of civil war.

Camden was thirty-five, inexperienced and untrained, and without any knowledge of Irish affairs. Situated as he was he found Robert's aid invaluable, and relied a great deal on him for information and guidance. He held office for three harassed years, and though in spite of constant threats of assassination he rode about the country attended only by a groom, and won the respect of the Irish, he became a nervous wreck, worn down by cares and anxiety, and but for Robert's assistance would never have been able to carry on during these difficult years.

Apart from the general unrest, there was the constant danger of a French invasion. Robert, who was firmly convinced that to save Ireland from France was the only thing that now mattered, felt that the time had come for him to throw his whole weight on the side of the Government, and in 1795 he left the Whig party. Writing to Lady Elizabeth Pratt, he said:

" You will not regret that I am an apostate with Lord Charlemont and many others from a set of them who compose a French party in this country, and are endeavouring to lead us through the same succession of horrors that has been produced in France by similar men and similar principles."

Parliamentary reform, to which he had pledged himself, seemed now of comparative unimportance. Although the Catholics, who had already received the franchise, were still not allowed to sit in Parliament, Robert was expressing his views in the Irish House of Commons that no further concessions could be made to them at that time without endangering the Constitution and the Protestant Church Establishment.

He is said to have been among the best speakers on the Government side of the House on this occasion, but the speech brought him little favour, and lost him many friends. He was growing in favour, however, with the powers that be, for Pitt invited him to second the

69

address to the King on the opening of the House of Commons at Westminster. Being a member of the House of Commons in England and in Ireland gave him little time for leisure. On 22 January, he had been chosen to second the Address of Thanks for the Lord-Lieutenant's speech in Dublin, so that he was to second the address to the Throne in two parliaments in the same year. When he returned to England he found himself in the midst of more stormy receptions.

On 29 October 1795, as George III drove from Buckingham House to Westminster to open Parliament, the royal coach was attacked by angry crowds. The populace pressed round the carriage, shouting "Bread!" "No War!" "No famine!" "No Pitt!" and even "Down with George!" Fists were thrust in the King's face; threats were uttered; and passing through Whitehall he was fired on.

The King behaved with his usual courage. He sat bolt upright in his seat, and never showed, even by a turn of the head, his awareness of the danger to which he was exposed.

Robert had had experience enough of such demonstrations in his own country, and he was not an uninterested spectator. It seemed to him that the state of affairs in England was almost as serious as it was in Ireland, that there was the same misery and discontent. On the surface the country seemed prosperous enough, there was the same gilded gaiety, but underneath there was poverty and starvation; it was the poor who suffered. Winter had already come, the price of coal was prohibitive, and the wretches shivered in their rags as they lined the procession route.

In spite of his experiences on the way, the King read his speech in the House of Lords calmly, and Robert, seconding the Address of Thanks, made his maiden speech. For nearly eighteen months now he had been a member of the House of Commons, and this was the first time he had spoken. He was never an orator, he had no gift for fine phrases, but with his modest bearing and quiet manner, he made a very favourable impression on the House. He was in full dress for the opening of Parliament, and looked more than ever handsome in his silk knee-breeches and rich lace ruffles. His speech was simple and impressive. Stating his grounds for the advisability of continuing the war, he said: " The system by which France governs is founded upon cruelty and terror, both of which are repugnant to a government that affects to ground itself on principles of equality, freedom and justice. Anxiety and eagerness for peace will not, I hope. allow our efforts to be broken, and I confidently expect that the period will arrive, when we may look back to the exertions we have made, as having been employed not less in preserving the safety of our country than in contributing to the general security of Europe."

Although Fox and Sheridan, who had always been opposed to the War, spoke strongly against the Address, it was carried by an unusually large majority.

But Robert's maiden speech, though it was well received, excited very little attention at the time. The speech had been adequate and dignified, but it held out no promise of the great talent and statesmanship for which he later became distinguished.

After the opening of Parliament the King, with great courage and against all advice, returned to his coach. "One person is proposing this, and another is supposing that," he said, "forgetting that there is One above us all who disposes of everything, and on whom alone we depend."

The reappearance of the Royal coach was greeted with a howl of fury by the mob. "Out with him! Out with him!" the people shouted as they surrounded his carriage. They clambered on to the coach, and were hurled down. Passing through St. James's Park the din was so great that one of the horses took fright, and a groom had his leg broken as he was flung from the coach. Stones were thrown into the carriage, several of which hit the King. He took one of the stones out of the cuff of his coat, and gave it to the Earl of Onslow who accompanied him, saying: "I make you a present of this, as a mark of the civilities we have met with on our journey to-day."

A few months later, seated in his box at the theatre, the King was fired at. When, for his protection, he was asked to move back a little, he replied: "Not an inch, not an inch."

The year 1795 was from all points a disastrous year, and the people were full of despair. There had been a series of bad harvests, and the country was faced with the prospect of famine. Robert noticed that the Press, full of good advice, was urging the wealthier classes to forgo food that was essential to the poor, to eat fish rather than meat, to be sparing of bread; but even if this rule was observed it availed the people little, for the loaf of bread had risen to a shilling, and even bread was beyond their reach. There was a serious shortage of flour, and the use of flour for powdering hair was from this time discouraged.

Victory was farther off than ever. The newspapers were full of the slaughter of our troops. The Duke of York's expedition to Flanders to assist the Austrians in their attack on Northern France had ended in bitter humiliation. The starving and demoralised survivors had now fallen back into North Germany, and the Government was sending transports to the Weser to evacuate them.

Charles, Robert's brother, who had returned home with the wounded, must have given him a sad account of the men and horses dying from starvation, and of the plight from which the Navy had rescued them.

Prussia had already deserted us. And now our other allies, Spain and Sweden, were signing a separate treaty of peace with France. On all sides Britain was threatened. But Pitt's optimism continued. Concerned now with his Budget he said to Addington: " If that goes off tolerably well, it will give us peace before Easter."

Robert, in spite of his admiration for Pitt, had never felt that peace was obtainable or even desirable with a France swollen to such proportions, and he viewed with apprehension Pitt's continued efforts to negotiate with France. He had made overtures of peace through the Danish Minister in London, and had been repulsed ; he had made overtures again through Wickham, our Envoy in Switzerland, but the offer had been ungraciously received and scornfully rejected. The French armies were doing far too well to desire anything but an unqualified victory.

4

In the spring of 1796 Robert left England to defend, in Dublin, Pitt's policy with regard to Ireland and the War, but he was back again in England in the summer of the same year, taking part in a General Election. He was returned for Orford, a pocket borough in Suffolk owned by his uncle Lord Hertford.

Though he had not yet been appointed to any office his services seemed to be required in both countries, and he spent much of his time travelling between the two.

He was not very happy regarding his position, and felt that his services should by now have received some recognition. Other young men of his age were already in office. George Canning, for example, had started his Parliamentary career in the same year as Robert, and was already at the Foreign Office as Under-Secretary. Canning was undoubtedly a brilliant young man ; he was witty and entertaining, but a little too full of assurance, and rather given to intrigue. He was a good speaker, but somewhat theatrical for the sober House of Commons. Camden, who used to sit next to him, had told Robert how Canning had hit him a plaguey hard blow on the shoulder when he was making his maiden speech ; Pitt, who sat beneath him, had managed to sidle a little out of the way, and Dundas had bobbed to save his wig from confusion. But Canning's flights of oratory must have impressed them nevertheless, for though he was a year younger than Robert he was already in office.

Robert was not unmoved by honours ; he was as ambitious as any young politician, and—as he did not neglect to inform Camden— he needed office to stimulate him to greater exertions. The chief offices in Ireland were closed to him, paradoxically enough because he was an Irishman.

Camden, who was handicapped by the failing health of his Chief Secretary, Pelham, had proposed him as Pelham's successor; but the Chief Secretary of Ireland had always been an Englishman, and Pitt felt at that time that he could not depart from this precedent. Robert began to wonder if his goal might not be more easily reached in England than in his own country, and wrote to Camden on the subject. Camden guardedly replied that Robert's feelings alone could determine whether he should make the Parliament of England or of Ireland his object. Personally he would prefer him to determine for England, as he would soon be leaving Ireland, although he wished him to be in Ireland as much as possible while he was there. Those were his personal feelings ; his judgment, he wrote, he left for Robert to discover. But Robert had already been marked down by Fate to serve his apprenticeship in the hard school of Ireland for the great place he was to fill in England's destiny.

5

In the summer of 1796, Robert landed again in Ireland. His father, owing to Camden's influence, had recently been created Earl of Londonderry, and Robert, from 9 August 1796, bore the title of Viscount Castlereagh.

His friends found him none the worse for being a lord, and thought the new honour became him well. He had intended staying only a short time at Mount Stewart, being anxious to rejoin his regiment, but his father confiding in him his alarm at the treasonable practices which were spreading to the north, and which existed on his very estates, Castlereagh made an extensive tour of the country on horseback to see for himself what was happening. He found that the whole of the north was infected, and that a serious conspiracy existed. Two of its leaders, he discovered, were Samuel Neilson and Thomas Russell, both connected with the United Irish newspaper, the *Northern Star*. He immediately informed Pelham of the danger, and was invited by Camden to attend a " Cabinet " at Dublin Castle.

Emily, who had accompanied him to Ireland, was persuaded to remain behind at Mount Stewart, as the family thought it wise for her to rest, but though he wrote to her continually, assuring her of his eternal affection, telling her " how ardently he longed to be with her again," how he " sighed perpetually to be restored to her," she replied that she would not remain another day unless he returned immediately to her side. He sent her tooth-powder, he sent her the locket he had had repaired for her, he had his horses waiting six hours in Merrion Street hoping he would be able to get back to her, but he was detained at the Castle. He implored her not to ride " Prince " unless his father was with her, and not to torture him with the idea of her being exposed to danger. Lady Louisa, he added, was in great hopes that her prudence " in remaining at Mount Stewart had its motives." But if Lady Louisa and the family were expecting her to produce an heir, they must have been sadly disappointed, for the marriage was childless.

After Castlereagh had made his report to the " Cabinet," Camden dispatched him to the north again to help in the work of rounding up the traitors. The scene in which he was now to be engaged was a very painful one, and the work distasteful, but the evil which necessitated it was, as he wrote to Lady Elizabeth Pratt, "a subject of much more serious anxiety to my mind." To many of his compatriots, who up to this time had had nothing but admiration and affection for him, it seemed a strange thing that Robert should become the "tool" of the Government.

Hitherto his influence and example had had an effect on all the young men of Northern Ireland, who were as proud of his talents and patriotic pledges as were his own family. In the gay and cheerful assemblies which distinguished the north, he had hitherto been a popular figure. With his unfailing courtesy and engaging address, his kindliness, his charm, he had endeared himself to many ; but now opinion changed.

At first Ireland witnessed his so-called "political delinquency" with sorrow, for even those who disliked his politics could not help loving him as a man. Grattan, and Charlemont, and those who knew him well, however violently they felt about his political course, never ceased to like him personally. But the mob, who never knew him, and who were to associate his name henceforth with imprisonments and repressive measures, began to pursue him with the bitterest hatred and abuse. Popularity, however, he had never cared about, opposition had never daunted him, and nothing ever made him abate one particle of his vigorous determination regarding anything which he undertook.

The work which he had now undertaken, distressing as it was to him, was necessary; for the United Irishmen had gained such strength, particularly in the north, that the whole country was rapidly drifting towards anarchy.

The United Irishmen, a society that had been founded as far back as 1791 by Wolfe Tone, a Protestant lawyer from Dublin, had been a perfectly legal and constitutional body to begin with. Its aim had been to unite "Irishmen of every religious persuasion, and thereby to obtain a complete reform of the legislation, founded on the principle of civil, political and religious liberty."

But its aims had gradually changed. In 1795 the United Irishmen took a solemn oath on the summit of M'Art's Fort, Belfast, "never to desist in their efforts until they had subverted the authority of England over their country and asserted her independence."

The Government, aware of their activities, had made a few arrests, but had only succeeded in driving the movement underground. Wolfe Tone fled the country, and was soon in France, plotting with the French an invasion of Ireland.

The Catholics at first held back, their priesthood disturbed by the atheistic ideas of the French, but they soon pressed into the ranks, their political grievances outweighing their religious scruples. Wolfe Tone had counted on the Catholics, because no change, he felt, " could make their political situation worse, and because they abhorred the English name and power."

Although the prominent leaders were Protestant—Wolfe Tone, Napper Tandy, Edward Fitzgerald and Oliver Bond—the real power lay in the number of Catholic rank and file. Religion was set aside, and every region of Ireland was honeycombed with secret societies.

" In the North," wrote Castlereagh to Lady Elizabeth Pratt, " the understandings of the lower orders are in a perpetual fever from the means taken to excite their passions." The treason was spreading even among his father's tenants and to the very servants at Mount Stewart.

In October 1796 directions were issued by their leaders to all the clubs of United Irishmen to form the societies into military bodies and to provide them with arms and ammunition. Lord Edward Fitzgerald was made Commander-in-Chief. The numbers of armed men in Ulster alone amounted to nearly 100,000, ready to take the field on the arrival of the enemy.[1]

Castlereagh had started out on his mission. Having to leave Emily behind did not lighten his task, and he had not been many days from her side before he was writing: " I am already tired of my liberty, and would walk on foot to Mount Stewart to recover my baggage, and to return to my obedience." But he had been entrusted with a grim duty, and he would carry it out to the letter.

Emily's friends were surprised to hear of her staying quietly at Mount Stewart in her husband's absence, instead of romping with her " old, faithful, riotous, joyous, noisy companions " at Dublin. Her cousin, William Connolly, wrote to her to express his amazement at her change of character. His letter written on 4 September 1796 is full of the treason that was undermining Ireland, and if there were

[1] Report from the Committee of Secrecy, by the Rt. Hon. Lord Viscount Castlereagh.

any doubt as to the necessity for the work Castlereagh was doing, this letter surely dispels it.

" They say the French are coming," Connolly wrote, " and I am glad of it, for they will alter all our manners. None of your long speeches in Parliament with rising or falling with Great Britain.
" We will jump and dance and leap and caper by ourselves.
" None of your stupid Castle balls with Lords- and Lady-Lieutenants sitting in state at the end of a long room.
" They say my uncle's regiment is a good one, but that as he is a poor decrepit old man, he will not be able to command it, but that your husband will do it, and as the regiment is certain of being employed, he will probably be killed, and then, my dearest Romp, you will be at liberty to choose again for yourself.
" Lord, what pleasure we shall have when these Frenchmen come, they are so lively, cheerful, and entertaining. Not at all like the grave English and Irish Politicians . . .
" In short, my dear Romp, I am quite delighted with those happy prospects that our charming minister, Mr. Pitt, has brought about for us, for no other man in Europe could have done the same. He was so tired of having all mankind our friends that he has brought matters so about as to make the greatest part of them our enemys."[1]

6

Robert was making his way to Ulster. He stayed the night at Lisburn Castle, the residence of his uncle, Lord Hertford, and early in the morning, accompanied by a magistrate before whom incriminating information had been sworn, he set out on horseback on his disagreeable mission. He had gone only a little way when he met Charles Teeling, a boy of eighteen, whose name appeared first on his list. Teeling was riding with his father, whom Castlereagh knew intimately, and he did not relish the task he had in hand. He accosted them with his usual courtesy, and turning his horse proceeded up the street with them. When they reached Lisburn Castle, and the Teelings were about to take leave of him, Castlereagh said to the boy's father: " I regret that your son cannot accompany you." And he conducted

[1] Londonderry Papers.

Charles Teeling through the outer gates of the Castle, which were immediately closed. Here the young man found himself surrounded by an armed guard.

After some expostulation, the father was allowed inside, and in deep anger inquired the cause of his son's arrest. "High treason," replied Castlereagh quietly. There was a painful interview between father and son. At length the boy's father departed, and the boy's horse was led home by a servant.

Several other arrests were made. Surrounded now by a large body of cavalry, Castlereagh passed on to Belfast. Here the garrison turned out, and numbers of foot soldiers, troops of horse, and a detachment of artillery patrolled the streets. Most of the shops put up their shutters, and hardly an inhabitant was to be seen.

Meanwhile young Teeling, who was confined to a front room in Lisburn Castle, leaning out of the window, began a conversation with some of his friends in the street below. A crowd quickly collected, some of them volunteering to waylay Castlereagh and assassinate him as he returned from Belfast. Teeling was opposed to any such action and dissuaded them from the attempt.

An end was soon put to these conversations by the removal of the prisoner to an inner apartment, where he was put under an additional guard. In the evening Castlereagh, who had returned from Belfast, entered the room. Teeling noticed that in spite of his elegant manner and apparent unconcern, he was tired and disturbed, and did not relish the task he had in hand.

"I regret," he said to Teeling, "that you should have been subjected to the painful restraint of an additional guard. It was not my desire that you should have been placed in such close quarters." And he pressed Teeling to share the light meal that had been brought in for him.

"I have had much fatigue to-day," he observed as they sat down. "We have made some important arrests."

"May I," asked Teeling, "inquire the names of those arrested?"

"We have arrested Neilson; do you know him?"

"Know him!" replied the prisoner. "I know him and respect his worth. A man of talent and devoted patriotism. An honest citizen, a warm and disinterested friend."

"Indeed," Castlereagh returned; and then, after a moment: "We have arrested Russell as well."

" Russell! " exclaimed Teeling. " Is Russell a prisoner? Then the soul of honour is captive."

Castlereagh was silent. He filled his glass, and passed the wine across the table. After a moment Teeling said: " May I beg to know, my Lord, what are the intentions of the Government towards me and my fellow prisoners? "

" You will be immediately conducted to the capital," Castlereagh replied. " His Excellency and Council will decide the rest."

A little later the guard entered and approached Teeling. " Treat the prisoner," Castlereagh said, " with every indulgence consistent with your duty and his safe keeping."

Outside a dense and almost impassable multitude thronged the streets. Castlereagh gave orders to the cavalry to clear a way, but it was some time before the prisoner, who was loudly cheered, could be moved through the excited crowds. Teeling was tried, and committed to gaol, but was later, through Castlereagh's influence, released.[1]

Castlereagh did his work very thoroughly, and most of the rebels were rounded up. There was one rebel, however, whom Castlereagh did not manage to capture; Wolfe Tone was still in Paris.

During the weeks that followed, arms were distributed by the rebels throughout the whole country, meetings took place night and day, and assassinations were a common occurrence. An attempt had been made on the life of Castlereagh's friend and former tutor, the Rev. John Cleland, but Cleland had fired two shots to the assassin's one, and it was the assassin who had had to make his escape.

When Castlereagh returned to Mount Stewart he rode round the estates trying to overcome the terror spread by the United Irishmen, who threatened vengeance on anyone who took the oath of allegiance. For days he was scarcely out of the saddle. The loyal were afraid to come forward; only the rebels would assemble. These gathered together in large numbers under the pretext of digging the potatoes or cutting the corn of any of their friends who had been arrested. Castlereagh, riding round the country, fell in with a large body of these " potato-diggers." He thought they looked a fine company of well set-up young men, and could not but admire the military style in which they marched, all of them in perfect formation, with an officer in front and rear. He rode along with them for some distance,

[1] Teeling's *Narrative of the Irish Rebellion.*

and had a good deal of amusing conversation, enjoying their jokes and their good humour.[1] At Comber, he left them, but instead of making a search for arms and a few arrests, as he had intended, he decided that, with hundreds of rebels " digging potatoes " within half a mile, it would be as well if he contented himself with merely examining the men suspected, and letting the matter rest for a while.

Besieged by letters from Emily, who was now in Dublin, waiting impatiently for his return, he wrote to her with equal enthusiasm:

" I am now Dearest Emily like a schoolboy before the holidays. I count every day, every hour which is yet to elapse before we are to meet . . . but there is that species of fluctuation in this neighbourhood that I cannot reconcile it to myself not to make every effort to redeem the people if possible. Not a moment shall be lost, and let the business take what turn it will, you may rely upon my embracing you the first moment. I still expect to get away this week. Dearest Emily can you doubt my eagerness to return to you, and can't you even approve of my endeavouring to render my Father as well as his people any service in my power ? "

A week or two later he gave a dinner to his father's tenants, many of whom had been terrorised, and persuaded between three and four hundred of them to take the oath of allegiance. Writing to Emily he said: " They did it with every mark of sincerity after the ice had been broken and their panic a little removed. They had been much deceived and much threatened. We had a very jolly dinner, Cleland quite drunk, the Rev. William Sinclair (the Presbyterian minister) considerably so, my father not a little, others lying heads and points, the whole very happy, and God Save the King and Rule Britannia declared permanent."

Barely a week earlier not a man could be prevailed upon to take the oath, soon over a thousand came in. Having completed his labours in the north to the satisfaction of the Lord-Lieutenant and of the Prime Minister, Castlereagh prepared to return to his regiment in Limerick, where Emily, whom he had not seen for some weeks, was to join him. " Dearest Emily," he wrote to her, " your last is such a *threatening* letter, that I am almost afraid of approaching you, yet I will e'en

[1] Letter from Castlereagh to Emily. Londonderry Papers.

expose myself to all your indignation, and shall set out to-morrow morning at six o'clock, you may expect me on Friday. So farewell, Mrs. Vixen. C."

7

Emily was overjoyed to see him again, but their reunion was short-lived, for, two days before Christmas, news was received that the French fleet had been sighted off Bantry Bay. Immediate orders were given to concentrate all available troops on the south-west coast and prepare for an enemy invasion. Emily was dispatched to Dublin, and Castlereagh took his place at the head of his regiment.

It was the sequel to Pitt's peace overtures. He had made a third attempt at negotiation but it had failed, and Lord Malmesbury, who had been sent out to Paris to treat with the French, had been ordered to leave the soil of France within forty-eight hours. As Castlereagh had long perceived, it was not the time for peace negotiations.

The Directory, swollen with power, believing that they had England at their mercy had now decided to strike at Ireland. A great fleet, carrying an army of twenty thousand men, under the command of Hoche, was on its way.

On Christmas Eve, 1796, Castlereagh marched out of Limerick at the head of a detachment numbering five hundred strong. Emily, who must by now have become inured to the vagaries of a public career, was left behind in the charge of Connolly.

The following day Castlereagh was writing her an affectionate letter reminding her of her promise not to ride at night, or sit up late, telling her how impossible it was to describe what he felt at parting with her.

The weather was cold, but he was marching on foot and did not mind it. The men were in great spirits, and only afraid that the Navy would run away with their credit. On the evening of Boxing Day, they reached Mallow and eagerly awaited orders from Headquarters, but none came. The following day there were still no orders; there was nothing but confusion; and Castlereagh was writing to Emily: " . . . the reports from Cork are so contradictory that we are yet in doubt whether the Fleet is French or English, and whether it ever

C. 81 F

anchor'd or not, and this day it is said to have been driven by the storm of Sunday night to sea."

Fastidious as ever about his attire, he ends the letter with a request for grey pantaloons and overalls, red waistcoats without lace, and a leather travelling cap to be sent to him.

Eventually orders came, and they marched to Cork to meet the enemy. But when they got there, they found that the wind had saved them the trouble of driving the French away; for there was not a ship left in Bantry Bay. It was rumoured that some had foundered and others had been taken, but "all that I can collect," Castlereagh wrote to Emily, "in the confusion of General Stewart's Orderly Room—the General and his Aide-de-Camps being complete fools—is that they are gone and that there is a prospect that they may fall into the hands of the English fleet." A few days later the regiment was ordered to Bandon as some of the enemy's ships were returning to Bantry Bay. "I believe," he wrote to Emily, "they have returned in distress rather than with any view of landing." It was true enough. They were a crippled fleet uncertain of their purpose. The ship containing Hoche, their leader, had got lost and never appeared at all. The others finding it impossible to effect a landing took their departure without doing any damage. Castlereagh rode over from Bandon where his men were stationed, and arrived at Bantry just in time to see the last two French ships prepare to sail away. At nightfall their sails were unbent, and in the morning they were gone.

A solitary figure silhouetted against the sky, he sat a moment in the saddle looking gravely out to sea, and as he scanned the horizon, the thought came to his mind that if the French had set sail a few days earlier, they could have disembarked the twenty thousand troops they had on board without opposition, and if they had done so there was little doubt that an open rising in the country would have followed, and Ireland would easily have fallen into their hands.[1] The whole country lay unprotected before them, barely three thousand men in all could have been rushed to Bantry, and these had only two pieces of artillery at their disposal. As for the British fleet it was nowhere to be seen.

Castlereagh turned back, and occupied his mind with the task of finding billets for his men. He had great difficulty in finding accom-

[1] Camden Papers.

modation of any kind and eventually he quartered half of them in
the parish church. They were wet through and hungry, their bread
and cheese had not arrived, there was no straw for them to lie on,
and there was but one candle in the church for illumination. But
suddenly, wrote Castlereagh to Emily, " your friend the Huntsman
appeared in the pulpit with his bugle horn and made the Church ring
with his music." This set them all laughing, and they forgot their
wet clothes and their empty stomachs till their bread and cheese
appeared, and they fell to.

Their discomfort did not last long, for soon they were ordered
back to their more comfortable quarters at Limerick, and Castlereagh
wasted no time in setting forth. Emily was growing more and more
impatient at his absence and suggested joining him, but Castlereagh,
expecting to be home before long, restrained her. On his way to
Limerick he found, when he arrived at the North Bridge of Cork and
was challenged by the sentry, that he had forgotten the password. It
was raining hard, and he was anxious to enter the town. Apologising
for his lapse of memory, he informed the sentry that he was Lord
Castlereagh, that the body he commanded was the Derry Militia, and
that it would be perfectly safe to let them pass. But the sentry, a
volunteer yeoman, imbued with a profound sense of his responsibilities, declared that his orders were to allow no one to cross the
bridge without the proper password, and that if his lordship attempted
to advance, he would fire. " You are right, sir," replied Castlereagh.
" I am glad to see such discipline among the volunteers." [1]

He then withdrew, and dispatching an orderly to the Bandon
Guard for the password, waited in the drenching rain till he returned.
Arriving at Limerick he found that there was a possibility of his
being stationed there for some time, and regretting his letter to Emily
in which he had dissuaded her from joining him, he wrote: " I feel
your heart is as impatient as mine under our present separation: and
bad as the fare is I can offer you, I cannot deny myself the only real
indulgence this world can offer me—so dearest Emily, if I am to
remain, come to me, and you will at least receive a most affectionate
welcome."

Before Emily could set out to join him, however, Castlereagh had

[1] Belfast News-Letter, 24 Sept. 1822. Quoted by H. M. Hyde. The Rise of
Castlereagh.

received orders for the return of the troops, and he was soon on his way home.

"God knows," he wrote, "I never undertook a more grateful journey. . . . I have no letter these four days. Have you expected me, or have you forgot me? May I believe the latter impossible, even were the absence as many years as it has been days! God bless you." He was still writing to her daily, and had to account for himself, if he missed a post. "Your letter of last night," he replied, in answer to a suspicious note, "gave me a little bit of a scold for leaving you two posts without a letter. Now Madame Soupçonneuse, I have only failed one day to write to you which was the day I went out of town, so you are a good for nothing toad to doubt me.

"I write to-night to desire Tuff to send no more letters here, which is the pleasantest commission I have given since my arrival. I told you I believe yesterday that I had been unwell—I am quite stout again.

"I have nothing, dearest Emily, to send you from this retired spot but assurances of eternal affection."

A few days later he was back in Dublin with his adored Emily. The invasion of Ireland was over.

8

It was good to be home again, with Emily beside him. Although she could be tiresome at times, tactless and indiscreet, her bustling, caressing presence comforted him; her spontaneity and gaiety cheered him; her ardent temperament warmed him. He did not mind if she were limited, unsubtle, frivolous; she was sensible, safe, reassuring. They went for long walks together, they went riding together. In the evenings he would sit in the drawing-room writing his long dispatches while she chattered to anyone who might be there, talking so quickly and with exactly the same expression of voice on matters trivial or serious, that the flow of words did not even disturb him. If on occasion her babbling proved too much for him, he would merely rise with a laugh and depart to his study. Often he accompanied her to the assemblies of the gay, fashionable world, of which she was so inordinately fond. But though he fitted in with Emily in the light, easy routine of her existence, his mind was dominated by political events, for the sky was heavy with cloud.

The state of Ireland troubled him most, for though the French invasion had been destroyed, it had been destroyed by the elements, not by the army. The French would come again, and unless immediate measures were taken for the defence of Ireland, they would find the whole country open to them. His first step when he took his seat again in Parliament was to bring forward a motion for the strengthening of the Militia, and he was relieved to find his scheme adopted.

The year 1797 was a bad year for England; it was perhaps the worst year she had ever known. The French were growing more and more powerful, and England more and more deserted. In April, Austria, the last of our allies, laid down her arms, and Britain stood alone. The victorious French armies were now posted all along the shores of the English channel watching for an opportunity of invading England. The whole French army—the " Army of England "—was turned against Britain.

Our Austrian allies had been driven out of Italy by General Buonaparte and pursued almost to the gates of Vienna. Buonaparte, who had proved himself a fine soldier, was becoming altogether too powerful. When he had been given the command of the army in Italy, no one had dreamed it would end by his making France mistress of Italy. Thin, small, sallow faced, and subject to uncontrollable fits of passion, he was beginning to intrigue society. The gossips alleged that he was put next to the wealthy and attractive widow, Josephine de Beauharnais, at dinner one evening, in order to vex General Hoche, who was pursuing her. If it were so, it had been most effective, for Josephine and Buonaparte were now married. He was being proclaimed the liberator of Italy, and was already the idol of Paris.

Robert turned the war situation over in his mind; it was not the most satisfactory subject to dwell upon. The only comfortable news he had heard was a report of some naval action, off Cape St. Vincent, where Admiral Jervis had defeated the Spanish fleet before it had had time to effect a junction with the fleets of France and Holland, and land an army on England's shores. Commodore Nelson had actually boarded the flagship of the Spanish Admiral, collected all the officers' swords and tucked them in a bundle under his arm.

The Navy was still England's safeguard; but there was trouble even in the fleet. With the navies of all Europe combined against England, with her finances in ruin,[1] and her people half-starved, the fleet had broken out in mutiny. It was little wonder that Pitt's attitude had become " dry and rejecting," that he had abandoned his liberal principles of government and was introducing legislation that trampled on the old national liberties of England. There was no longer free speech; harsh and vindictive sentences were passed on any persons on a bare suspicion of seditious intentions. At this very critical time there came a report that the French were planning to invade England and Ireland simultaneously, and against invasion neither country was prepared.

Although the Irish Parliament had taken Castlereagh's warning very seriously, and measures were being considered for the defence of Ireland, nobody knew who was to be trusted. There had already been a riot in the Militia itself. The search for arms was going on, but only a few rusty weapons had been surrendered. The whole country was secretly armed, secretly drilling, preparing to aid the French.

[1] In February, 1797, cash payments were suspended, and the Bank of England empowered to issue £1 and £2 paper notes as legal tender. Cash payments were not resumed till 1821.

CHAPTER IV

I

IT WAS while Ireland was in this alarming state that Robert received his call to the Government. In July 1797, while he was with his regiment, he heard from Camden that he had been appointed Keeper of the King's Signet. He was in office at last, although in a minor position; his foot was only on the bottom rung of the ladder, but he would climb. Accepting office in Ireland obliged him to vacate his seat for Orford in the English Parliament, and he did not sit again at Westminster for four years. But during those four years he was to play a very important part in the history of his country.

The whole of Ireland was at this time in a state of ferment, and the storm which was to usher in such dread consequences was near to bursting. The Irish had always been an oppressed and unfortunate nation; and now, roused by the French cries of "Liberty," and by the incitement of the United Irish leaders, they were being moved to such a pitch of excitement and passion that they were ready to commit any outrage against the Government. Assassination, plunder and theft were daily occurrences. Ragged men had nothing to lose, and when the only thing that came to them cheap was whisky, it was easy to get roaring drunk and forget their miseries, easier under the influence of liquor to be led by United Irishmen to steal arms from the troops and to take treasonable oaths.

All their lives the wretches had cursed and fought, with no hope and no salvation; now they were given grounds on which to fight; they were to fight for Liberty and Independence. The English they had always hated with a bitter, sullen resentment, as any country would hate a governing class imposed upon it. Their old, stubborn resentment now broke into a wild and terrible passion, which stopped at neither murder nor treason. All they wanted was the right to worship their own gods, to be responsible for their own laws, to be free of tithes, to be free of poverty; all they desired was a decent life, some hope for the future, some retribution for the past. The British Government was hacking at their liberties, clipping away their rights and privileges, adding burdens to their already overweighted load.

It might have been simpler and more humane to have given them what they wanted, or to have made very substantial concessions. Emancipation was their right. It might not have produced the good hoped for, or the evil feared, but it would at least have had the effect of tranquillising the public mind. In 1793, after the Militia had been formed, Castlereagh had been definitely in favour of concessions. " I trust, however," he had written to Camden, " that the happy change which has been operated in the aspect of Irish affairs, will not induce administration to withhold indulgences which it was in their contemplation to grant at a moment of more danger." By 1795 his views had changed, and he was beginning to resist further political concessions, since they could not be made " without endangering the present constitution." In 1797 he was definitely against concessions. Matters had taken a sinister turn, the whole complexion of affairs had changed, for the French had been called in.

Castlereagh had seen the extent and danger of the Irish conspiracy, but had felt, as he wrote to Pitt, that it would not produce any great calamity within, unless the enemy paid them a visit. At Bantry Bay he had seen for himself what would have been the fate of the country if the French had landed. It was France he feared, not Ireland. For six days, during which the shattered remains of the French fleet lay tossing on the waves within sight of the Irish shore, not a single British ship of war had made its appearance. That there would be another attempt at invasion, he did not doubt; that the Irish were arming themselves against the day, he was only too well aware. If their desperate designs were to take effect, the Constitution would be overthrown, and the country would become a dependency of France.

That the Irish were willing to exchange the yoke of England for the yoke of France seemed strange to him. Under the Directory the government of France was becoming more absolute than any Monarchy. Thousands had been deported to Cayenne; troops had been called to the capital; there was almost civil war. France had destroyed her Monarchy and her Church, yet so great was the Irish hatred of England that Catholic Ireland looked to an Atheist France for salvation.

It was a difficult time for Ireland ; it was not an easy time for England; for in the presence of an overpowering danger, she had as her nearest neighbour a country bent on undermining her, led by a band of conspirators who were daily urging the enemy to land on her shores. Wolfe Tone had even accepted a commission in the French Army.

There are two ways of dealing with Revolution, conciliation or coercion. The Government had tried conciliatory measures, but the Irish were not easily conciliated, nor were the British efforts very effective. In 1792 Pitt had given the Catholics the right to vote for members, but not the right to sit in Parliament. In 1795 he had sent out Fitzwilliam to try a policy of conciliation, but had immediately recalled him. He had it in mind to send out Cornwallis on a similar mission. But the country was at this time in such a state of confusion that Castlereagh began to feel that " some system of vigour must be acted upon."

As preparations for the rebellion grew, sterner and sterner measures were put into force. Putting down a rebellion is always a bloody and dreadful business, for desperate enterprises beget desperate measures. It fell to Castlereagh's lot to apply them. Although the responsibility for this policy cannot be laid at his door, he was the active agent in the harsh régime that followed. He learnt the technique of revolution only too well, and applied it without flinching or remorse. He accomplished his task, but he gained for himself an unenviable name in Ireland.

2

The United Irishmen were causing most of the trouble by creating organised disturbances all over the country, inciting men to commit endless outrages. Pikes were being forged on every blacksmith's anvil,

arms were being hidden, and secret preparations were being made for
a French invasion which was hourly expected, and which was to be
the signal for a general rising.

In an effort to prevent such an outbreak, Camden, in 1797, instructed General Lake to disarm all persons and disperse all unlawful
assemblies by any measures he thought fit. The troops behaved with
the habitual brutality of undisciplined soldiers, and hell was let loose.
Outrages were committed not only by the troops, but also by the
United Irishmen, who intimidated with threats of assassination all
those who would not join them, maiming their cattle and burning
down their houses over their heads.

Hangings, scourgings, assassinations took place daily. The soldiers
made no scruple of stripping suspected men, tying them to trees, and
flogging them with bits and bridles. Men were transported without
trial; scenes were enacted that can rouse only feelings of horror and
compassion for the miseries of that unhappy people. Numbers
perished under the lash. Many were strangled—sometimes half-
strangled and then revived—in attempts to extort confessions; rebels
were shot or hanged in front of their families; violence and disruption
were everywhere. The Government had set in motion a machine
which did its work ruthlessly. In spite of the punishments, however,
disaffection grew. It spread even to the Militia, and thirteen of the
men received sentences of five hundred to fifteen hundred lashes each,
the sentence being carried out before all the troops of the
neighbourhood.

A frantic hatred of England now united all Ireland, and passions
grew more and more inflamed. Being ordered to take whatever
measures they thought fit for the preservation of peace, the military
made ample use of the power invested in them, appointing themselves
both judges and executioners.

"That there was a necessity for a vigour beyond the law," wrote
an Irish Presbyterian Minister, the Rev. Edward Hudson, to Charlemont, on 15 July 1797, "I am perfectly convinced, as I am also that
it has been attended with many good effects. But in many, too many
instances, it has been carried to the most shameful excess. I saw a man
upwards of three score whose hands, drawn through the latches of his
own cart, were held by two soldiers, whilst forty lashes were inflicted
on his naked body by a clergyman who was not even a magistrate.

. . . I know these are the acts of individuals, and which would not be countenanced by Government, but it is impossible to convince the people of this."

The people were in fact far from convinced that the Government did not connive in these atrocities. There were many indeed who believed that the rebellion was the work of British Ministers, that it was provoked with a view to confiscations, that it had been stirred up by the Government to provide it with a pretext for bringing more and more troops into Ireland; there were many who believed that it was merely the old principle of " divide and rule " which was agitating this reign of violence, and that the Government were stirring up the Protestants and Catholics against each other.

Such views are hardly tenable. England needed all the men she could raise to protect her own shores, and had few to spare for such enterprises, nor could it have been of any possible advantage to her at this grim moment to have on her hands a rebellious Ireland. It was due without any doubt to the dangers with which she was surrounded that England put down the rebellion so ruthlessly.

The coercive measures taken by the Government caused an uproar in the Irish Parliament, where, in May 1797, one member suggested that the Government meant to coerce the whole country, and Grattan, rising to his feet, declared that he and his supporters intended to sit in the Irish Parliament no longer. Followed by a few members he walked out of the House, and did not enter it again for two years.

The coercive measures were defended to some extent by Castlereagh, who considered that " they were only justified by the alarming state of the country." He had been appointed a member of the Committee of Secrecy of the House of Commons, the object of which was to investigate treasonable conspiracies. He had now collected a mass of evidence proving that there was direct communication between the leaders of the United Irishmen and the French, whose assistance had been promised to aid the disaffected. A general rising was to take place throughout the north in June. It was Cleland, Castlereagh's old tutor, who had discovered the plans and submitted them to Castlereagh, with the result that the United Irish forces in the north were dispersed, and their leaders arrested.

Although the country was placed more strictly under Martial Law a free pardon was offered to all persons who took the oath of allegiance. In spite of all the measures taken, the United Irish conspiracy continued to spread, and every means had to be taken to disarm the rebels before the enemy landed. An invasion fleet was now being expected from Holland, where a formidable array of ships had been collected. For weeks all eyes were directed towards the coast, but the fleet never came; it was blockaded by Duncan, the British Admiral, and for months it dared not put out of port. Little did the enemy know that Duncan's ships had sailed off to join the Mutineers at the Nore, and that part of the time he was blockading them with only one ship beside his own. With this one ship he kept the Dutch in port by constantly running up flags with which he pretended to signal to the rest of his fleet. It was fortunate for England that the ruse succeeded, and that by the time the Dutch fleet ventured out, the mutiny in the Navy was over, and Duncan's ships were with him again. In a memorable action off Camperdown, which took place in October 1797, the British Admiral annihilated the Dutch fleet, and the second attempt on Ireland came to nought.

3

Castlereagh was still spending a good deal of time with his regiment, but he had numerous other duties to perform. He had been returned unopposed as member for Down in the General Election of 1797, and when Parliament was in session, he was in Dublin speaking nightly in support of the Government. He was also attending the Assizes at Downpatrick where a number of political trials were being heard. With great courage and a supreme indifference to threats and abuse he sat on the Grand Jury, and took on himself all the odium which Government measures roused. In spite of the dangers to which he was constantly exposed and the depressing state of affairs, which would rack the strongest nerves, he remained cool, courteous, detached; and as always he found time to write pretty notes to his dearest Emily:

"I have just come from dining with the judges," he informed her, " they are both so much in love with you that they have agreed in order to avoid pulling wigs, to have you as a toast, week about.

You belong to Lord Yelverton at present. I hope *my week* will come next."

Punctilious as he was in all his arrangements his consummate orderliness was sometimes disturbed, and just before a trial, discovering that he had left all the evidence behind on the piano, he wrote a harassed note to Emily saying:

"I am most excessively distressed in having forgot that shabby green pocket-book in which were the treasonable papers. I thought I had put it in my writing-case. I must have left it either in the black deal box, the key of which Quin carries with him, or on the harpsichord where I was employed the night before I set out in separating my papers. Dearest Emily look everywhere for it, and send it to me by Quin, seal'd up. I shall be ruin'd if I don't recover it: you may remember the papers we compared together—it has red lace round it.

In haste, ever your affecte.

CASTLEREAGH" •

It was, as Haliday informed Charlemont, "a sanguinary north-west circuit," and Castlereagh received a good deal of blame for his part in it; at one trial sentence of death was pronounced on twenty men together. Although Castlereagh did not relish such brutality he acquiesced in these methods, for there was disturbance and disaffection everywhere, and a few examples he hoped "might bring the people to their senses."[1]

His father had now to be protected in his own house, so serious was the situation, by a body of troops, for neither the house nor the family were safe from attack. For a short time the rebels gained complete possession of Newtownards, and a few months later an invading force entered Mount Stewart driving its garrison out. Six of the children just managed to escape in time.[2] It was an anxious

[1] There is no foundation for the accusation that Castlereagh was one of the Council which decided on the execution of William Orr, who was found guilty of administrating unlawful oaths to two soldiers. Castlereagh was with his regiment in Dundalk at the time, and Lady Londonderry exerted herself to get Orr reprieved, but without success. Orr is still regarded as a martyr in Ireland, and his death is quite erroneously attributed to Castlereagh.

[2] Percy MSS.   Pelham MSS.

moment, for many of the mansions in the neighbourhood had been burnt down; but the estate seems to have suffered little at the hands of the rebels.

Castlereagh's official duties were beginning to multiply, for in this year he became a Lord of the Treasury and a Member of the Privy Council. Camden was most anxious for him to be appointed to the office of Chief Secretary, but there were difficulties regarding the matter, for no Irishman had ever held this position. He wrote to Pelham, who had been away in England for some time on account of ill-health, informing him that a Chief Secretary who resided in the country would be of greater advantage to the public service, and suggested that Castlereagh would be a most suitable successor to him.

Pelham's answer was to return immediately to Dublin and resume his duties. The news he brought from England was disquieting. People were tired of the war; the Press Gangs infuriated them; taxation was soaring. Wherever Pitt went he was greeted with jeers and hisses. He had become so unpopular that he was insulted in the streets, and had to be brought back from St. Paul's under an armed guard. He was still bent on peace.

"I feel it my duty," he had said to Grenville, "as an English Minister and a Christian, to use every effort to stop so bloody and wasting a war." His overtures the previous year, as everyone knew, had been rebuffed. Now, against Grenville's advice, and in face of the King's disapproval, he was making another unreasonable attempt. It was his fourth effort. Castlereagh, although he was so great an admirer of Pitt, had always deplored his peace efforts. No responsible statesman, he felt, could have consented to make peace with a France in such a state of power and aggrandisement. No responsible statesman could have expected to make a desirable peace, a peace with honour; Pelham and Camden held the same opinion. But Pitt, against all advice, against even the King's feeling in the matter, had sent Lord Malmesbury once again to the Continent, and Grenville, as Foreign Secretary, had the unenviable task of drafting his instructions.

Canning, with his love of intrigue, was spending his time as Grenville's Under-Secretary guarding Pitt's instructions to Malmesbury from Grenville's eye, endeavouring to remember what each of his colleagues in the Cabinet was supposed to know, giving secret interviews to mysterious travellers who glided silently by his window, trying to circumvent as best he could Lord Grenville's control, and generally enjoying the world of diplomacy and the complexity of foreign affairs.

But the blessings of peace were not yet to be had. A week or two later came the news that Malmesbury had been once more ordered to leave the soil of France. Peace was not to be had at any price, and England was compelled to carry on with a war for which she was still unprepared. "If we suffer ourselves to be drawn into negotiations again," Canning was saying, "we are gone."

4

Although Pelham was back in Ireland, his health was still troublesome; he was unable to bear the full burden of Government duties ; and Camden was relieved to have Castlereagh with him at the Council Board. He had reassuring manners, and he exerted a steadying influence on the more violent members, who were always pressing for extreme measures. If Castlereagh was reassuring it was not because he did not fear more serious trouble ahead, for to him the Irish question was primarily a strategic one, connected always with the possibility of a French invasion, and it had been reported that Buonaparte himself was preparing to advance on Ireland. But he had the impersonal temperament which characterises the true statesman, he had the cool wisdom and infinite patience of the born administrator, he was in the habit of considering all public affairs in the same dispassionate manner. His unruffled spirit and his freedom from personal animosity inspired confidence and respect in Camden, to whom he was most useful at this time, for Pelham's health grew rapidly worse, and Camden came to rely more and more on Castlereagh's services.

Troubles in Ireland never ceased. In December 1797, Sir Ralph Abercromby had been sent out as Commander-in-Chief of the forces. He was a fine soldier, humane and efficient, but he only added to the general difficulties. Most of the time he was quarrelling with Camden and General Lake over proclamations which had already been made. He stated that the army was "in a state of licentiousness which must render it formidable to everyone but the enemy." He issued orders that in no case where military assistance was demanded by a civilian were the troops to act without the presence and authority of a civil magistrate. This may have been a wise measure, or in the disturbed state of the country it may have been inexpedient, but it was, in effect, in distinct contradiction to Camden's Proclamation, which expressly empowered the military to act if necessary without waiting for the authority of a civil magistrate.

The Council Board flamed with violent speeches against Abercromby, whom they felt should be forced to resign, or even be impeached; the Lord-Lieutenant was in a confused, uncertain and unhappy condition; for Camden was a tolerant man, kindly and affable, and he was beginning to feel entirely unable to cope with an Ireland which grew ever more disaffected. It was possible that Abercromby, who had only just arrived, did not understand the position in Ireland; it was undeniable that the men who knew Ireland and who had the greatest power—Beresford[1] and Clare[2]—were too violent in their opinions, and that their counsels might be dangerous.

In the midst of all these troubles, Pelham, who was at least a sane and impartial adviser, developed a fever, attended, as Camden wrote to Portland, " by the spitting of blood," and the Lord-Lieutenant was left without anyone in this most important office. He found it impossible to carry on, and entreated Portland to appoint Castlereagh in Pelham's place. The objection to his being an Irishman, he submitted, " is in the present extraordinary circumstances completely counterbalanced by his other qualifications." " Under the present circumstances of the country," he concluded, " and the unexampled difficulties of the moment, from the rebellion which exists and the impression made by Sir Ralph Abercromby's orders, I cannot really go on for the moment unless this measure takes place."

While Camden was waiting for a reply from the Home Secretary the situation in Ireland was moving towards its final dramatic scene; for a plot was now discovered to seize Dublin, assassinate the Ministers, and give the country over to the French. In this enterprise the young and ardent patriot, Lord Edward Fitzgerald, was the prime mover.

[1] John Beresford, District Commissioner of Revenue.
[2] John Fitzgibbon, Earl of Clare, Lord Chancellor of Ireland.

He had always been ready for the boldest enterprises; he had always intrigued with France, but though the Government knew it, many of its members regarded him with affection and always hoped he would not involve himself too deeply. He was generous, sincere and brave, and he was loved by the whole country. It did not make matters easier that he was connected with the noblest families in Ireland. He had always been a problem to the Government, and was to grieve its members further, for he was now concerned in the most sinister plot.

The plans were revealed to the Government by Thomas Reynolds, who had either been concerned or had pretended to be concerned in the treason. As a result when the leaders held a meeting at the house of Oliver Bond in Dublin they were all arrested; Lord Edward Fitzgerald, however, had been warned not to attend, and escaped capture. He was now wanted by the Government, but the whole country protected him ; all ranks were concerned for his safety; and though he changed his place of hiding frequently, and hundreds were at times in possession of the secret, no one ever betrayed him.

There was great distress everywhere regarding Fitzgerald and even the Government hoped that he would escape. It was for Castlereagh an even more difficult problem than for other members of the Government, for Fitzgerald was a cousin of his wife's. He did all he could to help matters, and was deeply distressed. When Lady Louisa Connolly, Fitzgerald's aunt, arranged to meet Fitzgerald's brother, Charles, at the house of a Government friend, she was surprised to find Castlereagh there instead. He tried to calm her, and explained that Charles had set off for the country to get out of the way. But when she began to question him about Lord Edward he said: " I fear I cannot answer your question, for you know I am bound to secrecy." He begged her, however, not to believe any reports she might hear. " For upon my word," he declared, " nothing has yet transpired. You may rely upon the earnest wishes of the Government to do all they can for Lord Edward, who is so much loved, and as he can't be found no harm can happen to him." He was most unhappy about Fitzgerald's wife. " I pity Lady Edward most exceedingly," he said, " and will do all in my power to send her back her private letters." [1] All

[1] Life and Letters of Lady Sarah Lennox.

Fitzgerald's papers had been seized, and there was great danger of his wife being implicated.[1]

What Castlereagh could not tell Lady Louisa was the fact that word had been sent to Fitzgerald that all the ports were being left open, and that all official facilities would be extended to him if he would escape. Unfortunately Fitzgerald refused. "I am too deeply pledged to these men," he said, "to be able to withdraw with honour."

Hoping that it might still be possible to rally his followers together for the rising, which had been planned for May 23, Fitzgerald remained in Ireland, going from one place of hiding to another, visiting his wife in secret, and taking the most foolhardy risks.

Castlereagh, unable to do anything further, rejoined his regiment, but he had hardly arrived in Dundalk when an express reached him from Camden, with instructions to return immediately and hold himself in readiness to take over Pelham's duties. Camden had prevailed at last, and Castlereagh was to be Acting Chief Secretary. It was an undoubted honour that was being conferred on him, and yet Castlereagh returned to Dublin with mixed feelings. He hesitated to take on himself the mantle of Pelham, and when he met Camden, suggested that his friend, Under-Secretary Elliot, who was more experienced than he, would be far better fitted than himself for the office. Since Castlereagh insisted, Elliot was approached, but he declined the position, feeling that the duties and responsibilities were too onerous and that his health would not sustain them. Castlereagh was at length persuaded to accept the office, and on 29 March 1798, he was appointed. He was to be Acting Chief Secretary, holding the position only during the indisposition of Thomas Pelham, but though Pelham lived to be seventy once he had shaken the dust of Ireland off his feet, he never returned.

5

Castlereagh was now established at Dublin Castle in Viceregal magnificence. He was part of the splendid train of the Lord-Lieutenant, with his pages and his secretaries and his aides-de-camp,

[1] *Life of Lord Edward Fitzgerald*, by T. Moore.

his gentlemen of the bedchamber, and his gentlemen at large. After the Lord-Lieutenant he was the principal figure in Ireland, for the government of the country was conducted through the Chief Secretary. He was the Government's head organiser, its leader in the House of Commons; he was the Minister through whom reluctant voters were pressed and patronage dispensed, through whom all official intercourse passed.

He sat in his spacious room at Dublin Castle, with two Under-Secretaries and a private secretary in adjoining rooms. He was barely twenty-eight, yet all the prestige and all the influence that belonged to high office was his, and it became him well. There was an urbanity about him, a courtly grace and manner, a blandness which were in the best traditions of Dublin Castle. He conferred favours with charm, and refused them with grace.

If he had any illusions when he entered Dublin Castle he lost them rapidly. But he had always known how corrupt was government, how glutted were its supporters with pensions, preferments and bribes in return for services rendered; he had always known that the British had no strength but the army. When he sat in Council the brutality and the bitter hatreds manifested by its members made him feel more than ever the ineptitude of the whole system by which Ireland was governed.

All day long he sat working in his room at the Castle, controlling from his desk a wild and embittered country. In an adjoining room was Edward Cooke, the Civil Under-Secretary, an old Etonian and Cambridge man. He had been at the Castle for twenty years, was forty-one and inclined to be overbearing. He did not welcome a young Irish nobleman as Chief Secretary—and yet they became the firmest friends, and in spite of differences of opinion, for Castlereagh was always for Catholic Emancipation and Cooke was opposed to all concessions, their relations were most cordial.

In another room was William Elliot, the Under-Secretary for War. He was a tall, thin young Scot, who had come over with Pelham two years previously. White-faced and attenuated he was known as " the Castle spectre." He, too, was a Cambridge man, and a warm friendship already existed between him and Castlereagh. Elliot had accompanied him on a visit to Mount Stewart the previous autumn, and when, after an illness, Elliot stayed with him for a while at the Chief Secretary's

Lodge in Phoenix Park, Castlereagh called him the "comfort of my life." [1]

As his private secretary Castlereagh had chosen Alexander Knox, a man of quite peculiar character. He was a little over forty, and was affected by strong religious principles which seem to have come on him late in life, causing him to revile himself immoderately for the frivolities of youth, and to pass such severe strictures on himself that one is led to suspect him of more heinous crimes. He shared his mother's bedroom till he was thirty, formed dubious connections later, and some years after he had resigned the secretaryship and left Ireland he almost destroyed himself by an act of physical mutilation, caused it was said by a passion for the wife of Sir Robert Peel.

In spite of these abnormalities Knox seems to have been a man of intelligence and culture and great conversational powers. He, too, had the deepest regard for Castlereagh. "Wherever I am," he wrote to him after he left Ireland, "in whatever circumstances I may be, I must still, until consciousness and recollection leave me, think of you."

6

Castlereagh's entry into office as Acting Chief Secretary, in March 1798, was marked by decisive action. After the arrest of the United Irish leaders Camden had vainly temporised. With Pelham ill and Castlereagh in Quarters he had felt himself incapable of action, and by delay and irresolution he had allowed the rebel forces to muster. Everything was working up to one of those alarming crises with which the Government of Ireland was only too familiar.

The day after Castlereagh entered on his new duties a meeting of the Privy Council was called, and a Proclamation was published announcing the existence of a conspiracy against the Government. Orders were issued giving the military power to suppress violence and rebellion with the utmost rigour, and to disarm the rebels and all persons disaffected to His Majesty's Government by the most summary and effectual measures.

On the same day Castlereagh sent a copy of the proclamation to

[1] Pelham MSS.

Abercromby, and ordered him to direct the military to act without waiting for authority from the civil magistrates in the dispersing of unlawful assemblies. Abercromby was compelled to withdraw his previous order, and was driven to resign. Military rule was now to be exercised throughout the whole country. Unless arms were surrendered troops were to be given free quarters among the people and authorised to demand forage and to commandeer horses and carriages as required. In many cases the troops behaved outrageously, burning down houses where arms were found, or where pikes were being manufactured.

Castlereagh had no deadly zeal against the liberties of mankind; but he was obsessed by the dangers of a French invasion, and he felt that Ireland, with her warring factions, her instability, her wild moods, must be subdued before the French landed. He did his best to govern Ireland, though Ireland was not in any governable condition, and he tried his utmost to calm the ferocious spirit of his colleagues, who demanded measures even more severe than those already in force.

In the Council Chamber there were angry explosions daily, and feverish harangues; nerves were jangled, and tempers short. Lord Chancellor Fitzgibbon, who had recently been made Earl of Clare, an arrogant and intolerant individual, full of violent animosities of furious personal antipathies, and hostility to all popular claims, lashing himself as ever into a fury against the Catholics, was now demanding that every political prisoner should be attainted and executed; he was even defending the use of torture for the purpose of discovering concealed arms. There were continuous wranglings. Beresford, another implacable foe of the Catholics, was advocating the policy of flogging to obtain information. Beresford controlled so many boroughs that Castlereagh had to exercise all his tact and diplomacy to keep him within bounds.

He did all he could to stem the tide of bloodshed. He stated publicly that every complaint of military licence would receive immediate attention, and redress would be afforded. He ordered that free quarters should be discontinued, but not before it had been violently abused.

Although the proclamation, which gave the military power to act without waiting for directions from the civil magistrates, was regarded as the highest mark of tyranny, it was apparently a necessary step in suppressing the rebellion. One of the rebel leaders[1] subsequently admitted in his memoirs, that up to the time of the proclamation the process of arming the people had gone on smoothly in the south, and that it was this proclamation and its accompanying precautions which alone checked it.

7

The arrest of the leaders at Oliver Bond's house seemed to have halted the conspiracy, but there were other leaders, unknown to the Government, meeting at Michael Byrne's bookshop in Dublin, planning the final preparations for a general rising. They had learnt caution, and the Government was completely unaware of their existence. But at the last moment they made one mistake. They took into their confidence a young captain of the King's County Militia, which was noted for its disaffection, and tried to bring him into the plot. He immediately communicated with his commanding officer who, greatly alarmed at the disclosures, took him to the Castle, where he saw Castlereagh. The pale face of the bland Chief Secretary must have gone paler still when he heard the news. He advised the young captain to accept an invitation he had received to dine with the conspirators, and he discovered in this way that the rising was to take place the following Monday. He issued warrants immediately for the arrest of Michael Byrne, and all who were concerned in the plot.

A proclamation was issued at the same time offering a reward of a thousand pounds for the apprehension of Lord Edward Fitzgerald, who was now on his way to Dublin to be in readiness for the revolt.

The Government had already been informed of his movements, and a few moments after his arrival in Dublin, Major Swan and Mr. Ryan who had been sent to arrest him forced their way into his room. As they entered, he sprang at them like a tiger, and a desperate scuffle ensued. Stabbing Swan with a dagger, Fitzgerald grappled with Ryan, whom he stabbed in the stomach again and again, till Ryan fell on the floor in a welter of blood, mortally wounded. Major Sirr, who had followed the two men in, aimed his pistol at Fitzgerald, and fired, wounding him in the arm. Even then it was not without a

[1] Michael Byrne's Memoirs.

desperate fight that Fitzgerald was taken. Bruised and bleeding he was conveyed in a sedan chair to the Castle, where Castlereagh saw him.

He sent immediately for a surgeon, and Fitzgerald lay back on two chairs while his wound was dressed. At the same time Castlereagh sent a messenger to Camden who was at the theatre. It was unfortunate that in an adjoining box Lady Castlereagh was entertaining a party which included a number of Lord Edward's relatives. One of them was so overcome at the news that Lady Castlereagh had to lead her out of the theatre, and together they went to Moira House to comfort his wife, the unfortunate Lady Pamela, who was staying with Lady Moira.

Castlereagh had hoped to lodge Fitzgerald in an apartment of the Castle, but the magistrates claimed him as he had killed one of their men, and he was taken to Newgate.

While he was in prison his wound became inflamed, and gave rise to a fever from which he never recovered. On 4 June 1798, he died, a martyr to the cause he had had so sincerely and honestly at heart.

Although Castlereagh had been unable to do anything for Fitzgerald he was able to arrange for the peaceful departure from Ireland of his wife. He silenced the Press as to her movements, and afforded her every courtesy.

8

The Irish Rebellion, in spite of the arrest of its leaders, broke out on the appointed day, 23 May 1798. With its massacres and retaliations, its outrages, its dark and bitter hatreds, it flamed through the country, and Castlereagh's first task as Chief Secretary was the unenviable duty of suppressing the revolt.

The rebels, deprived of their leaders, relied now on numbers, which they collected by force as they passed through the country—" poor creatures," Lady Louisa Connolly wrote, " who confessed that they did not know what they were going to fight for."

The rebellion spread in all directions. In the south it assumed the character of a religious contest, and, not content with fighting the British, the Irish fought each other—Protestant against Catholic, Catholic against Protestant—in religious frenzies. In spite of all

Castlereagh's attempts to prevent excesses, atrocities were committed daily. For these Castlereagh received the blame. The newspapers attacked him, bitter invectives were poured on him, but he met all onslaughts with the same calm indifference. His task was to assist the Government in putting down the rebellion, and his efforts never slackened. Cool and detached, displaying an exquisite appreciation of circumstances, a shrewd acquaintance with the conditions of Irish life and the temper of the Irish people, he went soberly about his duties.

Under his lead the Government proclaimed Martial Law throughout the Kingdom. Though it gave rise to more excesses, the extent and the enormity of the treason, he felt, made it essential for the preservation of the State. The country was ill-protected; it was almost defenceless; the troops he had demanded from England failed to arrive, and amid all the confusions he heard with dismay that Napoleon's fleet had sailed out of Toulon. It was the expedition which had been expected by the Irish as their signal for a general rising.

Although Buonaparte had changed his plans, and was on his way to Egypt, Castlereagh's nightmare was not yet over. At one time eight hundred of the Dublin garrison offered to give up the barracks if the leaders would only give the signal. In an hour they could have captured the capital and paralysed the whole Government. There was alarm for the Government's very existence. The small bodies of troops quartered everywhere were harassed to death.

Reports of cruelties were still coming to Castlereagh, but he heard of them on both sides, and with all his power he could not stop them. Horrors abounded. From his window in the Castle he saw, it is alleged, the carcases of the dead stretched out in the Castle Yard as trophies. They were cut and gashed in every part, covered with dust and clotted blood, a most frightful spectacle. On the gates, as he entered, he saw the severed heads of traitors. If he had a queasy stomach, such scenes must have sickened him.

How long ago was it that he had written so happily to Lady Elizabeth Pratt, " Our regiment has learned its duty so fast that they make now a very respectable appearance, and it has been all effected without flogging." So quickly does one grow old, and hardened, and disillusioned.

To-day he was writing to her sadly :

" As to myself, I have not sought the responsibility which for a time may rest on me—had I courted it I should tremble. As it is, I feel tranquil in the sincerity of my endeavours to do my duty."

But he hoped that Pelham would soon be restored to health, and relieve him of the responsibility which had fallen too heavily on his shoulders.

It was a dark, depressing world he lived in. In the towns, houses were shuttered and barred, shop windows were smashed, printing presses wrecked in the street, carts overturned. A pall of smoke rolled ominously on the wind, and everyone knew that somewhere houses were burning, and men being piked to death. In the streets people hurried on with set faces, slowed down suddenly, and hurried on again. It was a suspicious, surly land.

Wexford was the central point of the Revolution. Led by Father John Murphy, the Catholics of Wexford fought with fanatical passion. At Scullabogue they put a hundred Protestant prisoners to death, deliberately firing the barn in which they were held captive. Not one escaped. The Protestants behaved with equal vindictiveness and savagery.

The camp at Vinegar Hill, where the rebels fortified themselves, was carried at length by the military after a violent struggle, but the carnage was horrible. " I really feel most severely," said General Lake, " the being obliged to order so many men out of the world, but I am convinced that if severe and many examples are not made, the rebellion cannot be put a stop to."

Castlereagh did all he could to alleviate the evil. In a letter congratulating General Lake on his victory he said: " It would be unwise and contrary I know to your general feelings to drive the wretched people, who are mere instruments in the hands of the more wicked, to despair. The leaders are just objects of punishment." [1]

But the rebellion continued. The rebels, dispersed at Wexford, moved on to Wicklow, dispersed at Wicklow, moved on to Kildare. Camden, who felt that Lake was unequal to the emergency, and who was annoyed with the Government for not dispatching the reinforcements promised, sent in his resignation, urging the Government at the same time to send over General Cornwallis, to combine

[1] *Castlereagh Correspondence.*

the offices of Lord-Lieutenant and Commander-in-Chief of the Forces. On 21 June 1798, Cornwallis arrived in Dublin. He had been sent out to conciliate the Irish, and his first step was to issue a Proclamation authorising " His Majesty's Generals to give protection to such insurgents as should surrender their arms and take the oath of allegiance to the King." He recalled General Lake from Wexford, and appointed in his stead General Hunter, directing him " to put an end to the indiscriminate slaughter." Hunter was indefatigable in his exertions to restore confidence to the people.

Of Cornwallis the Irish historian, Plowden, writes: " This appointment under Providence was the salvation of Ireland. His Lordship had it in his special commission to put down the rebellion in Ireland by moderation and to check the ferocity of the Orange system by firmness."

The rebellion was nearly over. It had died down in Wexford only to flare up in the north, but in Ulster it began feebly, and met with little success. The only considerable body of insurgents took up their stand at Ballynahinch, on Lord Moira's demesne. " The rebels fought at Ballynahinch, as in Wexford, with determined bravery," wrote Castlereagh, " but without the fanaticism of the southerns. . . . The body there assembled was entirely dispersed. In their ranks were found two of my father's servants, a footman and a postilion." [1]

Under their leader Henry Monroe, a young shopkeeper of Lisburn, the rebels actually put up such a fight that they nearly defeated the Royal Army, but in the end they were routed. The town was pillaged and fired, Monroe was carried to Lisburn, and hanged at his own door, while his wife and family were in the house ; his head was afterwards exhibited on a pike on the market house opposite his residence. Ulster was settled once and for all, and no further attempt was ever again made to raise the standard of rebellion in the north; but throughout the country the troops behaved with incredible brutality, and the atrocities committed and the reprisals taken left an indelible mark on the mind and memory of Ireland.

[1] Castlereagh to Elliot. Pelham MSS.

9

The battle of Ballynahinch caused Castlereagh to lose one of his dearest friends, the beautiful Lady Moira, whose husband had been doing all he could in the English Parliament to get the repressive measures in Ireland repealed. Castlereagh was aghast one morning to receive a letter from Lady Moira written in the third person informing him that henceforth all intercourse between them must cease.[1] She returned, at the same time, a book he had lent her only the day before, when he had sat with her for an hour, and never saw her more cordial.

He was very much disturbed by the letter, and sent it on to his stepmother, telling her he scarcely knew whether it grieved or surprised him most " to have given such mortal offence and yet not be able in the smallest degree to divine the cause." They had parted the best friends possible. " Can she possibly resent," he asks, " or trace to me any of the acts of severity exercised by the military at Ballynahinch ? In short, it is impossible to comprehend what called forth so much indignation. I love her so sincerely, and have long felt myself so closely connected with her in friendship, that I cannot but feel most anxious till this strange business is unravel'd."

Notwithstanding the disastrous state of the country Castlereagh announced in the House of Commons on 17 July a general pardon to all who would surrender their weapons within fourteen days; he also presented a Bill for granting compensation to such of His Majesty's loyal subjects as had suffered losses in their property in consequence of the late rebellion.

On 30 July he wrote to Wickham[2] that " the earnest wish of the Lord-Lieutenant and himself was that the principle of pardon should be pushed as far as may be at all compatible with the public safety."

In the House of Commons when one member suggested that all persons already in custody, charged with high treason, should be tried by military courts and executed as quickly as possible, Castlereagh intervened, and the proposal was abandoned.

On the day before the rebellion broke out, Pitt was engaged

[1] Camden Papers. Undated. Unpublished.
[2] Under-Secretary of State for Home Affairs.

in fighting a duel with Tierney, who was temporarily leader of the Opposition. Tierney had taken exception to Pitt's taunt that he was obstructing the defence of the country, and since Pitt refused to withdraw the observation, the two statesmen met and exchanged shots. No one was injured, and honour was satisfied. But afterwards rumours began to circulate that Pitt was insane. His health was certainly impaired, he had begun to suffer greatly from headaches, and a continuous display of nervous irritability gave rise to this strange report.

Writing an account of the duel to his friend Richard Wellesley, who had just gone out to India as Governor-General, Pitt mentioned incidentally that there was a rebellion in Ireland which he trusted would be crushed before any attempt at invasion could be made by France. He added significantly: " We must, I think, follow up such an event by immediate steps for a Union." The troops, he observed, were " behaving incomparably."

CHAPTER V

I

THE REVOLT with its atrocities, its violence and its outrages, was over. Castlereagh had taken it by the throat and strangled it; he had stifled it so effectively that it had lasted barely a month. The troops promised by the War Office had been sent with customary optimism three weeks late. "With French assistance," Castlereagh said, "the people could have carried the country before a regiment from the other side found its way to our assistance." But the French delayed, and by the time the invasion arrived, the rebellion was over, and the country quiet.

Scarcely five weeks after the revolt had been suppressed, the French troops landed at Killala Bay, and even though the people did not rise, the invaders won a preliminary victory at Castlebar, where General Lake's Militiamen distinguished themselves by fleeing in panic at the first charge of the enemy. The engagement became known as the "Castlebar Races." What might have been the result of the invasion had the Irish Government been faced at the same time with open rebellion in the country it is not difficult to surmise. But Lord Cornwallis, who had been sent out in Camden's place, was already on the march with 30,000 men, and the invading army was rounded up.

There were other attempts at invasion, but they were all minor efforts. In October, Napper Tandy, an absurd, drunken, loquacious little Irish ironmonger, landed in Donegal with a corvette of French soldiers and marines, and a handful of United Irishmen. But nobody joined him. The few fishermen who espied the invaders took to their boats in terror, and the place was deserted when they landed. Napper Tandy issued a bloodthirsty proclamation to the deserted shore; he then got so drunk celebrating his arrival that he was unable to get back to his ship, and had to be carried on board. A day or two later he sailed away, having done no very great harm, returning to France a hero and a martyr, only to die there of dysentery.[1]

About the same time Castlereagh heard that another French squadron was sailing from Lough Swilly; he sent the information to Admiral Kingsmill, and the French ships were intercepted. After a short action the invaders surrendered to a British fleet; one of the first prisoners to step ashore was Wolfe Tone, the founder of the United Irishmen. He was a dynamic, heroic young man of twenty-eight, who had once been a brilliant lawyer; his sallow face and long lank hair now graced the uniform of a French general. Carried in irons to Dublin, he was tried by court martial and sentenced to be hanged, but he managed to avoid the rope by cutting his throat with a razor while he was in prison.

It was fortunate indeed for England that Buonaparte himself had abandoned Ireland for Egypt, and that France was able to launch only a few isolated expeditions which were easily crushed. Years afterwards at St. Helena, Napoleon realised his mistake. " *Si au lieu de l'expédition de l'Egypte,*" he said, " *j'eusse fait celle de l'Irlande—si de legers dérangements n'avaient mis obstacle à mon entreprise de Boulogne, que pourrait l'Angleterre aujourd'hui? A quoi tiennent les destinées des Empires!*" If he had gone to Ireland instead of Egypt, if chance disturbances had not upset his arrangements at Boulogne, what would England have been to-day? On such small matters depend the destinies of Empires.

Had he indeed come with all his forces at the outbreak of the rebellion, as the Irish expected, Ireland would surely have been lost and England's fate might have been sealed. But he had gone to Egypt and sealed his own fate, for it was there that he received his first check. Though he had taken Malta on his way out, he had fallen in with Nelson when he arrived, and his fleet had been utterly destroyed at Aboukir Bay. Early in October, Castlereagh rose in the Irish House of Commons to announce Nelson's victory over Buonaparte in the Battle of the Nile. With unusual warmth he moved a vote of thanks to " the gallant Admiral, Sir Horatio Nelson, the gallant officers of the fleet, and the brave soldiers and seamen, for the valour evinced by them on this glorious occasion." Nelson was

[1] Harold Nicolson: *The Desire to Please.*

wounded, but the French had been so completely defeated that all communications between France and her army were cut off. Buonaparte's army of England was now shut up in Egypt, and the fleets of Great Britain swept the seas.

2

Castlereagh was still Acting Chief Secretary. The position was his until Pelham should return, or until a new Chief Secretary should be appointed. For over six months he had borne almost unaided the burden of Government business in the House of Commons; he had shown unsuspected gifts as a parliamentary manager; he had kept within bounds the inflammatory members led by Clare and Beresford, who were still violently attacking the Catholics; and Cornwallis had found him as indispensable as Camden had done. But Castlereagh had as yet no fixed position and sooner or later he would be out of office.

Camden, who was at Walmer staying with Pitt, discussed his young relative with him, and was glad to hear Pitt say that he was impressed, as indeed were all the Ministers, with a very high opinion of Lord Castlereagh's capacity and conduct. He confessed that he had been prejudiced against an Irishman occupying the office of Chief Secretary, but that the perfect impartiality Castlereagh had shown in Irish affairs, and the line he had adopted, had so much taken off that prejudice in his mind that he had totally overcome it, and he wished that Pelham would decide not to return to Ireland, so that he might appoint Castlereagh in his place.

Camden was happy to hear these opinions expressed, but he knew that the matter did not rest entirely with Pitt. The King too had his prejudices. There was also Pelham, who, though he admired Castlereagh greatly, was not yet ready to take the step which might leave his office open to him.

"I have followed you," Pelham wrote to Castlereagh, "through all the difficulties and vexations attending your situation with the most sincere satisfaction and pleasure; my vanity in some measure gratified in observing that all I expected and foretold to others respecting you had been so fully accomplished; and having received the satisfaction which a friend alone can feel of hearing persons of different descriptions, both here and in Ireland, speaking with unanimous approbation of your conduct, which I consider a sort of victory and triumph on your part, as you must be aware that there was considerable prejudice both here and in Ireland against the appointment of an Irishman."[1]

But Pelham had nevertheless decided to return to his post. He suggested, however, that Castlereagh on vacating his office should be appointed Chancellor of the Exchequer, receiving at the same time an English peerage. Castlereagh declined the appointment, chiefly out of consideration for Parnell, who had held the office for nearly fifteen years; he also declined the peerage which would have removed him from the House of Commons, expressing himself with becoming modesty as " perfectly satisfied with the favours already shown me."

Pelham, however, did not return to Ireland; his health eventually compelled him to resign. Cornwallis now pressed in the strongest terms for the appointment of Castlereagh as Chief Secretary. Pelham and Pitt were equally anxious for his appointment, but it was some time before the King could be persuaded that the appointment of a stranger, after the recent events, would be dangerous, and that Castlereagh, although an Irishman, was the only man with the necessary qualities, who would be willing to accept the office.

On the 8 November 1798, Castlereagh received the news that he had been officially appointed Chief Secretary. It was a signal honour. He was the first Irishman to hold the office. Delighted with his new dignities he took a day or two off from his labours to carry the news himself to his father. But as he lay that night at Mount Stewart, listening to the soft tides of Strangford Lough, his more critical judgment must have given him some inkling of all that these honours would cost him, of the burden they would lay on him, of the loneliness they would bring him. For he knew what was in Pitt's mind regarding Ireland, and though his cool, controlled convictions coincided with the measure that Pitt meditated, he shrewdly guessed at the burning passions which would be roused in the hearts of his countrymen by the event already foreshadowed.

He had played his first conspicuous part in the unhappy scene of the Irish Rebellion, and had received more than his share of the odium excited by its barbarities; it was the only subject which in later years

[1] *Castlereagh Correspondence.*

CASTLEREAGH, AS A YOUNG MAN

By T. Lawrence

ruffled his temper in debate. He was to play his second great rôle in an equally tragic scene; for Pitt, finding the difficulties of reaching a settlement after all the recent disturbances almost insuperable, had come to the conclusion that now was the time for a sudden and daring step. He had resolved to put into effect a project which had long been in his mind—the union of England and Ireland.

Castlereagh was again to be the instrument chosen by the Government to bring about what Ireland considered to be the abolition of her freedom, and he was to incur even greater hatred for his part in carrying the Union than for his part in suppressing the revolt.

3

On 6 December 1798 he left for England to discuss the Union with British Ministers. Although there were complaints that his youth and inexperience rendered him unfit for such important work, the Ministers found him equal to it; and indeed for the task in hand, the ruthless suppression of opposition, the management of turbulent crowds, and of a violently divided House of Commons no one was better qualified than the cool, impassive, level-headed Castlereagh.

He was sworn a member of the English Privy Council, kneeling before His Majesty to take the oath of allegiance and rising to take the oath as a Councillor of State. He kissed the King's hand, shook hands with every Councillor present, and took his seat at the Board. He was the youngest of the few Irishmen on whom this honour had been conferred, and no one could deny that he carried his honours well.

During the discussions he informed the Ministers in his quiet, confident way, that if the British Government were determined to carry the measure, and would permit a proper military force to be kept in Ireland, there could not be any doubt of its success, nor could any reasonable fear be entertained of serious danger in the attempt.

His arguments convinced the Ministers, who found themselves well satisfied with his clear, long-sighted views, and he was instructed to introduce the Union in the Irish Parliament when it opened in January.

In spite of his confident manner he had no illusions about Ireland, nor was he ignorant of the difficulties that would arise. Writing to the Earl of Shannon after the discussions, he said: " Before we reach our port we shall have many a rude blast. I trust our friends will not mind it, and we shall yet do well."

He made various amendments to the Union draft, which the Ministers accepted, and in less than a fortnight he was back at the Castle with the amended draft in his portfolio. A few days later Portland, the Home Secretary, was informing Pelham that: " His talents, conduct, and manners very justly entitle him to the testimony you have long borne them."[1]

Back in Ireland Castlereagh began sounding leading personalities, interviewing possible friends and potential enemies, putting pressure on some, promising preferment to others, promising peerages, promising hard cash, suggesting quietly that His Majesty's Government would have no use for men who were against the Union. Sir John Parnell was actually dismissed from office for opposing the measure. As the Speaker, Foster, who was also against the Union, could not be removed, his son was discharged from his post in the Revenue.

There was nothing decent about such methods—" bribing knaves into honesty and fools into common sense "[2]—but it was the way Ireland had always been governed; and the Union, Castlereagh told himself, which could only be brought about by corruption, would end corruption once and for all; it was the only way of destroying the evil. His duty, as he saw it, was " to buy out and secure to the Crown for ever the fee simple of Irish corruption, which has so long enfeebled the powers of Government and endangered the connection."[3] It was the only means of healing the distractions of the country, and of securing its connection with Great Britain.

There was much for the Chief Secretary to do before Parliament opened. Work piled up for him, and he sat at his desk through the long night writing endlessly, writing letters, writing dispatches. His correspondence grew heavier and heavier, but he wrote every letter, every dispatch, with his own hand. His industry was enormous. Cornwallis sent him urgent messages: " There is no time to lose in

[1] Pelham MSS.

[2] Essays by Robert, Marquess of Salisbury.

[3] Castlereagh to Cooke, 21 June 1800: *Castlereagh Correspondence*.

this business. If you can come for ten minutes I shall be glad to see you. The ride will do you good." His horse was saddled, and he would canter across the park, begrudging every moment he gave. A letter would arrive from Camden, complaining that he had not even written to inquire after his health. He must write to Camden too. His own health was not very good either; he was completely exhausted by the strain.

4

On 22 January 1799 the debate on the Union opened. As Castlereagh took his place in the House he felt pretty confident of success. He had bribed and threatened all along the line, and he knew, or thought he knew, how most of the members would vote. It was four o'clock in the afternoon, the candles were already lit, and the House was packed. Up in the gallery, which was filled to overflowing, he saw Emily, and caught her eye.

The atmosphere was charged with excitement, and as soon as the word " Union " was mentioned there was an uproar in the House. Ponsonby rose, and, in order to prevent the Union being brought forward, moved an amendment to the King's Speech, pledging the House to maintain a free and independent legislation. A long and acrimonious debate followed. As speaker after speaker rose, torrents of invective were poured forth; the members grew more and more bitter and vituperative, and Castlereagh came in for a good deal of abuse. The evening lengthened, and it was not till after midnight that Castlereagh rose to address the House. Amid the rocking currents of the debate his voice was calm and steady, his bearing grave and courteous. As the excitement in the chamber grew more and more intense, his calm, elegant, and courteous bearing grew more pronounced; but in spite of all his measured arguments the House remained hostile. He spoke, it was said, " with great manliness and good sense." Indeed, as Barrington, one of his opponents remarked, " he far exceeded the powers he was supposed to possess." He was neither dramatic, nor rhetorical, he explained simply and sincerely what the Union would mean for England and for Ireland; and he trusted that no man would decide on a measure of such importance on private or personal motives. "If Great Britain calls for your subjection," he said, "resist it, but if she wishes to unite with you on terms of equality 'tis madness not to accept the offer."

After he had resumed his seat, Plunket rose and made a violent attack on Castlereagh's personal character. He described him as "a green and sapless twig"—a reflection on him apparently because the Lord had not blessed his marriage with children. He was "a young philosopher who has been transplanted from the nursery to the Cabinet, to outrage the feelings and understanding of the country." "During the administration of this unassuming stripling," Plunkett declaimed, "a system of black corruption has been carried on within the walls of the Castle." Neither did Pitt escape; he found Pitt's example "inimitable in its vices."

Plunket was cheered tumultuously, and when Ponsonby's amendment pledging the House to maintain a free and independent legislation went into a division, he nearly carried the House with him. His amendment was lost, however, by one vote. Castlereagh was aghast at the narrow escape, having expected from his calculations a majority of 45. Actually the Government escaped by the merest accident, for there was one member, Luke Fox, representing a pocket borough of Lord Ely's, an anti-unionist, who had been sitting with the anti-unionists and who had not registered his vote. When the doors were locked he had concealed himself in a dark corner of the House to avoid voting, but he was discovered, and the Sergeant-at-Arms was ordered to bring him forward to be counted amongst the opponents of the Union. Had this been done the numbers would have been equal, and the Speaker, who was against the Union, would have given his casting vote for the amendment; the Union would have been lost, and Castlereagh prevented from raising the question again ; but Luke Fox suddenly declared that he had accepted the office of the Escheatorship of Munster from Lord Castlereagh, which vacated his seat and precluded him from voting.

It had been a near thing, but the Government was saved. As the Opposition had done so well Mr. Ponsonby proposed fixing an early date for a debate on the principle of Union, but Castlereagh checkmated this move by informing the House that he would not persist any further in the measure at present. He was not desirous, he said, of forcing the measure with any precipitation, nor against the wish of the House, but if the public mind should change, in such a case he thought he would be justified in resuming the subject.

The question had been run too close for him to take any risk.

5

The debate had continued without interruption from four o'clock on Tuesday afternoon till one o'clock on Wednesday afternoon. But it was not yet over. The following day Sir Lawrence Parsons moved that the paragraph in the King's Address relating to the Union should be expunged from the records; upon this another debate ensued which went on without interruption for another twenty-two hours. The streets were packed with excited crowds, and the House surrounded by angry demonstrators.

During the debate one of the speakers stated that the Government was seeking to betray the country now that Ireland was weak from civil war and overrun with troops. Castlereagh immediately rose, and spoke with unusual heat, attacking the Opposition with great severity for its tactics. " I have heard alleged against Ministers," he said sternly, " facts of so base and false a tenor that I will trace them to the individual, be he who he may, from whom they originate, and force him to make a public disavowal." He deprecated the " equivocal language " used. " If gentlemen conceive," he said, " that any man on this side of the House has done them personal injury, let them come forward and seek redress like men, but let them not resort to that kind of language which is just so far short of personal offence as to shelter them from personal chastisement."

He faced the House fearlessly, and spoke with great vigour. But the cause was lost. Many of those who had promised their support had been bought over by the Opposition, which had paid, it was alleged, as much as five thousand pounds for a vote. Castlereagh's calculations had gone amiss. Parsons won his motion by five votes, and the paragraph relating to the Union was expunged from the records.

As the House was about to adjourn Ponsonby rose and informed members that in order to prevent the Union ever again being brought forward he would move a resolution in the words of his amendment rejected by one vote the day before, pledging the House to maintain its independent legislation.

Castlereagh jumped to his feet, and protested against such an unconstitutional attempt to bind the House. " A time may come," he said, " and I believe it will come soon, when the country and the House may view the matter in a different light, and they may then repent the precipitancy and temerity of the resolution which has been proposed." It was an effective move by Castlereagh, and it saved the situation. Ponsonby was compelled to withdraw his motion, but before the House adjourned Castlereagh had to give his assurance that he would not bring forward the measure again " so long as it appeared repugnant to the sense of Parliament and the country."

It was a disheartening moment. The Opposition had won. Dublin went wild with excitement, the city was illuminated, and the mob ran riot. Threatening crowds assembled before Castlereagh's house, and troops had to be called out. It was an unfortunate beginning. The Opposition laid bets that Castlereagh would be out of office within a month. But Castlereagh was endowed with indomitable courage and an iron will, and he held on. " For most assuredly," he said, " the language and conduct both without and within doors has been such on the late occasion as to satisfy every thinking man that if the countries are not speedily incorporated, they will ere long be committed against each other."

After all the effort he had put forward Castlereagh was depressed by his failure, but he was not discouraged. Writing to the Duke of Portland he said:

" However I may have failed, from inability, in the discharge of the important trust committed to me, I am confident your Grace will believe there has been no defect of zeal."

Portland was by no means dissatisfied with Castlereagh's efforts; he was in fact already writing to him, expressing the satisfaction of all the King's Servants on his conduct, congratulating him on the temper, the firmness, and the spirit he had displayed on both these important and most trying occasions, attributing to him the entire defeat and total rout of Mr. George Ponsonby's motion, informing him that he had " acquired a respect and confidence which would facilitate all the measures of his administration, and his future course in life."

As the year progressed Castlereagh continued preparing the ground, for he was determined that the Union should be carried. More work, more anxiety, more desperate struggles devolved on him; he was so loaded with duties and affairs that he scarcely had time to breathe. Although his health was again giving him trouble, he had no time to consider it; so many other things were occupying his mind.

It was a comfort that Buonaparte was still in Egypt, still cut off by the British navy from all communication with the Continent. In spite of the destruction of his fleet at Aboukir Bay he had stormed his way to Jaffa, had massacred the Turkish garrison of three thousand men who had surrendered to him, and had marched on Acre; but here another British seaman, Sir Sidney Smith, interfered with his plans and helped the Turks to hold out. Again and again Buonaparte tried to take the city. Again and again he failed. There was plague in his camp, his men were mutinous, and the flags of England and Turkey continued to fly over the white walls of Acre.

" If it had not been for you English," he afterwards declared, " I should have been Emperor of the East, but wherever there is water to float a ship, we are sure to find you in the way."

Baffled at Acre he had written to Tippoo Sahib, ruler of Mysore, that he was on his way with an invincible army to deliver India from the iron yoke of England; but Tippoo Sahib had been slain, and his armies defeated by the British troops at Seringapatam. Castlereagh must have noted with interest that it was an Irish acquaintance, Arthur Wellesley, who was largely responsible for these operations.

The political horizon seemed to be clearing. In Buonaparte's absence Pitt had formed a new coalition with Austria, Russia, Turkey, Portugal and the two Sicilies; the Russians and Austrians were now overrunning all Buonaparte's continental conquests. The fortunes of France were crumbling; it looked as though peace might be had within the year.

6

Although disaster was in the year 1799 overtaking the French everywhere, reports came that they were making preparations at Brest for another invasion of Ireland. It caused the usual agitation among the lower classes, and the usual rumours of intended insurrections.

Robberies and murders were again taking place, cattle were being destroyed, sentries on the bridges were being shot, the countryside was growing black and sullen. Castlereagh found it necessary to introduce into Parliament a new Martial Law Bill, and a number of British troops were stationed in the country.

In the meantime he went on canvassing votes for the Union. The bulk of the people were, in his opinion, by no means averse to the Union. The south was definitely for it, the north indifferent. Dublin and central Ireland were against it. But the chief opposition came from Parliament, many of whose members would suffer financial loss by Union, but here money and influence could still do everything. Votes had always been gained by the grossest bribery. Castlereagh used the old system but with greater effect. Over a million pounds in money and a vast number of peerages and places were distributed among the members of Parliament. A shameful traffic and a sordid bargaining began. "I despise and hate myself every hour," wrote Cornwallis, the Lord-Lieutenant, "for engaging in such dirty work; and am only supported by the reflection that without a Union the British Empire must be dissolved."

Castlereagh quietly continued his labours. He knew men, especially he knew their weaknesses, and he knew how to turn them to account. He knew how much they would bear, he knew how much would buy them. He had involved himself in an enterprise which could not be honourable to England, and which inflicted damage on his greatest interests. It may have been a fatal blunder, shrewd politician though he was, to force a Union on an unwilling people, but he earnestly believed it to be the only way of settling Ireland, and of saving the British Empire.

His path was beset with difficulties; it led through conflict and despair, but his confidence and courage carried him and the Government through all its dangers. He had an adroitness and a capacity in conducting state affairs which even his enemies came to respect. Whether he were offering favours or refusing them his gentle and agreeable manner never changed. Day and night he laboured to overcome the immense obstacles that faced him, to reconcile conflicting opinions, to restore order out of chaos.

As a result of his efforts the Government began to gain ground. In the autumn, accompanied by Emily, he crossed again to England, hoping to obtain a definite statement from the Ministers regarding the Catholics, for although during these past months a good deal of progress had been made he felt that the Union could not be carried without the Catholic vote.

7

It was not a propitious moment to be setting out for England, for the Ministers were engrossed by other matters. The War situation was perilous. Although Pitt had combined the whole of Europe against France, and the French had been driven back across the Rhine and across the Alps, it was in this hour, when Britain stood so well, that Pitt conceived one of his ill-starred plans. He had begun to prepare for the invasion of Europe. After having prepared so long *against* invasion, the people of England had welcomed the idea of preparing *for* an invasion. There had been great enthusiasm throughout the country, marshalling of troops, parades and drilling.

But the senior officers of the Regular Army were not so enthusiastic. Sir Ralph Abercromby had expressed the strongest disapproval of the project. What transport was there for guns? he had inquired. For the sick and wounded? For provisions? Where were the flat-bottomed barges that would be required? What about greatcoats for the soldiers? Tent-equipment? Fuel?

"There are some people," Pitt had murmured, "who have pleasure in opposing whatever is proposed."

To the Prime Minister these matters had seemed of secondary importance. He had grown more and more impatient with Abercromby's long list of obstacles, and the old soldier had been hurried to sea. Castlereagh's brother, Charles, had accompanied Sir Ralph Abercromby on the expedition, and Castlereagh must have received disquieting news from him, for everything had gone wrong from the start.

Before they had got to the Helder, where the army was to land, they had been overtaken by violent storms; when they arrived they had been met by a tremendous barrage of fire from the defenders, who were expecting them. In spite of this Abercromby had managed to get his men ashore, and two days later the British navy had been lucky enough to capture the Dutch fleet lying at anchor. Seven Dutch ships and eighteen smaller warships passed into British hands without a shot being fired.

Had Abercromby been able to press on, he would have encountered little resistance, but he was short of wagons, short of horses and artillery. He was short of food and water. Two thousand of his men fell sick. To add to the general mismanagement the Duke of York was sent out to take over the command. He was sent at the head of as large a force as any England had commanded on the Continent since the days of Marlborough, but he was a deplorable commander. Charles had been unfortunate enough to have served with him in the Netherlands when they had to evacuate the Continent four years before. There was the same inconceivable muddle.

The Duke of York decided to attack, but just as the troops began to make headway, he called a retreat. Across the soaking ground, the endless dykes, drenched and dispirited by the continual rain, the shivering troops retreated. Almost the first news that greeted Castlereagh when he arrived in England was the evacuation of the Continent. Charles was seriously wounded, and he waited anxiously for his return.

The only gleam of light in the whole expedition had been the capture of the Dutch fleet, which Britain managed to retain. "Whatever the British do," an Austrian official observed, "they always succeed in adding to the number of their ships."

In Parliament Pitt came in for a good deal of comment. He tried to blame the disaster on to the weather, and asserted that it ought to be a source of satisfaction that our army had been restored to us. Sheridan remarked sarcastically that besides the capture of the Dutch fleet, the nation had gained some useful knowledge; it had been found out that no reliance could be placed on the Prime Minister's knowledge of human nature, that Holland was a country intersected with dykes, and that the weather in October was not as good as it was in June. The question was whether the price paid for the information had not been too dear.

A good deal of blame was laid on the Duke of York, and Pitt informed the King that the Duke could not continue as Commander of the forces. The old King was deeply hurt. He acquiesced, but solaced himself by telling Pitt that it was not his son, but Pitt's brother

Chatham, now head of the Admiralty, who was responsible for our disaster. Whoever was to blame, our efforts at co-operation had only been an embarrassment to our Russian allies, who now retired from the contest.

As though matters were not bad enough, at this depressing moment came the startling news that Buonaparte had escaped from Egypt and was back again in France. The British Government was thrown into the greatest consternation. For months Buonaparte had been shut up in Egypt. He had been unaware of what was passing in Europe, but Sir Sidney Smith had mischievously sent him a pile of newspapers, from which he learnt of the new coalition formed by England, Austria and Russia, and of the defeats France was suffering on every front. His own army was still locked up in Egypt, blockaded by the British navy, unable to move.

Leaving his men behind, he ran the gauntlet of the British cruisers, and made his way back to France. While the British armies were evacuating Holland, Buonaparte made his dramatic appearance at Golfe Juan in the south of France. The inhabitants, when they heard the news, went wild with excitement. Swarming down to the waterside they bore their hero proudly ashore. All the way to Paris, crowds surged round his carriage. Three weeks later he had overthrown the Constitution by armed force and, as First Consul, had established himself as master of the country.

8

Castlereagh watched with painful interest the sudden reverse of fortune. He was not surprised that the Ministers could not give their attention to Irish affairs, and he waited patiently to be called. When he was at length summoned, he was pleased to find that the English Ministers seemed to be in favour of Catholic Emancipation; there was not one Minister against it; it was even discussed whether an immediate declaration on the subject to the Catholics would not be advisable ; but the idea of giving a direct assurance was abandoned on the ground that it might at that moment alienate the Protestants. Castlereagh was directed to convey to Cornwallis the assurance that he was fully warranted in soliciting every support the Catholics could afford him, and that he need not apprehend being involved in any difficulty with that body afterwards.

In the Cabinet there was another Irishman who was equally enthusiastic regarding the Union. Canning was writing to his cousin Bessy, saying: "I have been thinking of nothing else for these two months. And the result of my thoughts is that it must succeed, and will succeed, and that our poor country will be saved, in spite of the folly and fury of some of its mistaken patriots, and all its self-interested ones. Next year I hope we shall be one people."

When Castlereagh returned to Ireland he was able to give Cornwallis the assurance he desired, and the Irish Government now omitted no exertion to call forth the support of the Catholics in favour of the Union. The Catholics, who were given no actual pledge, gathered that they might expect emancipation after the Union was carried. They were to receive a rude awakening later.

The Union was brought forward again exactly a year after its first introduction. Cornwallis was doubtful of its success and hoped that Pitt and the Cabinet were prepared for the worst. He was in any case disgusted with the whole business, and was looking forward to a peaceful retirement. Castlereagh was in distress because sufficient instalments had not arrived from England, and as every day produced new symptoms of disaffection, money was urgently required before Parliament met. In due time the expected funds arrived, and some of the wavering friends of the Government were brought to a more favourable mind. For months Castlereagh had been making preparations for the approaching contest, and though he knew it would be heavy work, he was far more sanguine than Cornwallis regarding the issue.

He moved from his house in Merrion Street, which had become too small for the amount of entertaining and other business in which he was now involved, and took Mornington House, a grand mansion on the opposite side of the street, where Arthur Wellesley had been born. There, against a background of panelled staircases and spacious halls, Lord and Lady Castlereagh entertained the neighbouring aristocracy. Sumptuous dinner parties were given, and the guests full of madeira and champagne, resolved, as Barrington put it, " to eat, drink, speak, and fight for Lord Castlereagh."

On 15 January 1800 the last session of the Irish Parliament opened. It was a memorable occasion. As soon as the King's Speech had been read, Sir Lawrence Parsons rose and moved an amendment that a Free and Independent Parliament should be maintained in the Kingdom; he accused the Chief Secretary of packing Parliament, and of attempting to force an unpopular measure through the House while Martial Law prevailed, and while there was a considerable armed force in the country.

Castlereagh, in his anxiety to answer these charges, rose to his feet the moment the speech was concluded, and the Speaker, who was notoriously against the Union, raised a laugh by asking him if he wished to second the amendment of the Honourable Baronet. Castlereagh resumed his seat till the amendment was formally seconded, and then answered the charges with astonishing vigour. The debate lasted throughout the night. When dawn came, the weary members were still sitting in the cold wintry light listening to the endless discussion. Suddenly they were galvanised into life, for the doors opposite the Speaker were flung open, and there, framed in the doorway, supported by two members, stood Henry Grattan, the old Irish patriot.

He was ill, and could hardly stand; it was a long time since he had entered the House, but his re-election had been hurried through after midnight, and he had been carried down to College Green in a sedan chair in order to " register his last protest against the sale of his country's liberty."

Dressed in the old blue and gold uniform of the Irish Volunteers, and leaning heavily on the shoulders of his two companions, he advanced slowly and in considerable pain up the floor of the House.

Castlereagh rose to his feet, and remained standing with his head uncovered till Grattan had reached the table and taken the oath. There was a complete hush while Grattan took his place. He was so weak that when he rose to speak he found that he was unable to stand, and begged permission to address the House sitting.

In spite of his condition, he spoke for two hours, and with such vehemence and passion, that the whole House was electrified. At the close of his speech, utterly exhausted, he lay back in his seat, and pointing an accusing finger at Castlereagh cried: "The thing which he proposes to buy is what cannot be sold—Liberty. He proposes to you to substitute the British Parliament in your place, and to destroy the body that restored your liberties, and restore that body which destroyed them. Against such a proposition, were I expiring on the floor, I should beg to utter my last breath and record my dying testimony."

But Castlereagh had done his work so thoroughly and relentlessly, that in spite of the impression made by Grattan's appearance and his impassioned oratory, the Government remained undefeated.

The news of Grattan's appearance spread like wildfire through the city; the temper of the people was so inflamed that Castlereagh's carriage was stopped by a howling mob shouting for his blood. Unperturbed, Castlereagh threw open the door of his carriage and standing on the step, produced a brace of pistols, declaring he would shoot the first man who touched him. The crowd fell back, and the carriage passed on.

But the mob collected again outside his house, where they burnt his effigy amid shouts of execration. Riots broke out all over the town. Members of Parliament were beaten and stoned, their carriages thrown into the river. Members were compelled to go about armed, and detachments of cavalry were ordered out to patrol the streets. In spite of all opposition, and every threat, Castlereagh succeeded in piloting every clause of the measure safely through its committee stages.

The Union resolutions were brought before Parliament in February. Castlereagh, when he took his place, was unusually pale. He had had a severe attack of influenza, and was hardly fit to be present. His nervous energy had been drained by the strain of the past few months, and he had given himself no rest or relaxation. Night after night he had spoken in the House, where sittings had rarely broken up before midnight, and had often lasted throughout the night and till noon the following day. He was weak and exhausted, but he faced the House, which was full to overflowing, with his usual dignity, and explained and justified his plan.

In spite of the passionate efforts of Grattan, who continued with more and more eloquence to decry the passage of the Union through Parliament, the preliminaries were carried by a good majority.

"While a plank of the vessel sticks together," Grattan declaimed, "I will not leave her. Let the courtier present his flimsy sail and carry the light barque of his faith with every new breath of wind: I will remain anchored here—with fidelity to the fortunes of my country, faithful to her freedom, faithful to her fall."

Before the Union was finally carried Castlereagh had to submit to further ferocious attacks from Grattan and other members. He answered them with spirit and address. He declared his contempt for the idle parade of parliamentary spirit which led to nothing, and which denied in offensive terms what had never been uttered. Throwing back his head he looked round the House. "If any personal incivility is offered to me," he added, "it is not in Parliament that I shall answer it."

For a moment there was silence. His skill with pistols was not unknown. Then shouting broke out on all sides, and the galleries had to be cleared.

To avoid witnessing the final scene, nearly the whole of the Opposition rose and left in a body. When the question had been put, and carried without a division, in the face of all the empty Opposition benches, the Speaker flung the Bill on the table with a gesture of disgust.

The long struggle was over. The Union was carried. Lady Castlereagh gave a masked ball in the grounds of the Secretary's Lodge in Phoenix Park. The gardens were illuminated with a thousand coloured lamps suspended from the trees, and the chosen guests celebrated the settlement of a question which the British Government had been violently agitating for over a year ; it was a settlement which was to remain in operation for over a century.

On the day the measure was to receive the Royal Assent in the House of Lords, 1 August 1800, crowds collected all round the building. They were unusually quiet. But when the Chief Secretary descended from his carriage at the door of the House, someone behind him shouted: "Bloody Castlereagh."

The cry was taken up by the crowd. Castlereagh turned round and faced them, and the cries died down.

He had borne the whole weight of a struggle as unequal as any that had ever been undertaken; the contest had been long, the struggle at times unendurable, but he had arrived through a series of reverses at complete victory; and now the people were shrieking their venomous hate in his ears.

It was undoubtedly the work of the Opposition. They had done what they could to inflame the people's minds. Had they been left alone, the people, he was convinced, would have acquiesced in the Union. But the Union had been so distorted, he had been so abused, it had not increased their tenderness towards him. It hardly mattered; had they cheered him it would have meant as little. He had done what he could to pacify the popular mind, but it is easier to inflame than to pacify, and the Opposition had found material that was only too inflammable.

In spite of the Opposition, however, the Union had been carried. It had now passed through the Commons and the Lords. But even so Castlereagh could not rest. There were still so many matters to attend to. Portland was behaving very oddly about the British peerages which had been promised to certain Irishmen for their support; he had actually declined to confirm them. If they could not keep faith with those persons with whom they had made arrangements it was morally impossible for him or Cornwallis to remain in their situations.

There was another matter which was giving him and Cornwallis even greater embarrassment. Nothing had yet been done about the Catholics. Although the country could not have been saved, he was convinced, without the Union, it could not be taken for granted that it would be saved by it. "The Union will do little in itself," he had written to Whitehall, "unless it be followed up." But so far nothing had been done towards redressing the Catholic grievances, and the Catholics had given their support to the Union on the understanding that these would be dealt with. It was a matter he was very anxious to get settled, and as soon as Parliament rose he crossed to England again to impress on the Ministers the necessity for speedy concessions.

It was towards the end of August 1800 when he set out for London.

GEORGE CANNING

By T. Lawrence

The cold, fresh winds blowing across the sea were a tonic, the sway of the deck under his feet and the big expanse of blue sky overhead restored him; he felt vigorous again. Standing on the boat watching the coast of Ireland fade into a dim line he began to feel the satisfaction of something achieved. Though the people raged against him, his colleagues and the English Ministers had appreciated his colossal effort. Portland had written a very flattering letter to Cornwallis regarding him: he had seen Cornwallis's reply.

"It gives me," Cornwallis had written, "very sincere satisfaction to find that His Majesty's confidential servants are so sensible of the extraordinary talents and good services of Lord Castlereagh, to whom the success of this great and difficult undertaking ought in justice to be principally attributed." That was acknowledgment enough, but Cornwallis had also asked Portland to confer a British peerage on Castlereagh's father, in acknowledgment of the services his son had rendered his country. Cornwallis had been informed in reply that the family could have the peerage whenever they desired; but it was suggested that its acceptance should be postponed, because the British Government did not wish to lose Lord Castlereagh's services in the House of Commons. They did not want him, as Portland put it, to come into the House of Lords "till age, infirmity, or the desire of repose should make him wish to retire from the more busy and active scene of the House of Commons."

"No man ever was so flatteringly pressed to decline honours," Cooke had written him from London. "The real fact is," he had said, "that they hope you will make the same figure, and take the same lead which you have done in Ireland, and they sadly want some character on whom business may repose." Pitt's health had been troublesome for some time, and Dundas, Cooke wrote, was retiring. Canning had neither rank nor authority, nor had he yet shown himself a man of business, and they had nobody on whom they could rely. Pitt's "personal contest with Buonaparte may distress him, should he be driven to peace," he added. It did not surprise Castlereagh. Pitt had tried so many times to make peace with France, and on such slender chances; and yet when Buonaparte, in December 1799, had himself suggested peace, which might have been had on advantageous terms, he had rejected the offer out of hand. It was one thing, he felt, dealing with France, and quite another dealing with a Corsican upstart, who had had the effrontery to nominate himself First Consul. He would have no truck with Buonaparte; the offer of peace was ignored.

It was an extremely hot summer, and having at length arrived in London Castlereagh wished to see the Cabinet and return to Ireland without delay, but unfortunately most of the Ministers were out of town. He was travelling without Emily, who generally accompanied him everywhere, and he was already beginning to miss her. She was no doubt spending her time fluttering from balls to routs and assemblies, with jewels and ornaments in her hair that were quite formidable, and with a look of contented disregard of the cares of life in her round grey eyes; but her frivolities had never disturbed him. She may not have had the depth of feeling nor the intelligence of mind to make their relationship an inspiring factor in his life, but it had always been a pleasant enough partnership, satisfying all his needs.

As soon as possible he saw Pitt and the Duke of Portland, who promised to expedite his business; but things did not move very fast. In spite of their promised endeavours it took some time to summon the Cabinet. He grew bored with London. The town was empty, and he was half-dead with the heat. He went out with Elliott, and dined at a chop house; he saw his father who was over on a visit; he wrote little notes to Emily.

"You good-for-nothing wife, I have but one letter from you since we parted. Perhaps you will recriminate, which will only prove that you hate writing even to me. You will see if I am not angry I am at least sufficiently impudent, and I only expect you to be a little ashamed."

A day or two later he was writing again: "I long, Dearest Emily, to hear from you: indeed I hate my liberty, and wish every hour to be again chained to the oar."

Whenever a letter arrived from her, he replied immediately and always with the same tenderness.

" MY DEAREST EMILY,

Thank you for your absolution which arrived this morning. I send you mine in return with an embrace, which I wish I could bestow in a less spiritual form; but I trust it will in the meantime

130

be accepted as a pledge of affection, which I shall be most impatient to redeem."

The Ministers were still out of town. Restraining his impatience, he spent the time having his house redecorated, buying a new hat for his wife, and a jewel for her to wear " on a white gown." He went off for a short time to Sussex to stay with the Camdens ; he visited the Duke of Portland at Bulstrode. He reminded Emily to write to his sister Caroline. "Don't forget this, my dear Lazyboots."

From Bulstrode he was suddenly recalled, for news came that his brother, Alec, was seriously ill. The boy was only eighteen, and a victim of tuberculosis, yet he had entered the Navy, and fought at St. Vincent. He was now desperately ill, and was being brought to London. Castlereagh travelled as far as Liphook on the Portsmouth road to meet him. "Alec's fate, poor boy, is sealed," he wrote to Emily, "and nothing is looked to but smoothing the remainder of his existence, which to all appearances, cannot be prolonged many weeks. You cannot expect to receive anything but gloom from me at present."

On the 23 September he received at last the expected summons to Whitehall, but there was still intolerable delay. In the Duke of Portland's office, where he was waiting in anxious expectation of being called, he continued writing to Emily. "The Cabinet is sitting and I wait patiently, though not with patience . . . it was not my fault that the business has hung so long, but I at last told the Duke I must set out, which I suppose made the Ministers think of doing some business —what remains one Cabinet will finish, and the Duke assures me I may set off on Wednesday morning. I am really grieved, and quite determined never to come alone again."

Six years of marriage had not dimmed his affection for Emily, and he busied himself with commissions for her. "I have lost the name of your hatter," he wrote to her, "but shall execute your commissions as well as I can. You see what good order I am in, but I expect to be in better when you can punish me more immediately after the fault.

"I am going to dine with the Master of the Rolls at Hampstead, to meet Mr. Pitt.

"Alec, poor fellow, has gained strength upon the whole since his return, but I see no additional grounds of hope."

He was still waiting to see the Cabinet. He had packed his trunks, and was ready to depart, but from twelve till five he was kept in Downing Street while the Cabinet were employed on other business. He was then appointed for the following day, but after waiting for three hours, was again put off. He was out of all patience.

"I don't know what you feel," he wrote to Emily, "but I am quite determined, unless you differ, never to pass from one country to another, even for a day, without you. You know how little given I am to professions, but I have really of late felt the deprivation with an acuteness which is only known to those who are separated from what they most love.

"But I find I am in danger of committing the intolerable barbarism of writing a love letter to my wife—I shall therefore for the sake of my character in the Post Office trust all my experience of this moment, in the consideration of my return, to that imagination which is best acquainted with me."

II

There was reason enough for the postponement of Irish affairs. At the head of a large army Buonaparte had crossed the Alps again, had marched into Northern Italy, and on 14 June 1800, had crushed our Austrian ally at Marengo. The Austrians were being defeated now on every front. "Our own armies," Grenville wrote sardonically, "could not have done worse."

Our own armies, unfortunately, had not even come to the help of the Austrians as arranged; they had been left waiting for orders, they had been left waiting for a new Commander-in-Chief, they had been left "unemployed," as Grenville observed, "gaping after messengers from Genoa, Augsburg and Vienna, till the moment for acting was irrevocably passed by."

On the very day of Marengo, which had at one moment been very near a victory, the British Secretary of War began dispatching orders for four thousand men to be sent out, "for important operations on the Italian Riviera." But the operations were already over, and

Buonaparte, from the battlefield of Marengo, surrounded by fifteen thousand dead bodies, was dispatching a letter to the ruler of Austria recommending him to withdraw from the contest.

Pitt found this an opportune moment for making peace overtures; this time it was through our ambassador at Vienna. He had paid over to Austria two million pounds to pledge her not to conclude peace without England's participation. But it had availed him little. For when the Austrian plenipotentiary arrived in Paris, Buonaparte, with veiled menaces, insinuations and tempestuous outbursts, forced him to sign the peace preliminaries which he dictated.

Although Austria refused to ratify these peace preliminaries, it was of no consequence ; for Buonaparte inflicted on the Austrians a final defeat in the snows of Hohenlinden, after which they signed a separate peace at Lunéville. England could not participate in the peace as Pitt had desired; for Buonaparte now demanded that the blockade of Egypt should be raised before he would enter into any discussions.

" There must be a great taste for being laughed at amongst us," said Canning, " if we go on discussing after this answer. I give Talleyrand great credit for having discovered the fright in which we were. Gracious God! It makes me sick to see ourselves become the object of such broad, undisguised contempt. . . . Do people hold up their heads? And does the Cabinet meet by daylight? "

The Government declined to raise the blockade of Egypt, the war continued, and the Cabinet turned to Irish affairs. Castlereagh was astonished now to find that a new and sudden opposition had arisen ; it was voiced by Loughborough, the Lord Chancellor. To Castlereagh's amazement he delivered a violent harangue against any political concessions whatever being granted to the Catholics. The other members, even Pitt, said little. This new opposition, it appeared later, was the result of Loughborough's having betrayed the Cabinet's designs regarding the Catholics to the King, who had not yet been consulted in the matter. He had even shown the King a confidential letter from the Prime Minister, and had informed him that by assenting to Catholic Emancipation he would be violating his Coronation oath. The King, who had always been opposed to such a scheme, became incensed with Pitt for having contemplated these changes without consulting him.

Pitt had no doubt thought it best to promote unity in the Cabinet before confronting his Sovereign with the proposed measure, but Loughborough having betrayed him, nothing further could be done. The shrewd old King, though grateful to his Lord Chancellor for bringing the matter to his notice, was under no illusions about his character, and when Loughborough died, remarked: "He has not left a greater knave behind him in my dominions."

For Castlereagh the sudden change was a bitter blow. "Those things which, if now liberally granted," Cornwallis had said, "might make the Irish a loyal people, will be of little avail when they are extorted on a future day." His apprehensions were only too well grounded; it would be difficult, Castlereagh felt, to break the news to him. Deeply disappointed he returned to Ireland. The Prime Minister, equally disappointed, went back to the country to stay with his friend, Addington.

Pitt was at this time in very poor health, and badly in need of a rest. He was so weak indeed that the wags declared "he could no longer raise the port to his lips." All Cabinet business had to be postponed, since he was clearly unequal to the strain of it. But Castlereagh did not let the matter rest. The act of Union was due to come into operation on the 1 January 1801, and in December he was again in London endeavouring to persuade the Ministers "to adopt manfully the only measure which could ever make the mass of the people in Ireland good subjects." When he was summoned to Whitehall he received another rude surprise, for now the Home Secretary's attitude too had changed. Conscientious scruples had suddenly and most conveniently arisen in the mind of Portland regarding the emancipation of the Catholics, and Castlereagh sensed further trouble ahead. Everything now depended on Pitt, he felt, and on his influence with the Cabinet and the King.

He sat down at his desk and wrote a long letter to Pitt, reminding him of what had occurred at the Cabinet meeting the previous autumn, when he had been directed to inform Cornwallis that "as far as the sentiments of the Cabinet were concerned His Excellency need not hesitate in calling forth the Catholics' support in whatever degree he found it practicable to obtain it." He reminded him further that he had been directed to inform Cornwallis that he need not apprehend being involved in the difficulty with that body which he seemed to apprehend. He added that he did not then hear any direct objection stated against the principle of the measure by any one of the Ministers then present, that it had even been discussed whether an immediate declaration to the Catholics would not be advisable.

He recalled to Pitt's recollection all that had been said at that Cabinet meeting, and informed him that though His Excellency had not given the Catholics any direct assurance of being gratified, he considered the measure essential to the future interests of the Empire. He begged Pitt to give these matters their due weight in his decision.

Pitt was genuinely anxious for Catholic relief; but his mind at this time was distracted by a variety of troubles. His chief burden was the war, and the war was going badly. Negotiations with France, which he was still pursuing, were not progressing. Added to his public trials he had now considerable private worries. He was heavily in debt, so much so that he was indeed at one time in actual danger of arrest. To the last day of his life executions were threatened against him. Hearing of his difficulties, the merchants of London offered him a gift of £100,000, and the King begged him to accept £30,000 from his Privy Purse, but he declined both offers. Finally he accepted a loan of £12,000 from a few intimate friends, but this still left a heavy balance.

Even had there been no Irish trouble, Pitt was too overburdened and too ill to carry on. Castlereagh's letter seems to have spurred him momentarily to action, and a few days later he arrived in Downing Street, held a Cabinet meeting, and expressed his unalterable determination to proceed with a measure of Catholic relief. The majority of the members were with him, and Castlereagh, who had been called in to the Cabinet meeting, was now almost jubilant. If Pitt were firm, the measure would be carried.

The King hearing of these consultations flew into a rage. At a levée a few days later he declared in a loud voice that he considered all supporters of Catholic Emancipation as " personally indisposed " to him. He went up to Dundas, and pointing at Castlereagh, said: " What is this that this young lord has brought over, and which they are going to throw at my head? I hear he is to bring forward a motion in the House of Commons respecting the Catholics. I shall reckon any man my personal enemy who proposes or supports any such measure. The most Jacobinical thing I ever heard of."

" You'll find," replied Dundas quietly, " among those who are friendly to that measure some you never supposed your enemies." He tried to explain to the King that his oath was limited but he was cut short with the testy remark: "None of your Scotch metaphysics, Mr. Dundas! None of your Scotch metaphysics!"

A short and angry correspondence followed between the Prime Minister and the King, and a few days later, in February 1801—the month that Austria signed her Peace Treaty with France at Lunéville, without England, in spite of all Pitt's efforts, being able to participate —Pitt sent in his resignation to the King, suggesting Addington as his successor.

To many it seemed wrong and ill-judged to throw up the reins of government on whatever pretext at such a critical moment in the destinies of the country, and to hand them moreover to Addington, a well-meaning but inefficient nonentity.

The grounds which he gave for his resignation history has accepted as genuine, but some of his contemporaries questioned his motives for retiring. Even his faithful friend, Canning, says discreetly: "Pitt resigns, no matter for what reason, and I feel it right to follow him out of office."

Auckland declared in the House of Lords that Pitt's resignation was involved in mystery which the eye could not penetrate.

On 9 February 1801, Lord Glenbervie wrote in his diary that an idea was in circulation that "the whole was a game to give the go-by to the Catholic question and get rid of Windham and perhaps Spencer, and that Pitt then means to resume the government."

Castlereagh, who rated his motives at the highest, felt that the Prime Minister might have shown more perseverance in his dealings with the King, who had been known to give way before in matters to which he entertained violent objections, notably in the matter of American Independence.

But the King was in a sad condition at this time and Pitt may have thought it best to humour him. Whatever the cause, to throw away what almost amounted to a pledge to the Irish Catholics, and refuse to acknowledge or redress the rights of a whole nation on account of a madman's whim, seems peculiarly unjust, for it was no secret that the King was now suffering from one of his periodical fits of insanity.

After he had received Pitt's resignation, which he immediately accepted, he went to Church where he remained a long while praying. It was snowing hard, the day was bitterly cold, and he caught a severe chill. A few days later he threw himself into his physician's arms in an agony of weeping, and agreed that he must be very ill. After several nights of delirium he rallied a little, and sent a message to Pitt informing him that he was the immediate cause of his affliction.

Pitt now promised the King that he would not bring forward the Catholic question again during his reign, or permit it to pass, adding, strangely enough, that he was ready to resume office should Addington resign.

It seems inconsistent, even taking into consideration the King's condition, to have resigned on the question of Catholic Emancipation, and to have been ready to take office again, renouncing the measure he had given as the cause of his retirement. It is equally strange that he should have chosen so weak a vessel as Addington to follow him. Was his resignation merely a gesture, and did he intend to come back when Addington failed? Was it a respite required for his health's sake? Was it because of his failure to make peace with France? It was a common charge of the day, according to Temperley,[1] that Pitt's Catholic zeal was but the pretext of his retirement. Dundas had even observed to Malmesbury: " If these new Ministers stay in and make peace, it will only smooth matters the more for us afterwards." All we know is that Pitt was a broken man. Up to 1797, that blackest of black years, when England stood alone against Buonaparte, Pitt had managed to get through the affairs of state. But in this year he began to complain of illness, and to speak of retirement, naming Addington as his successor.

The month that Austria signed her peace treaty with France was a particularly trying one for Pitt. Four times he had attempted to make peace with France. Four times he had failed. The country was now in a perilous state. The scarcity of bread was mounting to a famine. England's debts were alarming. A new army was massing on the shores of France, and invasion seemed imminent. Buonaparte was preparing for a decisive conflict with Britain, and Britain once again stood alone.

Pitt shifted the burden on to other shoulders, and retired to the country. Castlereagh had the ungrateful task of breaking the news

[1] *Life of Canning*, by H. W. V. Temperley.

137

to Cornwallis, which he did as diplomatically as he could. But his dispatch filled the officers at Dublin Castle with the greatest consternation. There was only one course for a man of honour to take, and Cornwallis took it. He sent in his resignation. Castlereagh followed him out of office. He had given all his effort to the Union, he had succeeded against all odds; and the Union would be a failure. He was out of office; and in the streets of Dublin the people were singing:

> " A high gallows and a windy day
> For Billy Pitt and Castlereagh."

CHAPTER VI

I

IT WAS not a happy time for Castlereagh. The moment which had been so opportune for settling the Catholic grievances had now been lost. He wrote to Lady Elizabeth Pratt a little sadly:

" It is an age since I have written to you, but my silence, I know, is never misunderstood—the events that have filled the last six weeks, are of a description, which conversation alone could explain . . . what will be the end of all these things it is vain to guess . . . we are again to struggle as I feel unnecessarily, and I only hope, if our prospects are disappointed, that we have done our duty—Pitt has closed an unexampled career in a manner which places him in point of character above the world . . . whether the part he has taken is not too refined for this world, some persons may doubt, but that it is great beyond example, I am persuaded no man can deny—what may be my destiny hereafter, it is not worth inquiring—I shall feel happy myself in having been connected with him in what has occurred and shall return to my private situation without having any particular reproach to make to myself for what has happened whilst I have been engaged in the public service."

To Cooke he wrote: " If the King's feeling had been different, I think everything would have been smooth—but now feelings and parties will form—our line is most difficult . . . we shall both be grey before the results we promised ourselves are fulfilled." [1]

He was greatly distressed by the unexpected turn things had taken. After all his endeavours Ireland, he feared, was again to become a millstone about the neck of Britain, and to be plunged into all its

[1] Londonderry Papers.

former horrors and miseries. In spite of the fact that no definite pledges had been given to the Catholics the success of the Union would be tarnished, perhaps forever marred, by suspicions of broken faith.

All his plans so nicely regulated had collapsed. He was out of office. The future had seemed full of promise, full of the most dazzling hopes; and suddenly the air had darkened round him. He loved Ireland. It was home to him, a background of memories, a place where he had been born, where he had lived and worked and dreamed, a place to which he would always come back, lured by its enchantment. But nothing would ever be the same again. Ireland was now linked with memories of frustration, of half-fulfilled ambitions and defeated hopes. A sad finality hung over him. He had tried to give Ireland form and dignity; out of a shapeless chaos he had tried to mould a clear-cut image; and succeeding beyond all hope he had failed. Ireland's wounds would never heal, she would struggle on unheeding, undisciplined, uncompromising, unforgetting.

But there was still much for him to do. Until his new successor was appointed he was still in charge of Irish affairs, still a Member of Parliament, representing the county of Down at Westminster, instead of representing it, as he had done for the past ten years, at College Green.

When the first Parliament of the United Kingdom assembled he took his seat near Pitt on the back Government benches. It was over four years since he had sat at Westminster, but those four years had given him a new self-confidence. He was no longer a silent member, and at the first opportunity he rose and introduced a motion for continuing the Lord-Lieutenant's power to enforce Martial Law in Ireland. His oratory was never remarkable, but he made a masterly speech, which did not fail to impress those who heard him.

When Castlereagh rose, Sheridan raised an objection on the grounds that he was not a responsible Minister. Castlereagh quietly replied: " I contend that it is competent for any member to get up and make any proposition he thinks it his duty to make." Sheridan was disposed of, and Castlereagh, meeting all charges against him with a dignity and courage that disarmed criticism, carried the debate triumphantly. Later in the evening Pitt declared in the House that his noble friend had that night " given proof that there are among us talents of the first rate together with extensive knowledge of the true interests of the Empire."

Writing to Cooke after the debate, Castlereagh did not neglect to mention the Irish members who had supported him.

" I feel excessively grateful to, and proud of my Irish friends— they have done themselves great honour in the debate of Thursday, thoroughly convincing the House of the necessity of the measure, and of their own propensities being as humane as any on this side of the Water."

In spite of his drawbacks as a speaker, for he was often prolix and diffuse, and rarely eloquent, he was invited to lead the Irish supporters of the Government in the House of Commons; but he declined the offer, preferring no doubt a wider field for his activities. He had in fact acquired such prestige through his management of the Irish Parliament and his conduct of the Union that he was pointed out as the future Prime Minister. That he did not achieve this position was possibly due to the King's prejudices, for he always associated him with Catholic Emancipation and the violation of his Coronation Oath. Mr. Abbott, who was to be Castlereagh's successor in Ireland, noted down in his diary that the King was very angry with Castlereagh.[1]

The King was also very angry with Pitt, and even before Pitt had sent in his resignation he had asked Addington to form a Ministry. Addington could at least be relied upon to form a Ministry hostile to the Catholic claims, for he was strongly opposed to Catholic Emancipation. " Lay your hand upon your heart and ask yourself," the King had said to him, " where I am to turn for support if you do not stand by me."

Castlereagh expected little from Addington's Government. On the 14 March 1801, he wrote to Cooke: " Pitt resigns to-day—when I heard him on Thursday my heart bled at losing him, he was on his highest horse—alas how will Addington's party get over the ground . . . if you knew how little reluctant he has been to accept the change it would not add to your confidence in his means to save us and himself."

Nobody had much confidence in the Addington Ministry, except one old Tory, who remarked dryly: " Well, thank God, we have at last got a Ministry without one of those damned men of genius in it."

[1] *Colchester Diaries.*

141

Yet Addington did not hesitate to take over the reins of government. Castlereagh trembled for England, for the outlook was dark at home and abroad. In Europe the British army had done nothing to its credit; and now the Baltic powers—Russia, Sweden, and Denmark—had combined in an effort to break Britain's power on the seas. Britain's answer to the Baltic league was to send out a fleet to break it up.

Castlereagh had never had any doubts of the Navy, he had never had any doubts of Nelson, in spite of the scandals of his private life, and he rejoiced when in April 1801, there came news of Nelson's victory at Copenhagen. For it was Nelson's victory, even though Nelson had been second in command. In spite of heavy casualties and orders to draw off and cease action he had gone forward doggedly till he had wrested victory out of the mouth of defeat. His victory wiped Denmark out of the League.

A week or two later the Government heard without much sorrow that the Czar Paul, whose mad oscillations had been giving Britain endless trouble, had been assassinated in his Palace at St. Petersburg. Holy Russia too was out of the League.

Good fortune seemed to mark the beginning of Addington's Ministry; for, a day or two later, when Castlereagh was working at the Martial Law papers with Abbott, Pitt arrived with news [1] that the French troops which Buonaparte had left behind in Egypt had been defeated at Alexandria by Sir Ralph Abercromby. Castlereagh was sorry to hear that his old friend, Abercromby, had fallen in the action, but he had fallen covered with glory. The British troops had triumphed over the French at last, and had proved that when properly led they were not inferior to our seamen.

Suddenly after all the gloom there had come two brilliant successes. Although Castlereagh was too equable by nature to get unduly elated when news was good, or downcast when news was bad, he must have felt a new confidence. Prospects seemed brighter, there was less despondency in the air, and he was beginning to look forward to enjoying a little leisure. He was already sending music to his regimental band in Ireland, and arranging to spend the summer at Mount Stewart.

" I hope, dearest friend," he wrote to Lady Elizabeth, " you do not

[1] *Colchester Correspondence.*

mean to absent yourself from Mount Stewart next summer, the first for many years which seems to promise our reunion."

But his plans miscarried. Completely worn out by the strain of the arduous labours he had performed, and by the heavy responsibilities that had been laid upon him, he suddenly collapsed. The work he had got through would in itself have been enough to destroy a stronger constitution, the anxiety and disappointment which had followed his efforts brought on a crisis. His friends had noticed for some time that he looked pale and worried, but he continued to come down to the House till the physical collapse which had long been threatening came upon him. One morning he was unable to move from his bed. His head span, the world grew dark around him, and he lay in his room shivering with fever.

For weeks he lay in a critical condition, and for a time his life was despaired of. Emily was in the greatest distress, and hardly left his bedside; physicians bled him copiously and administered numberless purgatives, till even the little strength that was left him ebbed away. Patiently he bore it all. Pain racked his mind and his body, and at night, as he lay on his bed scarcely conscious, his spirit seemed to be swaying away from him, beyond the firelit room, beyond the realm of consciousness into a world that was peopled by distorted shapes and demons.

For weeks the fever continued, and anxiety increased among his friends. On 22 April, Lord Cornwallis, in a letter to Major-General Ross, was writing: "I have been for some days under great anxiety about Lord Castlereagh." A fortnight later he was still as anxious, and wrote again: "I have been, and indeed am still very uneasy about Lord Castlereagh, who has had a return of his fever. They tell me there is no danger, but I have no idea of a fever of so long continuance without danger."[1]

Castlereagh's life was indeed in danger. For weeks his temperature continued, but there came a day when the mists cleared from his mind, the fever died down, and hope revived. He was still seriously ill, his spirit sunk in a black despondency, but he was out of danger.

It was June, the weather was warm, and as soon as he was well enough Emily took him to Harrogate. They went by easy stages, resting on the way at Culford with Cornwallis, who had just returned

[1] *Cornwallis Correspondence.*

from Ireland. At Harrogate, away from all politics, he began to recuperate, and a month later was writing to Cooke:

"I have been very idle since I came, have forgot politics, and am grown *very fat*." It was not easy to forget politics, for disquieting rumours penetrated even to the Pump Room. Buonaparte was preparing to launch another expedition against Ireland; the French fleet had orders to sail from Brest. Castlereagh grew restive. He could no longer remain inactive ; he was anxious to get back to Ireland and rejoin his regiment. Now that he was well again, and free from official duties, this was his one desire. He was discussing the matter with Emily, who still did not find him strong enough to undertake the rigours of camp life, when news came that Tom Connolly, the Derry Militia's Commanding Officer, had retired. Castlereagh was next in command. He would remain at Harrogate no longer, and in spite of all arguments began to make preparations to get back into barracks.

By the middle of August, 1801, he was with his regiment again. The rumour of invasion seemed to be unfounded, but he was glad to be back in Ireland. However ill she treated him he would never lose his love for Ireland—Ireland with her grace and her despair, with her one single, undefeated, stubborn purpose—to be rid of the conqueror. The blood of the conqueror was in his veins, and yet for good or evil Ireland was a part of him.

He spent a few happy days at Mount Stewart ; he went riding, walking, sailing; everyone found him the same charming, sympathetic companion.

He spent some time in Dublin, assisting Lord Hardwicke, the new Lord-Lieutenant, who was grateful for his advice and help. Castlereagh gave him the welcome news that he had found the north quiet; he was convinced that its tranquillity would remain undisturbed so long as the French kept away from Ireland's shores; but they would never be free from that apprehension while war continued.

It was rumoured that he lived for a short time in a small house at Dundrum, not far from Dublin, in order to visit the son whom Nelly Stoal was said to have borne him, and who was a pupil, it was whispered, at Mr. Delaney's school nearby.[1] That he spent some time at Dundrum is evident, for his brother Charles reports an attack on

[1] Felton Reede.

his life in this district. He was returning from the mountains, where he had been out shooting one day, when he was set on by two men, and had the narrowest escape.[1] One of the men stopped him to inquire the time, and as he was about to reply the other seized his gun. Castlereagh, with his usual presence of mind, drew a pistol from his pocket and fired. The man fell, but another springing out from a ditch joined in the fray. Castlereagh's pistol missed fire, and he was in the gravest danger when suddenly a young naval officer, jumping over a gate, came to his assistance. One of the men escaped, but the other two were dealt with, and, tying their hands behind their backs, Castlereagh and his companion marched them back to Dundrum. The man who had come to Castlereagh's assistance was a Mr. Jennings, whom Castlereagh was able to reward later by giving him the command of a cutter.

2

He had not been more than two months in Ireland, where he had been hoping to remain for the rest of the year, when he was summoned back to Westminster. There was a new excitement abroad, for peace was in the air, and Parliament was meeting to discuss the preliminary articles. The first act of the Addington Ministry six months earlier had been to propose terms of peace, but Buonaparte had then repulsed its overtures. That he was ready now to come to terms seemed suspicious to Castlereagh. Did he require a little breathing space to prepare for greater activities? *Reculer pour mieux sauter?* Castlereagh still doubted the advisability of coming to terms with Buonaparte. War was preferable to an uncertain peace, and in spite of the war, Britain was prospering.

It was a curious phenomenon : Britain had suffered so many reverses during these eight years of war, and yet, in spite of all her setbacks, in spite of the financial burden she was carrying, of rising prices and soaring taxes, she was prospering. Even in the midst of war, her trade had passed all bounds, her exports had more than doubled. She had managed to appropriate the carrying trade of France, Spain and Holland, whose merchantmen she had either

[1] Londonderry Papers.

captured or blockaded; she had managed to capture isolated spots that were of the utmost benefit to her—Ceylon, the Cape of Good Hope, Minorca, Trinidad, Martinique. In spite of all her defeats she had not lost an inch of territory anywhere.

By signing a peace at this moment we might, Castlereagh feared, lose everything. We should lose the Colonies, which we had so hardly won, we should lose our Colonial trade, which would go to our enemies, we should lose our commercial monopoly. On the other hand, our finances were unfortunately low, and even though, as Pitt put it, we had " a revenue equal to all Europe, a navy superior to all Europe, and to make us quite gentlemen a debt as large as that of all Europe," peace was not going to stabilise our financial position; it might possibly aggravate it. A peace at this moment could not in any case be a lasting peace, for Buonaparte was still triumphant.

Taking into consideration all these facts, Castlereagh decided, nevertheless, to support the Government, for England too needed a breathing space. She had already lost all her allies, and if she could secure peace now on terms consistent with her safety and independence, it might be better than carrying on the war alone. But such a peace could in no way be a settlement of long duration, it could only be an armistice which would very soon be broken. With this conviction in his mind, when he rose in the House of Commons to support the Government, advocating peace he at the same time solemnly warned the members to " take proper measures that the nation, if again driven to extremities, might return to the contest duly prepared."

The Peace terms were far from satisfactory; Britain agreed to restore all the colonies she had taken, except Trinidad and Ceylon. She gave Egypt back to Turkey. She agreed to give up Malta. There were no lengths apparently to which she would not have gone. The British had a way when it came to reconciliation, of giving away casually all that they had fought for so violently, and had obtained at such sacrifice.

Although Addington was the instrument it was Pitt's peace, and Pitt seemed content. He argued that the security for which we had so long contended had at last been achieved.

The King, who had now recovered from his illness, was under no such illusions. After reading the preliminaries he lifted his hands and eyes to heaven, heaved a deep sigh, and kept silent on the matter.

Later he said to Lord Malmesbury: "Do you know what I call this peace?—An experimental peace; for it is nothing else. I am sure *you* think so; and perhaps you do not give it so gentle a name; but it was unavoidable. I was abandoned by everybody; allies and all."

3

It was Cornwallis, Castlereagh's "old master" as he called him, who was sent out to Amiens to conduct the peace negotiations. From the first they did not go smoothly. He found the French overbearing and insolent; they appeared to him to have all the disagreeable qualities of the old French without their accomplishments. He had an interview with Buonaparte, who talked to him "*en Roi*." He did not get very far with Buonaparte. And it certainly did not appeal to him, with his dignity and decorum and lengthening years, to be sitting at dinner with all the mistresses of the French Ministers, and to have "to hand out the ugliest of them," because she was in the keeping of the Foreign Minister, M. Talleyrand.

The negotiations dragged on for months, and he began to doubt if Buonaparte had any intentions of making peace at all. The powers of Europe were prostrating themselves at his feet, except for one little island; it might suit him better to gain time by protracted negotiations, and to continue the war. For six months terms were discussed, and it was only by giving way all along the line, that eventually in March, 1802, the Peace of Amiens was signed; but it was a Peace, as Sheridan declared, that everyone would be glad of, and nobody proud of. It was a Peace which contained in it, as another wag remarked, "all the elements of a just and durable war." It did not hold up for one moment the encroachments of Buonaparte, who continued with his annexations.

Castlereagh viewed the events passing on the Continent with great anxiety, and hardly was the Treaty of Amiens concluded, when he submitted to the Cabinet a memorandum on the situation, suggesting that Buonaparte be called to order and requested to abstain from further encroachments. The country should show, he declared, that it had made peace in a tone of moderation, but not of submission.

"Is there nothing left," he asked, "but submission to every insult and injury France may think fit to put upon us? The situation we are placed in is certainly both painful and critical: to submit to France at any time is little congenial to our habits and feelings; and it is difficult to persuade one's self that that line of conduct can be wise which tends to lower the nation even in its own estimation. . . . What I desire is that France should feel that Great Britain cannot be trifled with."

His Memorandum reviewing the Relative Political Situation of Great Britain and France was considered a diplomatic document of the greatest importance: his speeches on the peace treaty revealed him as a statesman of the highest order; there was a growing recognition of his qualities on all sides, so much so that Addington, in July 1802, offered him the post of President of the Board of Control.

Although it went against the grain " to embark under Addington," he was pressed by Pitt to accept the offer. He was not to make Catholic Emancipation a bar to his return to office any more than Pitt was to do later. He felt that in the critical state of affairs there were other matters which must for the time being take precedence. Greater and more immediate dangers claimed the first attention, and the question of Catholic Emancipation must sleep, he feared, till the difficulties of the moment were overcome.

4

During the summer recess he was in Ireland again for the elections. He received an enthusiastic reception from his constituents, and was returned for County Down unopposed. There was even a proposal in the *Belfast News Letter* to raise a statue to him. Happy as he was to receive these demonstrations from his countrymen he did not stay very long, but quickly returned to London to take up his new duties.

He was in office again, and glad to be once more "a man of business." The Presidency of the Board of Control was not one of the highest offices of state, the vastness of human destiny held more dazzling situations, but his foot was firmly planted now in the path of power. The following October he was admitted to the Cabinet. At thirty-three he was a Cabinet Minister. He was one of the pivots upon which the politics of Europe turned. A little while and he would be guiding the destinies of England.

The main duties of the Board of Control were the handling of Indian affairs, at this time a difficult and delicate task; for Castlereagh had to deal with an arrogant Governor-General in India, who was full of complaints against the East India Directors, and with the East India Directors in Leadenhall Street, who were full of complaints against the Governor-General. He had to provide not only for the safety of India, but for the contentment of all parties concerned in the government of India.

On his way back from Ireland he spent a week in the Highlands with Dundas, who had formerly been President of the Board of Control, and carefully studied the position with him. He also passed two days in Suffolk with Cornwallis, who had twice been Governor-General of India. He discussed the Indian question with Cornwallis, and was glad of his advice.

The Governor-General who was causing difficulties at this time was Lord Wellesley, brother of the future Duke of Wellington. Three times already he had sent in his resignation, complaining of the mortification and embarrassment imposed on him by the Directors. The Directors, on the other hand, cordially disliked Wellesley, who treated both them and their directions with contempt. Cornwallis felt that Wellesley might have been extravagant and acted with violence, but that the Directors had certainly used him ill. He advised Castlereagh to try to keep him in India for another year, and to get some of his objectionable propositions modified. Castlereagh acted on Cornwallis's advice.

Recognising Wellesley's zeal and ability, he warned him of the disapproval caused at home by his complicated conquests, but begged him to remain another season, assuring him at the same time of his staunch support.

After Castlereagh's appointment the situation was sensibly relieved. With perfect discretion he smoothed away difficulties and patched up quarrels. His " ready dispatch of business," as Wellesley afterwards testified, " his high sense of honour, and comprehensive and enlarged views," made him as effective at the India Office as he had been at Dublin Castle. He supported Wellesley in Parliament against all the assaults of his enemies, and although he differed from him regarding the war against the Marathas, he assisted him in the conduct of it, and gave him all his support.

There had been fierce fighting in India, which had brought great fame to Lord Wellesley and to his brother, Major-General Arthur Wellesley, between the brilliant schemes of the autocratic Governor-General and the military gifts of Sir Arthur the map of India had been transformed by conquests and annexations; but Castlereagh feared lest England should involve herself too much in the endless and complicated distractions of the turbulent Maratha Empire. He would have preferred to let the Maratha chiefs fight each other, rather than help one against the other.

Castlereagh's relations with the Wellesleys during this whole period were completely cordial, and it was already in the stars that Castlereagh should one day send General Wellesley to Spain, and bring the Napoleonic War to a triumphant conclusion.

He had met Sir Arthur in the Irish House of Commons; they had entered Parliament in the same year, and had formed an acquaintance in those early days. Castlereagh had a vivid recollection of the day the Speaker, Sir John Parnell, had introduced them to each other, and had carried them along with him to Barrington's house for dinner.[1] He remembered Arthur Wellesley's ruddy face and juvenile appearance, and his frank open-hearted manner. His friendship for him strengthened during these years, and each found a new confidence in the other.

Though Castlereagh's time was fully occupied writing dispatches to the Governor-General and his brother, interviewing the Directors, and settling their differences, his mind was occupied as much with the European situation as it was with India, which he regarded as only a part of the whole question of imperial policy. His primary concern was always the security and dignity of the British Empire, and though his field was India, he never ceased to take the closest interest in the affairs of Europe.

As a Cabinet Minister he was brought into close contact with the diplomatic relations between England and France, and within a few months of occupying office, while still holding only the position of President of the Board of Control, he began to take the lead in the determination of European politics.

[1] *Personal Sketches of His Own Time*, by Sir Jonah Barrington.

Buonaparte's encroachments in Europe still caused anxiety. He was imposing constitutions on Holland, sending forces under General Wey to occupy Switzerland; he had annexed Piedmont and the Isle of Elba. In view of these aggressions Castlereagh suggested that Malta, which we had engaged to return to the Knights of St. John, but which had not yet been handed over, should not be given up. " I think we must insist," he said, " on the permanent possession of a naval station." Malta he contended, was a stepping-stone to Egypt, and should be retained even at the cost of a renewal of the war with France, a contingency which he regarded in any case as inevitable.[1] Pitt felt at first that even Malta was not worth the risk of immediate war, but he finally approved Castlereagh's action.

" My opinion is," Castlereagh stated, " that with Malta for seven years, Lampedusa for ever, Holland and Switzerland evacuated, and the Turkish Empire and Naples under the avowed protection of Russia, if not formally guaranteed by her, you would stand well at home, and well with reference to France."

The Government found his advice worth considering, and refused to evacuate Malta. Buonaparte flew into a rage. He sent for Lord Whitworth, the British Ambassador in Paris, and demanded the immediate evacuation of the island. There was a stormy interview. Buonaparte shouted and fumed. He declared that the British Government were determined to drag him into war. He said he would put himself at the head of his army and invade England. He made the wildest threats, but the point on which British Ministers took the deepest offence was his remark about Egypt: " *Nous l'aurons malgré vous.*"

On receiving a report of this interview, the British Government refused to discuss the evacuation of Malta further, and Castlereagh drafted a memorandum stating the grounds for a renewal of war. The memorandum was adopted and published. Britain, taking a firm hand at last, demanded that France should evacuate Holland and Belgium, that Britain should retain Malta for ten years, and acquire Lampedusa, a small naval station, off the coast of Tunis.

Napoleon angrily rejected these demands ; and on May 18th 1803, without waiting this time for an ultimatum, England declared war on France.

[1] *Castlereagh Correspondence and Dispatches.*

5

Addington was getting out of his depth, and was quite unable to manage the situation. A little man, with a narrow outlook and mediocre abilities, it had surprised everyone that he should be called to such high office. Pitt's friendship for him was based on the fact that his father had been a patient of Addington's father. It was he who had prescribed port for Pitt in his youth—advice which Pitt had never neglected to follow.

Addington was despised by all the foreign governments, and equally by the Government of which he was head. He seemed to lend himself to ridicule. Once he advised the King to use a pillow of hops to cure his insomnia, which so amused Canning that he dubbed him "the Doctor." The nickname was adopted by Parliament, and when Addington inadvertently used a medical term in the House, the members rocked with laughter, and he had to appeal to the Chair for protection.

His Government was described by Canning as "meaning very little, nor meaning that little well." Addington himself was "like the small pox, since everybody must have him once in their lives." Nor could Canning resist circulating a few rhymes about him.

> " 'Twere best no doubt the truth to tell
> But still good soul *he means so well* ! "

Canning was still out of office, and he spent his time striving to oust Addington. His great desire was to get Pitt restored to the Premiership. He had come into Parliament under Pitt's patronage, he was among Pitt's closest friends, he had been indebted to him for his rapid rise. Apart from Pitt there was no one to whom he could look for lucrative and important office, and Canning was always on the lookout for office; he did not seem to mind *whose* office. "If Lord Castlereagh came to be seized with a desire of retirement," he had once suggested, "I might go to Ireland." "The death of an old man," he wrote to a friend, "would help me to a Privy Councillor's office here."

Canning was fortunate, for Mackenzie, the Privy Seal of Scotland, died most opportunely, and Pitt, before he resigned, had been able to appoint his friend Joint Paymaster-General, and admit him to the Privy Council. But these honours did not last very long. A few months later had come Pitt's resignation carrying with it the resignation of the ministry, which included Mr. Canning.

Out of office Canning exerted all his efforts towards undermining Addington's influence, and forcing Pitt back into the Premiership. But Pitt remained loyal to his friend Addington and would do nothing. His health at this time was very poor, and retirement was necessary for him. Yet Canning worried him night and day till his continual harangues began to prey on Pitt's nerves, and their friendship was for a time at straining-point. The longer he remained out of office the more petulant Canning became; his old, sunny carelessness was giving place to a malignant ill-humour that his friends found difficult to contend with.

While Canning continued to insult the Ministers, assisted by Lord Grenville, who took equal pleasure in pelting them, Pitt remained calmly at Walmer, or he took the waters at Bath, and dissociated himself entirely from the aims of both his friends. He was indeed far from pleased with their efforts, and declared that " nobody did his cause so much disservice as Lord Grenville in the House of Lords, except Mr. Canning in the House of Commons."

But they were not discouraged. On 28 May 1802, Canning had organised a great dinner at the Merchant Taylors' Hall, to celebrate Pitt's birthday. It was attended by nearly a thousand persons. From these celebrations Pitt himself was absent, but his health was drunk, and a song which Canning had written for the occasion was sung. It was " The Pilot that Weathered the Storm."

The song has given a somewhat false impression of Pitt's importance. He hardly weathered the storm; the storm engulfed him, and he went down in it. He had been unable to defeat Buonaparte, nor had he been able to make peace with Buonaparte, and now that the peace which he had inspired had come about, it had proved an ineffectual truce, and hardly an honourable one. The song was simply an electioneering tag: it was part of Canning's campaign to get Pitt back again into office, and as such it served. " It was a political engine," Lord Glenbervie noted down, " and it has been much criticised both as a composition and on account of the opinions it insinuates and the purpose it was meant to promote."

Pitt was not unmoved by the demonstration, but he still refused to sanction any efforts to get him back into the Premiership. Canning for all his shrewdness misunderstood Pitt, for actually, with improving health, he was growing tired of his inactivity, but he was too proud to take any step towards regaining office, and he knew that the King, who showed extreme partiality to Addington, had no desire to see him back. He had also a very small following in the House. But war had again broken out; the horizon was full of portents, and Pitt's time was coming.

A few days after war had been declared he appeared again in the House of Commons. There were cries of " Pitt, Pitt," as he strode to his seat. He looked far from well. His face was no longer red but yellow, and every now and then he gave a hollow cough. He looked dejected and melancholy, and the general impression on all was that he was finished. The Royal Family slighted him, and when, in the House of Lords, he stood behind the throne, the Princes passed him by without a word.

But when he rose in debate it was " the great fiend himself." He was for war, for war without end. For nearly two hours he spoke, and with such vehemence and such eloquence that even his enemies were silenced. Creevey, who bore him no affection, declared: " In the elevation of his tone of mind and composition, in the infinite energy of his style, the miraculous perspicuity and fluency of his periods, he outdid as it was thought all former performances of his. Never to be sure was there such an exhibition. Its effect was dreadful." [1]

Pitt's speech was unexpected. In office he had spent all his energies trying to bring about peace. But now he had yielded to the current, he was for war. The House was with him, and when Wilberforce, who followed, made a speech for peace, the members tried over and over again to cough him down.

War, in any case, had already been declared, and Pitt made it a stepping-stone back to office. Addington was certainly not equal to guiding the country through a major war, but, as is the way with

---

[1] Unfortunately the shorthand writers were excluded from this session, and there is no report of the speech existing.

great men and small, he was reluctant to relinquish office. He suggested that Pitt should *join* him in the Government. Pitt gave a peremptory and angry refusal. He would come back only on one condition, that he took the reins himself; he would come back only as Prime Minister. In high dudgeon he withdrew to Walmer, where he spent his time organising the local volunteers, parading and drilling, surrounded by a train of military attendants, while the country plunged into war, and the Addington Ministry continued in power.

Castlereagh, who had long been convinced that war was inevitable, had taken the precaution, while negotiations were still in progress, of ordering the Governor-General of India not to proceed with the restoration of the French and Dutch possessions, which he had previously instructed him to surrender. Wellesley had as usual disregarded his instructions, and the French and Dutch possessions were still in our hands. The outbreak of war gave Wellesley new opportunities, and he was soon engaged in further schemes of conquest.

The outbreak of war had its repercussions in Ireland, a country which Castlereagh always watched with anxiety. The Government already knew that Robert Emmet, a young Irish hothead, had had an interview with Buonaparte in Paris, and it did not surprise Castlereagh that it should be followed by another rebellion. Nothing had been done as yet to adjust the Catholic grievances. He had warned Addington of the need to " soften religious contentions " in that country; he had also written to the new Chief Secretary, Mr. Wickham, regarding the necessity of raising a militia for the security of Ireland in case of war, promising him all his support. But as usual there was gross mismanagement. It was fortunate for the Government that the revolt itself was ill-prepared and ill-contrived, and that it developed into a mere street brawl, for the city was in the hands of the mob for three or four hours before the authorities moved. During that time Kilwarden, the old Lord Chief Justice, who was driving through the city with his daughter and his young nephew was dragged from his carriage and murdered. Other murders were committed before the casual arrival of a patrol of soldiers, who fired on the mob and dispersed it.

Emmet, finding himself abandoned by his followers, made his escape, but he was taken later by Major Sirr, the officer who had captured Lord Edward Fitzgerald, and on 20 September 1803, he was hanged. He was only twenty-one, and his death roused the same deadly malice in the heart of every Irishman that has tinged the whole history of Ireland.

Castlereagh was deeply concerned for the fate of Ireland, for troubles seemed only to multiply. He was deeply concerned too for the fate of England, for her position was growing ever darker and more difficult. Buonaparte was still massing troops at Boulogne for the invasion of England. The Government majority was shrinking, and a Ministerial crisis seemed at hand. The King, who had always been behind Addington, was exhibiting those nervous, excited, irritable symptoms, which usually led to a fit of insanity. Addington was in a dilemma. He was still trying to compromise with Pitt, but Pitt maintained a haughty inimical attitude towards his old friend, and when Addington sent him a message begging him to state what could be done, he replied that to the King alone, or to any person deputed by the King, would he make such a communication. There was nothing else for Addington to do but send in his resignation. The King with great reluctance accepted it, and with equal reluctance recalled Pitt.

After three years' retirement, Pitt was back again in office. But his tenure was to be a short one. He was already passing into the shadow of death, and had but two years to run—two years of isolation and gloom—before death took him.

Castlereagh, who had become Pitt's principal confidant, remained for the time being at the Board of Control, but he was soon to be raised to higher office, and to conduct the whole progress of the war.

6

On 18 May 1804, the day that Pitt took his seat again as Prime Minister, Buonaparte was proclaimed Emperor, and henceforth called himself by his Christian name in the royal manner. He had summoned the Pope to Paris, and ordered him to crown him and Josephine at Notre Dame, and the Pope had come at his bidding. The new Emperor may have lacked breeding, culture and style, but he had conquered half Europe, and was now Emperor of France.

He gathered around him a court, and made the members of his

family Imperial Princes and Princesses. English papers caricaturing him depicted him in his throne-room, casting a glance round at his ragged relations, and saying to Talleyrand: " As these are part of our relatives, do you, Tally, get them washed and enrol their names in the Légion d'Honneur." In the midst of the magnificent coronation ceremony, he is said to have remarked to his brother Joseph: " If only father could see us."

He had ordered a plebiscite to be held on the question of whether the French desired him for their Emperor or no. The general feeling was that he would be Emperor in either case, and that it was advisable to say " yes." One voter wrote against his " *Oui:* "—" *Je crains, tu crains, il craint.*"

The prospect before Pitt, when he resumed office, was not a cheerful one. Britain was at war again, and with a tyrant who had grown tremendously in strength and power. More than ever England needed a firm hand, and Pitt, broken in health, was clearly unequal to the task that faced him.

The Tory party at this time was not overloaded with genius, and Pitt tried to form a Coalition Government which should combine the talents of both the Tories and the Whigs. To this the King, after a good deal of pressure, agreed, but bigoted as ever, he obstinately refused to include in the Ministry Charles Fox, the Whig leader, whom he considered a vicious, intemperate person, and an evil influence on his eldest son, the Prince of Wales. As Lord Grenville and other of Fox's friends declined to take office without him, the project failed.

Pitt had to fall back on a Tory Government, which was composed of such meagre talent that the Ministry was dubbed " the new Administration composed of William and Pitt." Nine out of the eleven members of the Cabinet were in the House of Lords.

Castlereagh was at first Pitt's only Cabinet colleague in the House of Commons. He became Pitt's chief lieutenant, and as Pitt grew daily less disposed to business, the greatest share of the work of government fell on his youngest colleague.

Castlereagh had always been one of Pitt's most devoted adherents, and regarded himself as Pitt's pupil. With his untiring energy and endless industry he became indispensable to a Prime Minister who was getting weaker and more and more averse to labour. He was always willing to shoulder the heaviest burdens. He was a shrewd diplomat, he had a grasp of general affairs which inspired confidence and respect, he was considerate, courteous and loyal, and he made for peace in the Cabinet.

In the new Ministry he worked untiringly, and had more of Pitt's confidence than any other member of the Government. Far more trusted than Canning, who as yet held no place in the Cabinet, he showed a steadiness which the other never possessed, and his freedom from jealousy and animosity promoted harmony where Canning's wit and waggery, and his love of intrigue, created only discord.

To Pitt he was the greatest asset, for the new ministry, weak as it was, was soon to be further weakened by the loss of two of its chief members. Lord Harrowby fell down the stairs at the Foreign Office, and retired with concussion of the brain. Henry Dundas, now Lord Melville, and First Lord of the Admiralty, Pitt's dearest friend and oldest supporter, became the object of a scandal which shook the House of Commons. A Commission had been appointed to inquire into frauds and abuses in the Royal Navy. In its Tenth Report Lord Melville was accused of having, when Treasurer of the Navy, used the public funds for private purposes. Although there was never actual proof of this, he admitted paying into his private account Admiralty funds which were used for Secret Service. The scandal caused great excitement in Parliament, and deep anxiety to Pitt.

Castlereagh and Canning came to the aid of the unfortunate Minister and doggedly defended him. When the question of Melville's guilt was finally put to the vote, the numbers for and against him were equal. The Speaker, Mr. Abbott, turned pale as he announced them, for the casting vote was his. After a painful silence, during which Pitt bent a glance of mute appeal on him, he gave the vote *against* Melville. From Melville's detractors there came a wild shout of victory. Hunting cries rang through the House. Pitt, unable to control his emotion, pressed his hat down on his head, and made for the door, the tears coursing down his cheeks. Castlereagh, Canning and a few other of his younger followers closed round him, and surrounded by them he moved out of the House.

Melville was later impeached by the Lords, but though he was finally acquitted his reputation never recovered. For Pitt it was a mortal blow. " We can get over Austerlitz," he said during his last days, " but we can never get over the Tenth Report."

During the inquiry Pitt suffered the further humiliation of being himself examined for money irregularities, and confessed to having lent £40,000 and £100,000 out of money voted for Navy services to two merchant members of Parliament (who had always voted with him) when he knew them to be bankrupt. At one time it almost seemed as if he would have to resign the Premiership. As Creevey remarked: " It was a damned unpopular business."

7

The Government's position was an unenviable one. Hemmed in as it was by difficulties, it was now menaced by the King's insanity and the fear that a Regency might have to be appointed, which would result in the overthrow of the newly formed Ministry and the return of the Whigs to power. The greatest secrecy was maintained regarding the King's health, so that the country might not learn the truth, but it was difficult to prevent the news from leaking out.

The King, so dignified and so prudent had changed sadly in manner. His conversation had become incoherent, wearisome, and indiscreet. He talked so incessantly that his medical adviser thought it necessary to recommend His Majesty to be a little more silent. He did not take this unkindly, but thanked him for his advice. As his condition did not improve, and fits of violence occurred, the Reverend Dr. Willis, a mental expert who had attended him before, was called in. The King asked him if he, a clergyman, were not ashamed of himself for practising such a profession. " Sir," said the reverend doctor, " our Saviour himself went about healing the sick." " Yes," retorted the King, " but he had not £700 for it." The King's wits were still a good deal sharper than those of many of his subjects.

Unfortunately, his symptoms were so disquieting that it was thought necessary to remove him to an apartment at Windsor separate from the Queen's.

One of his chief anxieties was to see his children, but the doctors forbade this. He was greatly distressed, and would send an attendant to request them to show themselves at the windows of the Lower Lodge for only a few minutes. It is painful that the doctors should have deemed it inexpedient to grant this simple desire.

One evening he became violent, and a page came out of his apartment to inform the physician. Dr. Reynolds and an equerry entering found His Majesty very much agitated. He complained of the rough treatment he had received from his pages, who had been obliged to hold him down in his bed.

As his malady seemed to be increasing, it was arranged to remove him to Kew. But when, on the day of the removal, the arrangements were cautiously mentioned to him, he stoutly objected, and refused to get up. When all persuasion failed, Pitt, who was in the ante-room, was asked to go in and inform the King that the Queen had already gone to Kew. Pitt entered the room, and after making his obeisances, said:

" What a fine day it is. Perhaps Your Majesty would care to rise, and set out for Kew, where Her Majesty has just gone."

" If Her Majesty has gone to Kew," the King observed, " she has gone without leave, and she should return to ask my pardon." Pitt tried again, but failed to persuade him.

At length, baffled in his endeavours, Pitt retired, and a favourite equerry was sent in. But when the subject was again broached the King became very angry, and hastily closing the bed curtains, hid himself behind them.

Finding that nothing could be done by persuasion, the physicians decided to go in together and get the matter settled. On seeing the four doctors bearing down on him, the King's agitation increased. He desired Dr. Warren to leave the room instantly. As Dr. Warren did not move he jumped out of bed and rushed at him. The pages laid hold of his arm, and finding himself helpless he retired to bed again. As he still refused to get up, a firmer tone was assumed and he was informed that, if he did not go, other means would be resorted to. He asked if they meant to use force. " Yes," Dr. Warren replied.

He was silent for a moment, then he said he would get up if the physicians went away. They retired, and after a little more delay, the King rose and dressed himself. He took a glass of water, and some bread and butter, then putting on his greatcoat, he walked to the entrance, accompanied by his equerry and three officers.

Orders had been sent to clear the Castle Terrace and lock the gates to prevent a crowd gathering. The closed gates did not escape his notice. When the carriage entered the Home Park, about twenty loyal inhabitants of Windsor, mostly tradesmen, suddenly appeared, and as the carriage passed, bowed respectfully, taking a melancholy leave of their sovereign. As the King returned their salute a tear started to his eye. " Why am I taken from a place I like best in the world ? " he asked sadly.

On arriving at Kew he got out of the carriage without hesitation, and walked leisurely through the Hall. But beyond the Hall he quickened his pace, and breaking into a run tried to enter the Suite of Apartments on the left, where he expected to find the Queen and his children. But the doors were locked, and he turned away in disappointment. The doors on the opposite side were then thrown open, and he was escorted to them. He found them empty. As he entered he looked round him with some surprise, for many disturbing changes had been made in the apartment. A bed had been placed in the room, and a water-closet added. These alterations discomposed him very much, and he repeatedly asked who had ordered them. Receiving no reply, he became more agitated and complained that he had been deceived. He declared he would not go to bed, but would sit up all night and tire out his attendants. He remarked that he was very strong and active, and in proof of this began to dance and hop about with great agility, a most affecting sight. The night was an unpleasant one. The King carried out his intention of not going to bed, and stayed up till four o'clock in the morning, when, becoming violent towards one of his pages, he was forced into bed. This put him in a state of great agitation, and his violence increased.

The change to Kew, far from doing him any good, only aggravated his disorder. He refused to eat or drink; he became depressed and declared he was tired of his life, and entreated his pages to put an end to it.

After a few days, in his more composed moments, he began sketching. He drew some plans of the house, and put in suggestions for alterations quite effectively. Having drawn a firm and accurate line he turned to his page and said:

" Pretty good for a man who is mad."

But his periods of composure did not last very long; often he became enraged and violent, and Dr. Willis, who was now in constant attendance, took a firm hand with him. He informed him that his mind was deranged, and told him he must control himself, or he would be put into a strait waistcoat. He went into the antechamber, and returned with the object in his hand. The King eyed it attentively, and somewhat alarmed, said he would go to bed. He went into the next room and undressed quietly. After Dr. Willis had gone, he abused all physicians, and complained that they had concealed from him his true condition. After this the poor man, overcome by grief, burst into a flood of tears, and wept bitterly.

8

The King's insanity did not ease the Government's position; it only made it more insecure. Pitt's difficulties increased daily: an injured reputation, declining health, a feeble Ministry, a mad King, and across the Channel, encamped at Boulogne, Napoleon's Army of England watching for the moment to invade. It was the year 1804.

The whole coast of France bristled with guns; 100,000 men and a host of flat-bottomed boats stood waiting. The Emperor appeared in the camp in person, reviewing infantry, attending embarkation rehearsals, riding among his troops, standing silhouetted against the sky in his old grey overcoat and worn black hat, with his telescope turned on Dover.

" Let us be masters of the Channel for six hours," he said, " and we are masters of the world."

" Fifteen millions of people," he said, " must give way to forty millions."

Wild rumours that the invasion had started kept sweeping the country, and for an invasion, if it came, we were wholly unprepared. The Volunteers, enrolled for Home Defence, were armed with pitchforks to meet the expected legions.

Invasion was expected hourly, and dwellers on the coast had already evacuated their homes. The Prime Minister warned his colleagues that if the enemy landed they would pass " with the rapidity of a torrent " over the sixty miles to London, but the officers of the Navy held other views. Although the ships were in poor condition, they were manned and officered as no other fleet had ever been; there would be no landing in England. The Officers of the Army were equally sanguine.

" We understand," wrote General Sir John Moore from Sandgate, where he was stationed, " that Government have positive information that we are to be invaded, and I am told that Pitt believes it. The experience of the last twelve months has taught me to place little confidence in the information and belief of Ministers, and as the undertaking seems to me so arduous, and offering so little prospect of success, I cannot persuade myself that Napoleon will be mad enough to attempt it. He will continue to threaten, by which means alone he can do us harm."

" One thing is perfectly clear," said Lord Nelson, " we shall never have a solid peace until the invasion is tried and found to fail."

Napoleon, on the contrary, was very certain of success. He had even ordered a medal to be struck to commemorate the invasion of England. On one side was the Emperor's head crowned with laurel, on the other Hercules strangling a sea-monster. He had had it marked " *Frappé á Londres*, 1804," as though it had been struck in London after the conquest of England had been effected.

He had three fleets now at his disposal, a French fleet at Toulon and at Brest, and a Spanish fleet at Cadiz. The three combined, he was convinced, would be sufficiently strong to hold the Channel long enough to enable him to get his armies across. Eighteen thousand men at Brest were to sail for Ireland, and march on Dublin, while the Grand Army invaded Kent. All that was necessary was to divert the British Navy while the three fleets combined, and made their way up the Channel towards the Straits of Dover.

It was a harassing time for the Government. Pitt, in an effort to divert Napoleon's attention from England, was ready to send an army to the Continent to assist any country against the common foe. He was ready with immense subsidies, and was courting Russia, Austria, Prussia, and Sweden, in an attempt to form another coalition.

Alexander, the young Czar of Russia, welcomed the idea of a European coalition. He already saw a vision of himself at its head— the saviour of Europe. His mission, he began to feel, was to restore peace to a stricken world, to bring happy tranquillity to every country, to convert Europe into a permanent Christian republic, with himself directing its destinies. He was a strange young man, a baffling mixture of impulsive philanthropy and shrewd egotism, full of vague and hasty ideas, mingling sentiment with diplomacy, mysticism with astuteness. All countries, he stated, should be governed by the sacred rights of humanity, and a league of nations should be formed to enforce these rights by a new code of international law. But in order to secure this happy tranquillity England should give up her maritime conquests, and should first of all surrender Malta, which should be garrisoned by Russia. On this condition depended Russia's alliance.

The idea was charming. But it was on this very subject of Malta that Castlereagh had persuaded the Government in 1803 to declare war on Napoleon. At that time Pitt did not think Malta worth a war, but his opinion had changed, and in his answer to the Russian Czar, he declared: " Whatever pain it causes us (and it is indeed great) we must give up the hope of seeing the alliance ratified, since its express condition is our renunciation of Malta. We will continue the war alone. It will be maritime."

Although Alexander's views were a little vague, and he sounded half-dreamer, half-charlatan, they contained all the elements of the European system established by Castlereagh at the Congress of Vienna ten years later. These hazy suggestions were developed in a remarkable document of 19 January 1805, which gives precision and clarity to the scheme. The document, which bears no name, is attributed to Pitt, but as Pitt was in very poor health at this time, and as the Foreign Minister, Lord Harrowby, had just retired, it seems more likely to have been Castlereagh's memorandum. It was the line in any case on which Castlereagh developed his policy at the Congresses; it foreshadowed the system of alliances and compromises carried out by him in the Treaties that followed Napoleon's downfall.

For the moment Alexander's dreams vanished into the air, for Napoleon was still unbeaten, and his continued annexations ended all hope of peace on the Continent. He had now annexed Genoa, and crowned himself King of Italy. Even Alexander saw that there was no hope of satisfying him, and he decided to waive Malta, and to enter into a definite alliance with England and Austria. It is interesting to note that to the general terms of the alliance the Czar added a clause that, on the conclusion of the war, a Congress should be held, to draw up a Law of Nations and to form an International Federation to enforce it. This treaty was the basis of the Grand Alliance, over which Castlereagh was to preside in 1814, and which actually effected the deliverance of Europe.

In June 1805, the same month in which Pitt dispatched to St. Petersburg his reasons for retaining Malta, Castlereagh was appointed Secretary of State for War and the Colonies. He succeeded his uncle Lord Camden, who gave up the War Office, but who remained in the Cabinet as President of the Council.

CHAPTER VII

I

As War Minister, Castlereagh had all the power he desired. From now on he was Napoleon's great opponent. He had long discovered what Napoleon's aims and ambitions were, and he saw that the struggle must be waged to the bitter end. At Pitt's request he retained the Presidency of the Board of Control on which he had now served for three years. The doubling of the two posts gave him a great deal of labour and also a great deal of influence—for the whole world was now his province. But work he had never shunned, and ambition had always spurred him on.

Canning, who had tried and failed to get the Secretaryship of State for Foreign Affairs, was not very pleased at Castlereagh's promotion, and voiced his displeasure in a letter to Pitt.

" I must mention another person in your Government—Castlereagh —for whom I have never at any moment entertained anything of dislike, and whom upon nearer intercourse I grow to like, as much as the difference of our natures admit, very cordially. . . . But you can't suppose that I can very patiently bear the accumulation of two efficient offices upon him—as if there were no one else capable of executing either of them."

But Canning had lost a good deal of Pitt's confidence, and disappointed of higher office, he had now to content himself with that of Treasurer of the Navy. " I hate the thought of the Treasury Board," he informed Pitt, " for except yourself, who is there I can sit near with comfort, or with whom exchange a word in the course of debate ? "

The Treasury Board was not in any way what he desired, and he accepted it with a bad grace. Peevishly he wrote:

" It almost proves to me that one has nothing to do in this world but to look straight forward to one's own personal interest, get the most one can, keep it as long as one can, give up as little as one can help, and think of helping nobody that is not essential to one's own object. I hate this philosophy, but a little more ill-usage from different parts will soon make me a convert to it."

He was growing cynical, disillusioned and embittered. Temperley tells us that it was the " years of disappointment and misrepresentation " which " told upon his temper and made him both irritable and nervous." [1] Had he been less inclined to jest at the expense of others, had he been less prone to intrigue against, and quarrel with, members of the Government, his friends would have been more numerous. As it was, few trusted him and there were few whom he had not offended. " I never hear the lock of the door turn," said one of his oldest friends,[2] " but I dread a visit from Canning."

2

At the War Office Castlereagh's career was not marked with any conspicuous success. His first effort, which was an attempt to set fire to the enemy's ships at Boulogne by means of Congreve rockets, was a complete failure. The rocket was a new invention which had been brought to him by Sir Sidney Smith. Castlereagh gave it the closest examination. In fact he explored its possibilities so carefully that he nearly got drowned in the process.

He took Mr. Pitt down the Thames at nightfall in one of the small, flat-bottomed boats that he intended using to launch the rockets. It was a very dark night, and as he stepped from one boat to another, he stepped into the water and sank. Fortunately he was now a good swimmer, and was able to keep under water for a few minutes and avoid rising under the boats. When he came up he called to the boatmen to keep away, and managed to swim to the nearest boat. It was his second escape from drowning.

When later he launched the rockets against the enemy fleet they

[1] *Life of Canning*, by H. W. V. Temperley.
[2] Liverpool.

did not reach far enough to do any damage. The idea was sound enough, but the invention was not yet perfected.

Castlereagh's next effort was to prepare for a new invasion of Europe, which Pitt was planning. Though Castlereagh prepared the expedition on an enormous scale, being the first to perceive that large scale operations were necessary for the defeat of Napoleon, the invasion was unsuccessful. The arrangements took too long, the decision to send a large army came too late, and the extraordinary rapidity of Napoleon's movements foiled all Castlereagh's well-laid plans.

Arthur Wellesley, who had just returned from India full of victories, was to be sent out with the expedition. Waiting in the ante-room at the Colonial office to see Castlereagh he found another person there whom he immediately recognised, from his likeness to his pictures and the loss of an arm, as Lord Nelson. As Castlereagh, who had been held up a good deal that day, kept them both waiting for nearly an hour, they were able to take stock of each other. Nelson very soon got into conversation with his companion, though he had not the faintest idea who he was. Nelson's conversation was entirely about his own importance, and Wellesley was a little disturbed by the vain, foolish chatter.

After a while, moved to curiosity by some remark Wellesley made, Nelson went out of the room to inquire about him. He must have been a little sobered by the information he received, for on his return his whole attitude had changed, all the vanity had disappeared, and he talked with such good sense and such sound knowledge of the state of the country and of the situation on the Continent, that Wellesley was as much surprised by his wisdom as he had previously been irritated by his foolishness. "In fact," said Wellesley, in after years, "he talked like an officer and a statesman."

When Nelson was at length admitted to Castlereagh's room, he received his sailing orders. He was to put to sea and intercept the French and Spanish fleets which were carrying invasion to the shores of England. It was the last time Castlereagh saw him.

Wellesley's orders were to sail for Northern Germany with the expedition then preparing. Sixty thousand men were to join the combined armies of Russia, Austria, Sweden and Prussia, whom Pitt had swept into a new coalition.

But Napoleon, hovering like a hawk at Boulogne with his picked army, waiting to swoop, heard of the coalition forming in his rear, and before the British force could embark for Germany, before the Russians could advance to meet the Austrians, he swept through the Black Forest, took the Austrian Commander by surprise, and forced him to capitulate at Ulm. He captured two hundred cannon, ninety flags, twenty thousand men, and all the generals.

Castlereagh was aghast; but Pitt, when rumours of the disaster reached him, exclaimed: " Don't believe it, it is all a fiction." The following day, however, in a Dutch paper, which Pitt brought to Malmesbury to translate, he found confirmation of the news.

3

It was a terrible disaster; but Nelson, searching the wide ocean, waiting for the French and Spanish fleets to put out from harbour, fell in with the enemy ships off Cape Trafalgar. As the two lines of the British ships moved slowly towards the enemy, Nelson said: " I will give them such a shaking as they have never yet experienced; at least I will lay down my life in the attempt."

Through a scene of falling masts and crashing broadsides, the *Victory* sailed. Her mizzen topmast was shot away, her wheel broken, her sails torn to shreds, her decks filled with the cries of wounded, but she sailed ahead, cutting right through the enemy lines.

Nelson walked up and down the quarter-deck. With the four stars of his Orders blazing on his breast, he was too easy a target. As he turned a musket shot struck him, and he fell.

He lived long enough to hear that the French Admiral had surrendered. Indeed the French and Spanish ships were almost entirely destroyed, and never again during the war did a French or Spanish fleet venture out from harbour. Yet so deeply was Nelson honoured, that when the news arrived, there was more sorrow for the loss of England's hero than joy for the victory gained. His body was brought home in his flagship and laid to rest in St. Paul's.

The funeral procession, as it came by water from Greenwich, was watched by a mourning nation. The streets overflowed with sorrowing people; for Nelson's courage, his generosity, his simple, frank, open nature, even his very weaknesses, had endeared him to all the people. His very name was magic.

Castlereagh, writing to his wife, said: " You will weep for Lord Nelson, whilst you and all around will rejoice in his glories. After an action of only four hours, with only twenty-seven sail of the line against thirty-three, he took nineteen and one blew up. We have lost no ship, but alas, the first Admiral in the universe."

If Nelson had decided to die, he could not have chosen a better hour.

" The public would never have sent him on another expedition," wrote Castlereagh's stepmother, " his health was not equal to another effort, and he might have yielded to the more natural but less imposing effects of more worldly honours—whereas he now begins his immortal Career, having nothing to achieve upon Earth, and leaving to the English fleet a Legacy which they alone are able to improve. Had I been his Wife or his Mother I would rather have wept him Dead than seen him languish on a less splendid day. In such a Death there is no sting, and in such a Grave everlasting Victory."[1]

4

Trafalgar had lost the country its greatest Admiral, but it had saved England from invasion. At the annual dinner of the Lord Mayor, Pitt, whose popularity had been on the wane, was received with wild acclamations. The crowd stopped his carriage in Cheapside, took off the horses and drew him in triumph to the Guildhall. He was hailed as the saviour of Europe. His speech on this occasion was a very brief one; but it was perhaps his finest effort.

" I return you many thanks for the honour you have done me. But Europe is not to be saved by any single man. England has saved herself by her exertions, and will, as I trust, save Europe by her example."

But Europe was on the brink of further disaster, for Napoleon had entered Vienna, and was sleeping in the Palace of Schönbrunn. A few days later he pushed on northward in pursuit of the Russian and Austrian forces which had now combined, and which he shattered on 2 December 1805 at Austerlitz. The third Coalition was at an end.

[1] Letter from Lady Frances to Castlereagh, in the possession of Mrs. Fanshawe Royle.

The Czar Alexander was in flight, the Emperor Francis was signing away his possessions to the conqueror, the whole of Europe lay at Napoleon's feet.

Castlereagh received the news of Austerlitz as he entered the house of Lord Aberdeen at Stanmore, where he and Lady Castlereagh had been invited for the Christmas festivities. The dispatches had followed close on his heels, and almost before he had entered the house he was leaving again and preparing to travel through the night on the Bath road to break the news to Pitt.

It was evil news that he was bearing, and Castlereagh did not relish handing the dispatches to his chief, whom he knew to be gravely ill. Fate had dealt them a cruel blow. If Napoleon had not struck so swiftly, the Austrian Archduke Charles, with ninety thousand men who were rapidly advancing from Italy, would have been there to face him. The Russians and the main Austrian army had only to retreat towards them and Napoleon would have been surrounded with forces three times as large as his own. But the Russians and Austrians with precipitate haste had given battle at Austerlitz, and were now suing for peace. The King of Prussia, instead of declaring war on France, had waited for the result of Austerlitz, and had now signed a treaty of alliance with the enemy instead.

When Pitt opened the dispatch which Castlereagh had brought him his face turned ashen. " Heavy news indeed," he said. He was silent for a moment, then he called for a brandy which he hurriedly swallowed, and asked to be left alone.

His haggard, emaciated appearance, his hollow voice and the pallor of his skin had long told that death was near. Austerlitz killed him. Bath, as he wrote to Castlereagh later, was of no further use to him, and he was setting out for home. He intended, he said, to be back for the opening of Parliament, but he never took his seat again. As he entered his house at Putney, his eye rested on the map of Europe. " Roll up that map," he said hoarsely. " It will not be wanted these ten years." His voice had almost left him; he was so weak he could hardly drag himself up the stairs of his home.

Castlereagh was now in the greatest difficulties regarding the army he had dispatched to Germany. Twenty-six thousand picked troops had already been sent out; these were marooned on the Elbe, and liable to be cut off at any moment by the freezing of the North

German rivers. He wanted the men back before they got involved in an engagement, for Austria, which they had been sent out to help, had already capitulated, and Prussia was not to be trusted; but the Prime Minister's signature was necessary for their evacuation, and the Prime Minister was in a desperate condition. It was painful to Castlereagh to trouble him at such a time, but his signature had to be obtained, and every moment counted. He approached Pitt's doctors, and since they gave their permission for a short interview, he went over to Putney. When he entered the sick room, he found Pitt in a sad condition: it was not easy to break the news to him, but it had to be done. With a deep sigh Pitt took the paper and affixed his signature. Castlereagh hurried away, and by his promptness was able to withdraw the army without losing a man; at the same time seven hundred Prussian vessels were seized in British harbours and on the seas.

A few days later Pitt grew delirious. Rallying for a moment he murmured: " My country; how I leave my country." There followed a few broken exclamations on the alarming state of public affairs, and in the morning, on the 23 January 1806, the twenty-fifth anniversary of the day he first entered Parliament, he died.

Castlereagh, meeting Canning on the road to Putney, told him that the worst had happened. They were both deeply affected. Writing to his wife, Canning said:

" Poor dear Pitt—how all his good now lives in our heart, and all his bad (and how little he had of that) fades away. God bless him. He is a loss not to be repaired."

Pitt's body was carried to Westminster with all the pomp and grandeur he had avoided during his life. Castlereagh and Canning were among the pall-bearers. A splendid train of Princes, nobles, and bishops followed. All dissension was now hushed, and he was laid in the Abbey by the side of his father, the great Chatham, amid universal grief.

5

Great as were Pitt's abilities he had failed miserably in his management of the war; he had failed to achieve either peace or victory. And yet, in spite of his crippling loans, his panic legislation, the failure of his sporadic expeditions, and of his Continental combinations, he has passed into history as the Minister who steered the country through the Napoleonic Wars, as " the Pilot that Weathered the Storm."

He died, however, nine years before the war was ended. He died leaving England in the most desperate straits. Napoleon was at the zenith of his power, controlling almost the whole of Western Europe. Italy, Holland, Prussia, Austria were all his satellites. But Pitt was a master of eloquence, and shining phrases are more easily remembered than sober achievement. " At the close of every brilliant display," wrote Sydney Smith, " an expedition failed or a kingdom fell. God send us a stammerer."

A " stammerer " was sent, for it was in Castlereagh that the country was to find its match for Napoleon. To him it was left to make good the breaches which Pitt had left, and to guide England safely and surely to victory. His time, however, had not yet come, for with Pitt's death he was out of office again.

The death of their leader had thrown the Tories into utter confusion. In spite of the incapacity which Pitt showed in his conduct of the war, he was a man of extraordinary powers, and his authority over the House of Commons had become more and more absolute. He was a born leader of men, and it was difficult to find a successor. The King's efforts to form a new Tory administration proved fruitless and he had no alternative but to send for the proud Lord Grenville. Grenville, however, refused to form a Ministry unless Fox were accepted, and Fox, with his revolutionary views and his reputation for profligacy, was more than ever unpalatable to the King. It was distasteful to the stubborn little man to be coerced. He considered the matter for several days and appeared extremely depressed. He then said to the Queen: " I have taken Mr. Fox for my Minister, and on the whole I am satisfied with the arrangement."

When Fox entered the Royal Closet he was shocked at the great change which had come over the King. He had aged considerably since they had last met. He was deaf and almost blind. Groping his way about with a stick he was a pathetic sight. The poor man had been tried by many afflictions. " My lord," he once said to the Archbishop of Canterbury, " I have twice read over the evidence of the physicians on my case, and if I can stand that, I can stand anything." He had stood more than that. He had borne the insults and jeers of the Prince of Wales without flinching. He had borne the scandal which his other sons provided.

The Duke of Clarence and Mrs. Jordan were producing an interminable family of illegitimate FitzClarences. Prince Edward was living with an elderly French woman in Canada. There were rumours that the Princess of Wales had given birth to an illegitimate child. In spite of the probity of his household there seemed nothing but levity and profligacy in the King's family.

"I am quite resigned," he said, "for what have we in this world to do but to suffer and perform the will of the Almighty?"

Fox he still considered the evil genius of the Prince of Wales, but he met him without a trace of rancour. "Mr. Fox," he said, "I little thought you and I should ever meet again in this place, but I have no desire to look back upon old grievances, and you may rest assured I shall never remind you of them."

The Ministry of all the Talents thus came into existence, but it did not last very long. In spite of all its talent it had no capacity for foreign affairs, and was most unfortunate in its conduct of the war. Its Foreign Minister, Fox, a brilliant orator, an agreeable character, and undoubtedly the foremost man in public life, was full of headstrong impulses, and as little capable of guiding the country through a major war as the proud, chilling, and scholarly Grenville.

The Whigs had always been opposed to the war, and Fox's first move was to institute negotiations for peace. Castlereagh combined with Perceval, a vigorous young lawyer who was making headway in the House of Commons, in leading a very active and energetic Opposition. He had never believed that Napoleon had any idea of making peace, and it hardly surprised him when the negotiations were broken off, not merely on the point actually in dispute, but on account of the evident insincerity of the French Government. There remained nothing else for the Ministry to do but to carry on with the war. The position was almost hopeless, for the power of Napoleon hung like a cloud over the whole of Europe. He was now proclaiming his brother Louis King of Holland as he had proclaimed his brother Joseph King of Naples. In the month of October 1806 he marched through Germany and crushed the Prussians, who had suddenly gone back on their alliance with him, at Jena and Auerstadt. No army collapsed before Napoleon so completely as those once invincible

Prussians. The French General, Bernadotte, had been bribed by English gold to keep his whole corps out of the engagement, but the French troops under Davoust, dispensing with Bernadotte, smashed through the Prussian lines, and marched on to Berlin. Napoleon entered the capital. At Potsdam he walked into the apartments of Frederick the Great, which had been left untouched since his death. Leaning over Frederick's tomb, he drew the dead king's sword from its scabbard, and carried it away as a trophy.

To the Abbé Sièyes he exclaimed: "I did not find any Prussia; what a people, what a country, what a government. . . . The Austrians are different; they have no energy, but they have honour. The Prussians though have neither honour nor soul. Sheer canaille."

From Potsdam, on 21 November 1806, he issued his famous Berlin Decrees, forbidding all commerce between England and the Continent. England now found herself isolated from the rest of the world. Without one ship Napoleon had placed the British Isles in a state of blockade. But he found he was unable to do without British commerce himself. A widespread contraband trade arose, and the French army were soon marching across Poland shod by Northampton, and clad in greatcoats made in Leeds.

At Eylau, in the month of February 1807, Napoleon met the Russians, and here his triumphal march received a temporary check. The Russians fought a hard battle and declared Eylau a victory; but such matters affected Napoleon little; he too declared Eylau a victory. Actually it was disastrous for both the Russians *and* the French. The earth froze, the snow beat down, frozen bodies strewed the ground, the carnage was horrible, and after the bitterest fighting there was no victory on either side. Had Alexander received the help he had expected from Britain the scales might have been turned in favour of the Russians, but not a soldier had been sent, and Napoleon pressed on to Friedland.

6

Although he was now free from the ties of ministerial responsibility Castlereagh was full of anxiety about Britain's loss of dignity abroad. The Ministry of all the Talents was frittering away England's strength on distant ventures which could not possibly affect the main issue. Expeditions had been sent to the Dardanelles, to Egypt, and to Buenos Aires, leaving no troops for essential activities nearer home.

In the House Castlereagh opposed the Whig policy of isolating England from Europe, and urged the Government to hold 60,000 troops available for Continental operations; he opposed the reduction of military expenditure at this critical time; but he was disregarded. Out of office he gave up hours to strenuous work which seemed to lead nowhere. He would lie awake at night, with that sore throat and headache which came from speaking in the ill-ventilated House, pondering over the general situation. But he was powerless to avert the catastrophe which he felt was coming. Though he went out of London for week-ends, staying with the Camdens or the Hertfords, most of his time he spent in the House. Often when Emily was waiting for him to escort her to the theatre, she would receive a last minute note sent by special messenger: "We shall be kept in the House for some time—you had better go to dinner, leaving the beefsteaks for us. We shall follow you to the Play." Catalani was singing at the Opera, and Castlereagh would manage to slip into his box in time to hear her. Music had always been his one relaxation; the piano and the 'cello were still a solace to him in the few moments of leisure he allowed himself. Even Emily was encouraged to play the harp.

At the Opera, as soon as he appeared in his box, his friends would drop in to discuss the war situation. Things were going from bad to worse, and while the present Ministry and the present policy continued, there could be no hope of improvement. It was an immense strain for him to feel himself unable to do anything except play an insignificant part in the platitudinous, quarrelsome atmosphere of the House. Government seemed to be an obstructive business of energetic factions ranged against each other, and all he could do was to add to the general confusion. What he wanted was power, the power to steer the country through all the stresses and conflicts of that chaotic time; but he was consigned to a period of inaction on the Opposition benches, and nobody knew how long the period would last.

Discouraged and depressed he crossed with Emily to Ireland. It was always a comfort to be in the peaceful surroundings of Mount Stewart. Its calm atmosphere soothed him, driving away the shadows that haunted him. He found the gardens in full beauty, and spent his time planting, grafting, pruning.

Emily at this time was waxing in size alarmingly. The comments on her growing bulk were hardly kind, but she was blissfully unaware of them. Lady Bessborough described one of the dancers at the Opera as being " like Lady Castlereagh in person, the fattest of the fattest, biggest animal ever yet noticed by naturalists."

Her looking glass must have ruthlessly betrayed those sagging contours, those unmistakable chins, those spreading hips, for she was nearly as broad now as she was long. But corsetted in whalebone and covered with finery she still believed in her beauty, and had the gratification of being collected in a series of miniatures of the handsomest women in the fashionable world. Judging by a portrait of her, which displays her ponderous flesh in florid tints, she had very little claim to be included in the collection. Castlereagh, however, was still attentive to her, and his affections never seemed to stray in any other direction.

He was happy in the bosom of his family, where he met with nothing but affection. He rode round the estate talking to the cottagers, or sailed on the lake. But his mind was obsessed with the menace Napoleon had become, and though he loved the quiet atmosphere of his home, and the green fields of Down, he was soon back in England, harrying the Government again from the Opposition benches.

Fox, who was now in very bad health, hardly came down to the House at all. His life indeed was ebbing fast, and in September of this year, only a few months after Pitt's death, he passed away.

" Little did I think," said George III, " that I should ever live to regret Mr. Fox's death."

The old, blind king, so honest, so ascetic, so wise between his intervals of madness, had never had any love for this Ministry, and when it brought forward a bill to open the higher offices in the Army and Navy to Roman Catholics, he gladly dismissed it.

7

Castlereagh was back again in office. In the new Tory Government that was formed in March 1807 by the aged Duke of Portland, he came back to his old place as Secretary of State for War and the Colonies. After a year of frustration, he was free to exercise again all his powers. The other members of the Ministry were Canning, Perceval, Wellesley (afterwards Duke of Wellington), Palmerston, and Hawkesbury (afterwards Lord Liverpool), all of whom became Prime Ministers. Castlereagh never became Prime Minister, but he was to become more powerful than any of his colleagues.

Since the Duke of Portland was too old and inept to be of any service, the burden of carrying on the war fell on Castlereagh, the War Minister, and on Canning, the Foreign Minister.

Canning was not an easy man to work with. His brilliance and his biting wit were a little disconcerting, his arrogance and his self-assurance irritating; but he was bold in conception and swift in action, and he held the same view as Castlereagh regarding the war, that victory was the only solution for the country, that France must be beaten, absolutely and irrevocably beaten, before there could be any peace or happiness again in the world.

With the combination of Castlereagh and Canning a new vigour entered into politics, a policy of action which took the place of the old slow moving machinery. The new combination, aggressive and adventurous, took Napoleon by surprise.

The first situation the Ministry had to deal with was created by Russia. Like a thunderbolt came the news that our Russian ally had made a secret treaty with the enemy. On 14 June 1807, France had defeated Russia at Friedland, and the two Emperors, Napoleon and Alexander, meeting a few days later on a raft in the middle of the Niemen, had signed the Treaty of Tilsit, dividing the world between them. One of the terms of the Treaty, according to Canning's secret information, was the disposal of the Danish fleet, which Napoleon was to take over. Canning wasted no time. Castlereagh had already assembled as many troops as he could collect, and in August 1807, with the utmost speed and secrecy the Navy was sent out to Copenhagen. At the same time Francis Jackson, a diplomatic agent, was roused from his bed and dispatched to the unsuspecting Crown Prince of Denmark to demand the surrender of the Danish fleet for the duration of the war.

King George was among the critics who deplored the arbitrary action of his new Government. When Francis Jackson reported to him on his interview with the Danish Prince, the old King asked him where he had found the Prince. " He was on the ground floor, please your Majesty," was the reply. " I am glad of it for your sake," said the King; " for if he had half my spirit, he would have kicked you downstairs."

The Crown Prince had in fact informed Mr. Jackson that he had no intention of surrendering his fleet, and that if Great Britain decided to bombard the unprotected city of Copenhagen he would meet the British General in Copenhagen, at the head of his army.

Copenhagen was bombarded. It was a ruthless move and only the law of self-preservation could justify such treatment of a friendly neutral. But we had held Napoleon at bay only through our mastery of the seas, and if Napoleon put himself in possession of the very efficient Danish fleet, having already obtained the assistance of the Russian fleet, Britain's naval supremacy would be gone. It was perhaps the most perilous moment of the entire war.

Sir Arthur Wellesley, who was now Ireland's Chief Secretary, had been dispatching urgent messages from Dublin pressing Castlereagh to release him for military duty. Castlereagh, whose eye had long rested on Wellesley, granted his request, with the result that Sir Arthur found himself in command of the Reserve bombarding Copenhagen. He bombarded the city till it surrendered. Copenhagen had fallen to Nelson in 1801: it fell to Wellington—or Wellesley as he was then called—in 1807.

The energy and action which entered the Government with the combination of Castlereagh and Canning infuriated Napoleon. He was enraged by the capture of the Danish fleet to such a degree that never since the murder of the Russian Czar had Fouché, the Prefect of Police, seen him give vent to such a violent outburst of temper. What amazed and angered him most was the promptitude and resolution shown by the English Ministry. It had frustrated all his designs. He suspected treachery in his Cabinet; but the source from which Canning had derived his information had been so secretly kept that even Fouché was unable to discover the betrayer.

8

Having captured the Danish fleet and roused the enmity of Denmark we now seemed to be inviting the enmity of America. American seamen had long been irritated by the arbitrary behaviour of British naval officers, and the Royal Navy had long been incensed by the open encouragement given to British deserters in American ports.

In June 1807 an incident occurred at sea, off the entrance to Chesapeake Bay, which excited the whole American nation and nearly led to war. Three deserters from the British Navy were alleged to be on board the American frigate *Chesapeake*, and though a protest was made by the British Ministry at Washington, the men had not been surrendered, the United States claiming that the three deserters were of American nationality.

Admiral Barclay, without waiting for authority from England, instructed all ships under his command, in case of meeting the American frigate *Chesapeake* at sea, to proceed and search her for the three men. On 22 June the *Leopard* hailed the *Chesapeake* and requested her to adjust the matter of the deserters. The Captain of the *Chesapeake* replied that he knew of no such men, and would not allow any search for them to be made. Before he was able to prepare his ship for action, the *Leopard* opened fire, and the *Chesapeake*, unable to defend herself, was forced to strike her flag. The officers of the *Leopard* then boarded her, took the three men, and another deserter who was definitely of British origin, and returned to their vessel, leaving the *Chesapeake*, disabled and dishonoured, to drag herself back to port.

The humiliation suffered by the American Navy over this matter was never forgiven. Jefferson, the United States President, sent an envoy to England demanding reparation, and also the abandonment of impressment and the right of search. He further required that all armed vessels of Great Britain should depart from American waters. Canning made no serious objection to the demands as far as the *Chesapeake* was concerned, but he declined to discuss the matter of Britain's right to search merchant vessels, which was the chief of America's grievances.

"America will engage in war," wrote the young British minister,

Erskine, from Washington on 21 July 1807, " rather than submit to their armed ships being forcibly searched on the high seas."

Canning still refused to enter into any discussion of the matter, but he sent George Henry Rose as his special envoy to America to adjust the affair of the *Chesapeake*. He carried orders, however, asserts Henry Adams,[1] the American historian, which made an adjustment impossible. Britain was ready to disavow the attack on the *Chesapeake*, but that was the limit of her concession. The Americans felt that this mission of peace and friendship was intended only to repeat the assertion of supremacy which had led to the original offence, and the *Chesapeake* affair was left unsettled.

Matters were now aggravated further by Canning's proclamation in November 1807 of the Orders in Council, which prohibited goods from any country passing to the Continent unless they had previously touched at a British harbour. The Orders were a measure of retaliation against France, but they ruined American commerce. The Americans believed that they aimed at checking the commerce of America, in order to stimulate the commerce of England, and a tension was created which lasted for five years and ended in war.

On 22 December 1807, the President recommended an embargo on all foreign vessels in the United States' ports. In the same month Napoleon was issuing the Milan decrees, declaring every vessel of whatever nation coming from Britain or bound for Britain or any British colony, liable to seizure.

The coast of Europe was lined with Napoleon's troops to enforce the Decrees, the seas were covered with British ships to enforce the Orders.

The situation was growing more and more complicated. With troubles accumulating on all sides the Czar began moving troops into Finland, which was under Swedish rule; and Sweden's king, Gustavus, appealed to Britain for help. Sir John Moore, one of the first officers in the Army, was immediately dispatched with 12,000 troops to co-operate with the Swedes. They were sent out with the same speed and secrecy as had marked the Copenhagen expedition, but unfortunately no preliminary arrangements had been made. On his arrival Moore found that Finland was already lost, that the state of the country was desperate, and that the mad King Gustavus had issued orders

[1] *History of the United States*, by Henry Adams.

forbidding Moore's troops to land. He had an interview with the king, who said: "Before I allow foreign auxiliary troops to land in my country I wish to be clear whether they are under my command or not." Moore was quite decided not to put his troops under a mad king—there seemed to be a veritable crop of mad monarchs at this epoch—and he wrote home for orders, suggesting that the troops be brought back to England at once. Receiving a vague reply and no definite directions, he discussed operations with King Gustavus, who put him under arrest. Fortunately he escaped from prison, and receiving no further orders he brought his troops straight back to England upon his own responsibility. Canning was furious with Moore for this action, but Castlereagh with his deep sense of justice supported him. Over this matter the seeds of dissension between Castlereagh and Canning were sown, and this disagreement developed into an antagonism which was to have grave consequences later.

CHAPTER VIII

I

AFTER THE unfortunate Swedish incident the Government turned its attention to Portugal, for Napoleon had sent one of his most able generals, Junot, to occupy Lisbon. With the French troops in the suburbs of the capital, the Prince Regent, who was governing the country on behalf of the mad Queen Maria, was only too happy to accept Britain's offer of protection. The British Navy shipped the Royal Family off to Brazil, and took over the Portuguese fleet.

Trouble now arose in Spain, where Napoleon had been stirring up Prince Ferdinand against his parents, offering to support him if he seized the throne, after which he had invited the King of Spain and his son to Bayonne to arbitrate between them. When they arrived, he betrayed them both, forced the king to abdicate, and nominated his own brother Joseph King of Spain.

It did not matter to the Spaniards that their King, Charles IV, was a half-wit, and that their Queen was living in adultery with her Minister: Godoy, every Spanish peasant felt his honour assailed by Napoleon's betrayal, the desire for independence flamed through the country, and Spain rose in revolt. It was the first sign of a people rising against the might of Napoleon. A nation ignorant and ill-armed, cried Lord Russell, was ready to fight in the field of battle, in the town, in the village, in the farmyard, and in the peasant's cottage for the sacred cause of national independence.

Castlereagh was quick to perceive the nature of the crisis, and at once supported the revolt. In a letter to Charles written on the 10 August 1808, from St. James's Square, he wrote: " I send you a Secret Note, which I propose to circulate to the Cabinet to-morrow—

of course the decision remains to be taken but it will give you the train of my own reflections upon our future movements—how glorious to England it would be, after recovering Portugal by her Command of the Sea, to meet the Enemy at the Foot of the Pyrenees, and to forbid his Return to France."

Many members of the Government feared the financial exhaustion which a war in Spain would entail, they also feared the inability of a British Commander to maintain himself in the Peninsular; but Castlereagh and Canning felt that it was the first and might be our last opportunity of turning the tide of Napoleon's success, that if we neglected it, if we wasted an hour, or gave way to doubts, or hesitations or delays, we deserved to perish.

The House of Commons decided that any nation that started up to oppose the common enemy became instantly an ally, and immediate help was sent to the Spaniards. Our troops were ready, for Castlereagh, during his time at the War Office, had re-organised the army so completely that England was able to provide at this critical moment all the men necessary for the Peninsular Campaign.

Castlereagh had at this time been working on the idea of assisting the inhabitants of the South American Colonies of Spain in their revolt against the mother country, and 9000 troops lay at Cork ready to embark for South America. Sir Arthur Wellesley, who had been sent to take command of these troops, was now ordered to sail instead for the Peninsular, a step which was to have such far-reaching consequences.

The plan for assisting the American Colonies in their bid for independence was temporarily abandoned, but it had been fully matured by Castlereagh, and when the scheme was eventually in 1823 put into effect by Canning, with the proud boast that he had " called a new world into existence to redress the balance of the old," he was merely executing a plan which Castlereagh had long projected, putting on it the seal of a brilliant phrase.

The opening of the Spanish campaign was marked by the usual blunders. Its only happy touch indeed was the choice of Sir Arthur Wellesley as Commander of the Forces, and this was not effected without difficulty. " Sir Arthur Wellesley," Barrington wrote, " never would have had the chief command in Spain, but for the ministerial manœuvring and aid of Lord Castlereagh; and Lord Castlereagh never could have stood his ground as a Minister, but for Lord Wellington's successes."

Wellesley's ability Castlereagh had long measured, but his appointment had to be made over the heads of much older officers, and it roused the greatest opposition. Wellesley was so young a Lieutenant-General, that the King and the Duke of York both raised objections to him, and for the time being something more ancient and venerable had to be found.

The troops under Sir John Moore had now been added to the Peninsular expedition, and Moore had a right to the command. He was a man of riper age, his abilities were respected, but unfortunately he had incurred the displeasure of Canning, and instead of sending him out to command the Peninsular Campaign, Canning resolved to irritate him into resigning.

Moore was not to be coerced in this way, and he ignored Canning's intrigues. He was not happy however about the arrangements that had been made, and after he had had his final interview with Castlereagh, and had already taken his leave, he opened the door again, and said: "Remember, my lord, I protest against the expedition and foretell its failure."[1]

When Castlereagh mentioned this to the Cabinet, Canning exclaimed, "Good God! And do you really mean to say that you allowed a man entertaining such feelings with regard to the expedition to go and assume the command of it?" An official letter was then sent after Moore equivalent to one demanding his resignation, but Moore merely sent a dignified reply, and sailed with the expedition.

A further insult was put on him by appointing over his head Sir Hew Dalrymple and Sir Harry Burrard, two aged generals who were quite unfit for their job. The Cabinet, who had only just been rendered aware of their existence, decreed that they should take command in the Peninsular. So that Sir Arthur Wellesley, arriving off Portugal with his army, received the disconcerting news that Sir John Moore, Sir Harry Burrard, and Sir Hew Dalrymple, were each on his way to the Peninsular to take the command out of his hands.

Castlereagh tried to lessen the blow by informing Wellesley that he had made every effort to keep in his hands the greatest number of

[1] This is Stapleton's version. Sir Frederick Maurice in his Diary of Moore asserts that Moore's words referred to an expedition sent out in July, two months earlier.

men, and for the longest time that circumstances would permit. Wellesley had already had to cope with a " second in command " as well, but with the latter he had come to an immediate understanding. He informed him that he did not know what a " second in command " meant, that he alone commanded the army, and that he would not only take, but insist upon the whole and undivided responsibility of all that should happen while the army was under his command. But the days of his command were numbered.

He had just landed his men, and launched an attack against the French, taking up his position on the hills above Vimiero, to cover the landing of two brigades that were just arriving and anchoring off the coast, when he found that the two brigades were accompanied by Sir Harry Burrard. Wellesley was inclined to advance, but Sir Harry Burrard preferred to wait, and Wellesley had to cancel his orders for a fresh offensive.

Sir Harry decided to spend the night on board. During the night the French moved. While his commander slept, Wellesley had the good fortune to defeat Junot and his whole force. When Sir Harry Burrard landed in the morning, he found to his surprise that there was an action in progress at Vimiero. Satisfied with Wellesley's dispositions he directed him to go on with an operation he had so well begun. A new shell invented by a Major Shrapnel was tried out during this action, and was completely successful.

As the French ranks broke under the British fire, Wellesley turned to the Cavalry, and said, with a lift of his cocked hat: " Now, Twentieth, now is the time," and his dragoons charged. To Burrard he said, as the shattered French drew off: " The enemy are completely beaten, and we shall be in Lisbon in three days." But Burrard decided now to assert his authority. His unfortunate experience having been limited to a few unsuccessful expeditions, he decided to call off the pursuit and wait. " A very good sort of man," Mrs. Jackson relates, " and if he was unfit to command an army, they who gave him the command ought to have known that, for I am sure everyone else knew it."

By the following morning, however, Burrard had lost his command, for Sir Hew Dalrymple now arrived, and Burrard was superseded in his turn by a general whose sole experience of active service had been in the unsuccessful campaign in Flanders with the Duke of York fourteen years before. Sir Hew likewise preferred to wait, and Wellesley was unable to press on to Lisbon. But the French had surrendered, and in September 1808 a truce was signed at Vimiero.

Wellesley disliked the terms of the armistice, and wrote to Castlereagh the following day: " I beg that you will not believe that I negotiated it, that I approve of it, or that I had any hand in wording it. It was negotiated by the General himself in my presence and in the presence of Sir Harry Burrard: and after it had been drawn out by Kellermann himself, Sir Hew Dalrymple desired me to sign it."

2

Wellesley's relations with his new Commander were far from easy. Castlereagh had expressly desired Sir Hew Dalrymple to make of Sir Arthur " the most prominent use permitted by the rules of the service." But Dalrymple had other views. The rules of the Service, he said, and his own feelings of what was due to himself and to the distinguished officers senior to Sir Arthur Wellesley, would not allow of his making any extensive use of the talents of that General. Sir Arthur, deeply mortified, wrote home to Castlereagh informing him that he would prefer to be recalled, and above all he begged that he would not be blamed if things did not go as Castlereagh and his friends in London would have wished.

The result of the armistice was most unfortunate. Wellesley had completely defeated Junot, and had been upon the point of pursuing the French army, with every prospect of forcing it to surrender, when a new General had taken the command out of his hands and stopped him. Within twenty-four hours a second new General had taken the command out of the hands of the other, and had confounded things completely. The result was that Junot and his army, instead of being shipped off to England as prisoners, were comfortably embarked for France under the Convention of Cintra. When the British nation and the Cabinet heard the terms of the Convention they were aghast. After fifteen years of defeat, when a victory had at last been snatched from the French, it had been thrown away by the British Generals. Castlereagh, for once in his life, became almost hysterical. The three Commanders were recalled, and a Court of Inquiry held. It pronounced that none of the three Generals was to blame, and that when the chief command of an army changes hands three times in forty-eight hours, things can not be expected to go well.

The Convention of Cintra widened the growing breach between Castlereagh and Canning, for Canning desired to sacrifice all the Generals. He drew no distinction between Wellesley and Dalrymple or Burrard, and was for throwing them all overboard to save the face of the Ministry. Castlereagh, on the other hand, insisted that the Cabinet must bear its share of responsibility.

It is difficult to decide on whom to place the blame for the general muddle, but as Castlereagh had done his utmost to secure the command for Wellesley, whose competence he had always admired, and as he was also in sympathy with Sir John Moore, and stood by him to the end, it may have been partly due to Canning's personal dislike of Moore and growing antagonism to Castlereagh, and partly due to the views of the King regarding seniority, that the two other Generals were sent out, with its unfortunate consequences.

3

Moore was still kicking his heels near Lisbon, awaiting orders from Dalrymple or Burrard or whomsoever the Ministry thought fit to put over him, when he received news that he was now in command of the Peninsular army. After all the bitter insults he had received, he was to command the largest British army that had been employed since the beginning of the war. The army had increased considerably in size, owing to a measure Castlereagh had brought in for augmenting the regular army and raising forty-four thousand new militiamen. The measure was unpopular, as many of Castlereagh's measures were; but when the necessity came for sending an army to the Continent, for the first time during these hapless years such an army was forthcoming.

Moore now received orders from the Cabinet to leave Portugal, to march into the heart of Spain, and co-operate with the Spanish Commander-in-Chief. He was reluctant to proceed, having no faith in the organisation of the Spanish army, having no funds, having no confidence in the optimism of Ministers at Whitehall who " fancied themselves military men" without knowing how far their projects were "susceptible of being carried into practice." He knew it would be impossible to march a large army through the Spanish passes, across mountains rising in places to 4000 feet, to march them for 300 miles without enough carts, without enough animals to carry their equipment, without any information as to whether the roads were fit for heavy artillery, and to arrive in time to succour the Spanish armies. But he was a soldier. He had been ordered to march into Spain to join the Spanish Commander-in-Chief, and he obeyed orders. He soon found that there was no Spanish Commander-in-Chief to join, and long before he could reach them the Spanish armies had been scattered by the French. Deceived by false information from Frère, the British Envoy, a man of more optimism than wisdom, Moore found himself isolated in Northern Spain.

In this position he received a letter from Castlereagh predicting an early advance by the Spanish armies; nobody seemed to be aware that there was *no* Spanish army, that the last remnants had already ceased to exist. To add to Moore's difficulties winter suddenly descended. The snow from the mountains began to fall, and the winds were so fierce and bitter that the men could hardly stand. Moore was completely in the dark as to what the French and the Spaniards were doing, for no one troubled to send him information. In this dilemma a sheaf of captured documents, taken off a French officer carrying dispatches, fell into his hands, and he learnt that Napoleon had taken Madrid, and was himself advancing on him with 300,000 troops. Soult with one army was already in front of him, Napoleon was now in his rear. Hopelessly outnumbered there was nothing for him to do but retreat to Corunna. He was in command of his country's only army, and it was his duty to preserve it, and not commit it to suicidal ventures.

Castlereagh's brother, Charles, accompanied Moore on this unfortunate campaign, and Castlereagh had a private as well as a public anxiety when he heard that the army was retreating. Charles was later to be rewarded for his "zeal, activity and gallantry" by being given the government of Charles Fort in Jamaica, a military sinecure. But at the moment he was suffering untold hardships.

The winter was severe, the roads almost impassable, the men were knee-deep in snow, soaked to the skin, cold and famished. They trudged by day through rivers of slush that froze at night, the rearguard fighting the pursuing French continuously all the way. The army, composed largely of raw, uncouth men, of criminals and wastrels, became completely demoralised, and took their revenge on whatever came their way. Their conduct was infamous, but they marched with untended wounds across mountain and ravine; their horses died in the snow, or slid over frozen precipices and were abandoned. And yet so skilfully was the retreat managed that no opportunity was given to the French of forcing an action till they arrived at last at Corunna. Napoleon, certain of the destruction of the British army, had already turned back and left the pursuit to Soult.

On 16 January 1809, when the troops arrived at Corunna, they found to their dismay that there were no transports to take them back to England. Having marched across three hundred miles of hell, they were now caught between the sea and the French. There was nothing for Moore to do but form his men into line under the walls of Corunna. From the stores in the city he took arms and ammunition, and distributed them among the troops. The French were already massing on the heights round the town when the British transports at length arrived. Straightway Moore embarked his sick and wounded and the whole of his cavalry. The French waited; for Soult had decided to destroy Moore's army as the men went down to their ships. The Reserve were marching wearily down to the quayside when the great battery of heavy guns on the rocks opened fire on them. They halted to a man, and when an aide-de-camp came spurring down to recall them, they turned and marched to the field. As Soult's troops surged forward, the British army met them, and enraged by the memory of all that they had suffered on the retreat, they fought like madmen, carrying all before them; soon they turned the enemy's advance into a complete rout. Moore saw that victory was his, but as he wheeled round, a cannon-ball struck him from his horse, carrying away his shoulder and part of his collar-bone. His men closed round him, and six Highlanders carried him on a bloodstained blanket through the streets of Corunna. "You know," he murmured, "I have always wished to die this way." It was growing dark, but the French attack was broken, and the men unmolested marched down to the quayside and embarked safely for England. Moore was left behind. He was buried on the ramparts of Corunna.

After his death Marshal Soult and Napoleon gave Moore unstinted praise, declaring that his firmness and his talents alone saved the British army from being destroyed in Spain; but the British army had been driven out of the Peninsular, and once again Canning was ready to throw all the blame on the dead Commander. Once again Castlereagh refused to agree with Canning, and took all the responsibility on himself.

4

A new scandal, however, was claiming the attention of the Government; for in this same month of January a certain Colonel Wardle rose in the House of Commons and charged the Duke of York with corrupt practices in the exercise of his duties as Commander-in-Chief of the army. He alleged that the Duke's mistress, Mrs. Ann Clarke, using her influence with the Duke, was selling commissions and promotions in the army.

Although the country was in so critical a condition nothing was discussed but the new scandal. An inquiry was instituted, chiefly at Castlereagh's instigation, and the war in the Peninsula was entirely forgotten while Mrs. Clarke, a vivacious, plump little Cockney, appeared in the House of Commons for interrogation. She was a woman who had never been overburdened with moral scruples. The Duke, it was reported, had accosted her at Blackheath, and had soon afterwards established her in guilty splendour at No. 18 Gloucester Place.

She had received from him many costly presents of diamonds that were never paid for, but no very generous allowance, and so found it necessary to obtain funds from less uncertain sources. At her residence in Gloucester Place a traffic started in commissions. Trade prospered, and she was able to live in even guiltier splendour. But unfortunately for Mrs. Clarke, the Duke suddenly broke with her, leaving her with a small pension, which he never paid. She threatened to publish her " Recollections," complete with love-letters written to her by the gallant Duke. To avert this, the Duke propitiated her with promises, which he never redeemed. Eventually Colonel Wardle, her latest protector, electrified the House of Commons by exposing the Royal scandal. At the Committee of Inquiry, Mrs. Clarke accused the Duke of participating with her in the proceeds of the outrageous sale of military appointments.

All the details of the "Duke and Darling" case, with quotations from the Royal endearments, became public property, and were bandied round the Clubs. Mrs. Clarke had even sold a commission to the footman who waited on her and the Duke at table.

The evidence was damning, but the Duke was a popular figure. In spite of his escapades and his incapacity, his good nature and courage endeared him to the army. As a Commander he had not shown any great efficiency, having come to grief in Flanders and at the Helder, yet he had improved conditions in the Army, and as a military organiser had shown a good deal of competence. Added to all this he was the King's son, and the members of the House of Commons felt it incumbent upon them to whitewash his character. But so much publicity had been given to the matter, that though he was acquitted, it was considered advisable that he should resign the office of Commander-in-Chief.

The "Duke and Darling" case exercised the minds of the Government, and provided scandal and gossip for the whole country, for several weeks.

5

Meanwhile Napoleon was overrunning the whole of Spain; he had even crowned his brother Joseph king in Madrid. In spite of these events Castlereagh was still pressing for the continuance of the Peninsular Campaign, and for the reinforcement of the army in Portugal.

Many years later, when the Peninsular War had come to its glorious end, Canning, with characteristic egoism, claimed that it was his opinion alone which was the cause of the continuance of the Peninsular War. There is no evidence of this; there does exist on the other hand a memorandum written by Castlereagh, in March 1809, based on a report of Wellesley's, in which he states: "I have always been of opinion that Portugal might be defended, whatever might be the result of the contest in Spain; and that, in the meantime, the measures adopted for the defence of Portugal would be highly useful to the Spaniards in their contest with the French."

He continued also to press for the appointment of Wellesley to the Peninsular Command. There was a good deal of opposition, but at length he prevailed, and the Cabinet submitted Wellesley's name to His Majesty. Knowing the King's prejudices in favour of seniority, Castlereagh, who was proposing the appointment of Wellesley over the heads of at least four senior officers, worded his letter to the King with extreme caution. His Majesty's confidential servants " begged leave humbly to propose to His Majesty that the chief command in Portugal should be entrusted to Sir Arthur Wellesley. . . . They were not unmindful of the inconvenience that might arise, in case of any considerable increase of forces, from Sir Arthur Wellesley's being so young a Lieutenant-General; but as any considerable increase of the army in Portugal could not then be looked to as probable, they humbly conceived that Sir Arthur might be employed where he had had the good fortune of being successful, and that it would remain open for His Majesty to make a different arrangement if it should appear proper to him to confide the command to a general officer of higher rank."

Wellesley, in a report to Castlereagh, had stated that in his opinion 20,000 or at the most 30,000 British troops could hold Lisbon against the French, more being impracticable on account of the difficulty of supplies. This modest demand on man-power commended itself to the King, and he gave his consent to the appointment.

Canning, not content with claiming the credit for the continuance of the Peninsular Campaign, claimed also in later years that it was he who had been responsible for Wellesley's appointment as Commander-in-Chief. When his Private Secretary, Mr. Stapleton, was writing his biography in 1824, Canning informed him as proof of this that he had written to his friend Charles Ellis, at the end of 1808, expressing his earnest wish that Wellesley should have the command in Spain. He had apparently forgotten that at the end of 1808, during the Inquiry into the Convention of Cintra, he was for throwing over all the Generals concerned, Wellesley included.

Mr. Stapleton made every effort to find the letter, but apparently it did not exist. He even wrote to Sir Charles Bagot, who had been

Canning's Under-Secretary, reminding him of the letter mentioned, which would serve to prove the exertions which Canning had made to secure the appointment of Sir Arthur Wellesley to the Command in Portugal. " The mere fact that such a letter exists is all that I want," he wrote, " because it will enable me to assert that of which I have at present only word of mouth testimony with more confidence than I have at present." No letter was ever produced.

But during the period when Canning was so enraged against Dalrymple, Burrard, and Wellesley, that he was for repudiating the Convention of Cintra altogether, and throwing over all the generals who had endorsed it, Castlereagh was writing to Wellesley in a letter dated 26 September 1808: " My first object is your reputation; my second is, that the country should not be deprived of your services at the present critical conjuncture. *I should wish to see you placed in a much more responsible situation*; but your reputation can never be lowered by whatever station the course of service assigns to you . . .

" I need not say how much my public and private feelings have suffered on the subject of the Convention. I hope the anxious solicitude which I feel for your fame and interest is not incompatible with what in justice I owe others." [1]

Even though Wellesley had signed the Convention, and had indeed " advised the principle of the arrangement," as he afterwards admitted, Castlereagh remained his staunch supporter, and never ceased to press Wellesley's appointment for the Chief Command.

But now, when Castlereagh had succeeded in persuading the Cabinet to resume the campaign in Portugal with Wellesley in command, Canning began that strange intrigue which was to have such unfortunate results.

6

On the 24 March 1809, the very day when Castlereagh induced the Cabinet to submit Wellesley's name to the King, Canning wrote to the Duke of Portland, asserting that the Government as then constituted was unequal to the great task imposed upon it, and that unless the fault was amended he would resign. He complained of Castle-

[1] *Castlereagh Correspondence.*

reagh's disposition to compromise, of his reluctance to throw over officers, thereby lowering the reputation of the Government in order to save individuals. He complained further of Castlereagh's delay in strengthening Portugal.

In all this there seems no very serious complaint except in the charge of delay in strengthening Portugal, and for this charge there does not seem to have been much justification. Four weeks before Canning's letter was written, Castlereagh had diverted the armament intended for Spain to Portugal, writing to Sir John Cradock at the same time that " it is the King's determination to use every exertion to strengthen the defences of Portugal." A fortnight later troops were assembled at Plymouth and ordered to the Tagus. There does not appear to have been any neglect or want of exertion on Castlereagh's part where Portugal was concerned.

All Canning's complaints were mere pretexts. The actual reason for his antagonism to Castlereagh, and his determination to have him removed from office, was more possibly his fear that Castlereagh would be a dangerous rival for the Premiership, when it fell vacant. The aged Duke of Portland was getting too feeble to continue in office much longer, and Canning had a great desire for the Prime Minister's place. Vain and vitriolic, he had long nursed a grudge against the quiet, resolute man, who stood like a wall of granite in his way. He noticed with dissatisfaction that Castlereagh was more respected than he, that in spite of his own shining talents, he could never overshadow him. Canning's origins were humble; Castlereagh had influential connections everywhere. In the Cabinet he had the support of his uncle, Earl Camden, in the Peninsular, of his brother, Charles Stewart; and now his friend, Sir Arthur Wellesley, was taking command of the Portugal expedition. Castlereagh, Canning felt, was already running the Peninsular Campaign as though it were a personal matter.

He was proposing further to organise an expedition to Antwerp, with the object of seizing the French fleet in the Scheldt. Canning was not opposed to a diversion on the Continent; he had indeed suggested that there should be one in the north of Germany; but what he objected to was Castlereagh directing both campaigns.

In Canning there was a restless craving to be always in front, always at the helm; he could not endure that anyone should outshine him. Swayed by envy and jealousy, he had always intrigued to get rid of those who stood in his way. Perceval, the Chancellor of the Exchequer and Leader of the House of Commons, his only other rival for the Premiership, he felt he could easily efface, but Castlereagh he could not. Canning had wit and eloquence; Castlereagh had only the dull qualities of industry, conscientiousness, perseverance. But he had the confidence of his colleagues, where Canning, with his quips and jibes, his lashing tongue and whispering intrigues, had only their mistrust. Although he had no pretty gifts, Castlereagh was a man of character.

Canning's letter of complaint to the Duke of Portland was shown to the King. Although the King had no great affection for Canning, he and Portland felt he was needed at the Foreign Office, and that it would weaken the Government if he were allowed to resign as he threatened to do. In order to retain him the King suggested that Castlereagh should change office with some other member of the administration. Portland agreed, but recommended that the change should be postponed until after the prorogation of Parliament, when Lord Wellesley, Sir Arthur's brother, should take over the War Office. Meanwhile not a word was to be said to Castlereagh. Canning seemed content with this arrangement, but within a month he was again agitating for Castlereagh's dismissal.

With intrigue going on behind his back all the time, Castlereagh was to continue for six months directing a war against a military tyrant who had already enslaved nearly the whole of Europe, and who was an ever-growing menace to the power of Great Britain. It is hardly surprising that things went amiss.

Supremely unconscious of the mischief Canning was brewing, oblivious of the fact that Lord Wellesley was to supplant him, Castlereagh was writing to his brother Charles, who was now Adjutant-General to Sir Arthur: " You will be glad to hear that Lord Wellesley goes immediately to Spain as Ambassador, so if you don't kick up a dust in the Peninsula during the summer, it's not our fault."

Satisfied that the Peninsular War was going favourably, Castlereagh now fixed his gaze on Antwerp. For some time the Admiralty had been issuing warnings that a great arsenal was being built at Antwerp, that the enemy were assembling a considerable fleet in the Scheldt, and that elaborate preparations were being made for an invasion of England or Ireland. Castlereagh felt that the time had come to deal a final blow at the naval power of France, and end the possibility of invasion once and for all. Napoleon would not be beaten, he was convinced, until we had complete control of the seas. He urged the Cabinet therefore to send an expedition to the Scheldt to destroy or capture the French fleet, and to destroy the arsenal at Antwerp, using the island of Walcheren as a base. Such an expedition, he declared, apart from breaking Napoleon's naval power would greatly aid the military position by dividing Napoleon's forces.

An expedition to the island of Walcheren had years before suggested itself to Pitt; and in 1805 and 1807 Castlereagh had investigated the matter. But the idea had been abandoned in favour of the expedition to North Germany which had proved unsuccessful.

Castlereagh was not unaware of the dangers that would attend an expedition to Walcheren, not the least of which was "the unwholesome state of the island," but he felt that the object to be attained was "of a magnitude to justify every reasonable risk."

The Cabinet however was not convinced. Canning still preferred diversions in North Germany; there were a few stormy debates, but Castlereagh continued to press his plan. At this moment Antwerp was wholly unprepared, and a blow against the enemy there would have been of the utmost advantage; for Antwerp was, as Napoleon had called it, "a pistol pointed at the heart of England." But speed was necessary, the whole thing depending on the suddenness of the raid. The Government however could not come to any decision, and continually postponed the matter.

Castlereagh went on with his investigations, but weeks dragged by, and the Cabinet was still undecided. The longer the expedition was postponed the more risk there was of the enemy learning the Government's plans, the more risk there was of the summer heat defeating the Government's schemes. But the Cabinet would not move. With all his power Castlereagh could do nothing but wait.

Pressed and harassed on every side by the arduous work of military organisation, by doubts of the Cabinet's intentions, by all the confusions that surround the preparations for a great expedition, and by fears that the Cabinet's sanction, when it did come, might come too late, Castlereagh went quietly on with his scheme, working out with sharp exactitude all the details of the plan.

The difficulties in the way of its preparation were enormous, for there was no superfluity of men, money, or munitions. But Castlereagh had long occupied himself with military schemes. For nearly two years he had been building up an army; and men, money and munitions, he found. Only the Cabinet's decision was wanting, and it seemed that that would never be obtained.

On 21 May 1809 there came sudden and startling news from the Continent. The Austrian people, inspired by the rising of the Spaniards, had rebelled against Napoleon, and had actually defeated the conqueror at Aspern. With his ammunition destroyed, and his one bridge broken behind him, Napoleon was now in the deadliest peril.

The hour for Castlereagh's expedition had come. He pressed for action, and the Cabinet, realising at last the far-reaching possibilities of a sudden *coup-de-main* at this moment, agreed at last that the expedition should go. But there were now discussions as to the practicability of a landing at Sandvliet, as to the number of troops stationed at Antwerp, as to the difficulties of carrying an army up the Scheldt. The King himself had always been doubtful of the success of the expedition, and though he endorsed the decision of his Cabinet, he informed his Ministers that he could have wished that " the information on which the practicability had been finally decided had not been so imperfect." But the King, Castlereagh felt, had always had a profound distrust of expensive expeditions, and had grown too accustomed to the bungling of continental campaigns. Castlereagh, however, was sure of his plan. For years he had been making the most extensive investigations. There was only one point on which there was not sufficient information and that was regarding the number of troops in Antwerp. But he had every reason to believe that the troops were few, and that the risk he was taking was not too great.

Events proved that his calculations were accurate, and there is no doubt that if, as Napoleon afterwards wrote, " the scheme had been executed with the same ability with which it had been conceived, important results would have attended it."

But now, when sanction had been finally obtained and it was realised that the whole outcome of the expedition depended on the suddenness of the raid, the command was given to Lord Chatham, whose habits were so leisurely, and whose manner was so grand that he could never be hurried.

When Castlereagh had first planned the expedition he had had Wellesley in mind for the command, later he had had thoughts of Sir John Moore; but Wellesley was now marching into Spain, and Sir John Moore had fallen at Corunna. The King favoured Lord Chatham, and Lord Chatham took the command. It has often been alleged that Chatham was forced on Castlereagh by the Canning faction, but if this is so, he seems to have shown no hesitation in accepting him. There was no one of the calibre of Wellesley or Moore to be found, and the weight of Chatham's name may have influenced Castlereagh.

The choice however was a grave fault; for Chatham was a politician rather than a soldier, and even as a politician he seems to have deserved his nickname of the " late Lord Chatham." He had always been late for Cabinet meetings: he was late for the Scheldt expedition. He had barely seen service more than once in his life. Ten years before, in 1799, he had commanded a brigade during the landing in Holland—a landing which had proved disastrous. Apart from that operation, for more than twenty-five years he had discharged no military duties whatever. His appointment was a strange and unfortunate one. In the high offices he had filled he had been remarkable for nothing but procrastination and inactivity. But he was the son of the great Chatham, he was the elder brother of Pitt, he was a friend of the King's, he was a friend of Canning's; he was in fact Canning's suggestion for the Premiership, should it not fall into his own hands. Being of the Canning faction he had no great friendship for Castlereagh, and for whatever reason disobeyed all his instructions.

Cold, aloof, and haughty, with his tight mouth, and forbidding manner, he was a complete contrast to Sir Richard Strahan, the

Admiral chosen to command the fleet, and there was friction between them from the outset. Strahan was bluff and hasty, full of zeal and ardour, and he fumed continually at the delay imposed on him by the noble lord. Even though the Cabinet had at last decided that the Walcheren expedition should be sent, orders and counter-orders followed one another in leisurely procession. Castlereagh urged in vain the dangers of delay. Chatham agreed with him; but cavalry transports had to be awaited from Spain, troops from Ireland, from Jersey and Guernsey; it seemed that the expedition would never get off.

While the Cabinet and the " late Lord Chatham " wavered, Napoleon, working furiously to restore his lines, and to gather new forces round him, trapped the Austrians at Wagram. On 6 July 1809, returning in all his strength he went through them like a thunderbolt, pursuing them with terrible havoc. Austria suffered an overwhelming defeat, and despairing of England's promised expedition, signed an armistice with France. Napoleon had not only quelled Austria, but his victory deterred Prussia and North Germany from rising.

8

It was already the height of summer, and the Walcheren expedition had not yet set out. It was no summer resort it was bound for, but a pestilential area that in mid-summer and early autumn would have defeated any army without the help of the French. It was by no means a defeated Napoleon the Army had to deal with, but a Napoleon gloriously triumphant. Castlereagh had been agitating so long for the expedition to be sent out, and it was beginning to look as though the armament had only been sanctioned when it was too late to be of any use. There was but one hope: Antwerp was still unprepared. If only Chatham would go ahead and act with speed, it could still be done.

He had given him the most precise and detailed instructions; never had his intellect functioned with more precision; but Chatham had replied to his memorandum that he had been so occupied with putting all the arrangements in progress that he had only been able very cursorily to look over the draft. As far as he could form an opinion respecting the instructions he would say that they were either a great deal too much in detail, as pointing out what it was the duty of the Admiral and General to decide, or they should have been a great deal more precise, and with accurate information on all points alluded to.

It was an odd communication. Castlereagh was beginning to get as restive as Sir Richard Strahan. The Navy had been ready since 9 June: it was already the end of July.

But now at last embarkation began and, with bands playing, the men were rowed to the ships that were waiting off the coast of Kent. Having completed all the arrangements, Castlereagh hurried down to the coast to meet Chatham, and accelerate as far as possible the departure of the troops.

Engrossed with the preparations, he was still unaware of the Cabinet's intentions regarding him; he was unaware that 21 June, the very day the decision to send the expedition had been taken, was the day the sanction of the Cabinet had been obtained for his removal from office. On that day the Duke of Portland informed Perceval of the arrangement that had been made in accordance with Canning's wishes. Perceval was shocked to hear of the underhand intrigue which had been going on for over three months behind Castlereagh's back, and he wrote to Canning remonstrating angrily, and protesting against further concealment.

Canning answered curtly that the concealment was none of his making, throwing the blame on Portland. In a note to his Under-Secretary, enclosing the draft for a reply to Perceval's letter, there is a phrase which sounds a little sinister. "This is something like what I think would do—leaving them to flounder, and not helping at all."

Sir George Jackson, a diplomat who was attached to various missions, makes an interesting note in his diary on the subject. "From what was at first," he remarks, "mere pique at the interference of one department in the business of another, the clash of opinions between these two Ministers grew to a settled purpose, on one side at least, of condemning and thwarting whatever measures were approved by the other."

This is obviously directed at Canning, for Castlereagh, so far from thwarting Canning, was even unaware of his enmity, which pursued him at that time so treacherously.

After a little more correspondence between them, Perceval and

Canning both wrote to the Duke of Portland, and it was decided that as Castlereagh had for months been toiling at preparations for the expedition, and would be held responsible for its issue, his removal should be postponed till the expedition was over.

But Canning now had another suggestion to make. Having magnanimously agreed that Castlereagh should direct the Walcheren expedition and be removed after it had ended, he now proposed that the Peninsular Campaign be taken out of Castlereagh's hands, and placed under his own direction.

From Sir Arthur Wellesley, who had sailed in April 1809, good news had come. He had landed at Lisbon, and marching north, had caught the French in the rear. Soult and his troops had been cleared out of the city. They were driven out so fast that they left behind their guns, their bullion, their stores, even the dinner that had been prepared for Soult, and which Wellesley consumed with great relish in his stead. In a fortnight he had outmanœuvred Soult; in a month from the time he landed he had cleared Portugal. He was now moving slowly into Spain. " The ball is at my foot," he wrote, " and I hope I shall have strength enough to give it a good kick."

It seemed an auspicious moment for taking over the Peninsular Campaign, and Canning rarely missed an opportunity. But Mr. Perceval did not find himself in agreement with Mr. Canning on this matter, and replied that whoever directed military affairs in one quarter must direct them in all. After further discussion it was finally decided that matters should remain as they were, and that again nothing should be said to Castlereagh. Perceval was not very happy about the whole affair. " This cursed business haunts me," he said, but in deference to the Prime Minister's wishes he endured the deception.

Castlereagh, still ignorant of all that was going on in the Cabinet, saw his expedition leave. It was the greatest armament that had as yet ever left England's shores. From Dover Castle he wrote to the King: " The wind is so fair and the breeze now sufficiently strong to enable the whole force with the exception of the reserve to reach the rendezvous before night."

As he predicted, the advance guard of the Fleet was at the mouth of the Scheldt as evening fell. But there three islands blocked the way, Walcheren, North Beverland, and South Beverland. Castlereagh's instructions to Chatham had been, " at the same time that you occupy Walcheren and South Beverland, to advance at once a considerable corps against Antwerp, which may be reinforced as soon as Flushing is invested, if not actually reduced." These instructions were disregarded from the outset. Chatham occupied Walcheren, whose total force was three battalions, and for a fortnight he did nothing more.

Lord Huntley, waiting at the mouth of the Scheldt, applied to Chatham for orders, but nearly a week passed before any orders arrived, during which time Huntley and his division remained in their transports off the coast blocking the entrance to the river. Another General, Sir John Hope, landed his men in South Beverland, and encountering no resistance of any kind, overran the greater part of the island, and took the little port of Batz at the farthest point. Hope was now divided from the mainland on which Antwerp stood by the merest strip of water. The city had very few defenders at this time, and he could have taken Antwerp at one stroke; but the barges and gunboats on which he relied for the crossing were fifty miles away, on the wrong side of the river. So there he waited like Moses, viewing the Promised Land, but could not enter.

Had Chatham invested Flushing on arrival, and pushed on to Antwerp, as Castlereagh had directed, Antwerp would have been taken, and the French fleet immobilised without much difficulty. But Chatham and the division assigned to take Flushing had landed on the Isle of Walcheren, as far distant from their objective as possible. Finding no obstacles in his way, Chatham had taken up his Headquarters at Middelburg in the centre of the Island, and there he remained, cool and tranquil, doing nothing. Huntley, still blocking the river entrance, waited for orders. Hope, still watching Antwerp, waited for barges. But Chatham fought in the grand traditional manner; he did nothing in a hurry. He never appeared before midday; if anything urgent arose, you called between certain hours, sent up your name, and waited your turn.

In the end, Strahan became so exasperated that he sent ten frigates under the walls of Flushing to force an entrance to the West Scheldt, without Chatham's help. The operation was effective. Chatham followed in a day or two, and Flushing, bombarded by sea and land, surrendered. The Scheldt was now clear for navigation, but a fortnight had been lost. Even now, had Chatham pressed on to Antwerp, he could still have taken the city. But he rested on his laurels, and did nothing more. Between him and Strahan there was no co-operation; the two commanders could agree on nothing, and while they engaged in endless disputes, the French fleet slipped off from Flushing to defend Antwerp, troops were brought up by the French, and the city was put into a good state of defence before the commanders could resolve how to attack it. The situation, if it had not been so tragic, would have been ludicrous. In the words of a popular rhyme:

> " The Earl of Chatham with his sword drawn
> Stood waiting for Sir Richard Strahan,
> Sir Richard longing to be at 'em
> Stood waiting for the Earl of Chatham."

It took Chatham yet another week, after Flushing had been reduced, before he joined Hope at Batz. By that time it was too late. Antwerp had received considerable reinforcements, while Chatham had lost nearly half his army through disease. For while the commanders had been carrying on their disputes the troops had been left waiting in the infested swamps of Walcheren, where a fever broke out which swept them away in thousands.

The cold malarial air sucked their vitality, disease spread among them so rapidly that soon more than three-fourths of the army were in hospital. Fever burnt their limbs, a white crust coated their tongues, they slaked their thirst with tank water that was poisonous, and swallowed unripe fruit rather than take the salt beef provided for them. Nauseated by the stench of decaying vegetation, deep in slime and mud, the wretched men waited.

The French now opened the sluices and let in the sea; water rose in the trenches; and all over the island a dense evil-smelling mist rose up and choked them. The emergency hospitals, unprepared for this heavy calamity, were so crowded that the men were forced to lie huddled together on the steaming ground unattended. By the time Chatham arrived at Batz there was nothing to do but turn back.

The month of August had seemed so good to Castlereagh. He had received dispatches from Chatham that the isle of Walcheren had been taken, that Flushing had been taken; he had received dispatches from the Peninsula that Wellesley, having cleared the French out of Portugal, was marching into Spain; he was now waiting impatiently for news that Antwerp and the French fleet had been taken.

Not till the 29 August 1809, when the greater part of the army had already been devoured by fever, did he receive disquieting news from Chatham. "I am sorry to say," Chatham wrote, "that I receive every hour the most alarming accounts of the progress of sickness among the troops. This island is by far the most unhealthy, and so much so, that even such of the natives as can, leave it at this season of the year. . . . I am hitherto very well."

The dispatch was followed by a report that Chatham had failed to reach Antwerp. To Castlereagh it came as the greatest shock. Two days later he was recalling the remnants of the British army and their leader. The expedition had cost England, it was alleged, fifteen million pounds of public money; and it had almost annihilated the British army.

CHAPTER IX

I

CASTLEREAGH HAD failed miserably, failed where he could hardly believe that failure was possible. The expedition had been so carefully planned and prepared; it was "feasible, and practicable." It was the only thing possible at the time. The responsibility for its failure "did not rest with those who had planned or who equipped the expedition," he was confident, but with those who had executed it.[1] If it had been carried out as designed we should have been in possession of Antwerp, and of the French fleet. But through Chatham's dilatoriness and sloth it had failed; yet Chatham, he knew, would be exonerated; and *he* would be saddled with the failure. Lord Lowther, who had been out with the expedition, had told him, and everyone else, how Strahan had urged Chatham by every consideration to mask Flushing with 10,000 men and with the flotilla, and he would engage to get round the island, either by the West or East Scheldt, and land the rest of the army, 25,000 strong, near Antwerp. But Chatham had answered: "We had better wait two or three days to see what would come of this first." Those two or three days, said Lowther, were decisive of the whole business.

Lord Chatham had now returned, proud and sulky, and out of humour with all his colleagues for not supporting him. The King's favour, and respect for the memory of Pitt, would exonerate him; but who would exonerate Castlereagh? And yet it was not the first time an engagement had been unsuccessful. The inevitable had to be faced, and faced with courage. But he had been subjected to an extraordinary strain, his nerves were frayed, his mind weary, his body worn. He

[1] Londonderry Papers. Castlereagh to Edward Cooke. Sudbourne Hall, Sunday.

was sitting to Lawrence for his portrait at this time, and the painter remarked that he had never seen a man so sunk in woe, and that more than once he had noticed him wipe his eyes. Lawrence put it down to the news of Wellesley's retreat. For now, following on the Walcheren disaster, came further tidings of misfortune.

Six weeks earlier, Wellesley had crossed the border and marched into Spain to join the Spanish forces in an attack on Madrid, but the Spanish forces had proved the greatest disappointment. Their leader, Commander Cuesta, was a man of eighty-three, who always crossed himself before he mounted a charger. His cavalry, escaping from its last defeat, had ridden over him in their haste, and now he always followed his troops in a coach. He had been lifted out on cushions to meet Wellesley.

As soon as Wellesley saw him and his outrageous army he knew the worst. Full of superstitions and obstinate to a degree, Cuesta had resisted Wellesley's suggestion to launch an attack, but when he heard later that the French were falling back, he became unnaturally enterprising, and determined to push on to Madrid.

Wellesley, short of supplies, decided to remain at Talavera, and let Cuesta and his troops go on; but they stumbled into 40,000 Frenchmen, and were soon back. That night, 28 July 1809, on the dusty hillside of Talavera, the French attacked. Two thousand Spaniards fled, and the British army had to fight against overwhelming odds; yet every attack was beaten off. There was havoc and slaughter; one brigade of cavalry charged into a deep ravine where men and horses lay heaped in agony; towards evening the long dry grass caught fire, and the British wounded were burned or suffocated to death. But after a desperate struggle, in which Wellesley lost more than 5000 of his men, the French were flung back in confusion. They slipped away in the night leaving 7000 dead on the battlefield. Talavera had been a victory, and Wellesley had been rewarded with the title of Viscount Wellington. But instead of marching on, Wellington had turned back and had retreated to Portugal. Castlereagh did not blame Wellington; he understood his difficulties only too well, but there was great dissatisfaction with him in many quarters.

He was blamed for gambling away the lives of his men at Talavera, which had proved after all a barren victory. He was blamed for having left his wounded behind. He was blamed for leaving his men to rot in the Guadiana marshes to which he had retreated. But Castlereagh never lost faith in him.

Before Talavera, when his brother Charles had written to him full of complaints because Wellesley was not pushing on, Castlereagh had sent him calm, wise, patient letters, praising all that Wellesley had done, and begging his brother to have confidence in him.

" I am not disposed to consider Wellesley or any other man as being without his drawbacks," he wrote, " or his faults, if you please, but I do deliberately believe him to unite more of the Essential Qualities of an officer, than any Individual in the Service—he deserves to Command great armies—we have already, under every difficulty, placed him in the most prominent Command the Service affords— can you hope to serve with any man who is more likely to lead you to Glory ? "

" I perfectly approve," he had written, " of everything Wellesley has done—I have no apprehension that he will not *enterprise sufficiently*, when there is a case to justify it."

" We have a *devil of a task* before us in the Peninsula," he wrote later, " now that Austria is disposed of. If any man alive can carry us through it, Wellesley will, and whatever may be the issue—I am confident he will *personally* rise with his difficulties." [1]

These sentiments he had expressed to Charles before Talavera, when the army was still halting and everyone was growing impatient. And the victory at Talavera had come close on its heels confirming Castlereagh's impressions.

" He has risen superior to his difficulties," he wrote to Charles again, " and left himself or rather his country nothing to wish for, but that he may be preserved to them." Although he praised Charles too for his brave conduct during the engagement, he could not forbear scolding him a little for his earlier impatience with Wellington. " You have a taste rather for a quarrel," he informed him. " This may do with your mistress, better than with your wife, but it will not do at all with your General—so for God's sake put an end to it. . . . Take my word for it, if you separate yourself from Wellesley, you will regret it the longest day you live, and you will in vain look for a better master. . . . If you blame him even in your manner for not *advancing*, without having fully examined his wants, or even if you

[1] Londonderry Papers.

208

had, it must do mischief. Rely upon it Wellesley does not require *the Spur*. I believe him to require neither, but of the Two, I should suspect the Check Rein was more call'd for, but if at this distance I can judge of any man's conduct, not being a Professional man myself, the whole of his proceedings, and none more than when he has omitted to push the Enemy, do appear to me to have been founded in the truest wisdom."[1]

And even now, when Wellington had retreated after a victory, and was back again in Portugal, Castlereagh was still upholding him.

But difficulties were closing in on all sides. The only thing was not to lose hope, and to hold on. Whatever happened, the Peninsular Campaign must continue, for it was the Peninsula that would in the end exhaust Napoleon.

2

Castlereagh, overwhelmed by the troubles that were gathering round him, did not know that he had yet another burden to bear. For Canning, as soon as the Walcheren expedition was known to be a failure, had written to the Prime Minister that it was due to the country and to himself that Castlereagh should now be removed from office.

The Duke of Portland informed him in reply that some of his colleagues were protesting against Castlereagh's removal, unless it should be effected with his concurrence, and that strong feelings of anxiety had been expressed that Castlereagh should not be suddenly placed in a situation of degrading dismissal. Perceval, who had protested against Castlereagh's removal from the beginning, regretted that Canning should urge fulfilment of the promise made to him, just in the moment of failure, and suggested to the Duke of Portland, who was decaying fast, that his retirement, which would necessitate a general recasting of ministers, should cover Castlereagh's removal from the War Department, and thus soften the blow.

The Duke, who had never wished for Castlereagh's removal, but merely for the addition of Lord Wellesley to the Cabinet, agreed to do all he could to ease the difficulty, and sent in his resignation.

[1] Londonderry Papers.

Matters now came to a crisis. Canning, in great displeasure, declared he would not serve under any third person. Although he had formerly suggested the Earl of Chatham as Prime Minister, he now insisted that the Prime Minister must be of the House of Commons. He also expressed his opinion that the Premiership must fall either to himself or to Perceval, remarking at the same time that he could not be expected to serve under Perceval. He was determined to be head of the Government, and having arranged for the removal of one rival, Castlereagh, he tried now to dispose of the other. He suggested to Perceval, who was the younger son of a peer, that he should go to the House of Lords. Perceval declined the honour. " I am persuaded," he said, " that Canning meant only to put an extinguisher on my head in the shape of a coronet." Unabashed, Canning even suggested that Perceval should take Eldon's office as Lord Chancellor, but Perceval did not wish to oust Lord Eldon, and stood his ground.

Finding that there was a general reluctance to remove Castlereagh, and that Perceval declined to be extinguished, Canning played his last card. He wrote to the Duke of Portland informing him that he considered retiring, unless the King should think he ought to undertake the conduct of Government, in which case he would not shrink from the undertaking. The letter was delivered to the King, who replied that he must take time to consider it. Canning then called on the King, but he received the same answer.

The King told Perceval later of Canning's interview with him, and remarked that his conversation was " the most extraordinary he ever heard." If His Majesty honoured him with his commands he would readily undertake to form an administration. " Not," said the King, " that he would advise with others, as you, or any other person, would have said, but he was fully prepared to undertake it. Now," continued His Majesty, " I do not believe, if he was to be the Minister, that there is any one of you who would continue with him, and he does not seem at all to think of that."

The King, astute as ever, realised that Canning with his plots and counter-plots, his hypocrisy and his conceit, had ruined himself with all parties, that he overrated his supporters, that he counted upon numbers who did not and would not follow him, and that his temper and arrogance were such as made it difficult to place him in the lead. The King had no intention of calling on Canning, and informed

Perceval that he would leave it to his present servants to find a successor to Portland.

Canning, finding that his plans were not prospering, declared that he was definitely sending in his resignation, and declined to attend the next Cabinet meeting.

Observing his absence, Castlereagh made inquiries, and Lord Camden had the unenviable task of informing him of the feeling against him, and of the Cabinet's intention of calling upon him to resign. In great surprise Castlereagh consulted Perceval, who showed him Lord Camden's private correspondence, and the whole intrigue was exposed.

Castlereagh was so amazed at Camden's connivance in the plot that at first he did not feel Canning's perfidy to its full extent. But when he came to trace the whole intrigue in all its complications, and learnt that Canning had demanded his removal six months previously, that for six months he had been permitted to remain in total ignorance of his situation, and that he had been allowed to plunge into the heaviest responsibilities after, as he put it, his death warrant had been signed, his face grew white with anger.

He saw only too clearly that his removal had been proposed by Canning merely to facilitate his own advancement. At a critical moment in the affairs of the country, he had threatened to resign if Castlereagh were not removed, and it was in order to retain Canning that he had been placed in a situation so full of danger and dishonour.

As he read the correspondence his anger and resentment grew. He had been duped and practised upon; he had been sacrificed to a colleague both unjustly and ungenerously, and no intimation had been given him even by his friends of the plot against him. So shabby a set of friends he had. As for Canning, he had surpassed in treachery and duplicity anything Castlereagh had thought possible. How could he have permitted a colleague to initiate so important an expedition, after he had denounced him? It was all the more disturbing that his friends had acquiesced in it—even Lord Camden, who was not only his friend, but a close connection.

" Preserve me from my friends," he said, " and I shall not fear my enemies."

Camden tried to explain that he had been restrained by Portland from informing him of Canning's designs; that it had been entirely against his inclination. He was even ready, in order to retain Castlereagh in the Government, to give up his own office, that of President of the Council, if Castlereagh would accept it. But Castlereagh's proud spirit did not know how to yield, and he declared that if he lent himself to such an idea he would deserve all the mortification that had been prepared for him. He declined the offer. Dignified and self-possessed he sent in his resignation.

There was only one more thing to do. Canning had condemned him without giving him an opportunity of defending himself; he had charged him behind his back in all quarters, and had only asked for the matter to be communicated to him, when sentence had already been passed without his being heard. He would have satisfaction.

The letter he sent to Canning was written in detail, with the precision of his official dispatches, and was quite unanswerable. He charged him with having acted with him, as though in full confidence, in matters of infinite delicacy, withholding from him all the time the fact that he had obtained a promise that he should be removed from the Cabinet after the expedition was terminated.

He informed him that his acquiescing in such a concealment was dishonourable between colleagues, and dishonoured him personally as a colleague and a gentleman, that others had concealed the matter from a mistaken regard for him, struggling to *prevent* his removal, but that Canning had concealed it from quite different motives, determined to *secure* his removal.

He did not deny that Canning had a right to say he would not serve with him; but what he had no right to do was to make him believe he was acting cordially with him throughout the expedition while insisting behind his back upon his being dishonoured at the end of it.

The letter covered three sheets of folio paper, and ended with the words:

" Under the circumstances I must require that satisfaction from you to which I feel myself entitled to lay claim.

I have the honour to be, Sir,

Your obedient, humble servant,

CASTLEREAGH "

Canning, casting his eye over the closely written sheets, exclaimed:
" I had rather fight than read it, by God."

He answered briefly:

> Gloucester Lodge,
> 20 September 1809.
> (half past ten a.m.)

" MY LORD,

The tone and purport of your Lordship's letter (which I have
this moment received) of course precludes any other answer, on my
part, to the misapprehensions and misrepresentations, with which it
abounds, than that I will cheerfully give to your Lordship the
satisfaction that you require.

> I have the honour to be, my Lord,
> Your Lordship's most obedient humble servant,
> GEO. CANNING "

3

The following day at six in the morning, accompanied by his cousin,
Lord Yarmouth, who was acting as his second, Castlereagh proceeded
to Putney. The parties were to meet at Lord Yarmouth's cottage on
Putney Heath. Cool and collected, and utterly detached, Castlereagh
chatted to Lord Yarmouth about the opera as they drove along, and
hummed an air that Catalina had made famous. It was a dull, un-
inspiring day, with heavy skies, and the river looked grey and murky
as they crossed the bridge.

As they approached the rendezvous Castlereagh could see near a
clump of bushes a second carriage waiting, a groom standing at the
horses' heads, and knew that Canning had arrived. A moment later
he caught sight of him talking to Ellis, his second, He had tried to
get Henry Wellesley, Castlereagh knew, but Wellesley had refused
to act for him. When their carriage stopped, Ellis came up and tried
to arrange the matter with Yarmouth, but failed. There was a little
discussion about distances, and the ground was measured.

Castlereagh took up his position calmly, standing sideways to his
man, presenting his lean body like the edge of a blade. Coolly he

took the pistol from Yarmouth and weighed it in his hand. He had not practised with pistols since he had left Ireland, but he had always been a good shot. He watched Charles Ellis trying to load Canning's pistol, and noticed that he was so nervous that Lord Yarmouth had to do it for him.

"Are you ready, my lord?" Yarmouth called. Castlereagh nodded.

"Are you ready, Mr. Canning?"

Mr. Canning was ready.

"Well then, gentlemen, fire as you please."

Canning fired immediately, but the shot went wide. Castlereagh aimed carefully, but he too missed. Was he satisfied, they were asking him? No, he answered coldly, he was not satisfied. Canning's second showed annoyance; Lord Yarmouth suggested that the matter had gone far enough, but as Mr. Canning had made no apology Castlereagh felt bound to proceed.

"Are you ready?"

Castlereagh heard a bullet whizz past him; it took a button off his coat. He raised his arm slowly, brought his pistol up along the line of Canning's leg and fired. Another moment and the seconds were running towards Canning who lay huddled on the ground. The surgeon followed on their heels.

After a moment Yarmouth came up to Castlereagh. It was a nasty wound, apparently, through the outer part of the thigh. Tedious but not dangerous.

They behaved to each other with their usual politeness, both before they went to the ground and after. Castlereagh's mind was relieved, the personal affront and injury atoned for.[1] There was nothing further for him to do, and he went back to his carriage and drove home.

Writing to his father immediately after the duel, he said: "We each fired two pistols, my second shot took effect, but happily only passed through the fleshy part of his thigh. Mr. Canning's conduct was very proper on the ground."[2]

He had hardly finished his letter before Lord Camden arrived at the house in a state of great agitation. "He broke into my room in

[1] Londonderry Papers. The Earl of Londonderry to his son, Charles.

[2] Written from St. James's Square, 21 September 1809. Londonderry Papers.

tears," Castlereagh wrote to his father, "condemning himself and stating his wretchedness."[1] Still burning from the wrongs he had suffered Castlereagh remained unimpressed by this demonstration. He informed Camden coldly that he acquitted him of any motive deliberately unkind, but that he could never forget the political injury to which he had been exposed. He told him in the strongest terms what he felt about the determination to sacrifice him to Canning, and how much he resented the danger to which his character and honour had been subjected.

Camden assured him that it was only through a desire to retain him in office that he personally had acquiesced in the concealment, hoping that with continual postponement the moment of removal would never come. He had been most uneasy about the whole affair, but the Duke who had been actuated by the kindest motives, but whose intellect was not very strong, had conceived this idea of retaining Canning, and at the same time of keeping Castlereagh till he should find another office for him.

He had been against it from the first, but had been compelled to acquiesce in the Prime Minister's wishes. Seeing now what it had all come to, he blamed himself bitterly for everything that had passed, and assured Castlereagh again and again that he had been most wretched over the whole business. He had always had the utmost confidence in him, as he well knew, and had even offered to give up his own office of President of the Council, if Castlereagh would take it. But he had refused. He could understand the bitterness in Castlereagh's heart, and his distrust now of all his colleagues, but he wanted him to believe that he had never done anything deliberately to hurt him, but had, on the contrary, mistakenly as it turned out, done all he could to save him pain. That he had only aggravated his injuries was the deepest misfortune he had ever suffered.

Camden appeared so distressed that Castlereagh gave him his hand, though he could not find it in his heart to condone what had been done. After they had shaken hands Camden turned the conversation, and said: "Let us now only look forward." He then began to talk about the forming of the new Government, and what he and his colleagues were doing; but Castlereagh stopped him short, and begged to decline the confidence.

[1] Written from Stanmore, 3 October 1809.

Finding he could do nothing further to remove Castlereagh's resentment, Camden took his leave, much to Castlereagh's relief. He was not unmindful of Camden's efforts on his behalf in the early days in Ireland, nor did he wish to be harsh to him, but hypocrisy was a thing he could not endure, and that Camden of all people should have practised it towards him, whatever the motive, was altogether incomprehensible and unforgettable.

On 1 October, he received a letter from Camden suggesting himself for dinner to discuss the measures that had been taken towards forming an Administration. Castlereagh wrote back declining the visit for the moment, as he wished to know nothing of the measures that had been taken. He thanked Camden for his kind intention, and hoped that he would not misunderstand his motive.

To his brother Charles he wrote: " I need not break my heart at losing so shabby a set of friends as mine have proved themselves." [1]

Turning his back on his former friends in the Cabinet, he declined to receive confidences from any of them. He preferred to know nothing of their progress, or to appear to know nothing, except what he learnt from the Press.

4

It was the end of September 1809, and the papers were full of more serious news than the fall of the Ministry. They were full of the retreat from Spain, and the starving, fever-stricken troops who were arriving along the Portuguese frontier, of the failure of the Scheldt operation, and of the disease that had broken out in the Isle of Walcheren. It was a bad moment for Castlereagh, and a bad moment for England.

The papers declared that Napoleon was insane—but his power ran from the Baltic to the Adriatic. He was forty years old, and it had been prophesied that after the age of forty he would not prosper; but he was prospering only too well. He had entered almost every capital in Christendom. He had incorporated Italy and half of Germany into his dominions; he had filled the thrones of Spain, Westphalia and Naples with his kinsfolk. He was now preparing to

[1] Londonderry Papers. Castlereagh to Charles. Stanmore, 16 October 1809.

discard Josephine for a younger woman. As Josephine had borne him no children he was contemplating a new marriage, in order to perpetuate the dynasty he had founded.

He had already made overtures to the Emperor of Russia for his sister's hand, but the Emperor had not encouraged the suggestion. He was now proposing himself as suitor for the eighteen year old daughter of the Emperor of Austria, and would soon be united to the ancient House of Hapsburg by a marriage with the Archduchess Marie Louise. The little Corsican was only too sane.

Marie Louise was the niece of Marie Antoinette, whose head had fallen to pave the way for Napoleon's rise to power, but the memory of her headless corpse did not mar the ceremonies.

The Walcheren failure and the retreat in Spain were not the only difficulties that faced the Government. There was trouble now with America, for President Madison had revived the Non-intercourse Act against Great Britain, and an American war seemed imminent.

During the previous year there had been a new spirit of accommodation in British counsels. Erskine, our Minister to the United States, had been instructed to settle the *Chesapeake* affair, and to inform the President that Canning was about to withdraw the Orders in Council. The United States had been full of rejoicing; commerce had opened up again, and ships and merchandise had been hurried to British ports; but Canning, without explanation, had suddenly rejected Erskine's arrangements. Erskine had apparently omitted to demand certain conditions, and President Madison had given offence by his unfortunate phraseology, stating that though he withdrew his demand for the court martial of Admiral Barclay, the Commander of the *Leopard*, he was " not the less persuaded that such an example would best comport with what is due from his Britannic Majesty to his own honour." His Majesty did not care to be told by America what was due to his honour. Canning recalled Erskine for transmitting such a message, and for acting on his own discretion in the matter of the conditions, and sent out in his place Francis James Jackson, who aggravated the position further by his unfortunate manner. He managed to embitter the whole of America against England. It was Canning's last step before the Ministry fell.

" Concerning the United States," records Henry Adams,[1] " Can-

[1] Adams: *History of the United States.*

ning had already done all the harm possible and more than three generations could wholly repair." Pitt had once said of Canning that he was like a mistress, always offended and always writing notes.[1]

Although Castlereagh appeared to know nothing of the Government's activities, a great deal penetrated to him. He heard of the King's attempt to form a Coalition Government. It was foredoomed to failure, for the Whigs were still against the war, and the war had to be carried on. However black things were, the British nation had a way of holding on and holding on till victory came.

He heard that the Prince of Wales, who was the virtual head of the Whig party, had written a letter to the King offering his services in forming an administration. He seemed mightily disposed to thrust himself into some negotiation or other, but his father declined the offer, reminding him of a former assurance never to interfere in political arrangements unless expressly requested to do so by His Majesty.

The Prince was very proud of the letter he had written to the King, and was showing it to all his friends. Sheridan informed Lord Holland, who was on his way to Carlton House, that he would like the Prince's letter extremely. "The fact is," he added, "the Prince had drawn it out at first himself, but in a way that would never have done, awkward in expression, forgetful of things that had passed, and pledging himself to others in future that would have been the devil and all. I contrived, however, just by hinting a thing here and there to recast the whole, and he is delighted with it."

When the Prince received Holland, he produced the paper with great complacency; "Sheridan will excuse me," he said—Sheridan also being present—"but though he is a clever fellow at such things, I must say he had drawn up a damned bad paper on this occasion. I just took the form and outline, but I have altered it myself, and was obliged to do so." At every word he read, he turned to Sheridan: "You will allow that's better, Sheridan?" To all of which Mr. Sheridan nodded assent.

Castlereagh was amused by all the rumours he heard, but he knew there would be no Coalition Government and no Whig Government. It would be a Tory Government again, and now that he and Canning

[1] Journal of Mrs. Arbuthnot.

were out, the only man who could form an administration was
Spencer Perceval. Although many considered Perceval a mediocrity,
Castlereagh had always had a great admiration for him. He had
no brilliance, but he was honest, amiable, and full of good qualities.
He had been the only one bold enough to protest against Canning's
deceitful operations in the intrigue against Castlereagh. Trusted by
everyone he was certain to get a following. He looked small and
insignificant, but he had made a very good Leader of the House of
Commons, and could hold his own in debate against any man. He
was opposed unfortunately to Roman Catholic Emancipation, but
was all the more in favour with the King on that account. As someone
remarked there was nothing wrong with Perceval except his opinions.
But Perceval believed that the struggle in the Peninsula should be
carried on at all costs, which was, after all, the major issue.

On 5 October 1809, Perceval took office as Prime Minister. The
Administration of which he was chief was not a strong one. Even
though it included three future Prime Ministers—Liverpool, Palmerston, Peel—it was not expected to last very long. "We have such
a set of dolts for Ministers," wrote General Calvert's lady, "that
it is most disheartening." And yet the Ministry lasted longer than
anyone expected. It lasted—with a few changes—for nearly eighteen
years.

5

Castlereagh's place at the War Office was filled by Lord Liverpool.
Canning's place as Foreign Minister was taken by Lord Wellesley.
This was not at all to Canning's liking. He had intended Wellesley
for Castlereagh's office, not for his own. "Oh—yes——" he wrote
to Bagot, "it is the Foreign Office specifically—nothing else—that
he accepts—— But he writes to people in office and out as if he
were accepting the whole Government." A day or two later he
commented bitterly: "He kisses hands for my office to-morrow,
and is to have the Garter (I understand) as an encouragement to
begin with."

The highest office in the State had been almost within Canning's
grasp, but his quarrels and intrigues had brought retribution on his

head, and he remained outside the actual Government of the country for twelve years. He had intrigued against Lord Liverpool (Hawkesbury) in the days of Pitt. He had quarrelled both with Pitt and with Addington. He had lost many friends in the past through this unfortunate trait in his character, he lost many more when the facts leading to the duel were made public. Trying to clear himself, he insisted that he had not known about the concealment, and that he had repeatedly remonstrated against it. But though Portland took all the blame on himself, he could not resist suggesting to Canning, in a letter only too logical, that it was strange he should have *remonstrated* against concealment, where he thought no concealment existed. Even his staunchest friends felt that it was vexatious that a man of such excellent abilities should have damaged himself so much.

Castlereagh on the other hand gained many new admirers. Everyone felt that he had been treated infamously; even in Ireland he was considered the injured party. But his sufferings were not yet over; for when Parliament met, a motion was brought forward by Lord Porchester condemning the policy of the Government in undertaking the Walcheren expedition. It was a painful moment for Castlereagh, but he stood the test. Even his bitter opponent, Creevey, states, that " everything that related personally to himself he did with a conscious sense of being right, and a degree of lively animation I never saw in him before. Base as the House is, it recognised by its cheers the claims of Castlereagh to its approbation, and they gave it." But when it came to his expedition, Creevey says, " he fell a hundred fathoms lower than the bogs of Walcheren." Another of Castlereagh's opponents, the Earl of Dudley, wrote: " Castlereagh has astonished all the world by his speech the other night. I am glad he succeeded, for, though an abominable Minister, he is an excellent man and a perfect gentleman."

Castlereagh has always been considered a very poor speaker, and yet the dignity and weight of his speeches have drawn admiration at times from many of his political enemies. Canning, on the other hand, who was a brilliant orator, was received very coldly by the House on this occasion. He was, however, sufficiently master of himself, Creevey informs us, " to let off one of his regular compositions, with all the rhetorical flourishes that used to set his audience in a roar; but he spoke from a different atmosphere. He was at least two feet separated from the Treasury Bench, and in the whole course of his speech, he could not extort a single cheer."

Canning was "like a dealer in a certain sort of ware," remarked another of his contemporaries, "very marketable up to a certain price and for some time, but base in its real nature, and which don't keep—I mean little prize essays of speeches, got up and polished, and useless, quite useless, for affairs."

The Inquiry into the Walcheren expedition clearly proved that its failure was due to Chatham's incompetence, indolence, and disregard of instructions. Chatham attempted to defend himself, in a private letter to the King, by throwing the blame on Strahan and the Navy. Universal indignation was roused in Parliament when this was disclosed, and the severest possible censure was passed on Chatham, on the King, and on the Ministers. The House was for fair play, and against Royal favouritism. So violent was the feeling against Chatham on this matter that he was forced to resign.

His friends regretted that all the blame should have been thrown on him alone, but they did not feel it possible to defend him. "I dare say he was not very active, but why did they send him?" was the general feeling. He was a man of good brains, it was said, but he found it more restful not to use them.

There was a great deal of controversy about the advisability of the expedition having been sent at all. In his speech vindicating his policy, Castlereagh declared that there was no other objective possible at the time, for there were not sufficient funds for an expedition to North Germany, which had been suggested as an alternative, and matters would have been no better if the troops had been sent to Spain, because there would have been no means of provisioning them.

The expenditure involved in the Walcheren expedition, he maintained, had been absurdly exaggerated. It had been put at a meeting of protest in the City at fifteen millions.[1] The actual expenditure involved, Castlereagh proved, was not more than eight hundred thousand pounds. After a heated debate, the motion condemning the policy of the Government in undertaking the expedition was defeated.

But attacks on Castlereagh were not yet over. In *The Morning Chronicle* there began to appear libellous statements made by an Irish

[1] It has been put by recent writers at 26 millions, but the estimate is quite fallacious.

journalist, Peter Finnerty, who had recently accompanied, as correspondent, the Walcheren expedition. He had been sent home on account of his indiscretions, and for this treatment he blamed Castlereagh. Finnerty had at one time been connected with the United Irish organ, *The Press*, a paper which had been suppressed.

He now accused Castlereagh of having "sanctioned torture," and "of having been guilty of tyranny, cruelty and oppression in his administration of Ireland." His assertions were so libellous that Castlereagh was compelled to institute criminal proceedings against him. The Attorney General did not think Finnerty would defend himself, and Castlereagh only "hoped for enough discussion to expose him," [1] but the trial which opened in July 1810 was a long one.

Castlereagh did not deny that there had been, during the Irish Rebellion, individual instances of cruelty which he declared nothing could justify, but the Government, he stated, could not be held responsible for isolated acts; and no torture had ever been inflicted with the sanction of the Government. The trial excited a great deal of interest and resulted in Finnerty being sentenced to 18 months' imprisonment in Lincoln Jail. In the House of Commons Castlereagh asserted that he entertained no bitter feelings towards Finnerty personally, and even pleaded for a mitigation of his punishment; he had taken proceedings against him very reluctantly, he stated, and only with a deep sense of public duty.

6

Castlereagh was forty-one. For over twenty years he had worked incessantly in the field of politics, superintending every detail himself, writing every dispatch with his own hand. He had forgotten what it was to have leisure. Now that he was out of office he decided to take a little place in the country where he could rest.

London was dull. Poor Princess Amelia, the King's favourite daughter, was dying, and the good old King was still fluctuating between sanity and insanity. A fresh attack of invasion fever was sweeping the country, and there were gloomy forecasts that we should

[1] Londonderry Papers. Castlereagh to his brother Charles, dated London, 14 July.

yet have to fight Napoleon on our own soil. Everybody seemed oppressed. Conversation generally was about the hardness of the times, about the necessity for economy, about giving up houses in town, about the high rents demanded.

Exploring the country round, Castlereagh found a small farm in Kent, about twelve miles from Westminster. The house was small, but in good condition, the situation retired, the surrounding country beautiful. The farm itself was bounded by a trout stream, which would give good fishing. He was delighted with the place, and as Emily was equally enthusiastic, in the summer of 1810 they settled at Cray.

Away from the cares of Government, Castlereagh revelled in his new-found freedom. He began to take a great interest in farming, which soon absorbed him completely. Writing to his brother Charles, he says: " I have not thought of anything of late but of sheep farming, I have been studying under Sebright and other learned breeders in Hertfordshire, and mean to have the best Merino Flock in England, on my new farm at Besley of 40 acres. Emily says I shall soon bleat, and be covered with wool."

The Comtesse de Boigne in her Memoirs describes the house at Cray as " a regular country parsonage." " The visitor's carriage drew up at a little gate," she tells us, " and a walk between two beds of ordinary flowers led to a six-roomed house. Though the entrance to the house was exceedingly mean it was situated in charming country, and enjoyed a magnificent view; behind it there was a considerable enclosure, with rare plants, a menagerie, and a kennel, which, with the greenhouses, divided the attention of Lady Castlereagh." Emily's " persevering attendance " on Castlereagh, she found " slightly ridiculous."

" She never left her husband at any time," she relates. " While he worked she was beside his desk. She followed him to the town and to the country, and accompanied him upon every journey. Nor did she ever seem to be vexed or inconvenienced by any difficulties. She would spend nights of cold, hunger, and weariness in miserable lodgings, without complaining or seeming to feel any inconvenience. In short, she did her utmost to be as little in the way as possible throughout this apparent devotion. I say apparent, because their most intimate friends believed that in this respect she was following her own desires rather than those of Lord Castlereagh. He, however, never offered any objection."

While she was at Cray the Countess witnessed an incident when Castlereagh showed great courage and presence of mind, intervening in a fight between Emily's bull-dog and a spaniel which he had attacked. Castlereagh was badly bitten in the leg and hand, and the spaniel nearly strangled before the dogs were separated. When Emily arrived the bull-dog was still growling with rage, but she calmed him with caresses, much to the indignation of the Countess and the others who had witnessed the scene. Castlereagh was badly mauled and in great pain for a while, but Emily persuaded him to keep the dog, though she herself was compelled to get rid of him four months later.

The Comtesse de Boigne noted that Lady Castlereagh had become " extremely stout, and though she preserved her beautiful features, had lost all her distinction." " Somewhat unintellectual," she informs us, " she was most benevolent, while her social manners were entirely ordinary and displayed no great knowledge of the world."

She " had the good taste," however, " to lay aside her finery at Cray, and was to be found in a muslin dress, with a large straw hat on her head, an apron round her waist, a pair of scissors in her hand, cutting away dead flowers."

Castlereagh loved the life at Cray. " I find it a very pleasant place to live in," he wrote to Charles, " when there is neither Parliament nor office to bore one. Idleness agrees with me marvellously. I wish to God we could pass the summer together." But Charles was still out in the Peninsula with Wellington, and there was little prospect of their meeting. Castlereagh continued to receive first-hand news of the campaign from his brother, but the news was far from good.

7

Throughout England the war in the Peninsula was becoming unpopular. For more than six months the British army had remained inactive; they had not fired a shot. Wellington was blamed for the idleness of his army when there was no action, and for the slaughter of his men whenever there was an engagement. The glamour of his former victories had faded, and it was estimated that he had lost a fifth of his army.

In May 1810, Napoleon sent his most famous general, Masséna, with added reinforcements, to the Peninsula, and Wellington, instead of driving all before him as the people expected, was calmly discussing evacuation. Transports were kept in the Tagus, in case this should be inevitable. Perceval was so much dismayed by the country's financial embarrassments that for a moment he too abandoned all hope of keeping the Peninsula. The troops had to be paid in the currency of the country, and the loss on the exchange alone cost England a million pounds annually. The soldiers' pay was six months in arrears, and the City of London had sent a petition for the immediate withdrawal of the forces in Spain. But it was only for a moment that the thought of recalling Wellington entered the head of Perceval.

Supported in Parliament by Castlereagh and by Canning, he stood his ground. "There was every motive," Castlereagh argued, "for playing the game as long as we could." "Every Frenchman that falls is in itself a gain," declaimed Canning. But Wellington was actually preparing to evacuate. Working secretly, he had three lines of earthworks thrown up across the Peninsula, between the Tagus and the sea. The third line was to protect the troops when they embarked; the second was for the army to fall back on, as its main line of defence; the first was to hold Masséna up for a while.

Wellington was some distance in front of these lines. As Masséna advanced, he began to draw back slowly, and as he drew back, he ordered the crops to be destroyed and the cattle to be driven off, so that Masséna pursuing the retreating army could find no provisions for his men as they advanced, and they were half-starved before ever they reached the "Lines of Torres Vedras." So much were the French hated in Spain that these lines of defence remained secret, not a single Spanish peasant betraying them to the French.

Completely unaware of the obstacle in front of him, Masséna marched on. At Busaco Wellington laid a trap for him, and checked the French for a time; but he had not sufficient men to enable him to continue fighting in the open field. He therefore continued to retreat. In the autumn of 1810, he took up his position behind his first line of defence. Masséna, when he came up to this barrier, was so amazed that he did not even attempt to storm it. Week after week he remained looking helplessly at the formidable barrier in front of him, while his army gradually wasted away through starvation and disease. More than 30,000 French soldiers perished, though not a single pitched battle had been fought.

At last Masséna ordered a retreat. A new game began, the French retreating, Wellington cautiously advancing. "If we can maintain ourselves in Portugal," Wellington wrote, "the war will not cease in the Peninsula, and if the war lasts in the Peninsula, Europe will be saved."

8

Castlereagh was still on his farm at Cray; he sent Charles, who was now Adjutant-General to Sir Arthur Wellesley, his opinions on the campaign, but informed him that he could give him little news excepting items from the Farmers' Calendar, into the mysteries of which he was deeply initiated. His Merino flock, he wrote, was prospering. "If you should capture a flock, and can send me some really fine, I shall be glad to pay for their import. But," he proudly adds, "as I have fifty of the very best, I should not wish to mix my flock with any but of the highest blood and the most established pedigree." Charles managed to send some sheep, but they did not prosper; they died one after the other of a mysterious disease.

Castlereagh found it pleasant enough to be without political cares. He enjoyed his new hobby and his new leisure, and life became far more tolerable. When Parliament rose he prepared to join Lady Emily, who was at Harrogate, and felt as happy at the thought as a schoolboy before the holidays. Afterwards they were to go on to Ireland to spend a few weeks with his family. He took a circuitous route to Harrogate in order to enjoy the countryside, and travelled on the box beside the coachman to see the landscape better. His servants he put inside the carriage to receive all the fine bows and curtseys. He found the box seat very comfortable, and the whole journey agreeable.

Passing through Lincolnshire he was amazed to see a Fen of 40,000 acres "over the whole surface of which four years since boats used to navigate," now covered with the most luxuriant crops. He was happy to see the wealth, the industry, the comfort of the country; and looking round on it all, it seemed to him a strange thing that there were "people ready to hazard all these blessings." It might astonish, he reflected, "if we did not know what human nature always has been, and always will be."[1]

In London there had been riots before he left, and the troops had been called out. Lord Carlisle, Byron's guardian, had got his noble nose well pelted with mud and dirt, and his friend, little Ossulston, had had to explain his politics to the mob. If he were not so small and inarticulate he might have got himself into mischief. As it was, nobody could hear him, so little harm was done.[2]

There were graver troubles. Napoleon had now marched into Holland; there would soon be no more countries left for him to annex. But he would overshoot his mark. His ally, the Russian Czar, was already getting restive. His Baltic trade having been paralysed by the Decrees, he was now refusing to break off intercourse with England, at Napoleon's behest. Russia, who had always had a weakness for British gold, should be encouraged.

9

The stench of the hot water baths at Harrogate was as nauseous as ever, and though there were good walks, and beautiful scenery, and exhilarating rides over the moors, Castlereagh was not ill-pleased when he and Emily set out for Ireland. The passage was rough, and the boat was late, but they were none the worse when they landed.

At Mount Stewart, there was an official-looking letter awaiting Castlereagh. It was from Perceval, and was an invitation to him to come back into the Government, with Canning. Without hesitation Castlereagh declined the offer, not "from any unbecoming feelings of a personal nature," he informed Perceval, but because he was convinced that such an arrangement could not command the confidence of the public, or give an impression that the Administration was united within itself.

[1] Londonderry Papers. Letter from Castlereagh to his brother, Sir Charles Stewart. Written from Hull.

[2] *Harriet, Lady Granville's Memoirs.*

It surprised him to hear that Canning, after all he had said, was ready now to serve under Perceval. Eventually negotiations fell through, and Perceval had to continue without either of them.

Castlereagh stayed at Mount Stewart for several weeks. The weather was fine, there was a good harvest, and he was happy to see everything so prosperous. He enjoyed the peace and quiet and beauty of the countryside, and occupied himself with the garden, planting bulbs with Emily and his sisters, and riding round the estate with his father.

But in October news reached him that the King's malady had returned, and that his mind was so seriously deranged that he might not be in a condition to open Parliament. It was the end of Castlereagh's holiday. If matters were as serious as he feared, there would be important discussions in Parliament when it opened, and reluctantly he set out for England.

He was not surprised at the King's condition. His favourite daughter, Princess Amelia, was dying of tuberculosis. It was sad that he should lose the only one of his children who had never caused him anxiety.

His sons had always behaved outrageously. They seemed to do nothing but pile up debts and illegitimate children, or embarrass the House of Commons with appeals for money. A few months earlier, in May 1810, one of the King's sons, the Duke of Cumberland, had murdered his valet, an Italian, who had apparently discovered the Duke with his wife. There had been a fight, and the valet was found cut to pieces. The Duke himself was badly wounded, but though the public was informed that he had been attacked by his valet, who had afterwards taken his own life, his plight did not cause general mourning. Hideously ugly, vindictive, and ill-tempered, he was the most destested of all the Royal offspring.

His brother, the Duke of Clarence, was still living with Mrs. Jordan, the actress. The Duke of Kent was living in almost domestic bliss with Madame St. Laurent, who had blessed him with innumerable children, all of whom had the right to use the " baton sinister " reserved for Royal bastards.

The Prince of Wales himself, who would become Regent, if the King did not recover, was notorious for his debaucheries. Although he was now so fat that tight-lacing no longer helped his figure, he was flitting from one mistress to another. He was slighting Mrs. Fitzherbert, to whom he was secretly married, neglecting Lady Jersey, who " went on like an old watch after the mainspring had gone," and was becoming entirely devoted to Castlereagh's aunt, Lady Hertford, a lady of over fifty, very dignified, and most respected.

10

Castlereagh returned to London to find that the King was mending a little, but there did not seem much hope of his sanity returning for any length of time. A Regency was inevitable, and Castlereagh was in his place at Westminster, in December 1810, when the Regency discussions opened, coming to the support of Perceval, who desired to limit the Prince's powers as Regent. Even though the Prince might be disposed to pursue a temperate course, certain restrictions, Castlereagh felt, were advisable, and he had the courage to vote for them.

" I had rather not give a vote which may be unacceptable to the Prince," he said, " but I don't like to shirk it on that account." He knew he would be incurring the Prince's displeasure, but he felt that the King was still monarch, and he did not like the idea of " turning his back on the old gentleman."

He made an effective speech, urging that the full powers of the crown should not be immediately conferred on the Prince, that restrictions should be imposed, but that these restrictions should be limited to a year. The Bill embodying this view was carried by a small majority.

Between debates Castlereagh went down to his farm at Cray. The workmen were still there, and he was happy to share his very small house with them. He gave them the kitchen and dining-room for their use, and was quite content with his restricted quarters. Proud of his progress as a farmer, he wrote to Charles, saying: " The cloth which has earned the prize this year in the west of England was made of *my wool*—I have received all sorts of congratulations and shall probably go down to Posterity as the greatest Shepperd of the Time in which I lived."

An unexpected letter came for him from Lord Camden, with

229

whom he had had no intercourse since the unfortunate quarrel. It was to inform him of some point which had come out in the Lords, and which he thought might be of interest to him. Feeling that it was time he made a gesture of forgiveness, he called on Camden, who was only too happy to put an end to a domestic separation that was tending to become permanent.

CHAPTER X

I

NOBODY KNEW what turn politics might take under the Regent. The Perceval Ministry were expecting to be turned out, the Whigs were expecting to come in; for it was generally believed, when the Regent was appointed, that as virtual head of the Whig Party, he would dismiss his father's servants.

"By God, they shall not remain an hour. Not an hour," he had said.

He had already taken the preliminary steps for forming a Whig Cabinet, and the principal places were all assigned, when, being informed that the King was recovering, he changed his mind.

"The powder in His Royal Highness's hair is much more settled than anything in his head, or indeed heart," Sir Thomas Moore remarked. On Sheridan's advice the Prince was now writing a letter to Perceval, announcing his intention of not changing his Ministers, declaring that his sole consideration for retaining them was his "filial duty and affection."

He was not ill-advised in keeping his father's Ministers, for the King was decidedly better, and it was rumoured that he would resume his functions as quietly as if nothing had happened, as soon as the Regent had got through all the arrears of business, and knocked off the many hundred signatures which had to be put to diverse papers. The King was allowed to see his family again daily, but though he was impatient to resume his duties, it was thought best to proceed with caution.

"It is true I have had a hard shake," he said, "a very hard shake; but I am now going on well, and the Prince's conduct will give me

time to recover quite, before I take to business again." But he refused
to remain unemployed for long. To the Chancellor, who counselled
patience, he replied: "Aye, aye, my Lord Chancellor, it's all very
pretty talking, but if you had been kept out of your place for six
months, you would have been glad enough to get into it again."

He seemed well enough at times, but it was well known that those
who suffered from his affliction were subject to violent relapses after
long intervals of apparent freedom from it, and the poor King was
no exception.

Meanwhile the Prince attended to business for seven or eight hours
a day. This was so novel a thing for him, that it occasioned "some
agitation in the blood," and he had to be "eased" before he was fit
for business again. In spite of his bulk and the agitation caused by
the many signatures he had to append, he was in good health. He was
already nearing fifty, and though his digestion must have been completely destroyed by the quantity of alcohol he had been pouring into
it steadily for at least thirty years, he continued to eat and drink and
revel all through the night. At the Pavilion, his fabulous palace at
Brighton, dressed in his full field-marshal's uniform, he would preside
over the band, singing at the top of his voice, and beating his thighs
to the music. He no longer wept tears for Lady Hertford or another;
now that he had the weight of the Empire on his shoulders, he was as
cheerful and as merry as a sandboy.

His private life had always scandalised the people, who gave all
their sympathy to his discarded wife, but though he was hissed wherever he went, he declared that no Prince was ever so idolised as
himself. His consort, Caroline of Brunswick, bold, crude and over-
painted, may not have been above reproach herself; whenever occasion
offered she could be relied on to act with the utmost indecorum and
lack of taste. All the same she attracted sympathy, for the whole
country knew how outrageously she had been treated by her reprobate
of a husband. When she had first arrived from Germany for her
marriage with the Prince, he had taken one look at her and, turning to
Malmesbury who had brought her over, said: "Harris, I am not
well. Pray get me a glass of brandy." The Government had forced
him to marry Caroline, but he had spent their wedding night drunk
in the fender. In 1806 he had brought charges of immorality against
her. Although she was acquitted of having borne an illegitimate child,

the Inquiry, or the "Delicate Investigation," as it was called, left her with no unstained character. The Prince behaved with untold meanness towards her: he had taken back the bracelets he had given her for a wedding present, and had bestowed them on Lady Jersey. He would not even allow her a house in London.

"The only *faux pas* I ever committed," said Caroline, "was my marriage with the husband of Mrs. Fitzherbert."

She took up her quarters at Blackheath, until the Prince, pressed by his Ministers, allowed her to reside at Kensington Palace.

"Damn the West! and damn the East! and damn Wellington!" he cried one day at Carlton House. "The question is, how am I to get rid of this damned Princess of Wales?"

He had been Regent now for four months, and was planning a grand fête, though the King, who had had a relapse, was desperately ill. The fête was the most lavish ever seen. In a tent supported by gilded ropes, and decorated with festoons of flowers, the guests were received by the Prince who wore a scarlet uniform and a hat studded with diamonds.

All the Royal family was present, except for the Queen and the Princesses, who, deploring the Prince's lack of feeling, absented themselves from the festivities. All the Dukes and Duchesses were present, all the Marquesses and Marchionesses, all the Earls and Countesses; but the Princess of Wales was not invited. The members of her Household were invited, but she was not included. Mrs. Fitzherbert was invited; but as, for the first time, she was not to sit at the Royal table, she declined the invitation.

"The two wives," someone remarked, "are sitting at home."

After the Royal fête was over, the fashionable world began to buy mourning; for the King, who was subject now to violent paroxysms, was not expected to last very long. Actually he lasted nine more years, but the poor man never regained his sanity, or his throne.

2

While the Regent revelled, the position in the Peninsula grew steadily worse. "The campaign in Portugal and Lord Wellington begin to be out of fashion with the Regent," Creevey noted in his Diary. It was not surprising, for the news from Portugal was far from cheering. Looking over the returns of the army one November morning, the Prince noted that there were 21,000 sick in Lisbon and in the field.

There had been three so-called successful actions during the year, but the slaughter had been terrible. They had been fought in an attempt to retake the frontier fortresses of Portugal; but the fortresses still remained in French hands. General Graham, in the spring of 1811, had won a " brilliant victory " at Barrosa, but it had been incredibly rash, and was quite fruitless; the waste of British lives had been colossal, and his army almost annihilated.

Wellington himself was as good as beaten at Fuentes d'Onoro, although he claimed it as a victory. He had followed Masséna's retreating army till he had forced it out of Portugal, but with Almeida, Ciudad Rodrigo, and Badajoz still in French hands, he could not advance into Spain. He had been about to storm Almeida, when he had found Masséna's army behind him at Fuentes, and had been compelled to turn and fight. He had stood his ground, and the French had not been able to relieve Almeida, but the losses had been stupendous. Wellington himself declared that " Lord Liverpool was quite right not to move thanks for the battle of Fuentes." The French, too, claimed it as a victory.

Almeida fell soon after, though even here the victory was marred by the negligence of two senior British officers, who seemed to be unaware one morning that the French garrison had destroyed their fortifications, and had moved off in the night. Wellington called it " the most disgraceful military event that had occurred."

Beresford had fared even worse in his attempt to storm Badajoz. Wellington had ordered him to concentrate his forces round Albuera, but Soult had pounded away at them, till, as Wellington said, " they were ready to run away at every moment from the time it commenced till the French retired." But they stayed, and fifteen hundred men were left out of six thousand British soldiers. Beresford would have declared himself beaten, if Wellington had not hastily intervened and declared him victorious. "We lost four stand of colours at Albuera," wrote Lord Temple, "and colours, cannon, and prisoners are enough to enable the French to claim the victory." Another such battle would have ruined us.

The end of the year 1811 did not bring any better news. Wellington made another attempt on Badajoz, and failed; he turned to Ciudad Rodrigo, but the war season was over by now, and his designs on Ciudad Rodrigo had to be postponed. It was a disappointing year. By the end of 1811, after three years of fighting, we had not shaken the French hold on the Peninsula.

Wellington cursed his men, though he was proud of their valour. When he had first seen his ragged army, he had said: "I don't know what impression they will make on the enemy, but by God, they frighten *me*." "The scum of the earth," he termed them, "the mere scum of the earth." "The English soldiers are fellows who have all enlisted for drink," he said, "that is the plain fact—they have all enlisted for drink . . . people talk of their enlisting from their fine military feeling—all stuff—no such thing. Some of our men enlist from having got bastard children—some for minor offences—many more for drink, but you can hardly conceive such a fine set brought together."

Whether it was the fault of the men or of their leaders, the Peninsular Campaign, in the year 1811, seemed doomed to failure. Unpleasant letters began to appear in the *Morning Chronicle*, criticising with much severity the military movements of Wellington.

It was a great surprise to Wellington when he discovered that the author of these letters was no other than Sir Charles Stewart, Castlereagh's brother. He immediately summoned him to head-quarters at Torres Vedras.

"Charles Stewart," he said to him, "I have ascertained with deep regret that you are the author of the letters which appeared in the *Morning Chronicle*, abusing me and finding fault with my military plans.

"Now, Stewart, you know your brother, Castlereagh, is my best friend, to whom I owe everything; nevertheless, if you continue to write letters to the *Chronicle*, or any other newspaper, by God, I will send you home." [1]

Charles was so affected by this threat that he shed tears, and expressed himself deeply penitent for the breach of confidence, and want of respect for the Articles of War, after which they shook hands.

Castlereagh was sadly embarrassed by his brother's disloyalty to Wellington. He had been so anxious for Charles to have a brilliant military career, but this unfortunate incident may have ended it, for soon afterwards Charles took up employment in the diplomatic field.

In Parliament Castlereagh defended Wellington against all attacks. He declared it his conviction that the fieldworks at Torres Vedras "would offer an impassable barrier to the advance of the French, and that, sustained by the British Navy, would enable us to prolong the contest in the Peninsula until the enslaved nations of the Continent should rise and throw off the yoke of their oppressor."

He was not wrong, for though the contest was at that time being carried on from a stern resolution not to be beaten, rather than from any hope of success, at the close of the year 1811 the tide turned.

3

The Regent at this moment was entirely indifferent to the state of affairs in the Peninsula. His attention was divided between his band of wind instruments at the Pavilion and his little toe, of which he had damaged a tendon. The injury had occurred at a ball, given by the Duchess of York to introduce the heiress-apparent, Princess Charlotte, into society. Someone was showing the Princess how to do the Highland Fling, when the Prince rose and said that *he* would show her how it should be done. He raised the princely leg, got his foot entangled in a sofa, and twisted his unfortunate toe.

There was a great commotion. He complained of violent pain, and went to bed for ten days. Every three hours he took a hundred drops of laudanum, prescribed by himself. The affairs of Government were at a standstill. He would sign nothing; attend to nothing; he

[1] *Captain Gronow's Recollections.*

would converse with nobody on " business." The agenda was now the Royal toe, and his only consolation, Lady Hertford.

A rumour started that his mind was affected, and Caroline went about saying: " They should let out the old one, and shut up the young one." The amount of laudanum he was taking affected his health, and he lost the use of his arm till his medical advisers persuaded him to exchange the laudanum for castor oil, after which treatment he recovered.

It was nearing the time when the Prince would be relieved of all restrictions, which had been imposed on him for a year. There was a feeling that, as soon as he was his own master, he would dismiss the Government and take for his Prime Minister Lord Wellesley, who was now in great favour; but how Lord Wellesley was going to make up a Government was a matter of speculation, for he was at war with every member of the Cabinet. He and the Regent, however, seemed to be warmly attached to each other, and would sit for hours together, remoulding the universe, and lost in wonder at each other's wisdom. He sought to gratify the Regent in every way, and there did not exist a doubt in his own mind that the Prince would put him at the head of the Government the moment he became " unrestricted." To Perceval, Lord Wellesley was not at all cordial. Nor for that matter was the Prince, who always spoke to him in his most sarcastic tones.

One of their minor differences was over the Bishopric of Oxford, which had fallen vacant. The Prince mentioned his intention of giving it to William Jackson, when Perceval said:

" On that point, sir, I am positively pledged."

" Positively pledged, Mr. Perceval? " said the Prince; " positively pledged to give away one of my bishoprics! I don't understand you."

" I mean," replied Perceval, " that it was the King's positive and declared intention to give it to Dean Legge."

" Mr. Perceval," said the Prince, " if I had any direct intimation of what were really the King's wishes upon the subject, I would not only make Dean Legge Bishop of Oxford, but Archbishop of Canterbury, if it were in my power; but as this is not the case, I shall make my own Bishop. And further, I desire never more to hear what were the King's wishes upon such subjects, through a third person."

Perceval was definitely out of favour. When the year 1812

dawned, Lord Wellesley was declaring to the Prince, that many personal considerations rendered it impossible for him to serve under Mr. Perceval any longer than it suited the Prince's wishes, and that he proposed to withdraw from the Government after a reasonable period. He wrote to Perceval to the same effect.

Perceval was quite willing to dispense with Wellesley, and went straight to the Prince, suggesting an immediate successor. The Prince was surprised, and declared that it was not an "immediate" resignation, and that he would not have his Government disturbed. He thought, moreover, that there should be some endeavour to dissuade Wellesley from his purpose. Perceval was against this, and insisting that an immediate successor should be appointed, suggested Castlereagh for the vacancy. The Prince received the latter suggestion graciously. He spoke in high terms of Castlereagh, whose dignity of character and whose knowledge of official business, he said, had impressed him.

"But have you Lord Castlereagh's consent to the appointment?" he asked.

Perceval replied that he had not sounded him, but that he had no doubt of obtaining his consent. He immediately sent to Castlereagh, desiring to see him on business of importance, and a meeting took place. When Perceval informed Castlereagh of Wellesley's intended resignation, and of the Regent's desire that he should consider the Foreign Office, Castlereagh's reply was most unexpected. He said he had no wish to stop a gap, nor did he feel that his emerging from retirement could in any case afford a fair prospect of doing good. His general disposition was to stand by the Prince where he felt himself unreasonably pressed, but there were questions, such as those of Ireland and Catholic Emancipation, on which he wished to remain free and unfettered. It was his opinion, moreover, that the Prince ought to prevail on some of his own friends, notably Lord Grenville, to take part in the Government.

When Perceval recounted Castlereagh's sentiments to the Regent, he was not displeased; he expressed his appreciation of the liberality, openness and honourable nature of the opinions and feelings transmitted. But Perceval himself was deeply disappointed at Castlereagh's refusal. He still persisted in the necessity of Wellesley's immediate resignation, and proposed bringing in Addington, now Lord Sidmouth.

The Prince looked at him with studied scorn, and in his most frigid manner remarked:

" Is it possible, Mr. Perceval, that you are ignorant of my feelings and sentiments towards that person? I now tell you, I never will have confidence in him, or in any person who forces him on me."

On this point the Prince would not be shaken, and his tone and his subsequent report to Wellesley of Perceval's impudence and folly, did not ease matters for the Minister.

4

The Prince still had it in mind to make Lord Wellesley head of the Government, and as soon as the restrictions on him were removed, he set about putting his plans into action. He invited Lord Grenville and Lord Grey to join Wellesley in a Coalition Government. Grey and Grenville declined to serve with Wellesley; they also declined to serve with Perceval; they also declined to accept the Government's policy, and demanded a total change of attitude towards the War, Commerce, Currency, America and Ireland. This was no small demand; it put Coalition entirely out of the question.

Another member of the administration was also retiring, and Perceval seeing his house tottering over his head, made renewed efforts to prop it up with Castlereagh and Sidmouth, but he was unsuccessful. Sidmouth was impatient for office, but the Prince would not have him; Castlereagh he could not get.

Castlereagh was not playing a game for office, which he could have had without manœuvring; he simply did not wish to be in office. His health and spirits had greatly improved since he had left the Government and it seemed to him that it would contribute neither to his fame nor happiness to be precipitated into " business " at this time. The Government's position was too precarious; the state of the country was such that Lord Grenville had declared: " There is no misery I should dread like that of undertaking, in such a state of the Court and country, any share in the government of either."

Castlereagh felt that it became him better to carry his weight in Parliament untrammelled by office, and he held aloof from all schemes.

He remained out of town as much as possible, not only because he preferred the country, but because he wanted to avoid all appearance of " caballing " with either parties.

He was at this time deeply troubled over personal matters. Lady Catherine, the wife of his brother Charles, had recently undergone a slight head operation. Charles being away she had asked Castlereagh to stay with her while it was being performed, and he had been by her side all the time. The operation had been successful, but unfortunately she caught a chill afterwards, and a few days later she died in Castlereagh's arms.

It had all been very sudden, and Castlereagh, greatly distressed, was afraid Charles might read the news in the Press before even his letters arrived. He wrote immediately to Wellington, apologising for expecting his assistance in matters of domestic calamity in the middle of his arduous duties, and asking him to give Charles the two letters which he enclosed, within a little interval of each other. The first was to prepare him for the sad news which the second contained. He also expressed a personal request that Wellington should facilitate and encourage Charles's return to England.

Deeply sensitive to his brother's sorrow he did everything in his power to soften the blow. Charles's young son, Fred, he took at once to his home, and did his best to comfort him. He wrote again to Charles, assuring him that the boy's health had not suffered in spite of his grief, and that he could be quite easy about him. Lady Castlereagh, he wrote, was very attentive to him, and it gratified him to see how well they got on together. Indeed, she took as much pleasure in the trust, he declared, as if he were her own son.

Later on he wrote to Charles that he would let his house for him for the season, as he did not wish to leave him the option of indulging his grief in that abode on his return to England. He did not know if Charles wished to return; he had mentioned it to Wellington, he said, desiring to take the responsibility for it, should it be Charles's wish, but he wanted him to do whatever he felt would best restore his mind. He hoped Charles would not think of withdrawing Fred from his care; he had arranged for tutors to come to him regularly. Lady Castlereagh had already established her authority over him, and the boy submitted to it with great good humour, and obeyed her without a single instance of mutiny on his side, or severity on hers.

CHARLES STEWART

By T. Lawrence

" I don't know how it has happened," he wrote, " that they have both hit it off so well. Whatever she says he receives as Law, as they are the best friends."

Charles's reply reveals the tender side of Castlereagh's character as nothing else could have done.

" Wellington on the 8th entered my room at Castello Branco," Charles wrote, " the same appartment in which our poor brother died[1]—I have ever felt a melancholy pleasure in inhabiting it! He desired me to prepare myself for the severest calamity. Having old political horrors in my brain at this new crisis at home, I ejaculated ' Castlereagh!'—the agonising truth then came forth—what followed I hardly know more than that I rode with Wellington to Moya and tears happily for me came to my relief.

" In confiding her boy to you she ratified my opinion and my judgment, in expiring in your arms she sealed our affections; making you with her last breath the bond of union between *herself, her boy and her husband.* How I have loved you my God can witness, what I feel to you now I can in vain describe. I have no fears for my blessed Frederic. If I were to die to-morrow, orphan as he would be he has found other parents.

" I have *one* (*letter*) *which I cannot part with*, but which you shall hereafter see. It will make your heart bleed—a history of the woeful operation, and what is more, a history of yourself, and my angel's opinion and love for you expressed *in such terms* as must penetrate very deep into your mind."

5

Proposals were still being made to Castlereagh to join the Government, but though the Prince seemed more stable, and Castlereagh was beginning to feel it his duty to serve him when called, he had some strange idea that it was a point of honour, when he returned to office, that he should go back to the War Department, which he had been forced to vacate. The old wound was still unhealed. Eventually, in March 1812, he was persuaded to return to the Government, not in his old place, but in Canning's old place, the Foreign Office.

[1] Thomas, another half-brother of Castlereagh's, had served with Wellington.

He was a great gain to the Administration, and Perceval went forward with renewed strength and confidence. Regarding Sidmouth, Perceval also wore down the Prince's resistance, and he brought Sidmouth and his friends in as well.

But two months later a horrible event occurred. On 11 May the House was sitting to examine witnesses regarding petitions against the Orders in Council which were ruining British trade; Perceval was absent, and a member started off to Downing Street to summon him. Hearing that his presence was desired, Perceval hurried into the House. The lobby was full, and as he entered, a man in tradesman's dress standing by the door drew out a pistol and fired at him. Perceval walked on one or two paces, then said faintly: " Oh, I am murdered," and fell to the ground.

His body was placed in the Speaker's house, and a doctor called, but medical aid was useless. Perceval was dead. In the House of Commons the shot had been heard, but business continued. Then a whisper ran round the House: " Someone has been shot." There was horror and distress when it was learned that it was the Prime Minister. The Speaker was summoned, and took the Chair, and the murderer was led up to the table between two officers of the House. He was identified as John Bellingham, a man of unsound mind, who thought he had been injured by some of the Minister's measures.

Bellingham was a man whose life had been loaded with misfortune. He had spent five years in prison for debt. He had been shipwrecked, bankrupt, his house had been burnt down, he had had an unhappy marriage, his father had been insane, all of which though quite distressing could not be laid to the charge of poor Perceval, who had never injured a man in his life.

He confessed later that he had meant to kill Lord Grenville, but Perceval came in his way, and he felt he must kill somebody. No one was more honest or more good-natured than Perceval, yet the people showed the most savage joy when they heard of his death. " Perceval is down," they shouted, " and the Regent must be down next." They tried to shake hands with the murderer on his way to the gallows. They tried to mount the coach. They clung to the wheels, and had to be whipped off. Bellingham was cheered and applauded like a conqueror.

By his colleagues Perceval was deeply mourned. Castlereagh, speaking in the House regarding the Prince's message of an annuity for Mrs. Perceval and her children, was so moved he was unable to finish his speech. He was " so much affected," it was said, " that he was obliged to sit down, amidst the loud cheers and strong sympathy of the House."

6

With Perceval's death the Prince Regent was in a complete turmoil. All the members of the Ministry tendered their resignation, and the problem of forming a new administration sent him nearly out of his mind. It might have turned a stronger mind than his, for none of the parties seemed able to agree on anything. The Prince's first idea was a Coalition Cabinet composed of Whigs and Tories; but the Whigs were against the Peninsular War and all for Catholic Emancipation, and the Tories were all for the Peninsular War, and for the most part against Catholic Emancipation.

The Regent sent for Lord Wellesley, and asked him to negotiate with the Whig leaders.

" Don't mention any names to me now, my lord," he said airily, " but make an administration for me."

Wellesley knew how incompatible were the two parties, and how impossible to combine.

" In a matter of such nicety," he observed, " I trust your Royal Highness will not press me for time."

" Take your own time," the Regent replied, " though there is not a shilling left in the Exchequer."

Off went Wellesley, but apparently nobody but Canning was anxious to serve with him. He did what he could to reconcile conflicting interests; he saw Grenville and Grey and Lord Moira, but had no success with any of them. He then returned to Carlton House to confer with the Prince; but he had hardly begun to speak when the Prince informed him that he was busy, and Wellesley was as good as turned out. The Prince now saw Liverpool and Eldon and conferred with them. When Wellesley saw him again, he warned the Prince that the country and the throne were in danger, and that it was perilous to leave the country without a Government. The Regent ignored his warnings. He informed him that no Prince was so beloved by the people as he was. He then began to abuse all his friends. Grey and Grenville, he declared, were a couple of scoundrels; as for Lord Moira, his once dearest friend, he was " a fellow no honest man could speak to." He raged and fumed and fretted, till Wellesley washed his hands of the whole business, and went out of town.

The Prince continued to see different people daily, and no one knew what was to happen. He went from one to the other, ran round in circles, came back to the first, interrogated the last, and was still where he was when he had started. Irresolute, changeable, capricious, full of irritation and nerves, in the end he could decide nothing. For nearly a month the country remained without a government.

Finally he sent for Moira, and flung himself upon his mercy. He cried loud and long, till he was very nearly in convulsions. "The afflicting interview," says Creevey, "was entirely occupied with lamentations over past errors, and delight at brighter prospects for the future under the happier auspices of his old and true friend now restored."

Moira told him that the country was in a grievous state. The Prince declared that this had been concealed from him by his Ministers, and that he had not seen a paper for three or four weeks. The upshot of it all was that Moira tried to form a Government. But a day or two later, when Moira was just beginning to feel his way, the Prince suddenly revoked his powers, and ordered his old servants to proceed with public business, under the leadership of Lord Liverpool.

The appointment of Lord Liverpool was a surprise to everyone. Although he had held nearly every office in the Cabinet and had proved himself able and efficient in each, he was far from being endowed with genius or even brilliance. But he was respected. When he had been at the Home Office under Pitt, and an intrigue of Canning's had led to his sending in his resignation, Pitt had informed Canning that if he must part with either, it should not be with Hawkesbury, as he was then called.

Liverpool was to be Prime Minister for fifteen years, through the most dangerous years of the war and through the more dangerous years of the peace, yet his name has left no mark on history. He has been ignored, forgotten, and even despised; for it was his fate always to be obscured by greater men. Even now, when he had attained the highest position, he was to be head of a Cabinet in which the principal figure was to be Castlereagh; for Castlereagh was soon to emerge as one of the greatest statesmen England has ever known.

7

In the new Cabinet Castlereagh remained at the Foreign Office. He also succeeded Perceval as Leader of the House of Commons, and this in spite of the fact of his being, as Lord John Russell asserts, a tiresome, involved and obscure speaker. But Lord John Russell, who sat on the Opposition benches, declares nevertheless that he never knew a man who had more influence in the House of Commons than Lord Castlereagh. "For there are qualities," he observes, "which govern men, such as sincerity, and a conviction on the part of his hearers that the Minister is a man to be trusted, which have more to do with influence over the House of Commons than the most brilliant flights of fancy and the keenest wit." It was this integrity that gave Castlereagh his power. He had no rhetorical gifts, like Pitt and Canning, with which to fire his hearers and inflame the imagination of posterity, but he had the dogged tenacity which never flinches, but holds on till the last battle is won.

The Regent now decided that he would like to have Canning, too, back in office. Castlereagh raised no objection, and a meeting was arranged. When they met, Castlereagh shook hands with Canning, and professed an admiration for his talents. Canning responded with a regard for Castlereagh's integrity, and they discussed the question of office. Castlereagh, in order to ease matters, made a gesture. He offered to relinquish his place, in order that Canning should return to his old situation, the Foreign Office; but he stipulated that he should continue to manage the House of Commons. Canning agreed to accept the Foreign Office, but he desired the leadership of the House of Commons as well. To this Castlereagh objected; he felt he had made enough sacrifice, and as Canning refused to agree on this point, the meeting broke up.

Canning admitted that the offer was perhaps the handsomest that was ever made to any individual, but his pride would not let him serve under Castlereagh in the House. Playing as usual for higher stakes, he was at length left out altogether; he was not to hold any office of importance till Castlereagh's death.

CHAPTER XI

I

FOR THE next ten years, from 1812 to 1822, Castlereagh bore the whole burden of Government in the House; at the same time he conducted the Foreign Policy of Britain at a most critical time in her history.

The state of affairs in 1812 was deplorable. At home the people were getting out of hand; the scarcity of food, the high prices, the lack of employment, were driving them to excesses. They broke into houses, and carried away arms. There were strikes and riots, and attempts at assassination. The temper of the people was such that outbursts of violence were always occurring. In the Peninsula there had been terrible slaughter, and Wellington had to be heavily reinforced. Apart from men, he needed money, and there was no money in the Exchequer. Castlereagh found, as he said, "a heavy job in every quarter." He could not recollect ever having "so tough a task." As though these difficulties were not enough, war broke out with America.

Castlereagh's first step as Foreign Minister had been to repeal the Orders in Council, but it was too late to ward off the dangers in which they had involved us, and nine days after Castlereagh had taken office, America, annoyed at our interference with her trade, declared war on England. With her strength so heavily taxed by the struggle with France, Britain felt she was being stabbed in the back. Everything seemed as black as it could be; but there was already a gleam on the horizon, for Napoleon had made a false move.

Enraged by Russia's determination to continue relations with England, he had summoned the Russian Ambassador, and had broken out in one of his famous tirades. War, he shouted, was bound to follow the Czar's repeated acts of defiance. He would march to Moscow with half a million men, with the greatest army that had ever yet been seen. He would enforce the independence of the West.

"It is the beginning of the end," murmured Talleyrand.

For Castlereagh it was the first happy day since he had come to the Foreign Office. He now took the precaution of revealing to Turkey, on whose help Napoleon was relying, the secret articles of the Treaty of Tilsit, under which part of her territories were to be annexed by France. The Sultan hastily concluded a treaty of mutual assistance with Great Britain and Russia. More than ever infuriated by this step, Napoleon began withdrawing large numbers of troops from the Peninsula for the invasion of Russia. It was the chance for which Wellington had long waited, and he did not waste an hour.

On 8 January 1812, he made a night attack on Ciudad Rodrigo, and stormed it. Although he lost heavily in casualties, he was successful. Unfortunately his men again behaved outrageously, and utterly disgraced themselves. Lost in the blazing streets, they fought for drink and plunder. Completely out of hand they started firing at one another, and into every door and window. "What the devil, sir, are you firing at?" an officer shouted at one of the soldiers. "I don't know, sir," he answered, "I am firing because everybody else is." But Ciudad Rodrigo had fallen, and Wellington was to receive an earldom from the Prince Regent.

In April 1812, he moved on to Badajoz, where he was again victorious. But the losses were so great that when he saw the casualty returns Wellington for once broke down. The gates of Portugal, however, were secured, and he marched into Spain. The French retreated, and early one June morning Wellington rode into Salamanca, cheered by the excited inhabitants. But Marmont was manœuvring in the district, and Wellington bided his time. When he attacked, he drove everything before him. Spain lay open to him, and three weeks later he was in sight of Madrid. King Joseph scuttled out of his capital, and Madrid made preparations to welcome the conquerors. Bells were pealed, olive branches waved, the road ran wine as the troops entered. New honours were showered on Wellington. He was created a Marquis. But after Madrid the fortress of Burgos barred his way, and he could not take it, nor could he maintain his advanced position without it.

The autumn passed, and the French gathered to north and south of him; the rain drove down; there was nothing to do but make an attempt on the fortress. The attempt failed, Madrid itself was threatened, and Wellington turned back, getting clear, as he said, of the worst scrape he ever was in. He retreated to Salamanca, but here again the French armies gathered around him, the rain continued, and he had to march his men right back to Portugal. The retreat was miserable; supplies went astray; the men starved; the rains drove down. " By God, it was too serious to say anything."

2

Help was to come however from another quarter. The Grand Army had crossed the Niemen; Napoleon had started on his Russian campaign. He had said he was going " only to free Poland," but no one was convinced by that. He had said he would defeat Russia in " two battles," and all would be over by the end of September; that had seemed at the time no idle boast.

Castlereagh, however, had been pouring subsidies and munitions into Russia, and he had every hope that Russia would hold out. On his farm at Cray he was in happy mood. In the spring, only two or three months before, he had written to Charles with grave anxiety that Napoleon had got Russia, Austria and Prussia in close alliance, and that the Turks were still our enemies. But since that time Castlereagh had managed to bring the Turks and Russia into an alliance with Britain; Napoleon, moreover, had drawn off his best troops from the Peninsula; he had ventured out without securing his back door, an imprudent move. Though Wellington had been unfortunate, Castlereagh still backed him; if he were kept well supplied, the trick, no doubt, would be done.

It was pleasant to lie on the grass during the warm summer days and think of Napoleon penetrating deeper and deeper into the mysterious depths of Russia, marching on and on across that endless plain. But it was a rude awakening when a few weeks later there came news that the French were in Moscow. At Borodino, at the very gates of the capital, they had fought the bloodiest of battles; it had nearly ended in Napoleon's defeat, but he had won. Berlin, Vienna, and now—Moscow.

Apart from the capture of Moscow, the war with America was giving the Government some concern. We were losing too many ships. The American Navy was small, but the Americans had excellent seamanship and gunnery, and were inflicting great injury on British trade and British prestige. Three British frigates had been captured, one after the other; the *Guerrière* had been burnt, and the *Macedonian* had been brought as a prize into an American port.

" It cannot be too deeply felt," said Canning, " that the sacred spell of the invincibility of the British Navy was broken by these unfortunate captures."

England began to mass a huge armament in Chesapeake Bay and in the Delaware River, and the following year was to see no repetition of the American victories. The Americans were not to meet with any great success in Canada either. In July 1812, they not only retreated before the British General, Brock, but the American General, Hull, surrendered his whole army to an inferior force and ceded a large extent of territory. Detroit and Chicago surrendered, and the British were soon masters of the whole of Michigan.

America had declared war when Napoleon was at the height of his power, but the face of the world was changing, for as winter descended there came news that Napoleon's army was in retreat.

Thirty thousand horses perished in one night, and half his men were buried in the snows of Russia. There followed a report that Moscow was in flames, but whether the French had burnt it down or the Russians, nobody knew. Soon the London papers were announcing that Napoleon himself had narrowly escaped capture; he had jumped out of the back window of a building just as the Russian cossacks were entering the yard.

London went mad with excitement. Castlereagh and Liverpool had reason to congratulate themselves. Although Russia had handled the campaign pretty well, she could never have held out if they had not kept her so well supplied. Without Britain's support it might have been Tilsit all over again.

But they had not finished with Napoleon yet. Though he had deserted his army and was now speeding across Europe in an old sledge, making his way back to Paris, he was full of new plans. His health, he said, was as good as ever. He had left 300,000 soldiers dead or captured in Russia, but his army, he declared, had not been defeated once. It was winter and hunger, not the enemy, that had decimated his troops. He would raise another 300,000 men, and would be back again on the Niemen in the spring.

But Castlereagh had already started putting into motion his great plan for a Grand Alliance. Three European coalitions had been formed by Pitt during the war, each of which had ended in allied defeats. The fourth coalition, which Castlereagh through so many difficulties was to form, established an alliance which brought the war to a successful conclusion, and settled the peace of Europe for forty years.

3

Castlereagh moved cautiously. For the moment he continued to pour subsidies and supplies into Russia. But subsidies were not enough. Alexander needed troops; he needed the help of Bernadotte, the Crown Prince of Sweden, whose army lay on Russia's flank. Although Bernadotte was a Frenchman, and had been one of Napoleon's generals, although he was married to the sister of Joseph Buonaparte's wife, he was ready, for a price, to abandon Napoleon and support Russia; but his price was Norway. Out of dire necessity Alexander now conceded to him a country which was not his to give away, and Castlereagh, knowing that the support of Bernadotte was indispensable to Russia, calmly acquiesced. He sent subsidies to Bernadotte to ensure his support, and coolly guaranteed that Norway, which was the property of Denmark, should be assigned to Sweden after the war.

In Parliament, Castlereagh received a good deal of criticism for this act, and even his admirers felt that it was hardly well done; but Bernadotte could not be bought for anything less than Norway, and Europe had to be saved. As a result of Britain's guarantee, Bernadotte agreed to take the field with 90,000 men.

Having given Russia every support Castlereagh turned his attention to Austria and Prussia, and made every effort to detach these Powers from the French Alliance. The sight of Napoleon's Grand Army staggering back from Moscow, pursued by the Russians, had emboldened Prussia, and a movement had started for Germany's liberation. This movement was fostered by Alexander, who crossed the Niemen on 1 January 1813, into Germany. Regarding himself as the heaven-sent saviour of Europe, and the guardian of international justice, he offered his assistance to all people who should abandon the cause of Napoleon. " Germans," ran his General's proclamation, " we open the Russian ranks to you: there you will find the labourer side by side with the prince. All distinctions of rank are effaced before the great idea of King, liberty, honour and country." Aided by British subsidies the proclamation had its effect, and by the time Napoleon got back to Central Europe with his new army, Prussia had been detached from the French alliance, and had joined Russia and Britain.

As soon as the alliance with Prussia was effected, Castlereagh sent his brother Charles to Prussian H.Q. as Britain's accredited representative. Arms and ammunition followed. Germany had been roused before Napoleon had had time to bring into action his new army, and in the Spring, when Napoleon reappeared in Central Europe he could not get to the Niemen because Prussia barred his way.

But Napoleon still had Austria in alliance, for Castlereagh's attempts to wean her from Napoleon's side had not met with any great success. Marie Louise was still Empress of France, and the Emperor of Austria would not proceed against his own daughter. Further, he had no desire to strengthen Alexander. It was not in the interests of Austria to have a too powerful Russia as her neighbour; but it was not in her interests to have a too powerful France either.

Her chief desire at this moment was peace. The failure of Napoleon's Russian campaign had so changed the position of France that peace seemed to Austria not only desirable but possible; but Britain was not ready to make peace with Napoleon until he was either overthrown or pushed back beyond the Rhine. The Emperor Francis was toying with the idea of acting as mediator between France and the allies, when Napoleon fell on the Prussian forces at Lutzen. Dashing from column to column with all his former energy, his young army fighting like veterans, he routed Blücher and his whole army. A fortnight later he crushed the combined forces of Prussia and Russia at Bautzen.

Recriminations began to arise between the Russians and their Prussian allies. " Better the French as enemies than the Russians as friends," the Prussians were already saying. It seemed to the Austrian Emperor a good moment for his offer of mediation, and his Minister, Metternich, was instructed to approach Napoleon.

Metternich had considerable gifts. Although he posed as a man of fashion, and had a great reputation with women, he was the wiliest of diplomats. He offered Austria's mediation to Napoleon on the basis of the natural boundaries of France—the Rhine, the Alps, and the Pyrenees. At the same time he gave an undertaking to Alexander that if Napoleon did not accept his terms he would join the coalition against France.

Castlereagh was not by any means in favour of an Austrian mediation, but he was inclined as ever to proceed cautiously. "The risk of treaty with France is great," he wrote to Cathcart,[1] "but the risk of losing our continental allies and the confidence of our own nation is greater": and he watched with great anxiety the development of the Austrian schemes.

4

On 26 June 1813, Metternich went to Dresden for an interview with the Emperor of France. It was a dramatic meeting. Metternich laid down his terms, and informed Napoleon that an Austrian army, fully mobilised and numbering 250,000 men, awaited his decision. Napoleon burst into one of his tirades. " So you too want war? " he shouted, " Well, you shall have it. I annihilated the Prussian army at Lutzen; I smashed the Russians at Bautzen; now you want to have your turn. Very well—we shall meet in Vienna." He blustered and fumed. He spoke of the terms offered him as though they were degrading. He had been offered the France of the Bourbon monarchy, the Netherlands, what he could hold of Spain, what he held of Italy, even the Illyrian provinces; but he was maddened by Metternich's attitude, and by the fact that an Austrian army was trying to coerce him. He questioned the strength of the Austrian army. Metternich coolly questioned the strength of Napoleon's army. "I have seen your

[1] British Minister at St. Petersburg.

soldiers," he said, " they are mere children. And when these infants have been wiped out, what will you have left? "

Napoleon was beside himself with anger. Flinging his hat into a corner he shouted: " You are not a soldier and you do not know what goes on in the mind of a soldier. I grew up on the field of battle, and a man such as I am does not concern himself about the lives of a million of men."

Metternich let the hat lie where it fell, and leaning against a little table which stood between the windows, said calmly, " If only the words you have just uttered could echo from one end of France to the other."

For a moment Napoleon was taken aback. He began pacing round the room talking all the while to cover his discomfiture. He had tried to weld the new world with the old, he said ; he should have known better ; he should never have married an Archduchess of Austria; it was a mistake. He went on walking round the room, and talking. On his second way round he noticed his hat lying in the corner, and picked it up himself.

Doubt must have begun to enter his mind, for he said: " It may cost me my throne, but I will bury the whole world beneath its ruins."

The interview lasted nine hours. When Marshal Berthier, who followed Metternich to his carriage, asked him anxiously if the Emperor had satisfied him, Metternich replied: " *C'est un homme perdu.*"

He waited at Dresden expecting to hear from Napoleon again. As no message came he made a show of packing his trunks for departure. The manœuvre succeeded, and a message arrived from Napoleon inviting him to return for another interview. At this second meeting, which took place in the gardens of the Marcolini Palace, Napoleon signed the four brief articles which Metternich had drawn up. These committed him to accept Austria's armed mediation, to send a representative to a conference which should take place at Prague between 20 July and 10 August, and to discontinue military operations between those dates.

From all these negotiations Britain had been shut out. Castlereagh was uneasy. He made it clear that Britain would never subscribe to a peace in which her own interests and commitments were disregarded, and that no further subsidies would be forthcoming so long as Britain was excluded from the inner councils of the allies.

At the same time he directed Cathcart to offer Austria half a million pounds if she took the field against Napoleon. But it was not Castlereagh's bribes or his warnings that broke up the negotiations, it was the news of Wellington's triumph in the Peninsula; for suddenly there came a report that Wellington had cleared the French out of Spain. Leaving Portugal in the spring he had again advanced across Spain, recovering half the country before the French could concentrate their forces. With the French falling back before him all the way, he had reached Vittoria, the last foothold of the Pyrenees on the great road to France. Here, on 21 June 1813, he routed the French armies, and sent King Joseph flying out of the country.

The news of the battle of Vittoria altered the attitude of the allies completely. They were on the eve of signing terms, which would have left Napoleon nearly as powerful as before. The news that Britain had cleared the French out of Spain encouraged them to abandon the negotiations and to continue the war. Napoleon's acceptance was rejected, rockets illumined the skies, bonfires were lighted, proclaiming to a weary world that Austria was marching against Napoleon ; hostilities had recommenced. By the middle of August the armies of Russia, Prussia, Austria and Sweden were ranged against France. Castlereagh had formed his coalition.

With his back to the wall, Napoleon was still to fight an un-rivalled campaign. Before the Austrians were ready, he was on them. At the battle of Dresden they retreated before him leaving their cannon and 20,000 prisoners in his hands. But he failed to take advantage of his victory, for his army was melting away, and the allied forces were now double his strength.

In the neighbourhood of Leipzig, in October 1813, the allies closed round him. At this moment, when a concentration of all the allied forces was necessary, Bernadotte began to give trouble. On the first day of the great battle which now opened, his army did not appear; he had actually declared that he would not cross the Elbe, and would merely look to operations that might secure him Norway. Instead of combining with the Prussians as directed, he detached himself entirely from the action, and exposed Blücher to very great danger.

Charles Stewart, discovering that Bernadotte had decided to take no part in the battle, wrote him a sharp letter, and followed it by calling on him. There was a stormy interview, and though it ended amicably with Bernadotte inviting Charles to dinner to meet the Emperor of Russia and the King of Prussia, it did not prevent Charles writing to Castlereagh that Bernadotte was a terrible cheat and quite artificial, and that if he had not been there Bernadotte's army would have played no part before Leipzig. Charles's efforts resulted in the army arriving on the second day. Combining with Blücher, Bernadotte's troops closed in from the north; Schwarzenberg with the Austrians and Russians moved up from the south; and the French were hemmed in by a great circle of fire. The Bavarians deserted Napoleon before the battle, the Saxon Corps during the battle, and Napoleon found his retreat cut off by his very allies. His last bridge was blown up. The Battle of the Nations was over. The allied troops were swarming into the city. Charles, without waiting for the news to be dispatched through the regular channels, immediately wrote off to Castlereagh and gave England the first intelligence of the great victory.

6

After the battle was over, while the allied forces were marching towards the French frontier, the allied sovereigns met at Frankfort and again started negotiations. The Frankfort proposals which were now drawn up were still favourable to Napoleon. They conceded to him, after the disasters of Moscow and of Leipzig, terms most advantageous, and a territory larger than Louis XIV had ever ruled at the height of his power. Yet Napoleon hesitated. He could not bring himself to give in. With his usual bluster, he declared that the conditions were unacceptable, that he was for war. But he was devoured by apprehensions, and he sent for Caulaincourt, who had long been

TSAR ALEXANDER

*By T. Lawrence, from the Waterloo Chamber
at Windsor Castle*

advocating peace, and made him his Foreign Minister. After a long delay a reply was dispatched to the allies in which Napoleon declared himself ready to accept in form the basis proposed. But he made many exceptions, protesting among other things against the Maritime laws of England.

There were three envoys now at H.Q. Charles Stewart, Cathcart, and Lord Aberdeen, who had lately been accredited to Austria. Lord Aberdeen, a very young and inexperienced diplomat, concealed the concessions that were being made to Napoleon both from Cathcart and from Stewart, and approved them. Stewart, when he heard of the negotiations, was deeply incensed and wrote off to Castlereagh post haste.

When he received the dispatch Castlereagh was greatly perturbed. Apart from the Maritime question, which was always of paramount importance in his eyes, he viewed with alarm the fact that France was to be left with a frontier on the Rhine, which gave her Antwerp, the Scheldt, and Flushing, as well as the whole of Flanders, from which point she would always be a menace to Great Britain. In return for these amenities Britain was to surrender the best part of her colonies.

Writing to Aberdeen in his usual calm, unruffled manner, he informed him that the terms would leave ungained the main object of the war which was security for the future, and he instructed Aberdeen to urge the continuation of the war until France could be restricted to the frontier limits of 1790. He made no demand for the dethronement of Napoleon, nor did he resist the return of the Colonies, and he assured Metternich of the disposition of the Cabinet to support Austria in every reasonable demand. But he objected to the clause regarding Britain's Maritime Rights, and he pressed for the destruction of the arsenal at Antwerp.

Although he appeared calm outwardly he was, as Lord Grenville wrote to the Marquis of Buckingham, " in a fever about it."

" I hear this morning from my brother," Lord Grenville wrote on 24 December 1813, " that Napoleon has notified the Senate of his acceptance of the basis of negotiations proposed by the allies. I do not wonder that Castlereagh is in a fever about it. My brother says that he is setting out for Mannheim; and certainly that is his only chance of having any finger in the pie. As to terms of peace, I am as little disposed as anyone to approve of a disgraceful or insincere termination of the contest. But, alas! the decision is not with us . . .

" If Lord Castlereagh does not make haste, I am confident he will find a separate peace signed. If he comes in time to put his name to it, that I fancy will be all the share he will have in it, except the honour of buying Holland or Italy with the best part of our conquests."

In spite of Lord Grenville's fears Castlereagh turned the situation, and managed to dissuade the allies from pursuing the Frankfort negotiations. The march of events aided him, for the allied troops had by this time crossed into France; Murat, the King of Naples, had joined the allies, and it was becoming more and more evident that there was no reason why the allies should not aim at the highest stakes.

The Prussians were burning to wipe out the disgrace of Jena; the Austrians saw an opportunity of regaining their ascendancy in Italy; the Czar himself became fired by the idea of entering Paris in truimph. They all adopted Castlereagh's view that the war should continue.

Metternich now returned an evasive reply to Napoleon. He stated that France had been very tardy in returning an answer to the Frankfort proposals, but he would nevertheless communicate her reply to the allied cabinets ; and the war continued.

It had been a critical moment for Great Britain. Peace had nearly been arrived at on terms most unfavourable to this country, terms to which Aberdeen had already agreed; but Castlereagh, taking advantage of the successes gained in the field and of the subsidies which were being poured into Europe, had by his intervention warded off disaster.

The war on the Continent was nearing its end, but the war with America was still giving us trouble. Although during the year 1813 the British Navy was blockading the whole of the coast of the United States, completely destroying American trade, American privateers managed to run the blockade, and actually captured British vessels even off the coasts of Ireland and of Scotland. Our Navy seized one vessel after another, notably the American sloop, *Argus*, which had been destroying one vessel a day in the British Channel, where it coasted for a month before it was captured. Practically the whole of the American Navy was shut up in American ports, yet the privateers continued to be the greatest menace. British cruisers caught them by the score, but faster and better vessels appeared; they rendered even transport to Ireland unsafe, and almost blockaded the British Isles.

But the Allied armies had now entered France; Wellington had driven Joseph out of Spain, and Britain was more free to deal with America. Castlereagh was most anxious for this futile war to end, but when Russia offered to mediate between America and England, he declined the offer, preferring, as he said, to negotiate with the American Commissioners direct. Albert Gallatin, Secretary of the Treasury of the United States, was sent to London therefore to hasten the approach of peace.

Writing to Clay, Speaker of the House of Representatives, Gallatin said: "Lord Castlereagh is, according to the best information I can collect, the best disposed man in the Cabinet." But though Castlereagh did all he could to effect a settlement, the negotiations did not prosper, for the President still insisted on the abandonment of impressment, which Britain refused to give up.

The war in Canada was full of vicissitudes, victories and failures following each other in quick succession. In January 1813, we gained a victory over the Americans at Frenchtown. In April the Americans captured York, the capital of upper Canada, where they burnt down the House of Assembly and other buildings. For this act severe retaliations were taken by the British. In September the Americans recovered Detroit, which we had captured in 1812, destroying Fort George and burning down the village of Newark.

The British replied by crossing the frontier and sweeping the country with fire and sword as far as Buffalo. Not more than seven hundred or eight hundred British soldiers ever crossed the Detroit river, but the United States raised fully twenty thousand men and spent at least five million dollars in expelling them.[1] American trade was ruined; the Americans could not sell their crops; but they refused to make peace till England abandoned her right of search. The American War was to continue for eight months after the war with Europe had come to an end.

[1] Henry Adams, *History of the United States.*

7

The close of the year 1813 saw the Allied armies marching towards Paris. The Cabinet was of the opinion that war was practically over, and all that remained to be done, was to settle the general terms of peace. After the narrow escape England had had, it was evident that some ambassador of greater weight and experience than the three accredited representatives should be sent to Allied headquarters.

Count Pozzo di Borgo had already been dispatched to London from Headquarters to inform the Government that a situation in which the three British envoys—Stewart, Cathcart and Aberdeen—all contradicted each other, was not one which could be allowed to continue, and that a representative with full powers should be sent out at once. To Castlereagh himself he said, "If you can resurrect Pitt, send him, but if that is not possible, come yourself."

As leader of the House of Commons, Castlereagh's presence in Parliament was not easily dispensed with. Liverpool could not do without him, but he was the only person who could be entrusted with the delicate work of deciding important questions on his own initiative without waiting for instructions from the distant Cabinet. It was decided, therefore, that he should go to the Continent when Parliament rose, spend his Christmas holidays settling the affairs of Europe, and when Parliament met be back again with the peace in his pocket.

"The march of events," wrote Castlereagh to Aberdeen, on 22 December 1813, "is so rapid, the points at issue so important, and the impossibility of keeping pace, by instructions from home, with the necessity for them abroad, is such as to require, were it practicable, that the Government itself should repair to Headquarters. As it is, they have thought it right that I should, during the recess, proceed there, to make such arrangements as the existing circumstances may require on the spot."

No one was more suited than Castlereagh for this office. It needed a mind patient, resolute, resourceful, an understanding competent to deal with all the complicated points at issue; it needed infinite tact. Castlereagh had these essential qualities; he had, moreover, that personal dignity, that cool detachment, which won him such respect and admiration in an assembly of foreign potentates, who could never take an impartial view on any question, or regard any issue without heat and rancour. It was little wonder that the British envoys failed to work in harmony when among the rulers and diplomats there was continual dissension. At the moment when Castlereagh was sent out to headquarters the coalition was at breaking point, the war was in fact far from over, and he could have had little inkling of the storm that awaited him.

CHAPTER XII

I

EMILY DECIDED at once to accompany her husband to Europe. She was delighted at the idea of travelling abroad, and immediately invited her niece, Lady Emma Sophia, and her nephew, Valletort, to join the party. On Sunday, the 26 December 1813, they were assembled at St. James's Square ready to start, but Castlereagh himself was absent. He had spent almost the whole of Christmas Eve and Christmas Day at Cabinet meetings, and even on the Sunday, when the little party was waiting to set out, and the carriages were at the door, he was in council with the Cabinet. His instructions he had already drawn up for himself, but there were many points still to be discussed.

His main object was not the dethronement of Napoleon, but the protection of British interests. He was determined that French territory should be restricted to the boundaries of 1792, but he was mainly concerned with Maritime Rights. "At all times," he had written to Aberdeen, "a Maritime question touches us to the quick." Apart from Maritime Rights his chief preoccupation was Antwerp. He was prepared to surrender any of our colonial conquests—provided they had no naval value—in return for the exclusion of France from any naval establishment on the Scheldt. To strengthen our interests in Antwerp he desired to unite Belgium with Holland, and he planned to bring these two countries into closer relationship with England by a marriage between the Prince of Orange and Princess Charlotte, heiress presumptive to the English crown.

Finally, he was anxious to establish a grand alliance of the continental powers, which should be continued after the war was over, to maintain the peace of Europe.

While Lady Castlereagh was waiting for her husband to return from the Cabinet meeting, a message arrived from Princess Charlotte who desired to see her before she left. At this time Princess Charlotte was not at all averse to a marriage with the hereditary Prince of Orange. He was a pleasing young man, good humoured and unaffected. Having lived five or six years in England, and having served with our army in the Peninsula, he seemed to be attached to everything English; whenever possible he wore his English military uniform, and when in full dress he never appeared without the Peninsula clasps. Princess Charlotte gave Emily a letter for the Prince, and they remained together for some time. When Emily got back to St. James's Square, Castlereagh was still absent. They had decided to start at 11 o'clock in the morning, but the day wore on, and it was not till 6.30 in the evening that he appeared. They took a hurried meal, and started at once on their journey.

There had been fog all day, and it was now so thick that the carriages went at a foot's pace with men holding flambeaux at the horses' heads. Misfortune followed them, for when the next day the fog cleared, and they went on board, they were becalmed, and for three days were obliged to anchor off Harwich. It was a bitterly cold winter, so cold that oxen were roasted on the frozen waters of the Thames. Such a frost had not been known, Lady Calvert noted in her diary, in the memory of man. To add to their discomfort, a violent gale arose as soon as they set sail, and they were tumbling about all over the deck together. Oscillating in calms and fogs and gales, ever up and down and never forwards, it was sad work, and they were happy enough when they at last sighted shore. But now there were further difficulties, for neither the captain nor the pilot seemed to know the Dutch coast, and for three wretched days and nights the ship tossed about in the open sea in sight of land. At one moment they were in great danger, but fortunately the captain of a frigate saw their plight from the shore and sent a Dutch pilot to their rescue. It was not till 5 January that they landed at Helvoetsluys. It had taken them eight days to reach the coast of Holland.

After the rigours of this journey it is quite surprising to find Emily protesting at being left behind at The Hague with Lord and Lady Clancarty,[1] while Castlereagh and his secretaries continued their weary

[1] Earl of Clancarty, British Ambassador to The Hague.

journey to Headquarters. The state of the roads and the movement of the armies, Castlereagh felt, made it too dangerous for her to accompany them, and he would not hear of her proceeding farther for the time being. One of the factors which unsettled her no doubt was a letter awaiting her from Castlereagh's brother, Charles. The gallantry of the soldier is far more evident in Charles's letters than the tact of the diplomat. At this moment he was writing to Emily :

" MY DEAREST LADY CASTLEREAGH,

I cry for joy—one word—don't be deterred by man, woman, or child. Remember I guarantee with my head your satisfaction, your safety, your delight. Put yourself by the side of your beloved lord, and come on to Headquarters. I'll be prepared for you, and if I don't take care of you, never say I am a soldier. We have ladies in abundance, Princess Wolkonski, etc., Lady Burghersh, Mde. Mademanhoff and our host. You will be as well with me as at the Hague. If Headquarters move across the Rhine or into Switzerland Friedberg is a nice town. We'll see the fall of the Rhine. I shall cut now all military and diplomatical concerns. Castlereagh has given me my quietus. I'll go pleasuring with you, so mind what I say and come to me. Bring your *side* saddle. I'll never forgive you if you don't come.

Ever your most affectionate

C. S."

To Castlereagh he wrote, " I am so perfectly enchanted, my dearest Castlereagh, that I know not whether to stand on my heels or on my head when the delight of embracing you is so near at hand." Things were " *dans une telle embrouillement,*" he added, that it was a matter of relief to everyone that Castlereagh was on the way.

Staying at The Hague but a few hours, during which time he arranged for the marriage between the Prince of Orange and Princess Charlotte—a union so well planned but which was never to materialise—Castlereagh pressed on to Headquarters travelling day and night. The journey was extremely difficult; the weather was so bad it took him ten and a half hours to do twenty miles. It was bitterly cold, the roads were worse than a ploughed field frozen, and he and Robinson,[1] who accompanied him, hardly saw any other object for

[1] F. J. Robinson, later Earl of Ripon, Treasurer of the Navy.

days than the four panes of glass of their carriage covered with a frost that no sun could dissolve.

Often Castlereagh would get out of the carriage and walk a great part of the way to spare the horses, as they slid over the frozen roads. But with his usual composure, he wrote to Emily: "The weather is cold but wholesome, and we have no right to complain." She was still agitating to join him, but nothing would reconcile him to her undertaking such a journey, on such roads, at such a season.

The journey was slow, and events moved fast, and by the time he got to Frankfort, Headquarters had already moved on to Basle. Stopping for a moment to buy some Frankfort fineries for Emily, which he dispatched with the hope that his lace would not prove English, he moved on to Basle. He had received a very confidential message from the Emperor Alexander, who wished him to know that he would be at Basle from the 1st to the 13th January, and especially desired that Castlereagh would see him before he saw any Minister either of Russia or of any other Power, as he wished to deliver his sentiments to Castlereagh first.

Up to this moment the fate of Europe had been in the hands of Russia, Austria and Prussia. England had not appeared. She was now to advance step by step on the scene until she gained the decisive rôle. The principal actor in the drama that was unfolding itself was henceforth to be Castlereagh. It was he who was to hold the thread of all the negotiations; from now on nobody could start a Congress or complete a Treaty without Castlereagh.

"With a mind direct and penetrating," wrote the French statesman and historian, Thiers, "a character firm and prudent, capable at the same time of vigour and of caution, having in his manner the proud simplicity of the English, he was called upon to exercise, and did in effect exercise, the greatest influence. He was, on almost every matter, furnished with absolute powers. With his character, with his instructions, one could say of him that he was England herself in the camp of the Coalition. Without him nobody would take a resolution or give a reply. Everybody wanted to see him first, to talk to him first, in order to gain him over to their side." [1]

Castlereagh was not to see the Czar of Russia first, for the journey

[1] Thiers, *Histoire du Consulat et de l'Empire*. Tome Dix-huitième.

from The Hague to Frankfort had occupied him six days, even though he had spent only one night in bed ; and though it was now thawing and he was able to press on, he did not arrive in Basle till the 18th January. By that time the Czar had departed. He had waited two days beyond the 13th, but had now had to move on to join his armies.

The Emperor of Austria and the King of Prussia, who were still at Basle, were equally anxious to see Castlereagh. They received him warmly, and assured him of their gratitude for the support they had received from Great Britain. He spent a few hours with the Austrian Minister, Metternich, and they went over the whole position together.

The main difficulty, Metternich informed him, would be not France's frontiers, but Poland and Saxony; for Alexander had now decided to annex Poland, and to give Saxony to Prussia in compensation for the Polish province she would be forced to relinquish. But Austria would never agree, he added, to Alexander's possession of the whole Polish frontier, nor to the disposal of Saxony for Prussia's benefit. Their meetings over these questions had become so heated that co-operation was now impossible. It was a perplexing problem. Castlereagh had no desire to see the Prussians at Dresden, and cared still less to see Russia in the heart of Europe.

Alexander had it in mind moreover, Metternich continued, to give the crown of France to Bernadotte. This piece of news startled Castlereagh considerably. Metternich's idea of imposing a regency on France under Marie Louise, for Napoleon's infant son, did not appeal to him either, but the idea of forcing Bernadotte on the French nation was far more repugnant.

He was delighted, however, to discover that Maritime Rights did not interest Austria at all, and that he and Metternich were in complete accord regarding the balance of power, both of them fearing the danger which Europe might have to meet in the growing power of Russia. Napoleon later declared: " Russia is the Power that marches the most surely and with the greatest strides towards universal dominion . . . for now there is no France and therefore no equilibrium."

Quietly Castlereagh adjusted his views. Very soon his charming manner, and his careful consideration of every point, resulted in his gaining the confidence of the other negotiators. Between himself and Metternich a friendship was early established. Metternich found him " absolutely straight." " Castlereagh behaves like an angel," he wrote to Schwarzenberg: and in his memoirs he noted down: "A stranger to all prejudice, as just as he is kind, Lord Castlereagh knew at a glance how to distinguish the truth in everything." Although their relations were harmonious, Castlereagh took a shrewd view of Metternich's character. "Metternich," he said, "is constitutionally temporising; he is charged with more faults than belong to him, but he has his full share, mixed up, however, with considerable means for carrying forward the machine, more than any other person I have met with at headquarters."

By the time Castlereagh met the Emperor of Russia at his Headquarters at Langres he was pretty well informed. Writing to Liverpool on 30 January 1814, he said: "I think our greatest danger at present is from the Chevaleresque tone in which the Emperor Alexander is disposed to push the war. He has a personal feeling about Paris, and seems to seek for the occasion of entering with his magnificent guards the enemy's capital. The idea that a rapid negotiation might disappoint this hope adds to his impatience." And he issued a discreet warning: "The Russian cavalry is a most formidable military power."

The discussions at Langres did not go very smoothly. Caulaincourt, Napoleon's envoy, was at this time urging that the Frankfort proposals, which Napoleon had accepted and to which Aberdeen had agreed, should be put into force, but the Czar, who was chiefly responsible for the Frankfort proposals, flushed now with success, was determined to dictate peace terms from Paris, as a reprisal for Moscow, and had no desire for negotiations. The Austrians on the other hand would not consent to march unless negotiations continued.

It seemed to Castlereagh that the only means of saving the Coalition from disintegrating was to form a General Alliance. But neither Russia nor Austria was willing to enter into any such compact until a settlement of the Polish question had been reached. Distrust and prejudice and hatred ruled the allies, their disputes were interminable, and there seemed no way of adjusting their differences.

Castlereagh took a firm hand; he informed them that Great Britain would refuse to surrender any of her colonial conquests until an agreement had been reached, an agreement such as would insure "that having reduced France by their union, they were not likely to re-establish her authority by differences among themselves." He insisted that France should be confined to her ancient limits, that

Caulaincourt should be informed that maritime rights were to be excluded from the discussions, and that Belgium should be united with Holland. After some discussion the allies agreed to these demands; and the vexed question of Poland and Saxony, which concerned Castlereagh less than British interests, was left to be settled at a Congress to be held in Vienna. Without even committing himself to the surrender of a single colony, he had gained all his points.

" We may now be considered," he wrote home, " as practically delivered from the embarrassments of the Frankfort proposals." Years later, Napoleon asserted that it was Castlereagh, and Castlereagh alone, who had prevented peace being concluded on the basis of the Frankfort proposals.

Although Castlereagh was anxious for military operations to continue, he was equally anxious for peace negotiations not to be broken off, and on 2 February 1814, the Ministers assembled at Chatillon to discuss terms. On that same day Blücher gained a victory over Napoleon at La Rothière. The victory went to Alexander's head and increased his determination to march on Paris. The Prussians supporting him, enthusiasm ran high.

Writing to Emily the following day, Castlereagh said: " Charles went over yesterday to old Blücher to pay him a visit after his battle. He says the old boy invited them all to dine with him at the Palais Royale on the 20 February with all the *mamselles*."

Alexander was now declaring that he would enter Paris, dethrone Napoleon, and set up any claimant likely to win the support of France. He was under the impression that Napoleon had been decisively defeated, and that the road to Paris lay open. Without consulting the allies, and to the great annoyance of Castlereagh, he sent an order for the negotiations at Chatillon to be suspended.

2

Charles, who was also under the impression that Paris was the next step, was writing to Emily urging her again to come to Headquarters, in spite of Castlereagh's instructions that she should remain at The Hague. " Metternich and all Headquarters say you should have come," he wrote to her, " mine would have been the task, and only mine, to take care of you, and if I did not execute it satisfactorily, mine would have been the Disgrace.

" Castlereagh wants my Princesses, this is the fact. He is as buxom and prinkety as 15, and Paris and triumphal arches puts the Hague and Dutch fraus out of the heads of the settlers of the world. You don't know how pleased his newly arrived Excellency is, by Count Razumowski asking me in perfect gravity which was the eldest brother of the two? What think you of this? Is it not time for me to hand over Princesses! . . .

" It is all nonsense to stick at the Hague—why not come and see the fun, fighting is all a farce now. I am very happy having nothing to do, but I want some Princesses to escort, so pray set out, and bring Lady Emma. As to Castlereagh he has not a word to throw to a cat on this sort of business. He thinks you are comfortably stow'd, and you know he spits on what I say, and I never can move him, nor have I any particle of influence.

" We march to-day for Chaumont and Troyes. Keep it snug, but the *Autocrat*[1] has set his soul on going to Paris, and nothing will prevent him. I wish, however, one could know what he would do when he gets there. I don't think your conjuror can fish out this.

" . . . Castlereagh is in high health, and vigour, still I believe he is not over happy in an Herculean labour. Tell Clancarty I have shut up shop and if he has any new trade in his Quarter I can turn to I am the man. In diplomacy I am voted incapable. . . . Adieu, dearest Lady Castlereagh. You shall hear from me in a day or two again, at present I am bored and out of sorts, as I have my humour, and things are not going my way to-day.

Yours most affectionately,

CHARLES STEWART "

Charles must have shown this letter to Castlereagh, for Castlereagh hastens to calm Emily's suspicions. " I suppose after Charles's long and humbugging epistle I shall be in your black books," he writes her, " but I am the honest man and he is the gay deceiver. I have now made acquaintance with all the great wigs here. The Emperor Alexander would be your favourite. He has 30,000 Guards here that are the finest soldiers I ever beheld. When I can calculate at all

[1] " The Autocrat " was Charles Stewart's nickname for Alexander.

movements or events, you shall have my plans. Till then don't stir, lest I should give you the slip and return by Paris.

" I am quite well. Work is hard—and never see a single Princess. So God preserve you. C."

However difficult the position he had to face, however harassed he might be, he always wrote to Emily in the same light, playful vein. At the moment he was deeply concerned about the Czar's attitude. He felt that if the allies could obtain peace now on the basis of the ancient limits it was wrong for them to risk further casualties. Metternich and Hardenberg [1] were in agreement with him, but Alexander declined to accept their decision, and even declared that he would not accept a " majority vote." Metternich again threatened to make a separate peace, and Castlereagh hurried to Headquarters at Troyes, where he had a stormy interview with the Czar.

Alexander was determined to suspend all negotiations till Paris was taken. Castlereagh informed him that his determination to dictate peace from Paris was full of hazard and at direct variance with the principles upon which the confederacy had been cemented, that it might lead to disgrace and disunion. He pointed out that it was one thing to take Paris as a natural result of military operations; it was another to go there to set up a new government, the character of which was not yet determined. And what would be the attitude of the French people, he asked, towards a sovereign whom the allies had forced on them at the point of the bayonet?

The interview was not a pleasant one. It ended by Alexander suggesting that Castlereagh was not accurately representing the views of the Prince Regent, or of the Cabinet, or of British public opinion. He informed Castlereagh that the Prince Regent had no desire for a peace with Napoleon, that Count Lieven had had an interview with him, in which he had declared that he was in favour of a Bourbon restoration.

Castlereagh took his stand. He denied in the first place the Czar's right to question his powers. He then informed him that he did not consider it either honourable or politic to support a Bourbon claimant while in negotiation with Napoleon. Regarding the information which the Czar might have received from the Prince Regent through Count Lieven, he declared he had no knowledge of it, and should feel

---

[1] Prussian Plenipotentiary.

it his bounden duty, as the responsible servant of the Crown acting on the spot, to deliver his opinion, on the part of his Court, in direct opposition to the instructions which Count Lieven's dispatch was supposed to convey.

The dispatch which caused Castlereagh so much bitterness originated in a new influence at Court. This was exercised by Countess Lieven, wife of the Russian Ambassador. She was a woman who had a finger in every political pie. A thin, angular creature, with a giraffe-like neck, a dark tangle of hair, and deep caressing grey eyes, she managed to attach many great men to her side. Although she had no remarkable beauty, she had an indefinable fascination, which was to captivate even Castlereagh at a later day. Piquante and provocative, a graceful dancer, a brilliant pianist, a clever conversationalist, adroit in the management of men and hearts, she had already captured the Regent. It was she who had persuaded him to inform Count Lieven, in a secret interview, of his desire to dethrone Napoleon, and restore Louis XVIII to the throne of France. The information was passed on to the Czar, and did not reach Castlereagh till everyone else had heard it.

Infuriated, Castlereagh wrote to Liverpool, protesting against the admissibility of "this system of acting by double and contradictory channels," which was so much the system of foreign courts that it might not seem unnatural to them, but which had placed him in the most distressing predicament. He had never had anything to do with tricks or intrigues. and he refused to countenance them now.

He informed Liverpool further that he would never support a war prolonged merely to dethrone Napoleon, if other objects were secured, however much he would welcome Napoleon's fall; and he sent Robinson home post haste to bring back definite instructions that he had the full support of the Government.

Castlereagh received by return full powers as he had requested, but the whole matter had been distressing to him in the extreme. His responsibilities were heavy, the work harassing, and he could not have gone on, he felt, without full support from home. "Castlereagh works hard writing all day," wrote Charles to Emily. "I know not how he finds room for so much as is in his head—poor things all around him are to him . . . God bless you, I hope to embrace you soon somehow or other."

The difficulties were at their height when there came news that Napoleon was again victorious. He had transferred his army from the Seine to the Marne, had surprised Blücher's troops as they were marching on Paris, and on 11 February 1814, had defeated the Prussians at Montmirail. Blücher had lost two-thirds of his army. A few days later, on the snow-covered hills of Montereau, Napoleon's army burst upon the Russians, whom he likewise defeated. In the midst of danger, when the gunners entreated him to retire to a place of safety, he replied serenely: "Courage, my friends, the ball that will kill me is not yet cast."

He pursued the allies up the valley of the Seine till they took refuge in the village of Chaumont. He had no intention now of approving the conditions sent him. Writing to Caulaincourt, who was still at Chatillon, he said: "Sign nothing without my orders, because I alone know my position." His position was surprising. He had performed one of the most brilliant achievements of his whole career. He had forced his way between the allied armies so that they could not combine, and had defeated them both; the allies were now in retreat. The Czar and the delegations had to evacuate their Headquarters at Troyes during the night. "We are uncertain," wrote Lady Burghersh,[1] who had accompanied her husband, "dilatory, and (*entre nous*) frightened." "The Czar," recorded Hardenberg, "has gone to pieces, and the King talks all the time like Cassandra." Metternich himself was alarmed. It was even feared that the delegation at Chatillon might be captured by the local population, who were forming themselves into armed bands. In consternation, the allies held a council of war. Prince Schwarzenberg, the Austrian Commander-in-Chief, urged a general retreat, and advised the sovereigns to ask for an armistice. In a panic Alexander decided to act on his advice, and Prince Lichtenstein was dispatched to Napoleon's Headquarters with the allies' request.

[1] Lady Burghersh was a niece of Wellington, married to Lord Burghersh, British Military representative to the Austrian army.

3

Hearing the news at Chatillon, Castlereagh hurried back to Head-quarters, which were now at Chaumont. There he found an alarming situation. The recriminations between Russia and Austria were at their height. Alexander, considering himself betrayed by the Austrians, who had remained inactive during the battle of Montereau, was now ready for peace at any price.

In the midst of all the panic and the recriminations, with excited voices crying out all round him, Castlereagh quietly informed the allies that their position would be hopeless if they shrank now from the contest. To solicit an armistice, he declared, was so inconsistent with their proceedings hitherto, and of so little dignity in itself, it could not fail to invite the enemy to assume a tone of authority. " If we act with military and political prudence," he said, " how can France resist a just peace demanded by six hundred thousand warriors ? Let her if she dare, and the day that you can declare that fact to the French nation, rest assured that Buonaparte is subdued."

He did not neglect to inform them, moreover, that Great Britain would not continue her subsidies unless she secured a peace such as she desired.

Calm and unperturbed in the midst of chaos and danger, his courage and wisdom carried the day. The crisis of Troyes dissolved, the panic subsided, and Alexander consented that the conference of Chatillon should be resumed.

To continue the campaign, however, reinforcements were needed, for the allies had lost half their armies. The only troops within reach were Bülow's division, which was lying inactive in the low countries, under Bernadotte's command. Bernadotte, obstinate as ever, had refused to bring them into action. The only way of escaping disaster was for this division to advance, but Bernadotte would not move, and the majority of the council of war feared that if the allies directed Bülow to advance without his orders, Bernadotte might be provoked into falling upon the allied communications. There was a moment of intense gloom, but Castlereagh rose and declared that the order to advance must be given, and that he would take upon himself the whole responsibility of any consequences that might follow. As regarded the

Crown Prince of Sweden he undertook to remove all difficulties with him. He was convinced that Bernadotte would not be likely to risk losing the English subsidy, nor his hope of Norway, and that a firm line was all that was necessary. The vigour and energy displayed by Castlereagh at this crisis decided the fate of the campaign, for Napoleon manœuvred Blücher into such a position that his destruction seemed inevitable, when Bernadotte suddenly arrived on the scene with a powerful army. Castlereagh had made himself responsible for bringing Bernadotte, and Bernadotte had come. On 9 March 1814, Napoleon's little army was terribly beaten at Laon by the forces of Blücher and Bernadotte combined. After the battle Napoleon sent word to Caulaincourt to treat on any terms.

His position had changed indeed. He had been offered terms which no sane person would have rejected, but he had altered his tone daily according to the way the war was going. What Caulaincourt accepted one day, Napoleon the following day would reject. Even Castlereagh had by this time lost all patience with him, and his desire to treat was therefore disregarded. Napoleon's offer, Caulaincourt was informed, had come too late; negotiations were closed.

But it was heavy work guiding the destinies of Europe, and Castlereagh gave himself no rest or relaxation. He was at conferences during the day, writing dispatches during the night, sending reports to the Cabinet, sending instructions to Cathcart, to Aberdeen, to Charles. He had interviews with Metternich, and private talks with Alexander, who begged him now to call on him without formality. His quarters at Chaumont were not very luxurious; he had only one small room in which he slept and wrote, and in which " the whole Chancellerie dined, when they could get anything to eat."

Castlereagh found Chaumont a dull, dirty town, which had nothing to reconcile one to it but a sense of public duty, yet it was here that he completed what was in a sense the greatest diplomatic act of his career; for the treaty of alliance which had never been out of Castlereagh's mind was now formed. By exercising endless patience and diplomatic skill he had gradually marshalled the allies into line, and on 1 March 1814, the Treaty of Chatillon was signed between Austria, Russia, Prussia and Great Britain.

It was an alliance of the great powers to protect one another against any attack by France. It was a league of nations formed to safeguard the world's peace. It was the origin of that Quadruple Alliance which was to dominate European politics for forty years. It was "perhaps the most far reaching treaty" Metternich wrote, "that had ever been signed." The four powers pledged themselves to protect the peace of Europe for twenty years, and to continue the war until their objects were obtained. These were for the most part an enlarged and independent Holland, a confederated Germany, an independent Switzerland and a free Spain. Great Britain's contribution in men and money was to be double that of any continental power; she had the right, however, to employ foreign troops.

Writing to his Government, Castlereagh said: "I send you my treaty which I hope you will approve. We four ministers when signing happened to be sitting at a whist table; it was agreed that never were the stakes so high at any former party. My modesty would have prevented me from offering it . . . but as they chose to make us a military power I was determined not to play second fiddle."

Castlereagh had got his Grand Alliance at last. It was no small achievement, for it governed Europe till 1848. It constituted the executive power of Europe, of which the Treaty of Paris and the Treaty of Vienna were to form the Charter.

4

Charles, who had replaced Castlereagh at the conference, was still waiting at Chatillon. He was a soldier, preferring action to diplomacy, and did not care for his position. Unburdening himself to Emily, he wrote on 4 March 1814, "How Castlereagh could ever stick me down to make a peace is what is most inexplicable to me. However, I am not sure it is not better to be spitting over a bridge than to be attempting a lame work.

"I shall play my good brother a trick or two yet for keeping me from the Marne to watch his dignified ambassadors. Oh dear! I wish you were here, and at least I should have a little fun . . .

"Castlereagh is at the top of the tree here. He has long governed England and is in a fair way of governing the Continent. I left him yesterday at Chaumont, and Robinson arrived here at night when I came home. So I dispatched him with his budget next day, and I am anchored here again until we get our dismissal, which I trust in God will be soon.

"I have sent horses to Castlereagh to ride, as also a cook, provisions, etc., as they are starving in Chaumont, and we in clover here, so you see I take care of his body for his Princesses, and as to his mind, I leave that to be fed on by *Europe's Salvator*.[1]

"Now Dearest, if you have charity, write some of your inimitable letters to me to make me laugh.

Believe me your most affect.

CARLO"

The allies were already marching on Paris. Napoleon flung himself in the rear of his enemies, distracting them as much as possible; the roar of cannon could be heard in the capital, and frightened peasants were crowding into the city.

5

Castlereagh had been recalled by Liverpool, who found it impossible to manage without him, and was already on his way home when he was overtaken by messengers requesting him to proceed to Paris. He found himself now between the two contending armies. He could not get to Headquarters because he was in the rear of the allied armies, which were now as it were the front line of defence against Napoleon's troops. Owing to the brilliant tactics of Napoleon's final campaign, Castlereagh was being driven from pillar to post. At Bar-sur-Aube the French entered the city the evening he left it. The Baron de Vittrolles, an envoy of the Bourbons, saw him on the road, dressed in a white cape, eating a hurried luncheon in the courtyard of the Château Vandoeuvre. He had propped his luncheon up on the rumble of his carriage, and was standing on tiptoe to reach his salmis of partridge and his glass of champagne. His digestion must have improved since the days when he lived on vegetable nourishment and fruit pies.

Vittrolles thought him handsome but cold. But Vittrolles was a representative of the Bourbons, and though Castlereagh was by now

[1] Alexander.

convinced that there would be a declaration for the Bourbons, he had not yet received instructions from his government on the line he was to take, and proceeded cautiously.

Lady Burghersh, on the other hand, who was also retreating and advancing with the army, delighted in Castlereagh. She thought he looked handsome, bronzed and picturesque, in his red breeches and jockey boots, and his fur cap with its golden band. " I had no idea he had so much fun in him," she wrote, and yet she too remarked that he was " impenetrably cold."

Emily, who was now besieging him with letters demanding to be brought over, was always quoting Lady Burghersh as an example, to prove that the roads were safe. It was the " mamselles " she feared and the " Princesses " that were keeping her away from her husband's side.

"I see I am in disgrace," Castlereagh wrote to her, " but I do not deserve it. Whatever nonsense you may get travellers to talk to you, about following the army, believe me it is not what you ought to encounter, even when everything is going smooth; but when the troops are in retreat it is still less fit for a woman. I can assure you Lady B.'s undertaking is so commented upon, and I can promise you she is herself heartily sick of it. When Robinson left us for England, the sort of hearty wish with which she said ' How much I would give to be of your party,' proved that following an army is not quite so joyous a life as you suppose it."

Castlereagh did not press on: the roads, he declared, were too unsafe to permit of his coming to Paris. He may have preferred to remain with the Emperor of Austria and Metternich until he saw what policy the Czar might adopt. If so, the roads afforded him every excuse. But Lady Burghersh managed to get to Paris alone, a few days later, and in the dangers which surrounded Castlereagh, for the roads were certainly unsafe, he had to protect himself first and foremost from his wife.

" When I am tried for leaving my wife behind me," he wrote to her on 30 March 1814 from Dijon, " I shall call Lady Burghersh as my first witness, who was obliged to fly from Chaumont and live at a bivouac with all the heavy baggage of the army, without the possibility of changing her chemise unperceived, except the ceremony was performed in the dark of the night. Another proof how pleasant the

277

travelling is, Wassenberg was laid hold by the armed peasantry, plunder'd of everything, and produced for Buonaparte's inspection I believe without a fig leaf, there being none to be found. He left there yesterday morning, at Donlevant on the Aube, in no very pleasant temper, having two days before lost 100 pieces of Cannon, 8 Generals and 6000 prisoners. The allies were near Paris, where perhaps we may yet meet on our way home. . . . The Emperor of Austria and Austrian and Prussian Ministers returned here from Bar-sur-Aube to avoid the enemy, we could not get to the Headquarters."

6

The following day, the 31 March 1814, the Czar, accompanied by the King of Prussia, entered Paris in triumph. Paris had fallen. Charles was with the conquerors, regretting the absence of Castlereagh. The crowds were enormous, and the acclamation so great that it was difficult for the procession to move forward. From the enthusiasm and exultation exhibited, Charles declared, one would have thought that the downfall of Napoleon and the restoration of a Bourbon king was the first and dearest wish of every Frenchman. The white cockade appeared everywhere, and the people thronged in masses round the Czar, waving their hands and crying: " *Vive l'Empereur Alexandre— Vive le Roi de Prusse—Vive les Rois libérateurs !* "

Preceded by the cossacks of the Imperial Guard, in a vast green hat with a cascade of cock feathers, huge shining epaulets, and stirrups of gold, Alexander rode slowly through the streets of Paris. He installed himself in the house of Talleyrand, since the Palace was said to have been mined. Talleyrand had been directed by Napoleon to accompany Marie Louise when she fled from the capital but, full of contrivances, he had arranged for a messenger to recall him on the way, and was thus back in Paris in time to receive the Czar.

The news of the fall of Paris reached Castlereagh at Dijon, and he wrote to Emily that he had now arranged for her journey to Paris, confident that the roads were at last safe. "I have laid in a stock of silks and old Sèvres china for you here," he told her, "but you must come for it, or else I will give it *en dépit* to some *Belle* at Paris. God

Bless you dearest friend. I am a bad boy but you will forgive me when we meet which I trust will be in the fewest days possible."

Napoleon was galloping through the dark night along the road to Fontainebleau. He knew that Paris had fallen. When he reached the ancient palace of the Kings of France, he dispatched Caulaincourt to see the Czar, and waited anxiously to know his fate. Caulaincourt returned to inform him that the powers would not treat with him; they required his unconditional surrender. He dismissed Caulaincourt from his presence, but after a few hours of anguish sent for him again, and presenting him with a paper said: " Here is my abdication, carry it to Paris." He had declared that he was ready to give up the throne, to give up France and even life itself for the good of his country.

He embraced Caulaincourt, and said: " Depart, Caulaincourt, depart immediately," but when his Minister had left, in a frenzy of despair he sent messenger on messenger after him ordering him to bring back his abdication. It was too late. That same night he took poison, but even this would not kill him, and a violent fit of vomiting saved his life.

The faithful Caulaincourt, blinded with tears, was on his way to Paris. When he arrived he was received by the Czar with great courtesy. Alexander informed him that the Allies would not deprive Napoleon of all hope of existence, but would give him a kingdom of his own. He was full of charming ideas, one of them was to give Napoleon the isle of Elba in full sovereignty. The Bourbon partisans suggested St. Helena, but the Czar decided on Elba, though Talleyrand and the Provisional Government strongly disapproved of the plan.

Ten days after Alexander's triumphal entry Castlereagh and Metternich arrived in Paris. They found the Czar arranging the peace and liberation of Europe, and proclaiming the doctrine of liberalism. His only interest seemed to be the universal happiness of mankind. Castlereagh and Metternich were a little suspicious, knowing that besides the happiness of mankind he also wanted Poland.

They were both opposed to the idea of the Isle of Elba as an asylum for Napoleon, Castlereagh objecting that the island was too close to the Italian coast, and within a few days' sail of France. He was anxious for a less dangerous retreat to be found. Metternich contended that to send Napoleon to Elba would be to invite another war within two years. But the evil was already done, and Castlereagh, not wishing to push his demands to an extreme, acquiesced. Only on those points which he regarded as vital to the interests of his country did he take a stand.

"Regarding the island of Elba," he wrote to Liverpool, "I did not feel that I could encourage the alternative, which Caulaincourt assured me Buonaparte repeatedly mentioned, namely an asylum in England."

Napoleon, after he was beaten, was actually given the island of Elba in full sovereignty; he was to receive, moreover, an annual revenue of two million francs. The revenue was never paid, even though Castlereagh protested to the French Government when he heard of the omission.

Napoleon listened to the news of his banishment with apparent calm. "I am a man condemned to live," he said. He took up his pen, and wrote a brief letter to Josephine, with whom he still corresponded.

"Adieu, my dear Josephine. Be resigned as I am, and never forget him who will never forget you. Farewell, Josephine. Napoleon." And then he added, even more pathetically: "I expect to hear from you at Elba. I am not very well."

The Imperial Guard was drawn up as he went to his carriage. For an instant he hesitated, then he stepped into the square and addressed his men. "Generals, Officers, Subalterns and Soldiers of my old Guard, I bid you farewell: for twenty years I have been pleased with you: I have always found you on the road to glory . . ." His voice broke. After a moment he said: "Let them bring me my eagle," and he kissed the colours. He embraced General Petit, and turning once more to his soldiers, he said: "Farewell, my children. My wishes will be always with you. Keep me in your memories." Then he turned and entered the carriage which was to take him into exile.

7

News had already reached Lady Castlereagh of the Allied armies' entrance into Paris, and all was excitement. Her new destination was not yet settled, but a few days later a messenger arrived from Castle-reagh to conduct her via Brussels to Paris, and she set off in the greatest haste.

After four months at the Hague she was in a passion to rejoin her husband, but there were many formalities to be overcome, there was a great deal of passport examination on the way, and she and her niece were quite worn out by the time they reached Paris. But they did not think of fatigue, narrates Emma Sophia, in the joyful meeting with Lord Castlereagh.

They found him established in the Hotel of the " Ministre des Finances " within easy distance of the Tuileries and the Boulevards. The atmosphere of Paris was more than ever exciting. The town was filled with soldiers, bands were playing, and the people were still shouting: " *Vive le roi, vive les Bourbons!* " At Montmartre, where the last fierce struggle took place before the Allies entered Paris, dreadful exhalations arose from the dead buried all around, and on a house sufficiently distant for safety there was still a notice: " *Ici on voit la bataille pour deux sous.*"

The King had not yet arrived. Writing to Liverpool, Castlereagh said: " If you hurry the King off, I may be with you this day month. It may appear presumptuous in me to say so, but my remaining till this new scene takes a shape is beyond all comparison more important than my original mission. You must therefore manage it."

It was not a simple matter to hurry the King off, for Louis XVIII could hardly put his gouty leg to the ground. On 4 May, however, he arrived. In a white waistcoat which reached to his knees, and gaiters that bagged like a petticoat, he was not a very inspiring figure. He was probably aware of the fact, for alluding to his divine right, he said: " Apart from that right, what am I? A sick old man." The Old Guard with lowering faces looked like thunder clouds as they lined the route of the gouty sovereign who had come to take the place of their Emperor.

Wellington arrived from Toulouse without notice, in time, in his blue coat, to see the Russian and Prussian guards march past the allied sovereigns. He was on horse-back, riding between Castlereagh and Charles. When he saw the Russian cavalry he said in his blunt way: " Well, to be sure, we can't turn out anything like this."

In the evening of the same day, he appeared at a ball given by

Charles Stewart. It was a very splendid affair, but unfortunately Charles's conduct was deplorable. The Grand Duke Constantine, the Czar's brother, who was one of the guests, asked for a waltz to be played. He and his partner were just beginning to dance when Charles stopped the orchestra and asked for a quadrille. Lady Burghersh, to whom he was now devoted, had apparently made the request.

The conductor hesitated, looked at the Grand Duke, and continued playing the waltz.

Charles lifted his voice and called out: " Who has dared to insist on having this waltz played ? "

" I," replied the Grand Duke.

" I alone give orders in my house, Monseigneur," Charles rudely observed, and turning to the conductor he said, " Play the quadrille."

The Grand Duke left the house, accompanied by all the Russians. It was an embarrassing moment for everybody, but especially for Castlereagh, who had the unpleasant task of placating the Russians and patching up the matter.

" That, I fancy," wrote the Countess of Boigne, who records the incident, " was the first of the impertinences which Sir Charles scattered throughout a progress which he began as Lord Stewart and continued as the Marquess of Londonderry."

Wellington was received rapturously in Paris. On one occasion, when he accompanied Lady Castlereagh to the theatre, his presence caused almost a riot. As soon as he was noticed the whole pit rose, and turning to his box called out: " *Vive Vellington !* " continuing their cries till he stood up and bowed to them. At the end of the performance, on opening the door of the box, he found the passage crowded with people waiting to see him come out. Lady Castlereagh was nervous and shrank back, but the Duke in his short way said, " Come along," and drew her on. As Mr. Planta and Emma Sophia, who were with them, followed, they heard one man say to another: " *Mais pourquoi l'applaudissez-vous tant? Il nous a toujours battus.*" The reply, Emma Sophia tells us, was charming: " *Oui, mais il nous a battus en gentilhomme.*"

Lady Castlereagh gave *de petits soupers* nightly, to which all those she knew could come without invitation. One evening, when a pale handsome woman was announced as La Duchesse de Sagan, Prince

Louis de Rohan nudged Lady Castlereagh and said: "*C'était autrefois ma femme.*" It was his divorced wife, who was now being courted by Charles Stewart. The incident seemed to cause embarrassment to no one, but when they were all gone Lady Castlereagh said: "Emma, I am afraid we live in very bad company." "Too true," comments Emma Sophia, "but we could not help ourselves and got used to it."

One morning Lady Castlereagh received a message from Josephine, Buonaparte's divorced wife, asking her to come and see her at Malmaison. Various engagements obliged her to postpone the visit for a week, at the end of which time, accompanied by Emma Sophia, she drove to Malmaison to pay her respects to the former Empress. They were both inexpressibly shocked on arriving at the lodge to find that the Empress had died that morning.

8

Although Castlereagh put in an appearance at most of the festivities he was working as hard as ever, but Paris was a bad place for business, and the balls, dinners, reviews, and fêtes, did much to distract the Sovereigns and their Ministers from the more serious work on hand. The Cabinet was anxiously awaiting Castlereagh's return, but he could not get away. Writing to Liverpool on 5 May 1814, he said, "I am truly sorry to occasion any embarrassment at home, by being absent from my post; but I really work as hard as a man can well do in such a town as Paris to finish my work, and I cannot persuade myself that it would be safe to leave it incomplete." Eventually it was only by a threat to transfer negotiations to London that he obtained all the signatures to the Peace Treaty by the end of May. It was a remarkable feat. In four weeks the most difficult peace treaty in history had been drawn up and signed. There had been a general feeling that the Treaty should be based on humanity and justice. Montesquieu, one of the greatest writers of the eighteenth century, had laid down a precept for all civilised people, that in peace men should do each other the greatest possible good, and in war the least possible harm. It was in this spirit that the First Treaty of Paris was drawn up.

The allies renounced all reprisals, vengeance, and humiliating measures, and offered France the same conditions as they had offered her at Chatillon, when they had been uncertain of victory. France received territories even beyond her boundaries of 1792.

Castlereagh was inclined to a liberal line on all subordinate questions, but on such matters as the French move to extend their frontier on the side of Belgium he was adamant. There was a lively exchange of words between him and Talleyrand, whom he informed that no peace would last unless the French people gave up " this false notion of Flanders being necessary to France."

On the question of the colonies England had taken, though she pledged herself to restore these, Castlereagh insisted on retaining Santa Lucia, Tobago, and Mauritius. Having spent six hundred million pounds in the war England was not being too harsh, he asserted, in demanding three small islands from France. He also displayed great firmness regarding the abolition of the Slave Trade, and on this matter Talleyrand, who found him as unshakable as a rock, was forced to give way.

Although peace was signed on 30 May 1814, there remained almost half of Europe, which France had conquered, still to be dealt with. It was from this enormous and formless mass that the new Europe was to take shape. Castlereagh, Metternich, Hardenberg and Nesselrode decided that the disposal of these remaining territories should be postponed until the autumn, when a Congress was to be held at Vienna, to which all the powers who had been engaged in the war would send plenipotentiaries. The purpose of the Congress of Vienna was to complete the settlement of Europe, but the four great powers intended from the first that the main points should be decided by themselves before the Congress met.

CHAPTER XIII

I

CASTLEREAGH ARRIVED home with the peace in his pocket. No one could deny that he had acquitted himself very creditably in matters of the greatest delicacy, in functions of the highest importance. Whether he had a claim to the character of a statesman was no longer contestable: he had won his laurels. He had triumphed over Napoleon. He had settled the Allies. The whole world was now in the palm of his hand; he had only to mould it a little nearer to England's desire. All his ambitions led to one end—the interests of England; and England was not unappreciative of his efforts. "Be assured," Cooke had written to him, "that the fullest justice is done to the great abilities you have displayed through the whole of the transactions which you have so successfully and wonderfully managed. Your superiority and authority are now fixed. . . . I long to see your victorious entry into the House of Commons."

The historic entry took place on 6 June 1814. It was about five o'clock in the afternoon when he arrived. The House was full, and he was greeted with loud and prolonged cheers. The whole House rose to welcome him, and business was for some moments suspended. A little flushed Castlereagh bowed and took his seat. Although he had never sought applause it was not unpleasing to receive it; he was almost moved to eloquence, his speech on this occasion being one of the greatest of his whole career.

"If the country," he said, "has for twenty years sustained the most severe burdens, and done so with a noble fortitude, it is at least gratifying for her to find that she has come out of the tremendous conflict in which she has been engaged with the acquisition of that

285

security for which she contended, and with a reputation unstained by
reproval. .... We have thus, Sir, at length closed the war as conquerors
certainly, but enjoying the rare felicity of receiving the benedictions
not only of those with whom we fought, but ultimately of those
against whom we fought. There is no feeling more powerful in Paris
at this moment than respect for the English character."

Castlereagh's old rival, Canning, expressed his entire approbation
of the Treaty, which he had no hesitation in declaring to be the
most glorious that had ever been concluded by the Government of
England.

There was no difference of opinion now as to Castlereagh's talents.
When the House of Commons offered to the Crown its congratulations
upon the treaty of peace, even Whitbread, who had always pursued
him with invective, retracted his former denunciations. His enemies
could no longer contest his capacity for affairs, and joined in
applauding him.

The Prince Regent honoured him with the Order of the Garter,
a distinction rarely if ever bestowed except upon crowned heads, or
persons of the very highest rank. In recognition of the great services
he had rendered, his father was created a Marquess, his brother a
Peer.

London went wild with excitement. The war was over. The Czar
Alexander and the King of Prussia, who had been invited by the
Regent, had arrived, and every night there were banquets, balls, and
gala performances. There were courts, levées, and drawing-rooms.
There were endless processions of horsemen and carriages. The town
was illuminated, and the whole population of London was in the
streets. At the Poulteney Hotel, where he was staying, the
Emperor of Russia appeared on the balcony and bowed to the
admiring crowds.

It had at first been intended that the Russian Czar alone should
be invited by the Regent, but Castlereagh had suggested that the
Emperor of Austria and the King of Prussia should be included in
the invitation.

" When I recommend you," he had written to Liverpool from Paris,
" to dilute the libation to Russia, I am the last to wish it should be
less palatable. The Emperor has the greatest merit, and must be held
high, but he ought to be grouped, and not made the sole feature for

admiration. The interview in England will have a sensible influence on the politics of the Continent."

But, even grouped, Alexander stole the picture, and was to cause nothing but havoc during his unfortunate visit to England. While the Czar was bowing from the balcony, the Prince Regent had to remain indoors, for the mob, who greeted him now with hisses, had threatened his life if he showed himself. He was even unable to call on the Czar, and the royal meeting had to be arranged at Carlton House.

The crowds were so enthusiastic, however, about the foreign visitors, that Blücher, attended by Charles Stewart and Lord Burghersh, was nearly crushed to death in the streets; the old warrior told Lord Burghersh afterwards that he had never been so frightened in his life.

Processions and pageants continued. "We are full of nothing," wrote Lord Grenville to Buckingham, "but very ridiculous preparations for very foolish exhibitions of ourselves to foreign sovereigns in that character which least of all becomes us—that of courtly magnificence."

One of the spectacles which delighted the crowd was the departure of the royal barge for Woolwich at eight o'clock on the morning of 14 June. Under an awning of purple silk embroidered with gold sat the Prince Regent attended by Castlereagh. Grouped about them were the Duke of York, the King of Prussia, the Emperor of Russia, and his sister, the Grand Duchess. The sun shone out as the barge glided away from Whitehall stairs, amid shouts of admiration from the people. Passing by Strand Bridge the royal party was greeted again with acclamation. There were scores of boats filled with spectators on the water, apart from the sixty boats, magnificently decorated, which provided an escort.

With all the festivities Castlereagh had scarcely time to breathe or sleep. He would gladly have retired from the glare and dazzle, but many of the functions he was forced to attend. He was somewhat disturbed at this time by an unfortunate renewal of the dispute between the Regent and the Princess of Wales, which could not have come at a worse moment. Caroline had published in a daily paper a letter from the Regent declaring that he would never meet his wife either in public or in private, and the whole country had turned against him.

The Czar's sister, a tactless little woman, who irritated everyone,

Castlereagh

infuriated the Regent by announcing her intention of visiting the
injured woman.

She annoyed the Regent further by reproving him at dinner for
exercising too strict a discipline over his daughter. She even began to
influence the Princess Charlotte against her intended marriage with
the Prince of Orange. The Opposition had already been working on
the Princess, and the combined tactics resulted in her suddenly
announcing to the Government that the marriage was broken off.

This development embarrassed Castlereagh not a little. Writing
to Lord Clancarty on 26 June 1814, he said: "The circumstances
attending the rupture of the marriage are yet mysterious: there can
be no doubt that faction had been busy at work upon the Princess
Charlotte's mind, and to add another complication to the family
embarrassments. . . . We all feel the deepest grief and disappointment
at this event."

The Grand Duchess continued to annoy the Regent. At a dinner
at Carlton House, where the Prince Regent's band always played, she
insisted that the band be sent away; music made her feel sick. Hearing
that a banquet was being given at the Guildhall, she insisted on accompanying the Czar. Although it had been pointed out to her that it
was not customary for ladies to be present at these functions, ladies
had to be invited.

During the banquet she asked the Italian opera-singers to stop
because music made her vomit. She even objected to *God Save the
King* being played. There were embarrassed mutterings all round.
"When folks don't know how to behave," Lord Liverpool said to
Countess Lieven, "they would do better to stay at home, and your
Duchess has chosen against all usage to go to men's dinners." It was
only with difficulty that they persuaded her to agree that the National
Anthem might be played after the royal toast; her nerves apparently
bore it.

The impertinences of the Grand Duchess irritated the Prince beyond
words. The Czar annoyed him equally. He would keep the Regent
waiting while he stopped to speak to leaders of the Opposition. When
the Prince introduced his beloved Lady Hertford to him, the Czar
merely bowed, and turning away, said, "She is mighty old." He
began a flirtation with the Regent's former mistress, Lady Jersey, who
was "still coasting round the Prince." At a Ball where the Czar

288

waltzed with Lady Jersey, the Regent went off five minutes after his arrival, sulky as a bear. "All agree," wrote Creevey, "that Prinny will die or go mad, he is worn out with fuss, fatigue and rage."

The Grand Duchess Catherine fanned the jealousies. She had an extraordinary power over the Czar, who succumbed to her in everything. She was only twenty-four, not very prepossessing, but vivacious and sparkling, and very sure of herself. She had refused the hand of Napoleon in marriage, she also refused the hand of two of the Regent's brothers, the Duke of Kent and the Duke of Sussex. At one moment she hoped to marry the Emperor of Austria. "He may be dirty," she wrote, "but I can wash him." The Emperor of Austria apparently did not desire to be washed.

As for the Czar, every day he became more and more unpopular, and it was with a sense of relief that London saw the departure of both the Russian royalties. Alexander's last gesture was to send for Lady Jersey on the night of his departure. No good had been done in any direction by the social festivities, certainly no profitable business. The royal visit had served only to create a gulf between Britain and Russia.

Castlereagh, who had hoped that much might be settled during the visit, was disappointed. He was still hard at work in the House of Commons. He had to obtain a vote of credit for his Kingdom of Holland, he had to obtain funds for the army of 75,000 men which he was maintaining on the Continent. Not the least of his difficulties was the Regent's domestic affairs, for the matter of the Princess of Wales was causing the greatest scandal.

In an effort to persuade the Princess to carry out a wish she had expressed to go abroad, he introduced a motion in the House to increase her allowance from £35,000 to £50,000 a year. As no conditions derogatory to her honour as Princess of Wales had been annexed to the offer, Caroline was pleased to accept it. But the Opposition was enraged with her " for snapping eagerly at the cash," and Brougham and Whitbread badgered her until finally she gave up the £50,000. There was further trouble when the Prince Regent refused to allow her a seat in St. Paul's Cathedral, on the occasion of the National Thanksgiving for peace. It seemed that the ferment would never die down, and Castlereagh sighed with relief when he heard that she was definitely leaving the country. On 8 August 1814, she departed for the Continent, mourned by nobody but the Opposition.

Although Castlereagh had tried to extract from the Foreign Ministers some definite statement of their intentions regarding the settlement of Europe during the Royal visit, nothing had been effected. The summer was passing and the Congress was soon to assemble in Vienna. Fearing that Bourbon France might throw her weight on Russia's side, Castlereagh decided that he would accept an invitation from Talleyrand to visit Paris on his way to Vienna.

He set out in August 1814, intending to interrupt his journey at Ghent, in order to see the American Commissioners who had been sent there to negotiate. Peace had been established with Europe, but we were still at war with America, and Castlereagh was more than ever anxious to bring this war to a close.

Although the American Navy had disappeared from the seas, owing to our effective blockade of the coast of the United States, we had not met with any great success in Canada during this last year of the war. In August 1814, Sir George Prevost was so seriously defeated at Champlain, that he was threatened by a Court Martial, which he only escaped by dying before the trial could be held. But the war in the Peninsula was over, and Britain was already sending heavy reinforcements " to effect a diversion on the coast of the United States in favour of our army employed in the defence of Canada."

While Castlereagh was on his way to Ghent, Major-General Ross arrived with his reinforcements at Benedict, about fifty miles from Washington. On landing, he received a report that American troops had crossed Lake Erie to Long Point, and had destroyed flour mills, distilleries and several houses in the neighbourhood, and that Admiral Cochrane had issued an order for retaliation.

For five days the British troops marched along in a leisurely manner, showing commendable respect for private property, and met with no show of resistance, until they came in sight of Washington. Ross hesitated whether to attack Washington, but the American militia that had been mustered to meet the British troops made a stand at Bladensburg, where they were easily routed, and retreated by the road that led to the Capitol.

Their Commander, who was wounded, was treated by the British, as he said, " with a most marked attention, respect and politeness, as if I was a brother "; but unfortunately, as the British troops, with General Ross and Admiral Cochrane advancing before them, reached the first houses of the town, some men fired on them from a house, and Ross's horse was killed under him. He immediately ordered the house to be burnt down; then followed the burning of the Capitol and the White House, an act which even the burning down of York, the capital of Canada, hardly justified. The British army then withdrew. A few days later in an ineffectual attack on Baltimore, Ross was one of the first men to fall.

2

When Castlereagh arrived at Ghent, though these facts were not yet known, he found relations between the commissioners extremely strained. He did not see any of the Americans. " They did not call upon me," he wrote Liverpool, " or desire to see me."

The American and the British commissioners had each put forward demands which were considered inadmissible. There had been disputes about frontiers and fisheries and impressment. Castlereagh felt that the British note sent to the Americans had been very strong; he would have been inclined, if he had prepared it, to have stated the propositions less peremptorily; but the English Commissioners at Ghent seemed to attach so much importance to not weakening at this stage of the discussions, that Castlereagh did not wish to cause them any awkwardness by originating an interview.[1] Although he gave instructions to the British Commissioners to make peace on any reasonable terms, the war with America continued.

His visit to Paris was more successful. He explained to Talleyrand, whom he found courteous and charming, the object of the conferences which the Four Powers intended holding at Vienna before the opening of the Congress, and hoped that Talleyrand would not interpret unfavourably their conferring on engagements which had been undertaken before they could count France among their friends. He assured the French Minister that he did not intend excluding France from any essential part of the negotiations. Before he left he obtained from the King and from Talleyrand a pledge that France would co-operate with

[1] *Castlereagh's Letters and Dispatches.*

Britain in putting an end to the Slave Trade, one of the chief questions to be settled at Vienna. Having come to a complete understanding with France he proceeded on his way in good humour.

3

It was 13 September 1814, a fine, autumnal day when Castlereagh arrived in Vienna. The city was crowded, for visitors from all countries had congregated to gaze on the sovereigns and celebrities assembled within its walls. With Castlereagh were Lord Cathcart and Lord Clancarty, Joseph Planta and Edward Cooke, Under-Secretary of State. There was also his brother Charles ; but Charles gave him little assistance and was only a source of embarrassment to him. His vanity, his airs and his innumerable indiscretions soon made him the laughing-stock of Vienna. But Castlereagh had a great affection for him, and always condoned his weaknesses. Everyone was puzzled by the influence which Charles seemed to exercise on his brother. John Croker thought Castlereagh had a real respect for Charles's understanding and a high opinion of his good sense and direction. "This seems incomprehensible to us who know the two men," he observed. But Castlereagh was not unaware of Charles's limitations. "You know," Charles had once written Emily, " he spits on what I say, and I can never move him, nor have I any particle of influence." It was a real affection for Charles, and a desire to help his family, that made Castlereagh appear to respect his judgment, though he was under no illusions about him. Calm and dignified himself, he could not but deplore Charles's incorrigible conceit, his eccentricities, his lack of taste. Nor could he approve of Charles with his carriage and four horses trying to eclipse the elegance of the Royal Sovereigns. But it was difficult to restrain his young brother. Charles was lavish by nature and loved display. The Congress nicknamed him "Lord Pumpernickel," and the "Golden Peacock" and "Prince Charles." The ladies described him coming into a room "all over stars and tenderness." Having his ears boxed at the theatre by some outraged beauty, quarrelling with a cab-driver, who gave him such a thrashing that he had to remain in retirement for days, he provided the Congress with a good deal of gossip. Castlereagh provided them with none. The Austrian police agents, who spied on Castlereagh's letters, found nothing in his private correspondence to amuse or even interest the Emperor of Austria, to whom all reports were submitted, and they gave up searching his wastepaper basket as a barren pastime.

The people of Vienna were less astonished by Charles's magnificence than by Castlereagh's simplicity. They watched Britain's envoy, clad in the soberest apparel, walking arm in arm with his wife along the streets of the city, entering all the shops, asking the price of everything, and then walking out again without buying anything. Among the glamorous throng which Charles tried to outglitter, Castlereagh moved quietly and unobtrusively. "Lord Castlereagh showed his long-drawn face with ennui stamped on every line of it from a coupé," narrates the Comte de la Garde-Chambonas. "It did not even light up when a hackney cab ran into the Calèche of the Pasha of Widin."

Every night during the Congress there were balls and masquerades. Alexander and Metternich outrivalled each other in the pursuit of fair women. Castlereagh danced when it was required of him, disporting himself in an Irish jig or a Scotch reel, but for the most part he could be seen standing erect against a wall, or leaning against a mantelpiece, listening with a courteous air to the Czar or the King of Prussia, or the Austrian Chancellor, all of whom were intent on winning him over to their side.

Another foil for Castlereagh's simplicity was his wife. Covered with diamonds and wearing clothes which Lady Grenville describes as being "fitter for Wapping," she was in evidence everywhere. On one occasion she created quite a sensation by wearing her husband's "Garter" in diamonds in her hair. "That is a little bit of facetious vanity," said the Prince de Ligne, "not contemplated by courteous Edward III when he picked up the blue ribbon that fastened the stocking of the handsome Alice of Salisbury."

Le Comte de la Garde-Chambonas, who did not care for Lady Castlereagh any more than he cared for her husband, remarked that the pride and pretension that she had displayed in attaching to her brow the honoured Garter had followed her into the gilded and brilliant halls of her residence. But the sumptuousness of her suppers failed, he observed, to thaw the iciness of the atmosphere. As for the host, amidst all the festivities where everything was given over to pleasure, he seemed preoccupied and smitten with care.

Castlereagh had no doubt other things on his mind than dancing. The quantity of business he had to attend to was enormous. The frontier of every state had to be reconsidered, and territorial adjustments made; there was the abolition of the slave trade to be accomplished, the navigation of international rivers, the emancipation of the Jews; there was the problem of Naples, and the German States; there was above all the vexed question of Poland and Saxony, which gave him endless trouble.

4

The formal opening of the Congress of Vienna had been fixed for 1 October 1814, but on the 15 September, two days after Castlereagh's arrival, informal meetings of the four Big Powers began. Only Castlereagh, and the Austrian Chancellor (Prince Metternich), the Prussian plenipotentiary (Prince Hardenberg), and the Russian envoy (Count Nesselrode) were present.

Metternich was the official President, the Congress having been convened in the Austrian capital, but Castlereagh's power was not in any way diminished. "England appeared at Vienna," wrote Friedrich von Gentz, Metternich's adviser, "with all the brilliance which she owes to her immense successes, the prominent part which she had played in the coalition, to her influence without limit, to a condition of strength and solid prospects which no other power has attained in these days, and lastly to the respect and fear which she inspires and which governs her relations with all the other governments."

Friedrich von Gentz, apart from being Metternich's adviser, was also Secretary to the Congress. He was a Jew, a writer, a scholar, and a close observer of all that passed in the innermost circles of the Congress. His opinion of Castlereagh was not always flattering. He admitted that he was guided by the purest intentions, but asserted that he held some radically false views, observing a neutrality where Europe was concerned that was often astonishing. How difficult it was for Castlereagh to observe this neutrality, to conciliate all parties without embroiling himself in their disputes, and finally to bring harmony out of chaos, and effect a settlement which kept Europe at peace for forty years, Gentz, who had only Austria and her interests to consider, was not ready to acknowledge, or competent to judge.

The Congress of Vienna, to which every Power in Europe sent representatives, was too large and cumbersome a body for the delicate negotiations of a peace, and the Four Big Powers had from the first decided that they would keep matters in their own hands. At their first informal meeting they occupied themselves chiefly with the problem of procedure, the nature and scope of the business to be transacted, and the formal arrangements for the assembly of the Congress. Castlereagh insisted from the first, Gentz noted down, that France should not be excluded from any essential part of the negotiations; Prussia was opposed to the plan, but eventually agreed to a compromise, by which France and Spain were to be invited to attend conferences which dealt solely with the future arrangements for the assembling of the Congress, the Big Four still reserving to themselves the final decision on all territorial questions.

On 23 September 1814, Talleyrand arrived in Vienna. He found himself in a chilly atmosphere. The allies were no longer interested, as at Paris, in the universal happiness of mankind; their main object at Vienna was the division among the conquerors of the spoils taken from the vanquished. Except for Britain, the Great Powers treated Talleyrand with a haughty reserve. But he soon divined the weakness of the allies, and drew up his plan of action. The first move in the game which followed was made by Alexander, who invited Talleyrand to a private audience, arranged for 1 October.

On the morning of 30 September, the day before he was to meet the Czar, Talleyrand received a note from Metternich asking him to attend a preliminary conference of the Great Powers at two o'clock that same afternoon. Labrador, who represented Spain, was also invited. Gentz tells us that the real purpose of this conference was to get France and Spain to accept the resolutions which the Four Powers had already passed. The chief among these was the decision that only the Four Powers could legally decide on the distribution of countries to be disposed of as a result of the war. Talleyrand had other ideas.

Looking like an old fuddled schoolmaster in his long coat, with his half-closed eyes and heavy countenance, he waddled into the conference chamber. The Ministers were already assembled round a long table, at the head of which sat Castlereagh. At the other end of the table sat Gentz. Talleyrand, with a quick glance round, took the vacant chair beside Castlereagh, and from this point of vantage, began

operations. For two hours, reports Gentz, he rated the Sovereigns.[1]
"Why had he been invited alone, and without his fellow plenipotentiaries?" he asked, his deep hoarse voice vibrating through the
room. He was informed that it was because it had been considered
more convenient to confine the preliminary discussions to the heads
of the delegations. In that case why had Hardenberg been accompanied
by Humboldt? He was informed that it was because Hardenberg was
unfortunately very deaf. Talleyrand, who had been lame from childhood, tersely replied, " We all have our infirmities, and can exploit
them when necessary." Castlereagh quietly intervened.

"The object of to-day's conference," he informed Talleyrand, " is
to acquaint you with what has been done by the four Courts since we
have been here." And he asked Metternich to hand the Protocol,
which they had drawn up and signed, to the French Minister. Talleyrand noticed that the word "Allies " had been used in every paragraph
of the document. He remarked on the fact, saying that it caused
him to wonder whether peace had been made or not, or whether
they were still involved in a quarrel. "Allies against whom?" he
asked.

Metternich replied that they had only used the word for the sake
of brevity. Talleyrand observed that however valuable brevity might
be, it was not worth the cost of inexactitude. He then read the paper
through and said he did not understand; for him there were two
dates, 30 May when the Congress was stipulated, and 1 October when
it was to meet. Everything which had been done in the interval he
did not recognise. It was illegal, and, as far as he was concerned, did
not exist. The assumption of control by the Big Four possessed neither
legal nor moral justification.

To all of which the plenipotentiaries weakly replied that they did
not in any case attach much importance to the document, and did not
mind eliminating it. They took it back, Metternich put it away, and
there was no further question of the Protocol. After having withdrawn
the document they produced another, which Talleyrand and Labrador
were to sign if they agreed. This document dealt with Committees
which were to be formed before the Congress assembled.

Talleyrand, suspecting that the four allied powers would themselves have the selecting of the Committees and that the whole affair

[1] *Dépêches Inédites.* Gentz.

was merely a ruse to put themselves in control of all the operations of the Congress, asserted that the idea of settling everything before the Congress assembled was new to him, and that the authority for selecting the Committees could only be given by the Congress itself.

Castlereagh remarked that he appreciated the weight of Talleyrand's opinions, but what other expedient could be found that would not involve inextricable delays?

Talleyrand asked why the Congress could not be assembled at once, and what delay would that involve?

Several difficulties were suggested, but the brilliance of Talleyrand's tactics so unsettled all the allies that they actually agreed to tear up the document which they had signed, and to start with Talleyrand's assistance all over again.

The most striking thing about this first clash was the weakness of the Great Powers. They were the victors, they occupied the whole of Europe with their armies, yet at the first objection from conquered France they withdrew all their proposals and adjourned. The reason for this attitude was the fact that Castlereagh and Metternich were having the greatest difficulties with Russia, and were anxious to win Talleyrand over to their side. On arriving in Vienna, Alexander had made it clear that nothing would satisfy him but the Duchy of Warsaw. Metternich had had private conferences with him on the subject, but could not move him. Castlereagh had had no better fortune with him. They needed Talleyrand; for if France threw her weight on the side of Russia, who already had Prussia in alliance, there would be no withstanding Alexander. Talleyrand, knowing their weakness and his strength, had won the first round.

Although the formal opening of the Congress had been fixed for 1 October, it was impossible to convene it on that date owing to dissensions among the allies. Three months had elapsed since their meeting in Paris, and during that period the allies had drifted farther and farther apart. Alexander's relations with England had been sensibly disturbed during his visit to London, and there was a new orientation in politics. Up to the signing of the Treaty of Paris the predilection of England for Russia had been felt in all European affairs. It had been established for a century, and had been reinforced during a quarter of a century of warfare. But now the balance of power was exposed to a new danger, for if Russia gained Poland as she was determined to do, she would be within striking distance of the heart of Germany, and a menace to all Europe.

Castlereagh, in his fear of the expansion of Russia, and his desire for a "just equilibrium" in European affairs, was at first inclined to the view that a stronger Prussia was a necessary condition for European stability. He even informed Hardenberg that if the incorporation of Saxony was necessary to her, Britain would acquiesce in the act, providing that Prussia opposed the Czar's annexation of Poland. But this attempt to wean Prussia from Russia failed; Hardenberg at first agreed, but after some weeks of apparent co-operation with England and Austria he declared that Prussia was on the side of Russia. It was clear to Castlereagh that Prussia was not to be trusted. He began to accept Talleyrand's view that if Prussia were put in possession of Saxony, in a few years she would form a militarist monarchy that would endanger the peace of all Europe. France was so opposed to the acquisition of Saxony by Prussia that, as Wellington wrote to Castlereagh from Paris, she would have been prepared to go to war, providing England was not against her, rather than acquiesce in Prussia's aggrandisement.

There seemed, in any case, no real justification for taking away his kingdom from the King of Saxony, even though he had been Napoleon's staunch ally; but Prussia was determined to annex Saxony, to indemnify her for giving up Prussian Poland to the Czar. "Prussia," says Gentz, "only brought to the Congress an immoderate desire for extending her possessions at the expense of all the world and without regard to any principle of justice or even of decency."

Backed by Alexander, who grew more obstinate and defiant daily, the pretensions of Prussia increased. The Congress was in an uproar. Alexander's interviews with Metternich had grown so stormy that by the end of October, Metternich was declaring that he would never again see the Emperor in private, and Alexander was declaring that Metternich had offended him mortally, and that he would never again have any personal connection with him.

The great powers in Europe had assembled to make a lasting peace, but they were already as distrustful of each other as if they had been at war, and it seemed as though the Congress would leave affairs in a greater tangle than before. The opening of the Congress had been postponed till 12 October, for some agreement had to be reached before the allies met the lesser powers. But on 12 October the opening was postponed till 1 November. By that time the allies were in a state of frenzied confusion; and the Congress had still not been convened. The quarrels grew more bitter day by day, and Castlereagh's idea of a lasting peace, founded on a just division of strength, seemed to be receding farther and farther.

Police reports in Vienna, issued on 20 October 1814, stated that there was talk of the approaching dissolution of the Congress and the departure of the Sovereigns and their Ministers, that there was also a growing fear of war. Preparations for war were indeed being made. Troops were being concentrated on the frontiers. The attempt by the Big Four to settle all the problems by informal meetings and a confidential approach had awakened only panic.

On 30 October it was decided to postpone the plenary sessions of the Congress indefinitely, and no further date was ever given for the assembly of all the Powers. As Gentz remarked, *there never was a Congress of Vienna.* There were only conferences of the Ministers of England, Austria, Russia and Prussia, to which Talleyrand was later admitted. These informal meetings continued, the Great Powers regulating the affairs of the lesser states without even consulting the representatives of the latter.

Finding it more and more difficult to resist Alexander's claim on Poland, Castlereagh decided to secure the Low Countries against his arms and his intrigues. Belgium had always been one of Castlereagh's main interests. "I had rather give the Prince of Orange something more to defend," he wrote to Liverpool on 11 November 1814, "and fortify the Low Countries than assist the credit of a Calmuck Prince to overturn Europe." He was able to get Holland confirmed in the possession of Belgium and Luxemburg; and Limburg and Liège were added to her dominions. But over Poland and Saxony there was a complete deadlock. In the midst of discussions Alexander would lean over the map, put his hand over Poland, and say with a tone of finality: "*C'est à moi.*" Eventually, finding that short of war there was no way of stopping Alexander where Poland was concerned, Castlereagh began to treat with him regarding a reasonable frontier, determined at least to stop him on the Vistula. Writing to Wellington, he said: "However it is something to find that we are allowed to treat, and not bound to receive the Emperor's pleasure as law."

By 1 December, he had broken down Alexander's resistance to the extent that the Czar was ready to accept Poland without the towns of Cracow and Thorn, which would become free cities under the protection of the allied powers, but he would only agree to this on condition that the whole of Saxony was ceded to Prussia. Metternich would not consent to Saxony going to Prussia on any terms, and there was still a deadlock. On 5 December 1814, Castlereagh wrote to Liverpool informing him that the discussions had become so acute that they might end in war.

The British Cabinet became seriously alarmed. England was still involved in the American War, and the Government felt that we had no immediate interest in the questions that were agitating Europe. Castlereagh was informed that the Government would not consent to involve the country in hostilities for any of the objects which were under discussion at Vienna. It was an awkward position for Castlereagh. He had done all he could to force the allies to an agreement, but the task seemed to be beyond him. In his desire to propitiate all parties, and to construct a Europe which would survive the test of time, he had restored the colonies captured by Britain (except for those which had a maritime interest) and had indemnified with large subsidies the countries which had suffered the greatest losses.

He now declared in the name of the Government that he would cease to pay subsidies from 15 January if the Congress did not come to a settlement, and that he had, besides, orders to leave Vienna, his presence in London being necessary on account of the meeting of Parliament. He also paid a visit to Talleyrand, who had not been admitted to the Conferences on the Polish-Saxon question, and they discussed the problem. The French Minister suggested that they should acknowledge the rights of the Saxon King. Castlereagh replied that he and Metternich, and Talleyrand himself, had already done so. Talleyrand then suggested that the three of them should make a private agreement regarding the matter.

"An agreement," Castlereagh exclaimed. "Are you proposing an alliance?"

"An agreement might be possible without an alliance," said

Talleyrand, " but it will be an alliance if you wish; I have no objection."

" But an alliance implies war, or else it may lead to it; and we should do everything to avoid war."

" I agree with you," replied Talleyrand. " We must do everything except sacrifice honour, justice and the future of Europe."

" War would not be looked upon favourably in England," said Castlereagh.

" War would be popular in England if you were to give it a noble aim, an aim with significance to all Europe."

" What would that aim be? "

" The restoration of Poland."

Castlereagh considered a moment, and replied, " Not yet."[1]

On the 29 December began the famous meetings which caused an explosion that nearly blew up the whole Congress. Alexander had summoned Metternich, Castlereagh, Hardenberg and Razoumoffsky (who had replaced Nesselrode) to a conference, to settle the problem of Poland and Saxony. At this meeting Castlereagh and Metternich accepted Alexander's proposal that Russia should take over the Duchy of Warsaw, with the exception of Gnesen and Posen and the former provinces of Western Prussia, and that Cracow and Thorn should be declared independent cities; but they refused to accede to the demand that Saxony should be incorporated with Prussia. Alexander took a high hand, and insisted that Saxony should be given to Prussia. Castlereagh was extremely irritated by his attitude, and when Hardenberg, emboldened by the Czar's tone, announced that if Prussia's claim to Saxony were any longer denied, Prussia would regard it as a declaration of war, Castlereagh took a risk. He rose, and informing the Prussian Minister that if such a temper really prevailed it were better to break up the proceedings, he walked out of the Congress.

A panic ensued. It looked as though war might at any moment break out. Castlereagh had completely disregarded the instructions he had received from his Government, but he knew that he had France and Austria with him. And he knew that the Treaty of Ghent had just been signed by Britain and America, and Britain's hands were no longer tied.

Castlereagh called on Talleyrand again, and informed him that

[1] *The Reconstruction of Europe*, by Guglielmo Ferrero.

Alexander was behaving in a dictatorial manner that he would not brook. " The Russians are trying to lay down the law," he said. " England will not take it from anyone."

Talleyrand again mentioned the subject of an alliance, and Castlereagh drew up the draft. A day or two later, on 3 January 1815, England and Austria signed a treaty of alliance with France, the enemy they had just beaten, to defend the Treaty of Paris by every means which might become necessary, including war. Each of them agreed to contribute 150,000 men if attacked by Prussia.

On that same day, another meeting of the Big Four was called. The Russian and Prussian Ministers attended it, neither of them having the least suspicion of what had taken place. Their surprise was great indeed when Metternich, backed by Castlereagh, proposed that Talleyrand should be admitted to the negotiations on the Polish-Saxon question. It was obvious that England and Austria had made an alliance with France. The alliance profoundly changed the aspect of the Congress, and from that moment the crisis melted away.

Alexander, realising that Castlereagh was not to be trifled with, lowered his tone prodigiously. He even promised to do his best to persuade Prussia to content herself with half of Saxony. On 5 January Castlereagh was able to inform Liverpool that the alarm of war was over. A fortnight later he was officially informed by Lord Bathurst that his Defensive Alliance with France had been approved by the Cabinet and would be forthwith ratified. Although he had disobeyed instructions, he received the Prince Regent's entire approbation of his conduct, " under circumstances very critical and deeply affecting the tranquillity of Europe." " The spirit," wrote the Regent, " with which your Lordship resisted the menacing language of the Prussian minister upheld the dignity of the Court you represent, and was well calculated to check an impetuosity, from which much might have been apprehended, had it not been so seasonably rebuked."

Castlereagh's courage and confidence had carried the allies through yet another crisis.

Talleyrand too had gained a victory. France was no longer isolated in Europe. At all the future conferences on the Polish-Saxon question Talleyrand was present. The Big Four had become the Big Five; and it was the Big Five that worked out the European frontiers.

Prussia was now forced to agree to the suggestion that Saxony should be divided in half, one-half to remain with the Saxon King. But there was further trouble about the portion to be made over to Prussia, who was now claiming the important town of Leipzig. The Police Reports relate that Castlereagh did not know where Leipzig was, and was surprised to find that it was in Saxony. He was able, however, to keep Leipzig out of the claws of Prussia.

Regarding Poland, Castlereagh contented himself with restricting Russia to the line of the Vistula as her frontier. Having settled the Polish problem as satisfactorily as he was able he abandoned his opposition to the Czar. It was always his aim to conciliate wherever possible, and he continued this line with Russia. A letter which he wrote to Charles a year or so later gives a clear statement of his general attitude to Russia.

" My notion of managing this great Power," he wrote, " is to indulge the Emperor a little more in tone, and to watch him not less closely in the long run. I think Austria ought not to be jealous of our coquetry with the Emperor, for if we can keep him in the right path it is everything to the Court of Vienna. It will also prevent the connection of Russia with France from becoming too close, which is bad for us both, but much more formidable to Austria. . . . My belief is that the idea of a German League, countenanced by us, has been the principal cause why Alexander has kept up his army on a war footing. . . .

" . . . My politics with reference to the Emperor Alexander may be stated in a short compass, and they are formed upon an attentive observation of his course since I joined him first in France. Up to the period of the Congress my fears were that Conquest was his passion. I changed my impression there, and my notion now is that if you treat him as Emperor of Russia in Europe, and do not attempt by alliances to shut him up and exclude him from his influence in continental affairs, that there is a fair chance of his reign being pacifist; and if it is, or can be made so, the tranquillity of Europe is secured, for there is no other power that has the means systematically to disturb us.

" I am rather inclined to this view of the Question from the disposition he has invariably shown, from the moment of our Polish controversy at Vienna to concert his measures with us. This I found particularly the case at Paris, nor have I ever found him impracticable or unreasonable in details, and if you except the Polish point, on which his honour was committed by Austria imprudently letting his troops get possession of the Duchy of Warsaw, I cannot upon a review of his whole conduct charge him with having been unjust or overbearing in his demands. . . .

"I hope Prince Metternich will concur in the expediency of fanning to the utmost His Imperial Majesty's pride as the Grand Pacificator. We should not despair of his choosing this as the best Pedestal for his Fame, and if we can bind him down in the trammels of his own Christian Maxims, it is a very cheap protection; at all events we lose nothing by the attempt, as little is to be gained by crying wolf, when we cannot justify a policy of a jealous and expensive nature."[1]

5

All through the month of November and of December, while Castlereagh was trying to settle the Polish-Saxon controversy, Liverpool was writing urgent letters to him, pressing him to return; for his presence was badly needed in the House of Commons. The latest day to which Parliament could be adjourned, Liverpool wrote, was the 9 February and Castlereagh's presence was of the utmost importance, as the Opposition were harassing the Government on every issue. In spite of the peace there was more unrest and more party spirit and rancour prevalent than had been known during the war. If the Government in the House of Commons should lose credit and be beaten in debate before Castlereagh returned, it would be no easy matter for him or any man to recover the ground that had been lost. It was even rumoured that Liverpool and Vansittart would be forced to resign, and that Castlereagh would become Prime Minister. True it was that Liverpool would not risk opening Parliament till Castlereagh returned. But Castlereagh felt that the fate of Europe depended on the decisions of the Congress, and he desired to conduct to their conclusion measures for which he stood so deeply responsible.

Writing to Bathurst, on 30 January 1815, he said: "You might as well expect me to have run away from Leipzig (if I had been there)

[1] Londonderry Papers. Undated, but probably 1816.

last year, to fight Creevey and Whitbread, as to withdraw from hence till the existing contest is brought to a point, and I think you do both injustice to your own supporters, and too much honour to me, in supposing my presence so necessary."

In a postscript he adds: "I beg you will not give any money at present to any of the Continental Powers. The poorer they are kept the better, to prevent them from quarrelling. Time enough to settle accounts when we know who deserves it." But he was making arrangements for Wellington to leave Paris and replace him at Vienna as soon as the problems facing the Congress were solved.

For months the Congress had been debating without coming to any agreement. "*Le Congrès danse*," observed the Prince de Ligne, "*mais ne marche pas.*" Castlereagh began now, as Chambonas remarked, to put some life into the deliberations and hurry on the conclusion of affairs. Day and night he worked to get an agreement on the chief points effected.

On the 3 February Wellington arrived in Vienna, and they spent some days together going over all the details which had to be arranged. There was still the question of Naples—whether to expel Murat or recognise him—there was Parma—whether to restore the Bourbons or establish Marie-Louise there—and there was the question of the confederation of the German states. There were also the final details of the divison of Saxony to be settled. On 6 February Castlereagh at last reached an agreement with Hardenberg. The more populous half of Saxony was to be left to her King, including Dresden, Leipzig and Bautzen; the larger part, though of less importance, was to be given to Prussia, who was also to receive Thorn from Alexander to console her for giving up Leipzig. Cracow alone remained a free city. Metternich, Talleyrand and Wellington were to go to Pressburg and invite the Saxon King to make certain sacrifices for the general peace. That the Saxon King declined this invitation made little difference; he was forced to accept.

Regarding Naples, Castlereagh refused to declare for or against Murat, and departed from Vienna without giving a definite opinion. It was a wise evasion, for the question of Naples was to settle itself. Murat's treachery to the allies in the days to come was to settle his own destiny.

On 14 February 1815, Castlereagh left Vienna, and after two busy days at Paris, was home again. At Dover he was welcomed by immense crowds with the wildest enthusiasm. In London, when he appeared in the House of Commons, the members rose again and cheered him. It was his second triumphal entry. The newspapers were full of his praise. But the Opposition members began to attack him with great violence. They were determined to discredit him, and through him the Tory Government.

He was attacked for not keeping Parliament properly informed of the Vienna transactions, for deserting Saxony and abandoning Poland, for repudiating Lord William Bentinck's promise of independence to Genoa.

Castlereagh rose to face his critics with that courtesy and calm which never failed to impress the House. So far from disclaiming responsibility, he accepted it. He had been obliged to take action without reference to the House, for had he delayed his decisions " the whole machine of Europe would have been arrested." Lord William Bentinck's promise of independence to Genoa had been totally unauthorised. The absorption of that city within the kingdom of Sardinia had been essential to the security of Europe, and it was on those grounds he had consented to it. But Parliament was not to be appeased, and the controversy continued. Attacks were becoming more and more heated, when an incident arose which was to absorb even the Opposition. For in the midst of recriminations, news suddenly arrived that Napoleon was missing from Elba.

At Vienna, on 6 March 1815, Charles had been awakened at an early hour in the morning with a dispatch from the English ambassador in Florence, informing him that a messenger had entered the town inquiring whether anyone had seen Napoleon. For five days Napoleon was missing. It was not known where he was, nor which road he had taken. Then came the thunderclap. He was in France. The soldiers were rushing to meet him ; he was being welcomed everywhere by enthusiastic crowds ; he was marching to Paris. " Castlereagh has taken to his bed with the news," wrote Mr. Bennett to Creevey.

In Vienna, Alexander, who had by this time decided to challenge Metternich to a duel, believing he had misrepresented his intentions to Prussia, dropped the idea, and the two made up their quarrel.

It was in Metternich's ballroom, where they were still dancing, that the King of Prussia first heard the news. He gave a sign to the

Duke of Wellington, and they left the room together, followed by the Emperor Alexander and the Emperor Francis. The ballroom gradually emptied.

" The Congress is dissolved," Napoleon had said on setting his foot on French soil. And indeed the Congress was dissolved. An agony of apprehension swept over Europe during the terrible hundred days when, regiment by regiment, the French army rallied to Napoleon. In Paris the French Government prepared for flight, without striking a blow. Louis XVIII stated in public that he would not leave his arm-chair, but in private he said: " So you want me to die on the curule chair. I am not in the mood." He was already planning flight. Fouché and Talleyrand were holding themselves in readiness to leap into the victor's camp, whichever it might be.

Castlereagh wrote post-haste to Wellington, informing him that the Prince Regent left it to Wellington to decide either to remain at Vienna or to put himself at the head of the army in Flanders. Wellington had already made up his mind ; he was off to the Low Countries to take command of the army. Meanwhile Napoleon had been carried shoulder high up the stairs of the Tuileries.

The allies hastened to renew Castlereagh's Treaty of Chaumont; the Grand Alliance was in operation again. As the days passed news came that Napoleon, at the head of a formidable army, was marching to the Low Countries. But the Duke of Wellington, with the English, Brunswick, Belgian and Hanoverian forces, and Blücher, with the Prussian army, were there to receive him. England stood breathless, waiting for news.

6

On the 21 June 1815, Lord and Lady Castlereagh were dining two or three doors from their own house, to meet the Prince Regent, when there suddenly came the sound of shouting and the rush of a crowd. A post-chaise and four, with three French eagles projecting out of its windows, and four French flags draped over the seats, was rushing at full speed across the square. It stopped for a moment at Castlereagh's door, and then away it went towards the house where he was dining. Major Henry Percy, A.D.C. to the Duke of Wellington, had arrived with dispatches, announcing that a battle had been fought at Waterloo three days earlier, at which we had been gloriously triumphant.

The Prince Regent and Castlereagh retired to another room to read the dispatches. Though they were greatly relieved to hear of the victory, they were horrified at the list of killed and wounded. Most of those who had fallen were men who had distinguished themselves in the Peninsular Campaign and whose names had become almost household words. The Guards had suffered severely. When the Prince returned to the drawing-room he looked very sad, and said with great feeling: " It is a glorious victory, and we must rejoice at it, but the loss of life has been fearful, and I have lost many friends." And while he spoke the tears ran down his face. Outside the mob was cheering. He went to the window, and bowed from the balcony, and the party broke up.

It was reported that Lady Castlereagh went on to a ball at Sir George Talbot's afterwards, but her niece indignantly denies this, as it was not considered correct to go to a ball in such circumstances. Indeed, like Trafalgar, the Battle of Waterloo at the time was regarded as great a disaster as it was a victory.

Wellington, the victor of Waterloo, was as distressed as the Regent. When Creevey congratulated him on his great triumph he said: " It has been a damned serious business. Blücher and I have lost 30,000 men. It has been a damned nice thing—the nearest run thing you ever saw in your life. Blücher lost 14,000 on Friday night and got so damnably licked I could not find him on Saturday morning, so I was obliged to fall back to keep up my communications with him. My God, I don't think it would have done if I had not been there."

Castlereagh made hasty preparations to leave for Paris for the final settlement. When he arrived he at once took the direction of affairs into his own hands. He sent immediately for Croker and Fouché to take measures for Napoleon's capture ; but Talleyrand decided that they should all meet at his house in the evening. When they assembled Talleyrand proposed that Napoleon should be arrested and shot. Fouché supported him, but Castlereagh demurred. Napoleon, however, settled his own fate by giving himself up to the British Navy.

He had boarded a frigate intending to sail for the United States when he found himself suddenly in the shadow of H.M.S. *Bellerophon*. His resolution and his courage were gone. All he could do was to surrender. Writing to the Regent, he said that he came "like Themistocles to sit down at the fireside of the British people, placing himself under the protection of their laws, which he claimed from His Royal Highness as the most powerful, the most constant, and the most generous of his enemies."

On board he showed Captain Maitland the portraits of his wife and child, and made himself agreeable to all. He seemed to believe that he would receive a warm welcome in England. When he arrived off Plymouth, crowds flocked to see him. For over 20 years the English people had been fighting him ; their sacrifices had been enormous, and yet there was a glamour about the fallen monarch that fascinated even the Captain of the *Bellerophon*.

The Government took no risks, and Napoleon was shipped off to St. Helena. He could hardly believe his ears when he heard what his fate was to be. "I am the guest of England, not her prisoner," he said. "I have come of my own accord to place myself under the protection of the British law."

7

The English army were again in Paris, encamped in the Bois de Boulogne. The Prussians were there too, behaving like boors. The Russians were so insolent they were hardly less offensive to the English than to the French. It was as well that Castlereagh and Wellington were in Paris, or the city would have been levelled to the ground.

"The immediate difficulty," Castlereagh wrote to Liverpool on 8 July 1815, "is how to keep Blücher and the Prussians within any bounds towards this town . . . they are at this moment mining the bridge of Jena, with a view to blowing it up. The Duke has written to urge them at least to suspend all measures of this nature till the arrival of the Sovereigns: and we propose to-morrow morning to pay the Marshal a visit at St. Cloud together, to stop, if possible, these measures of arbitrary and unconcerted severity."

On the 20 July, all being quiet again, Louis XVIII arrived at the Tuileries. Portly and good-natured, dressed in a blue coat with a red collar, a white waistcoat and a cocked hat and white cockade, he took his place again on the throne Napoleon had vacated.

The following day when Castlereagh and Wellington came to pay their respects to the restored monarch, they received a great ovation. The crowd was immense, and so loud were the shouts of the people that during their long audience they found it almost impossible to converse. As the shouts continued the King took them to the open window, and candles were brought to enable the people to see their monarch with Wellington and Castlereagh on either side of him. The crowds ran in a solid mass from every part of the garden, rending the air with acclamations; and singing and dancing and shouting continued for hours under the King's windows.

From all these festivities Talleyrand was missing. On Louis's flight he had been prepared to discuss the future of his country upon any basis with almost anybody; he had begun playing with endless possibilities. Castlereagh, who had the shrewdest insight into character, had written to Lord Clancarty: " I agree with you that Talleyrand cannot be relied on, and yet I know not on whom His Majesty can better depend." But the King had no intention of depending on Talleyrand. When the latter sought the presence, His Majesty said ironically: " So you are leaving us, Prince of Benevento? The waters will do you good. You must let us have news of you."

Talleyrand's career of shuffling politics and changing sides was temporarily suspended.

8

Lady Castlereagh, who had lost no time in following her husband to Paris, found a great change in the city. Instead of the small sprinkling of English there had been in 1814, there was now an English army and almost the whole of the English aristocracy. She was soon giving dinner-parties and suppers again, dances and picnics.

Her parties, thought Lady Shelley, who was in Paris following the Duke, were extremely stupid. She only enjoyed them, she decided, when she was put next to Lord Castlereagh, whom she found very " agreeable and strikingly handsome when he is animated, his conversation most interesting." Apart from the dinner-parties and suppers, Emily beguiled the time planning excursions. On one occasion, she took a party to Ermonville, where an unpleasant incident was only avoided by Castlereagh's tact. When the party arrived at Ermonville, donkeys were required to carry the ladies, but the messenger sent to a neighbouring village to procure them returned without any, because of the extortionate charge demanded. Blücher, who was among the party, grimly nodded to one of his men. Accompanied by a few Hussars, the man went off, and in a short time appeared with three times the number of donkeys required, followed however by an angry, gesticulating crowd.

Castlereagh moved forward, and went quietly amongst the villagers, sending them back with more money than the whole stud was worth. He did not care for Blücher's tactics any more than the Prussians understood such treatment of a conquered people.

Castlereagh was the star of Paris that autumn. Scrutinised by everyone he moved gravely amid the enthusiastic crowds. He was tired and far from well; and the mass of business he had to transact was becoming increasingly burdensome. To relax his mind and body he would spend hours every day in a bath at the Bains Chinois, but the relaxation did little to restore his exhausted faculties. Anxieties weighed him down.

One day he asked Dr. John Howell, Surgeon General to the Forces, where the carotid artery was situated, and learnt that it passed down the neck below the ear. The left carotid artery, he was informed, sprang directly from the aorta and supplied the brain: it was never interfered with, for even the smallest incision in the artery would cause instant death. The doctor was surprised to find him so interested in anatomical subjects, and must have wondered what prompted his inquiries, but if any dark thoughts were forming in that overweighted mind, nobody at that time had any intimation of the fact.

Overworked and overtired, Castlereagh's life had become a daily grind, a round in which he did his work enclosed in himself, a prison from which he could not escape. Sometimes he would get away from the crowds with which he was continually surrounded, and go for long solitary walks. He was wandering along the Champs Elysées one afternoon deep in thought when he was knocked down by a horse, and brought home in a carriage in a fainting condition. He had been kicked on the knee, and was in great pain. The blow brought on an attack of gout, and he was confined to his room for several weeks. But though he was compelled to stay in bed, he took no rest. He wrote his dispatches and gave them to Emma Sophia to copy for him. She had always had a deep affection for Castlereagh, and was glad to be of use to him during this trying time. She had always loved and admired him, and indignantly repudiated the accusation that he was cold.

"The calm dignity of his manner," she asserted, "gave an impression that he was cold: but no one who had seen his kindly smile, or been greeted by his two hands stretched out in welcome, could have thought him so. To all those connected with him he was most affectionate."

The injured knee gave him a good deal of trouble, and when he was able to get up he had to walk on crutches for a while. Vansittart, writing to him, said: "I have never known the public more anxious about any individual, or more sensible of anything, than of the detriment which the interests both of this country and of Europe must have suffered by even a temporary interruption of your services." But there was no interruption of his services; conferences proceeded in his bedroom, and the peace terms were settled.

Castlereagh was at this epoch more powerful than ever before. He could have acquired for his country great accessions of territory and immense financial and commercial gains, but he preferred security and peace. To Napoleon he seemed an imbecile for throwing away so many advantages, but Napoleon could better understand the attitude of the Prussians, who were out for revenge, for fantastic reparations and war indemnities, than the desire of Castlereagh for moderation, for a just and reasonable peace which would satisfy all parties.

The Prussian claims he opposed with vigour. The Prussians were demanding Alsace-Lorraine, the Saar valley, Luxemburg and Savoy; the war indemnity they desired was no less than twelve hundred million francs. But Castlereagh was opposed to a policy of revenge, and would not countenance their claims. Although he felt that the magnanimous policy towards France displayed in the First Treaty of Paris had hardly had the desired effect, and that the allies must look more than ever to security, his desire was to obtain security without undue severity. He did not feel that any stability would be attained if he allowed the Powers to take from France territory which she might in the future reclaim, and involve us any day in another continental war.

He did not hesitate to cut down the boundaries of France to what they were in 1790 instead of 1792, but he saved her from dismemberment and ruin. He also insisted on an indemnity, feeling that it was hardly to be expected that Britain should pay all the expenses of a war which France had imposed on her; but the indemnity was one that she could bear; it was fixed at 700 million francs. The north of France, he agreed, should be occupied by an army of 150,000 men, but only for a period of three to five years.

From the British nation there had come cries for revenge. Liverpool demanded the punishment of " traitors," and some blood had to be spilt. It did not escape Castlereagh's notice that Fouché gave warning to all concerned, but it did not trouble him. Only Ney refused to escape, and preferred to face the firing squad.

The Regent decided that France should not be allowed to retain the statues and works of art plundered from other nations. Castlereagh agreed that these should be restored to their owners, but he declined to accede to the Regent's proposal that some of them should be claimed for his Galleries.

The peace terms were at last settled. " Having signed everything to my entire satisfaction on the 20th at night," Castlereagh wrote to Charles, " both with the French Government and the Allies, I am now, my dearest brother, in all the misery of winding up, paying visits and getting away from this place in which I hope we have done some good, but not without slaving hard." " Slaving hard " had become part of his nature ; leisure and recreation a crying need that was denied him.

But he was satisfied that they had all, as he wrote to Charles, been acting an honest part towards Europe and each other. He was especially pleased that he and Wellington had seen eye to eye with each other. " Nothing could go on better than Wellington and I did to the last," he informed his brother. " I do not recollect a single divergence of opinion between us throughout the whole." All his efforts had been crowned with success. He had overthrown Britain's deadliest foe and had constructed the new Europe in such a manner that Britain obtained the longest interval of peace she had ever enjoyed. " Such achievements," states Sir Charles Webster, " should be sufficient to place him for ever amongst the greatest Foreign Ministers of his country." [1]

Before leaving Paris, Castlereagh brought up another matter which had been exercising his mind a good deal. He felt that no frontier rectifications would suffice to maintain security unless backed by a guarantee of the Great Powers. Having each obtained from the war all reasonable satisfaction, they should, he urged, form a council of united nations to safeguard the stability achieved, and prevent the threat of war wherever it might arise. His desire was to preserve that Alliance to which Europe already owed her deliverance, and to secure peace by discussion rather than by the threat of armed force. He achieved his aim, and the Quadruple Alliance was signed on 20 November 1815, the day the Treaty of Paris was signed. The Powers agreed to meet at fixed periods for the purpose of discussing measures for the maintenance of the Peace of Europe.

But the Quadruple Alliance, which Castlereagh considered his great achievement, was regarded with suspicion by the British people, who were afraid of continental entanglements. It was also condemned by later generations, because it ignored the principle of nationality and self-government, which were to be the master forces of the nineteenth century. Yet it secured its chief object, the maintenance of peace in Europe, and the peace it established lasted twice as long as the settlement of 1919, which was based on the national principle. The Quadruple Alliance was also prejudiced from the outset by the mood of spiritual exaltation which took possession of the Czar at this time. He had always been addicted to mysticism, and was now in the hands of the Baroness von Krudener, a woman who filled his heart with love for his enemies, and convinced him of his pre-ordained mission. The upshot of this mood of exaltation was the Holy Alliance. The Sovereigns, the Czar solemnly declared, should henceforth take for their sole guide the precepts of the Christian religion, namely justice, charity and peace.

Austria and Prussia, the two most rapacious and reactionary of the powers, duly endorsed the scheme. The Prince Regent, however, though he conveyed to the august signatories " his entire concurrence

[1] Webster. *Foreign Policy of Castlereagh.*

The Holy Alliance

in the principles they had laid down," and stated that he had no objection to the Czar making the divine precepts of the Christian religion the invariable rule of his conduct, expressed his regret that " the forms of the British constitution precluded him from acceding to the Treaty."

In Parliament Castlereagh, when he returned, defended the Holy Alliance; he was anxious to placate the Czar, but though he upheld it in public, in private he called it " a piece of sublime mysticism and nonsense." He even expressed his doubts of the Czar's sanity, and confessed that when Alexander first produced the draft for the Duke of Wellington and himself to read, it was not without difficulty that they went through the interview with becoming gravity.

The Holy Alliance, which has often been confused with the Quadruple Alliance, was entirely the Czar's contrivance; the Quadruple Alliance was the work of Castlereagh. Unfortunately, Castlereagh's desire that controversial questions should be settled by international arbitration instead of by war was completely misinterpreted by the people, and used for their own ends by the monarchs, and these assemblies came to be regarded as a conspiracy among the Sovereigns to protect each other. In this matter Castlereagh was in advance of his age, and was so misunderstood as to be considered a reactionary.

9

Amongst his papers, when he returned to London, was a report that Buonaparte had arrived at St. Helena. He was out of sorts on landing, the report ran, and did not like the aspect of the island. The news did not surprise Castlereagh.

There was also a letter from Charles, troubling him with a list of complaints. Castlereagh advised him to get married. " I wish," he wrote, " you would weigh one point well, viz. whether you have not lived a vagabond life long enough, and whether you would not upon the whole be more happy if your home, wherever it may be, be made both more creditable and comfortable to yourself by having a wife *chez vous* than a mistress *dehors*—you are young enough to marry well and to encounter a person whom you would like and who would like you—if you put it off too long you will find it a more precarious experiment."

However tiresome Charles might be, whether he was wanting honours, or merely leave of absence, or an advance, Castlereagh was kind but firm, helping wherever he could, admonishing when necessary, but always with affection. "Believe me, my dear Charles," he assures him, "that although I sometimes appear to forget you in the pursuit of business, my heart and affections are ever growing." Charles tried that affection sorely. Even in the matter of finding himself a wife he provided Castlereagh with endless vexation and embarrassment, for at the age of thirty-seven he centred his affections on a girl of eighteen—one of the richest heiresses in Britain—in such perverse circumstances, and with such lack of reserve, that assertions were made against him which necessitated his appealing to the Government to allow the marriage to proceed, for Frances Anne's [1] guardians were determined to oppose it. Again Castlereagh had the task of smoothing matters out, and the business ended happily with a fortune and wedding bells.

Finding town as dull as ever, in spite of its so-called gaieties, Castlereagh hurried off to his sheep at Cray. It was with a sigh of relief that he saw his farm again. "Thank God I am once more unsaddled," he said, "and may roll on the grass."

10

Although the war was over Castlereagh's position was no easier, for the blessed change that had taken place in the general state of Europe by the restoration of peace, after twenty years of savage warfare, was marred by the very real distress which now fell upon the poor. The sacrifices, the sufferings of England, throughout the long and terrible war, had been as great as those endured by any of the continental states, even though her soil had not been invaded. The sufferings did not cease with the advent of peace; if anything they grew more acute. Numbers of people had been thrown out of employment, through the cessation of the war and through the introduction of machinery; the cost of living had increased; but wages remained exceedingly low.

[1] Daughter of Sir Harry Vane Tempest.

Children were practically slaves, working in the mills fifteen or sixteen hours a day even at the age of six. Discontent was growing, acts of violence increasing; the temper of the people showed itself in gusts of popular fury which assailed the Regent, Wellington and Castlereagh alike.

Castlereagh was not insensitive to the cries of distress in the country. "They were such," he wrote to Charles, "as hardly to admit of exaggeration, and yet I hope," he said, "that things are somewhat mending"; but things were far from mending; the position grew steadily worse.

In the last year of the war, the landowners in Parliament had put pressure on the Government to pass a Corn Law Bill, forbidding the import of foreign wheat, unless the price of wheat reached 80s. a quarter. Although the law was inoperative, because a good harvest followed and the price of wheat fell, the Corn Law Bill roused the people to fury. In 1816 came a bad harvest and more distress ; the price of wheat reached 103s. a quarter, and the people were starving.

There were petitions to the Regent, but he waved them airily aside, saying: "My family have never attended to the prayers of the people." Misery and insurrection filled the land. Machines were broken in the dead of night, frames destroyed, work scattered on the highways; armed bands of desperadoes held the countryside in a state of continuous terror.

Castlereagh's only hope was a better harvest, and in the meantime a strong hand to put down the treason that was brewing; for seditious meetings were being held everywhere. The country was going through a great crisis, and it looked as though a temporary distress caused by industrial changes would be converted into permanent ruin for the people and the country. Our financial position was hopeless, but when Castlereagh supported the Chancellor of the Exchequer's proposal to continue the income tax, at the modified figure of 5 per cent, it roused the country to the deepest hostility. He had asserted in the House that he "felt assured that the people of England would not, from an ignorant impatience to be relieved from the pressure of taxation, put everything to hazard, when everything might be accomplished by continued constancy and firmness." This mild observation was considered offensive by the Opposition, who used it as a battle-cry, with which to enrage the people further against the Government.

A new movement by agitators calling themselves Radicals was formed. Stimulated by the French Revolution they besieged the Government with demands for annual parliaments, voting by ballot and universal suffrage. Castlereagh knew well enough the defects of the constitution, but he doubted whether sudden changes would alleviate the situation. " It is impossible," he had written Lord William Bentinck as far back as 5 May 1814, " not to perceive a great moral change coming on in Europe and that the principles of freedom are in full operation. The danger is that the transition may be too sudden to ripen into anything likely to make the world better or happier."

It was not that he was opposed to reform, but he had little faith in democracy, which at that time was associated with revolution, murder, violence and aggression. The country was too unsettled, he felt, for any sudden changes.

The Radicals were already becoming a very serious danger. On the 15 November 1816, they held a meeting at Spa Fields with flags and banners, bringing with them arms and ammunition. After a stormy meeting the leaders jumped down from their wagons and, followed by the mob, began attacking the shops of gunsmiths to obtain more arms. When a gunsmith remonstrated he was shot. Marching down Cheapside and Cornhill they fired off their arms, and rushed on to take the Tower. On the way they were met by the Lord Mayor and a few constables, and were easily dispersed. The leaders were arrested, but they were acquitted by the jury who were in complete sympathy with them.

The situation grew daily worse. On 28 January 1817, when the Regent was returning from Parliament with his escort of Life Guards he was grossly insulted, the state carriage was pelted with mud and stones, bullets from an air-gun were discharged, and a glass pane was broken.

There were reports of conspiracies, and of preparations for an armed rising. In alarm the Government passed a Bill to prevent seditious gatherings, and a month later the Habeas Corpus Act was suspended. It was suspended only till the 1 July but it had its effect, for the boldest of the leaders withdrew to America until the season of danger had expired. But the fact that men could be imprisoned without trial, though it may have suppressed treason for a while, brought more opprobrium on Castlereagh, who, though he was neither Prime Minister nor Home Secretary, was held responsible for every odious measure that was passed ; a responsibility which he never denied.

CHAPTER XIV

I

WITH HIS party and with the House generally Castlereagh was popular, but he was beginning to be hated more and more by the people. He began to feel a hostility in the air whenever he ventured out, a hostility directed towards himself. Sinister faces surrounded him, curses followed him; he was pursued by threats of assassination. He had felt the same hostility years ago when he was in Ireland, but danger never moved him. He put his pistols in his belt, and bore himself with the same indifferent air.

Riding one day through the streets on horseback he was attacked by an agitated mob shouting for his blood and threatening to drag him from the saddle. Instead of quickening his pace, he lowered his reins on to his horse's head and slowed down, proceeding quietly on his way, and not even the boldest of them dared to lay a finger on him.[1]

O'Connell, the Irish patriot, who had no reason to love Castlereagh, once said of him: " Castlereagh, with all his faults was a fine fellow, and as brave as Achilles."

But nobody had ever questioned his courage. Once, when an excited mob attacked his house, one of the Life Guards who had been called out, recognised Castlereagh among the crowd. He was standing looking up at his own house on which the people were wreaking their vengeance. Dressed in a blue coat buttoned up to the chin, with a white neck-cloth and long gaiters, he stood among the shouting rabble as calm and unconcerned as though he were in the House of Commons. He was not even ruffled by the abuse which was being heaped so liberally upon his head. When the Guards Officer warned

[1] Toynbee. *Glimpses of the Twenties.*

METTERNICH

*By T. Lawrence, from the Waterloo Chamber
at Windsor Castle*

him to go in, he said quietly: " The mob is not as dangerous as you think." Stones were being hurled through his windows, and when he returned eventually to the house he went round the drawing-room closing the shutters, with stones falling all round him, taking not the slightest precaution against being recognised.

The following day when Lady Castlereagh's niece, Emma Sophia, called to hear what had happened, she found him on the point of walking out. As she knew he would have to encounter the fury of the mob, she persuaded him to go in her carriage. While the carriage was moving at a foot's pace through the crowd he kept his face at the window. Fearing that he might have a stone thrown at him, she said: " Pray do not let your nose be seen, for it might be recognised, and my father would not like to have the panel of his carriage broken." He smiled and turned his head away.

It was a melancholy smile. Though he did not expect gratitude from the people for the way he had toiled to bring England to safety, he did not deserve to be so abused. He had never cared for public opinion, or attempted to make himself popular, but he had hardly expected such demonstrations of hatred. The country was in a bad state: it had been so for some time, and there seemed no way of improving conditions. If the Government took strong measures it was attacked for interfering with the people's liberties. If it refrained from taking strong measures it was attacked for being weak and ineffectual. If it prosecuted for libel on Ministers, or for high treason, the offenders were acquitted. There was nothing but opposition to everything the Government attempted. He worked as hard as a man well could. Eight or nine hours daily in the House of Commons; Committee meetings, Cabinet meetings, Agricultural Distress meetings, Poor Law meetings;[1] it was sapping his strength, and the temper of Parliament was such that every session was to give him a sharp campaign.

" I never found the House of Commons so dead to my voice," he wrote sadly to Charles.

[1] Inquiries into the condition of persons entitled to relief dated back to the Statute of Elizabeth.

2

The session fortunately was coming to a close, but there was no peace for Castlereagh ; for on the very last day, when the Opposition had exhausted all its other cries, Brougham took up an old question, accusing Castlereagh of tyranny, cruelty and oppression in his administration of Ireland. Castlereagh did not conceal his surprise that Brougham, without warning, should have chosen the last day of the session to bring up such an outworn subject. His defence, however, was so fine that it put an end to the charge once and for all, and it was never raised again in Parliament.

"With respect to Ireland," he said, "I know I never shall be forgiven. I have with many others incurred the inexpiable guilt of preserving that main branch of the British Empire from that separation which the traitors of Ireland, in conjunction with a foreign Power, had meditated. . . . Because I exerted myself to defend the people of Ireland from the conspiracy which surrounded them, my conduct has been the constant theme of invective. But I think those who are acquainted with me will do me the justice to believe that I never had a cruel or an unkind heart. I believe they would not think that I went farther in prosecuting even the guilty in Ireland than necessity demanded, or that I had recourse to measures beyond what the danger of the times imperatively demanded.

"If there were cruelties committed in Ireland (and I never denied that there were), they must fall on the heads of those who provoked that guilty and unnatural rebellion. I say, if the loyal men of Ireland took steps which they abhorred and ever must deplore, it was because they were the persecuted and not the persecuting party. Standing in that situation, they were authorised to use those means which God and nature had placed in their hands, for the protection of their lives and properties against lawless force and violence."

His speech made a great impression on the House. Canning, among others, supported him with one of his most brilliant speeches, ruthlessly exposing the injustice of Brougham's charges. His references to Castlereagh's clemency were greeted with loud approval in almost every quarter of the House; and Brougham, who had led the attack, subsequently acknowledged that so far as the accusation of cruelty was concerned he was mistaken. [1]

3

It was in this year, 1817, that the Prince Regent began to agitate for a divorce. Castlereagh feared that it would be an imprudent measure; he had no doubt that Caroline was lost to all sense of decency, that she was an utterly depraved character, but he was of the opinion " that this woman, loaded as she is with disgrace in the eyes of the whole Continent, will never presume to present herself again for factious support in England." He was mistaken; Caroline was to come in her own good time; but Castlereagh had all his evidence collected against the day. He was fully aware that she had been making herself conspicuous abroad with an Italian, black haired and moustachioed, of the domestic class. Reports had come from Naples of a gilded phaeton driving through the town, with a fat woman of fifty reclining in it, dressed in a pink hat, with pink feathers floating in the wind, a pink bodice cut very low, and a short white skirt, which showed two stout legs and a pair of top boots. Beside the carriage rode her handsome Italian, dressed in royal robes. At Geneva she had been seen dancing " en Vénus " naked to the waist. " Since de English," she said, " neither give me de great honour of being a princesse de Galles, I would be Caroline, a happy merry soul." In Milan her conduct was so disgraceful that all her English attendants left her. " She must be deranged," said Castlereagh, " vice and folly will not explain her proceedings."

The Prince Regent—who was equally grotesque—was now over fifty. He was florid and corpulent; his hair was dyed, and fluffed into curls, his face rouged and powdered; his costumes were most elaborate, his hands so heavily ringed that he could hardly sign his name. At Brighton, emblazoned with orders, he still drove his yellow tilbury along the Steyne. His Pavilion grew more and more fantastic, with its oriental dome and its litter of little domes, its Chinese mandarins, and its lacquered cabinets. He had always affected artistic tastes, acquiring, it was said, Old Masters and new mistresses. For the

[1] *Historical Sketches of the Statesmen of the Reign of George III.* Brougham.

moment Lady Hertford, Castlereagh's aunt, reigned as queen of his heart. She was dignified, decorous, and elderly, and there was much speculation as to what their relations really were.

In spite of his absurdities, his affectations, his voluptuous habits, the Prince still retained his evasive charm. It was his affability, his wit, his graceful turn of a phrase, his courteous manner that had gained him the title of the "First Gentleman in Europe." With his daughter, Princess Charlotte, he was now on friendly terms. Having satisfied himself that there was no personal objection to Prince Leopold of Coburg, whom she seemed to prefer to any other of the possible aspirants for her hand, he invited the young man over to England, entertained him at Brighton, and eventually gave the union his blessing. "The Coburgs are said to go on very lovingly," wrote Castlereagh to Charles a few months after the marriage: but their happiness was pathetically short-lived.

In the autumn the country was awaiting a royal birth, and there seemed no reason in the royal household for aught but rejoicing. On 4 November 1817, a message that his daughter's labour had begun reached the Prince at Lady Hertford's house in Suffolk. It was already night, but he set out at once for home. The messenger bringing him the sad news that the child was still-born, passed him in the dark, and he did not hear of the tragedy till three in the morning when he reached Carlton House. Tired and gloomy he went to bed, but an hour later he was roused by the Duke of York, who came to tell him that the Princess Charlotte had died in childbirth. She was only twenty-one.

Castlereagh, who saw the Prince in the morning, thought he bore the dreadful news "with very great manliness and feeling." There were demonstrations of grief throughout the whole country, for the Princess had been very popular with the people. About ten days before her death she had said: "Certainly I am the happiest woman in the world. I have not a wish ungratified. Surely this is too much to last."

In Italy Caroline received the tidings with apathy. It did not deter her from carrying on her frivolous pursuits, but she was an unhappy woman. Some time later, hearing that the old Queen was ill, she said: "The old Beguine, Queen Charlotte, is on her last legs I hear; *mais ça ne me fait ni froid ni chaud* now. There was a time when such intelligence would have gladdened me, but now, noting in de world do I care for, save to pass de time as quickly as I can, and death may hurry on as fast as he pleases—I am ready to die."

The throne being left now without a direct heir, two of the royal princes, the Duke of Clarence and the Duke of Kent, married hurriedly in the hopes of producing legitimate offspring. Clarence had given the Ministry a little trouble at first. He had thought it proper to propose to a Miss W., " a fine, vulgar miss," who had accepted him. It caused the greatest consternation at Court, and the Prince Regent, Castlereagh, Liverpool and the Duke of York talked, scolded, and threatened Clarence out of his love match. They informed him that there would be intervention by the two Houses of Parliament to prevent the marriage, and at length persuaded him to marry a Princess of Saxe-Meiningen. The Duke of Kent married a Princess of Leiningen, and gave a Queen to the throne of Great Britain.

The accounts which were reaching England of the conduct of the Princess abroad were so outrageous that some official notice had to be taken, and Castlereagh, who had done all he could to alleviate the position, now handed the matter over to the Cabinet. An inquiry was instituted by a body called the Milan Commission, which established the fact " of a continued adulterous intercourse," but, though the Prince Regent was more than ever determined on a divorce, the Ministers still thought it expedient to abstain from any public proceedings as long as the Princess continued abroad.

When his remonstrances and solicitations produced no further results, relations between the Prince and his Ministers became a little strained, and Castlereagh, who had gained an ascendancy over the Prince's mind, found himself shut out from his confidence. It did not ease his position that the Prince had transferred his affections from Lady Hertford to Lady Conyngham, who not only ousted Castlereagh's aunt from the Royal bedchamber, but who began to influence her lover against his Tory Ministers.

Castlereagh was uneasy and full of qualms. He needed the Prince's confidence, for he was making preparations to represent England at the Congress of Aix-la-Chapelle, which was to take place in September 1818. It was the first of those conferences which Castlereagh had outlined three years ago for the settlement of European problems.

" Never," remarked Metternich, who fell in love with Countess

Lieven during these negotiations, "have I known a prettier little Congress." It had its amusements, no doubt. Lady Castlereagh, who accompanied her husband, added little to them. Loaded with gold and diamonds she gave parties of such inconceivable boredom that everyone fled.

Castlereagh applied himself to business. Before he left Aix-la-Chapelle he had created a better understanding between the Powers and saved them from lapsing anew into hostile combinations against each other. The Congress among other things settled the reparation problem, confirmed the rights of the Jews, addressed to Bernadotte a sharp reminder that he must now pay to Denmark those compensations to which he was pledged, and relieved France from military occupation.

When he returned Castlereagh found that the position at home had deteriorated. Sedition was still spreading, and the cloud which had been darkening the political horizon was ready to break. Manchester, the centre of all the turbulence, had long been preparing a decisive demonstration, and in the month of August 1819 a mass meeting, with military formations and revolutionary displays, was held in the field of St. Peter's. There were red banners, bands playing the Marseillaise, and eighty thousand men and women wearing the Cap of Liberty.

Their leader, Mr. Hunt, addressed the crowd, but he had not proceeded very far when a detachment of sixty men of the Manchester Yeomanry Cavalry entered the field. As these advanced towards the wagon that contained Mr. Hunt and his colleagues, panic seized the people's battalions. The mob broke and ran, and in the fray men were trampled underfoot or cut down by sabres. Forty-four people were injured, four killed, and Mr. Hunt and his colleagues were taken into custody.

In London the incident was denounced at Radical meetings as " a massacre " and a foul attempt to destroy the liberties of Englishmen. It was used as a cry to rouse up the rest of the country, and mass meetings were held everywhere. There was plunder and murder and incitement to treason. Reports came of preparations for a general rising, and the ferment increased.

Demands were made by the terrorised for the increase of the Yeomanry Corps, but the men and officers were receiving such threatening letters that many withdrew from the Service, and none would join it. Castlereagh incurred a little more unpopularity by supporting the action of the magistrates in the Peterloo affair: they had done nothing, he stated, which was not strictly and legally justifiable, though whether they had acted with discretion was not very clear. He felt that the urgency of the crisis demanded that vigorous precautions should be taken ; but the root of the cause, the distress in the country, was not dealt with. The weavers were literally starving; the utmost a weaver could earn a week was two shillings and sevenpence, working from fourteen to sixteen hours a day; and these matters were not remedied.

The Government receiving threats of assassination, a Seditious Meetings Bill was passed, but Castlereagh was so bullied by the Opposition that the Bill was made temporary instead of permanent as many members had demanded, and Castlereagh was attacked for his indecision.

The year 1819 was fraught with difficulties. Notwithstanding the measures taken by the Government, organised conspiracy existed. So deep was the terror created by the offenders that witnesses dared not come forward to testify. All the symptoms of the French Revolution and the Irish Rebellion were present.

A great deal of the trouble had started with the Corn Laws, which had done more mischief than anyone could have conceived. The detestable project of keeping up the price of corn had reduced the country to a state that was little short of absolute famine.

Castlereagh, who had been suffering from a bad attack of gout, had just started on his way to Mount Stewart for a very much needed rest when he was recalled by express messenger to attend a Cabinet Council. An alarming plot had now been uncovered which had for its object the assassination of all the Ministers. Serious measures had to be taken; and as soon as Parliament met, the notorious Six Acts were proposed, and carried by a large majority in both Houses. The Six Acts, some of which were as harmless as they were necessary, prohibited unauthorised military training, forbade meetings for the consideration of grievances against the State, subjected periodical pamphlets on political subjects to a duty similar to that on newspapers, gave magistrates the right to enter houses by night or by day for the purpose of seizing arms. In the inflamed state of the country the measures were not unreasonable; they were defended in Parliament by Canning who has never been considered a reactionary. But they roused the greatest indignation amongst the people, and Castlereagh bore the brunt of their anger.

4

The year 1820 opened sadly. On the 29 January the great bell of St. Paul's sent forth its deep knell for the passing of George the Third. Wandering about in his castle, a shadowy, bearded figure, playing on his organ, blind and deaf and feeble, he had faded quietly away. In his coffin he was allowed to keep his beautiful white beard. " He has as fine a Rabbi's head as you could imagine," said the Duke of York.[1]

The King's death brought up the matter of the Princess of Wales again; for the Regent, who had waited so long for the throne, was now George IV, and his absent wife was Queen of England. He refused, however, to recognise her as such, or to allow her name to be included in the Litany. The horror of having the Queen made an object of the prayers of his people " haunted his imagination " and " distracted his rest." To ease him, his physicians bled him almost to death, but that did not relieve him of his malady. He wanted a divorce.

His Ministers with anxious solicitude weighed the whole of the perplexing and painful subject for days on end, but since, after due deliberation, they advised him *against* divorce proceedings, the King flew into a rage and sent them an ultimatum. If they were not prepared to advise His Majesty to proceed by way of divorce, his determination was to change his Government, and if he could not form a Government to relieve him to that extent it was his intention to retire to Hanover.

Castlereagh, who had a strong aversion to the whole affair, sent in his resignation. He wrote to Charles that the Government was virtually dissolved, that he deplored the view His Majesty had taken of what was due to his honour, in contrast with what his servants felt was due to his interests, and those of the monarchy.

The King did not accept Castlereagh's resignation for strangely enough the new elections, which were taking place in the country,

[1] *Letters of Princess Lieven.*

only established the Ministers more securely, and he felt that it would be impossible to form another administration.

After much discussion, Castlereagh consented to remain in office but on the understanding that no proceedings should be instituted against Caroline, unless she returned to this country.

In a letter to Charles, Castlereagh said: " Had I gone out I should have done so from a sense of public duty or I can more truly say personal duty towards the King, not only without any feeling of resentment, but, in truth, with an earnest wish that His Majesty might feel as little inconvenience as possible from the change. Under this sentiment I should certainly 'not have encouraged any of my friends to follow my example . . . remembering how much misery Pitt created amongst his connections by forcing them to embark with Addington."

Although Castlereagh's position was more than ever secure, he was in sombre mood, for the King, having been forced to give way, sulked like a child, and withdrew his confidence from his Ministers entirely.

It did not ease matters for Castlereagh that a feud existed between his wife and Lady Conyngham, the King's mistress. Lady Castlereagh, tactless and indiscreet, had announced that she would no longer invite Lady Conyngham to her evening receptions, and had made damaging remarks about her in public. Incensed by her behaviour the King gradually withdrew all the friendly favours which he had bestowed on Castlereagh, and the breach between them became so wide that Castlereagh no longer came near the King, even to speak to him on matters of State.

Matters of State, in any case, did not interest the King, for he was at this time entirely occupied with Lady Conyngham. Obese and gouty, he must have provided a ludicrous spectacle, sitting beside his mistress, kissing her hand continually with a look of the most devoted submission. The fact that she was a vulgar, grasping woman, plump and fifty-one, and the mother of five grown-up children, did not disturb him; he never left her side. He was growing fatter and fatter, and trundled about without his stays, which the doctors had forbidden him to wear. " His belly," said Creevey, " now touches his knees."

5

It was early in this year that the conspiracy which had been detected in the autumn of 1819, and which had been delayed by the passing of the Six Acts, came to a head. Its leader, Thistlewood, who had been imprisoned, had come out of jail thirsting for the blood of the Ministers, and was now planning with his confederates to murder the whole Cabinet. Learning that there would be fourteen or sixteen Ministers dining at Lord Harrowby's house at 44 Grosvenor Square on a certain day, he decided to get them all together. The Ministers had full knowledge of the plan, but Castlereagh was for their meeting just the same, so that the conspirators might not be aware that their plot was discovered. The rest of the Ministers considered this scheme overbold, and it was eventually decided to allow the arrangements to go on as if nothing were known, but to hold the meeting elsewhere.

All the details of Thistlewood's plan were in the Government's hands. The Cabinet was aware that some of the conspirators were being stationed outside Lord Harrowby's house to see that no police or soldiers were brought there. One of them was to call with a note while the Ministers were at dinner, the others were then to rush in, commit the murders and carry away the heads of Sidmouth, Wellington and Castlereagh in bags provided for the purpose. Thistlewood himself chose Wellington as his victim; there was a long fight over Castlereagh, everybody wanting the honour of cutting his throat. After the assassinations they were to set fire to Cavalry barracks, take the Bank and the Tower, and set themselves up as the Government of the People.

The Government made its arrangements. While the Ministers were at dinner, the police, reinforced by detachments of the Guards, made their way to Cato Street in Edgware Road, where, in a hayloft above a stable, the conspirators were collected. Some of them had already left to watch Lord Harrowby's house, but there were about twenty still congregated there. When the police reached the stable they found it almost impossible to get into the loft, as the only entrance was by a ladder, and the first man who mounted it was stabbed by Thistlewood in the darkness. The conspirators resisted the police fiercely, and, but for the arrival of the military, would have overcome them. Even so, half of the conspirators, including Thistlewood, escaped. He was discovered the following morning in a little house in Moorfields and, after a trial of three days, was condemned to death and executed.

The conspiracy was over, but the preparations for a general rising continued. There were midnight drillings of armed bands, firearms were collected, pikes manufactured. In the north were hundreds of idle Irishmen only too ready to help the Radicals against the Government, and there was close imitation of the Irish methods.

At a dinner party at Castlereagh's house, where the Duke of Wellington and the Hertfords were present, Countess Lieven, who was sitting beside Castlereagh, asked him if it were true that he went about armed. For answer he put his hand in his pocket and drew out two small pistols which he carried about with him everywhere, even at his own dinner table.[1]

6

Apart from the internal crisis, which gave Castlereagh so much concern, he was anxiously watching the turn of events abroad; for the revolutionary spirit was spreading everywhere. Liberal ideas were being repressed in Germany, where Metternich instituted the Carlsbad Decrees against the Universities and the Press; insurrections were breaking out in Spain and in Portugal; every country seemed to be in a state of unrest.

Metternich appealed to the Great Powers to intervene by force, and stamp out revolution in Europe, but Castlereagh did not wish to meddle with the internal affairs of other countries; his system of conferences had for its purpose the settling of the peace of Europe by arbitration; it was not a league which might at any moment involve Britain in war for issues which did not concern her. He was ready to condemn the licence of the revolutionaries, to voice his belief in the repression of such movements as that which was causing havoc in his own country, But he was not ready to join with the other Powers in using force to settle disputes which were purely local. Nor

[1] *Von Neumann Diaries.*

would he give his approval to the Carlsbad Decrees. He believed that intervention was not only inadmissible, but dangerous.

In a memorandum of 5 May 1820, extracts of which were later published by Canning, who adopted it as the basis of his own policy, Castlereagh made his views very clear.

" When the territorial balance of Europe is disturbed," he stated, " Great Britain can interfere with effect, but she is the last government in Europe which can be expected, or can venture, to commit herself on any question of an abstract character." In his opinion the principle of one state interfering by force in the internal affairs of another, in order to enforce obedience to the government authorities, was always " a question of the greatest possible moral, as well as political delicacy." The Alliance, he held, had no such purpose in view in its original formation.

He stood his ground firmly, but his influence in Europe was waning. The Czar, as well as Metternich, was now demanding intervention in Spain, where Royalist risings and revolutionary risings were the order of the day. Castlereagh was determined that Britain should remain neutral.

While the question was being debated a revolt broke out in Naples. Castlereagh felt that Naples presented a rather different problem. Although he was opposed to intervention by the Alliance, he recognised the right of Austria herself to act against Naples if the rebellion threatened her position in Italy and Germany.

Metternich was not satisfied with this policy. He desired a league of the Great Powers against Naples. His position was strengthened by the attitude of the Czar, who demanded that a conference be held at Troppau, and that intervention, if approved, should be collective.

Castlereagh, who wished to localise the dispute, was against any formal conference on the subject, but in spite of his opposition a conference was arranged by the European Powers to take place at Troppau in October 1820. The news was not very pleasing to Castlereagh, who suggested, at a meeting with Liverpool and Wellington, that Britain should not send a plenipotentiary, but that his brother Charles, who was then in Vienna, should, as a concession to Austria, be present as an observer. This would avoid a declared and open rupture with the Allies, and might prevent Russia and Austria from being driven into each other's arms.

Austria was the natural ally of Britain in the Mediterranean, and though her demands were now in direct contradiction to Castlereagh's policy, he did not wish to disturb their relations. The Austrian Ambassador, who was striving to get a British plenipotentiary sent to Troppau, was granted an audience with the King, but the King informed him that Castlereagh was absolutely indispensable in London, that Wellington was not sufficiently skilled, and that Bathurst would be no better than Lord Stewart, and there the matter ended.

7

During these days, when difficulties seemed to be multiplying everywhere, there arrived in England one fine summer day the despised wife of the new king. Her Majesty made her entrance in a chaise, with a man in Turkish costume seated on the box, and a troop of ragged men and boys running round the carriage cheering her. She had exchanged her fair hair for a black wig with a mass of long curls, had painted her eyebrows black, and plastered her cheeks with rouge. But the people of England were delighted with her, and gave her a rousing welcome.

The King now demanded that divorce proceedings be at once instituted. Wishing to avoid the scandal of a public trial, Castlereagh tried to come to an arrangement with Caroline, suggesting an annuity of £50,000 a year if she would remove herself from the country and renounce the title of Queen. His negotiations proving fruitless, a Bill was introduced in Parliament to deprive the Queen of her titles and privileges, and to dissolve her marriage on the ground of adultery.

Castlereagh, who was not looking forward to the Queen's trial, went down to Cray for a few days' relaxation. It was a pleasant, sunny August, but he had little time to browse among his sheep, for Lady Castlereagh was giving a grand fête, to which the ambassadors and their wives, and all the diplomatic circle were invited.

Among the visitors was Countess Lieven, the Russian Ambassador's wife, who liked to feel herself the pivot of affairs. She loved politics and had a weakness for great men. Castlereagh, whom she captured whenever she was able, found her entertaining and sympathetic, and devoted a good deal of time to her. He showed her round the house, pointing out the changes he had made, and introduced her to Don Quixote, whose story was embodied in the carpets in his study, and to Sancho who was being tossed in a blanket in front of his desk.

His strong character and personality attracted her. His impregnability seemed to challenge her, and practised as she was in affairs of the heart, she used all her graces to ensnare him. Politics, she told him, were the very breath of her nostrils. But they soon found themselves talking of other matters, and before long he was unburdening himself of all his private worries and distresses. He sat beside her while she played the piano; and in the evening, when dancing was in full swing, he crossed over to her and asked if she would attempt a waltz with him. "Heavens, what hard work to keep the minister in revolution," she observes. But she persevered. The majority of the guests, with sentimental preoccupations, went for a stroll in the dark night along the little paths in the garden, and left the two of them at their waltzing.

But affairs of the heart were not for Castlereagh. In a few days he was back in London for the degrading business of the Queen's trial. Caroline drove to Parliament in a State carriage drawn by six cream-coloured horses. She was cheered by an immense crowd, and everywhere she passed the sentries presented arms.

The Queen was being tried for adultery. Details about the yacht where she and Bergami slept were given, details about her underclothes, details about her very bath. She had the sympathy of all the people, who insulted the Ministers on their way to the House. Even the Duke of Wellington was hissed and hooted, and nearly maltreated by the crowd. The roadmenders in Grosvenor Place stopped his horse, and insisted on him saying: "God Save the Queen."

"Well, gentlemen," the Duke said dryly, "since you will have it so, God Save the Queen, and may all your wives be like her."

Castlereagh ran serious personal danger every time he left the House, and was continually threatened by the mob. It must have been an ordeal coming out of the Houses of Parliament every day with thousands of Radicals waiting outside. The Guards themselves were disaffected. The mob rioted in the streets, smashing windows and compelling the occupants of every carriage to say, "God Save the Queen." More troops were brought up to London, and at night cavalry pickets occupied the principal quarters of the town.

The Queen had changed her lodgings, and taken up her quarters

in a house, embarrassingly enough, next door to Castlereagh. He said
it would not disturb him in the least, except that the mob might begin
to pull down his house. "Few men," said Countess Lieven, "have
Lord Castlereagh's intrepid coolness." More than once nothing but
his unruffled appearance had overawed the mob. But he was obliged
all the same to put up a bed in the Foreign Office, having been told
that however courageous it might be to brave danger, his courage
became criminal when it provoked a disturbance. He had always
known how much feeling would be worked up in the country by
the Opposition over this matter, and he had done all he could to
avoid it. The country was now on the brink of civil war.

Through continual tumult and anxiety the trial dragged on, till
on 10 November 1820, the Government majority having dropped to
nine, which they considered a virtual defeat, the Bill was dropped.
The Queen would retain her title, but her name would not be restored
to the Prayer Book. Caroline shrugged her shoulders. " I have second
sight," she said, " and I tell you that in a few months' time my name
will be heard in all the churches."

Her prophecy was fulfilled, for within six months the injured
Queen of England was dead.

8

While the Queen's trial was proceeding, the Sovereigns of Europe,
in the winter of 1820, were in conference at Troppau discussing
intervention in the affairs of Naples. Castlereagh's suspicions that the
Conference would assume a shape entirely contrary to his ideas was
soon confirmed ; for Austria, Russia and Prussia—the Holy Allies—
issued a protocol binding themselves, by peaceful means or if need be
by arms, to bring back guilty states into the bosom of the Great
Alliance ; they invited Great Britain and France to adhere to this
scheme.

Castlereagh did not hesitate. In a dispatch of great vigour he
denounced the principles enunciated at Troppau. He protested against
the general claim of the European Powers to interfere uninvited in the
internal concerns of Sovereign States, and he refused to make Great
Britain a party to such interference. His memorandum created a

sensation at the Congress, but it did not deter the Holy Allies from their course, and they continued their deliberations in the same mood. Charles, as an observer and as a personality, carried no weight, but he incurred a good deal of ridicule, running back to Vienna in the middle of business to comfort his young wife. "The fool and his accursed wife," was the gentle comment of Gentz in his diary. In the English papers it was reported that Charles had challenged Prince Metternich to a duel at Troppau,[1] and on the latter's refusal to fight, had struck him. How far this is true is not known, but it is easy to believe anything of Charles.

Although Castlereagh had spoken so clearly and openly regarding the Troppau protocol he was anxious to avoid an open breach with the Allies. He informed Count Lieven, the Russian Ambassador, that his heart bled at having to dispatch such a paper, and he reiterated his attachment to the alliance, and his hatred of revolutions: but he warned him that if their protocol was published he would have no alternative but to issue a counterblast.

The Allies, undeterred, published their protocol, and invited Ferdinand, the King of Naples, to appear at Laibach, whither the Conference was adjourned. All the Italian States were invited to send representatives.

Britain sent no plenipotentiary to Laibach, but Charles went again as observer. His marital anxieties came to a crisis during the conference; his arrival had been delayed by the coming of age of his wife, and he only stayed three weeks, because of his wife's confinement. He seemed to be of very little use, however, even when he was present, for Castlereagh's views were ignored, and Austria secured Russia's support for her march on Naples. Metternich was triumphant, and could do without Britain's co-operation.

Castlereagh immediately published his counterblast to the Troppau protocol. He condemned in sweeping terms a system which was repugnant to the fundamental laws of this country. He did not deny Austria's right to intervene where her own interests were in danger, but he denied the right of the Powers to interfere generally in the internal affairs of other states.

The breach with the Alliance, which he had wished so much to avoid, was now complete. In the House of Commons, where he was

[1] *Von Neumann Diaries.*

PRINCESS LIEVEN
By T. Lawrence

attacked by the Opposition for Austria's policy towards Naples, and for his recognition of her right to interfere, Castlereagh observed that it was too much to be told that the British Government ought to dictate moral lessons to Europe.

While the Holy Alliance sat in conference, revolution continued to spread. The Austrian army was moving towards the frontier of Naples when news was received at Laibach that a revolution had broken out in Piedmont. The Austrian troops took this in their stride; the revolt was crushed as easily as the revolt in Naples, and Austrian dungeons were crammed with prisoners.

The Neapolitan outbreak, however, had hardly collapsed when the flame of revolution reached the Ottoman Empire. Armed with scythes and clubs the Greeks, who were still under Turkish domination, rose up and massacred every Turk on whom they could lay their hands. There were incredible scenes of butchery; women and children were slaughtered, and the streets ran with blood. By way of reprisal the Turks, on Easter Sunday, seized the Greek Patriarch, a man of eighty, as he descended from the altar, and hanged him on the door of his cathedral. On the same night Greek bishops were dragged from their altars and sacrificed on the steps of their churches, many of which were burnt to the ground.

A cry of indignation went up throughout Europe. Many saw in the Greek uprising a revival of the glorious past of Greece, and volunteers were drawn to the scene from every country. The most notable of these was Byron, who gave up his life for Greece and liberty.

The Czar, who desired to protect the Greeks, and incidentally to overthrow the Turkish Empire and get into the Mediterranean, began sending ultimatums to the Sultan. The situation was critical, and a Russo-Turkish war seemed imminent.

Castlereagh and Metternich were ready to forget previous differences in face of the new crisis, for both feared the expansion of Russia. Anxious to avert the war which threatened, Castlereagh wrote a personal letter to the Czar informing him that he was uneasy about the dreadful events taking place in Turkey. But whilst we could not refuse to the Greeks our sympathy and compassion, it could not be denied that they had been the aggressors on this occasion. He felt that Turkey was an excrescence in Europe, that the Turks were a bigoted, resentful and uncivilised people, but he feared that any attempt

C.   Y

to introduce order by external interference might expose the whole frame of our general system to danger. What he feared beyond anything was the spread of revolution.

Castlereagh's policy was clear and consistent. His sympathies were entirely with the Greeks, but Russia must be restrained from intervention, and from any tendency to move towards the Mediterranean.

" If," he wrote to our ambassador at St. Petersburg, " a statesman were permitted to regulate his conduct by the counsels of his heart, instead of the dictates of his understanding, he would use every effort to redeem from Turkish bondage their suffering and Christian subjects."

But Castlereagh's immediate task was to provide for the peace and security of Europe. To encourage the Greek insurrection might ultimately bring to the Greeks a measure of self-government, but it would throw into chaos the whole political system of Europe. The revolutionary movement had already reached Mexico, Peru, the Brazils; the whole world was in a convulsion. But not even Castlereagh could stem the tide. The desire for liberty could not be crushed; it was one of the deepest instincts of human nature.

9

In the middle of all this confusion and anxiety the Regent was preparing for the Coronation. The preparations had been going on for months, but the day at length arrived, and a magnificent spectacle was staged. In the Abbey the King walked down the aisle under a canopy of cloth of gold borne by the Barons of the Cinque Ports. Clad in a train of crimson velvet ornamented with golden stars, and a hat with spreading plumes, he managed to appear a very regal figure; and the singing and the firing of guns were drowned by the shouts of enthusiasm that went up from every corner of the building, as he entered the Abbey.

Castlereagh, too, with his good looks, dressed in the magnificent garter costume, brought a cheer from the crowd. He was now Marquess of Londonderry. Two months before, he had heard with the deepest distress of the death of his father, whom he had always loved and revered. He should have taken his place now in the House of Lords, but the event was postponed in order that he might continue to lead the House of Commons, which he did until his death.

At the Coronation there was one person who was conspicuous by her absence. Queen Caroline was not present. The King had decided that she was neither to be crowned Queen nor to take part in the ceremony. Late in the afternoon the unfortunate woman drove down to the Abbey in an open carriage, and was refused admittance at each of the doors in turn. She was denied even sympathy, for there was by now a general impression of her guilt, and people were getting tired of her story. The crowd assailed her with cries of " Go to Como." They had a new rhyme for her:

> Noble Queen we thee implore,
> Go away and sin no more,
> Or if the effort be too great,
> Go away at any rate."

Soon she would be indifferent to the jeers of the fickle mob, but at this moment the gibes came sadly amiss. It was on 31 July 1821, when the King, who was visiting Ireland, arrived off Holyhead, that he received a message that the Queen had been taken dangerously ill. He waited expectantly. A few days later, Castlereagh joined him with news that the Queen's condition was unchanged. For three days there was no further news. Then a letter arrived addressed to Lord Sidmouth, who had already preceded them to Ireland. Castlereagh decided to open it and read it to the King. The letter announced that the Queen was suddenly much worse. He was reading it aloud when he stopped, with a look of embarrassment, at a sentence beginning: " The Duke of York——" " Come, come," said the King, " you must go on with it now." Castlereagh read on: " The Duke of York is in despair at an event which so much diminishes his chance of the Crown." The King was fortunately amused at the suggestion that he might marry again and provide an heir, and he laughed uproariously. The following day was too rough for the crossing, and they remained at Holyhead. In the evening there came the expected news. The Queen was dead.

" The King was affected," said Croker,[1] " but not afflicted." He arrived in Ireland with a black band on his arm.

[1] Croker, Secretary to the Admiralty.

The Queen, who was a pathetic figure in spite of her follies, had said to Brougham, "I am going to die, Mr. Brougham, but it does not signify. I tell you I shall die, but I don't mind it."

Castlereagh wrote to Liverpool informing him that the King wished the Queen's funeral to go the whole way from Hammersmith by water. He was anxious to avoid demonstrations, but through some blunder his instructions were not carried out. The King was so angry with Liverpool that he said to Croker: "I will not go on with him any longer." His dislike of Lord Liverpool had been increasing for some time. He blamed him for his humiliation in the matter of the divorce, and had never forgiven him for having rejected a nominee of Lady Conyngham's for a Windsor canonry. Castlereagh had to bear the brunt of the King's ill humour, and was treated with marked coldness.

In spite of this he found the visit to Ireland entirely satisfactory; there was not a drunken man in the streets, nor did he hear an unkind word anywhere. Every village they passed through was illuminated, and there was general enthusiasm for the King and his Foreign Minister.

To a friend who congratulated him on his success, Castlereagh said: "I am grown, it seems, very popular, but with quite as little merit, I am afraid, as when I was most unpopular; and after all you must agree that unpopularity is the more convenient and gentlemanlike condition of the two." It was his last visit to Ireland—but it left a pleasant memory; he had conquered even that country of bitter animosities.

Lady Castlereagh had been unable to go on the visit to Ireland on account of her quarrel with the King's mistress, who accompanied him. Apart from the embarrassment which the quarrel caused Castlereagh, it ruined him with the King, who continued to treat him with cold indifference. In spite of this, Emily persisted in behaving as impertinently as possible towards Lady Conyngham. Her tactlessness annoyed everyone. "There is the bitterest prejudice against her," wrote Countess Lieven, "though her husband is regarded with affection." The Countess, anxious to help Castlereagh, tried to mediate between the two women, but in spite of all her efforts not a single act of courtesy could be obtained on the side of Lady Castlereagh. In a moment of confidence Castlereagh told Countess Lieven with great bitterness that the quarrel filled him with disgust, that there was so much pettiness on either side. To Lady Arbuthnot, however, he declared that Emily was incapable of doing anything unkind or tending to injure the character of anyone.

He was beginning to see a good deal of Countess Lieven; she was at all the dinners he went to, and all the receptions. Reserved as he was with others he found himself opening out to her, finding relief in their long and intimate talks. Tormented by so many troubles, tortured by a need for rest, he seemed to find relaxation in her company. He also found her services useful with the King; and when George, in October 1821, decided to visit Hanover, he arranged for Countess Lieven to find herself in Frankfort at the time, near enough for the King to send her an invitation to join the Royal party. After waiting at Frankfort for some days in expectation, the Countess obtained her invitation, and Castlereagh sent a courier to Frankfort to expedite her arrival.

Lady Castlereagh, who happened to find herself in Paris at the same time, was not invited. Although the King had not been able to take his mistress with him to Hanover, and Emily was probably hoping for an invitation, she was not included.

Castlereagh, in spite of his growing attachment for Countess Lieven, had nevertheless invited her lover, Prince Metternich, to meet the royal party in Hanover, confident that the Austrian Minister would co-operate with him in his attempt to dissuade the Czar from going to war with Turkey. The Austrian Minister received as rapturous a welcome from the King as from Countess Lieven; he records that he was delicately kissed by the English monarch on both cheeks, and compared to great men of all the ages, among whom were specified Minos, Cato, Cæsar, Gustavus Adolphus, Marlborough, Pitt and Wellington.

Relations between the King and his Ministers were still strained. Ever since the royal attachment for Lady Conyngham, who had Whig tendencies, there had been continual rumours of the King bringing in the Opposition. Liverpool, whom he detested, had exasperated him again by refusing to appoint Lord Conyngham as Lord Chamberlain; and George, determined to force his resignation, refused to transact any sort of business with him. In the event of Liverpool retiring, Castlereagh, as Esterhazy, the Austrian Ambassador, had written to Metternich, would have been the most likely person for the Premiership, had not the quarrel between his wife and Lady Conyngham turned the King against him.

Metternich and Countess Lieven, who both had a sincere regard for Castlereagh, set to work together to restore his fortunes with the King. Metternich felt that the character of Liverpool was obstructive, and that if the Ministry were reorganised under Castlereagh as Premier, England would take a more vigorous grasp of the world's affairs, and the whole position would be relieved. Under Metternich's influence the King's humour changed, and he began to smile on Castlereagh again.

For Castlereagh it was an embarrassing situation. It humiliated him deeply to require the assistance of two foreigners in his relations with the King of England. The matter preyed on his mind, and although his relations with the King were easier, he was not at all happy. He had been checked so long by the ineptitude and the caprice and the faithlessness of his monarch that he could no longer meet his smiles with any confidence.

He was also far from well. He had caught a bad chill on his first arrival, being quartered " in a Garden House, fresh painted, long untenanted, and icy cold." " However we have no right to complain," he wrote to Emily, " as they are very good to us, and do their best to make us comfortable." But he was in the lowest spirits, and ended his letter with the words, " God Bless you, my dearest Em, I don't know why or when I have been so low. So farewell. Yours ever, L."

The chill must have left him tired, and despondent, and weighed down with an unaccustomed depression, since there is no evidence of his ever having spoken in this way before. He was not the type of man who could unburden himself with any ease to others. All he could do was to close himself up in the solitude of his soul, and surround himself with an icy atmosphere which nobody would dare to penetrate. Even to Emily he said so little.

The King, however, was in great spirits, and continued to favour Castlereagh. Their reconciliation was complete, and it was arranged that on their return to London, Castlereagh should persuade Liverpool to offer the Marquis of Conyngham a post at Court which would place him officially near the King. The King now treated Castlereagh with the greatest distinction, and even mentioned to Metternich his idea of Castlereagh becoming Prime Minister. Castlereagh, who was not opposed to the Premiership, made it clear, however, that the final decision must rest with Liverpool himself. If the latter refused his proposal regarding Conyngham, he would go out with him. The King left the whole matter in his hands and suggested that Castlereagh should go to England in advance of him, in order to sound Liverpool before his return. Castlereagh was glad enough to be leaving Hanover. He tried to arrange to meet his wife in Paris on the way back, but his plans waited on the King's decision, and he had not yet been informed when he was to set out. "It is one of those vexatious combinations which belong to the sad trade I follow," he wrote to Emily.

When he was at length dispatched to England, he was unable to meet Emily in Paris, for the King desired him to proceed direct to Walmer, where Liverpool was staying. When Emily heard that he was unable to come to her, she wrote immediately that she would curtail her Paris visit and meet him at Calais on his way home.

His reply is charming: "I should be very unworthy, my dearest Em, of you, if I ever doubted that you would do whatever was most kind and most affectionate to me: and although I grieve to have cut short your Paris visit, and still more not to have enjoyed it with you, yet I receive the tidings of your meeting me at Calais with the greatest possible delight, and shall never forget your giving me this fresh proof of your attachment."

"As I must stop at Walmer," he added, "I hope you will not leave me so soon after our meeting. . . . I am writing to Liverpool to ask leave to bring my Baggage, which he is too gallant a man to refuse."

It was easier for Liverpool to accept Emily than to accept Conyngham, and it needed a good deal of persuasion to win him over to the King's new caprice, but as soon as Castlereagh saw that a compromise was possible, he worked loyally to keep Liverpool in Office, and managed to effect a reconciliation between him and the King. Lord Conyngham was to be created Grand Marshal, and various changes were to be made in the Ministry, the King making no secret of the fact that he accepted the whole arrangement only because of his Foreign Minister, and because of his understanding with Metternich. At a dinner he said: "I regard Prince Metternich as the first statesman in Europe, and after him Lord Londonderry."

Castlereagh was now stronger than ever, or as Croker wrote: " He is *better* than ever, that is colder, steadier, more procurante, and withal more amiable and respected. It is a splendid summit of bright and polished frost which, like the travellers in Switzerland, we all admire; but no one can hope and few would wish to reach."

The visit to Hanover had been a great success. The breach between the King and Liverpool had been bridged, relations with Austria and Russia had improved, and it seemed as though war would be averted. The King was in such spirits that he folded Metternich in his arms three times before he left. He had never been in better humour. When he arrived home he told everybody that at Calais the people were almost as glad to see him as the Irish had been, and he never ceased talking about it. He was delighted with his reception. He informed everyone that Brussels had been illuminated for him, and that he had been loudly cheered; but somebody noted down that he " only got two ' Vive le Roi d' Angleterre's,' and they were feeble cries uttered by children under age," and that an adult spectator had added: " Pardonnes leur, Mon Dieu, car ils ne savent pas ce qu'ils disent." [1]

He was overjoyed at having done a little sightseeing on the way. He had seen the field of Waterloo, though the rain was so heavy and the fog so thick he might as well have been at Carlton House. However, he got out in spite of the rain at the Farm of Hougemont, and under cover of Lord Jersey's cloak, paddled about a little. [2]

" By God!" Wellington said to Creevey, " you never saw such a figure in your life as he is. Then he speaks and swears so like old Falstaff, that damn me if I was not ashamed to walk into a room with him."

On 29 November 1821, Countess Lieven who had gone on to Paris from Hanover, arrived back from the Continent. " You cannot

[1] Londonderry Papers.   G. W. Chad to Lady Londonderry.   Brussels, 28 September 1821.

[2] *Idem.*

imagine how pleased Lord Castlereagh was to see me again," she wrote to Metternich. "He came in with open arms, and I simply had to open mine half-way, so that we gave each other a kind of semi-tender embrace."

They talked of the Austrian Minister a good deal. He asked her rather naïvely if Metternich really liked him, and spoke of the satisfaction and the pleasure of meeting him in Hanover, and of the impossibility of their opinions ever differing. "It is extraordinary," he said, "how much at ease I feel when I talk to Prince Metternich. It is the same with you, my ideas are all fluid." Countess Lieven told him that "fluid" was charming, and that she would tell Metternich what he had said, at which he gave a loud "Ha! Ha!"

Afterwards he told her all he had done to reconcile the King with Lord Liverpool. "The result of my negotiations," he said, "is good in fact, and it will be good as experience; for the King will learn that it is not so easy to dismiss a Minister, and the Prime Minister will learn that it must be remembered above all things that the King is master."

He seemed convinced that the Government was now solidly established, and he gave Metternich a great deal of credit for the reconciliation between the King and his Ministers.

Countess Lieven was not the only woman who has expressed her deep affection for Castlereagh. Mrs. Arbuthnot, whose husband was Joint Secretary to the Treasury, tells us in her *Journal* that she loved him more than a brother, that for eleven years he had taken the most affectionate interest in all that was a subject of joy or sorrow to her, that it was impossible to look at him and see the benevolent and amiable expression of his countenance without a disposition to like him, for over his whole person was spread an air of dignity and nobleness such as she had never seen in any other person.

CHAPTER XV

I

THE FRIENDSHIP between Castlereagh and Countess Lieven was ripening. When the King invited his Ministers to Brighton he informed Castlereagh slyly that Countess Lieven would be there. At table he told him to come and sit next to her. He had a passion for encouraging any affaires he suspected. But he talked to her himself all the evening, without stopping, and as Castlereagh had a member of the Opposition on the other side of him, he was reduced, Countess Lieven narrates, to falling on two enormous helpings of roast mutton.

In London he met her frequently. She had already informed him that she took a daily walk in Kensington Gardens, and he went riding there at the same hour. As soon as he saw her he would get off his horse, and they would walk along together talking. They talked of his position, of the King, of Metternich, discussing all the endless subjects which interested them both. He was full of a friendly tenderness towards her that charmed and moved her. "I really believe," she wrote Metternich, " that he loves me with all his heart." But she hastened to add: "If you hear any remark about my intimacy with him please do not think there is any harm in it. When he meets me he fastens on to me; we spend whole evenings sitting together and he never leaves me. The reason is quite simple. He knows very few people in society, which consists mostly of members of the other camp and of women who do not know him well enough to find him amusing." For herself she found him most entertaining. His French was quite original. His phrases and his images intrigued her. Speaking to her one day about Austria he said: " We regard her as the pivot of Europe, and our shoulder is always ready to support her. We are like

346

a lover whom she will always find waiting for her; and we like her to help her other lover, Russia, who is perhaps not always so faithful, but who must be treated all the better for that very reason."

She admired him greatly. He had about him an air of lofty distinction which attracted her, and a melancholy that her Russian soul so well understood. It pleased her that he trusted her with confidences that were never bestowed on another. He told her now that the quarrel between his wife and the King's mistress was disturbing him night and day, that it never ceased to prey upon his mind. She was very anxious to help him, and decided she would leave no stone unturned till the wretched quarrel was ended. Setting about the matter with energy and determination she got as far as persuading Lady Conyngham to call on Emily. There was great joy at the report that this unseemly quarrel was soon to end, but unfortunately Lady Conyngham altered her mind at the last minute, and the meeting never took place.

The climax came when the King was making out his list for a large dinner party, which was to be given for the Princess of Denmark who was on a visit to England. He had headed the list with the names of Lord and Lady Londonderry, but when Lady Conyngham saw the list, she declared she would not come herself if Lady Londonderry were invited, and forthwith crossed out her name. The King on his side declared that if Lord and Lady Londonderry did not come, he would not give a dinner at all. Pressed by Lady Conyngham, who persisted in excluding Lady Londonderry, he agreed finally to invite neither her nor her husband, but he begged Countess Lieven to use all her influence to persuade Lady Conyngham to revoke her decision.

After a week of endless entreaties, in the course of which the dinner was cancelled and re-ordered three times, Countess Lieven succeeded in inducing Lady Conyngham to allow Lady Londonderry to be included among the guests.

Castlereagh was delighted. Emily, however, was only to commit another faux-pas. At the Ball which followed the dinner she placed herself in the seat next to the King, a seat intended for Lady Conyngham, and the Royal favourite was more than ever incensed.

At a dinner party a few days later, Castlereagh told Countess Lieven how delighted he was that Emily had been invited again to Court, and asked her how the invitation had been managed. She told him what had happened, but instead of appreciating her victory, as she had expected, his face paled with anger. " You have shown me my position, our position, clearly," he said. " Things cannot go on like this. We cannot put up with a Lady Conyngham who is powerful enough to offer us such affronts."

She pointed out to him gently that Lady Conyngham could not be opposed, that consequently one must put up with the inconvenience, which after all was not very serious. But he was not to be appeased. " From now on," he replied coldly, " I shall be nothing more than His Majesty's very humble servant—we shall see how long these relations will last. If they do not last I shall resign. I have done enough for my country and my master to be independent in that respect—and nothing can stop me."

Countess Lieven expressed her surprise that he should be prepared to sacrifice for a woman's quarrel his entire political existence, and all the good he had done and might yet do. But he was so deeply mortified by all that had passed he could bear no more.

" I cannot sacrifice my honour and my pride," he said. " Both are more wounded than I can say. I have served my master with all my heart, but I am in a position to serve him no longer. Let him give orders to Lord Liverpool, the Duke of Wellington or to whomever he pleases. Whatever it may mean to me I can no longer receive them, if he thinks, that through the patronage of a foreigner, I can accept without difficulty an act to which my position alone entitles me."

Countess Lieven flushed at being called a foreigner. She had never known anything but kindness and courtesy from him, and was too grieved at this sudden attack to make any reply.

Later in the evening, when he was calmer, he talked to her of the intended visit of the King and himself to Vienna, where another congress was to be held to discuss the affairs of Italy. Though the affairs of Italy did not concern England, Castlereagh felt that by going to the congress he would be able to confer with the other Powers on three problems which were pending, the Greek revolution, the situation in Spain, and the recognition of the Spanish Colonies. All the necessary arrangements had been made, but Countess Lieven now informed him, that the King and Lady Conyngham could not agree about the journey. Lady Conyngham wished to meet the King only in the capitals, and the King wanted to travel the whole way with her. In a huff the King had now refused to go at all.

Castlereagh was amazed that Lady Conyngham should have an influence over such very important matters.

" The King's journey," he said, " will or will not take place; that is no more my concern. I wash my hands of it. The King has Liverpool; let him arrange with him. I shall accept his orders, and if I continue to serve him I shall decide, according to whether my wife is or is not included in the expedition, what course I have to take."

A gloomy silence fell between them. He stared down at the floor in an abstracted way, and then began to talk darkly of treachery. He mentioned the Duke of Wellington as an example of the treachery of those whom he considered his closest friends. Suddenly he turned towards Countess Lieven, and looking into her face, he said, " And you, you are also a traitor."

Distressed beyond words her eyes filled with tears, and she left the reception. In the carriage she told her husband what had happened. He thought first of all that she had by some foolish remark provoked this strange outburst, but when she recounted all that she had said he exclaimed, " Well, either I am mad, or he is."

2

On his way home from the dinner Castlereagh called at his brother's house in a state of great agitation. He told Charles that he had been humiliated to the last degree, that he had been reduced to owing his wife's invitation to a foreign ambassadress, and he could no longer remain one of the King's servants with any self respect. He was in a strangely excited state, and suddenly burst into a tirade against Countess Lieven. She was trying to goad him, he said, into resigning his office. She had introduced the Duke of Wellington into the King's good graces because she wished the Duke to have his office, hoping to find some one easier to deal with in Eastern affairs. She had been preparing this change behind his back, knowing full well that Wellington was not his friend and had long coveted his office.

It was a curious statement. Countess Lieven had certainly restored the Duke of Wellington to the King's favour, but though she was a great intriguer and was becoming altogether too influential at Court, her action could in no way have harmed Castlereagh. But Castlereagh's views had become sadly distorted. He was full of grief and anxiety and weariness, sick with apprehension and alarm. He was in such distress that he could control himself no longer, and he broke down and wept.[1]

Charles, who had never seen him in such a condition, burst into tears himself. The following morning he called on Countess Lieven and told her what had passed. She was deeply moved to hear of Castlereagh's agony of mind, and could not bear to think that he distrusted her.

" I have never wished to harm your brother," she said. " Whatever influence I have had, I have used actively and loyally in his service. He has had more than one proof of it. I have the most sincere regard for him. As for Wellington, Lord Londonderry has not a more sincere friend than he."

Charles, who was greatly distressed on his brother's account, told her that Castlereagh's spirit was deeply wounded, that his wife worried him ceaselessly, that their nights were spent in quarrelling, that between these night watches and the fatigues of Parliament his nerves were shattered, and he feared his mind would collapse.

" He is disgusted with everything," he concluded. " This woman's quarrel and the cup has overflowed. He suspects everybody. He is broken-hearted."

" In his place," said Countess Lieven, " my mind too would be filled with suspicion, but I hope that time will destroy the doubts and apprehensions which now exist in his mind."

A day or two later she was walking in Kensington Gardens when she became aware of a tall, solitary figure wrapped in an elegant cloak walking in her direction. Castlereagh saluted her gravely, and turning, fell in beside her. His attitude towards her seemed remote and detached. He did not allude to the scene he had made, but asked one or two questions about the King, whom she now saw every day. Although the King had already promised her that he would go to Vienna, he had asked her to keep his new plans secret, and she said very little about the journey.

[1] Lieven MS. Unpublished.

They walked along for a while in silence. He seemed anxious to make some confidence, but at any word she spoke he would bridle and suddenly withdraw into himself. There was distrust in all his remarks, but when she began to grow indignant he would give her a queer, disarming smile that tore at her heart.

He tried again to speak of something, but broke off in the middle and fixed her with haggard eyes. " Good God," he said, " can I trust you? " She turned to him and said: " Look full in my face, what do you see there? "

" A charming face, a clever face," he replied mockingly.

She flushed scarlet.

" No, my lord," she replied, " nothing of that, but an honest face."

There was an awkward pause. She wished she could say something to calm him, but when she tried he only grew more bitter and ironical. She had the deepest affection for him, and knew that he had the greatest friendship for her. Once he had said to her: " If only I could see you every day." And yet these seeds of suspicion had so suddenly been planted between them. Now he was becoming a torment to her and to himself.

She began to talk to him about his plans for the congress, but when she mentioned the month of August, he replied ominously: " In August I shall no longer be the King's Minister."

She could do nothing to disperse his strange mood, and when they parted, in spite of her efforts, they seemed to be on even less friendly terms than when they had met.

Later in the day he sent his brother to her to find out what the King had told her about the journey to Vienna, but Charles discovered nothing. She was reserved in her comments, and merely said that the King and she had talked about the expedition, and that he was counting on Londonderry to go. Charles told her that Castlereagh still suspected that Wellington was planning to supplant him.

" If Wellington is moved up a step," Charles said, " my brother will resign, for he will never suffer this rival, or indeed any rival."

She told him that there was general unwillingness to let his wife go on the journey, but it was absurd to suppose that for such a motive they would get rid of Londonderry, or that Wellington would intrigue to advance himself. She could not understand his distrust of

Wellington, and she grieved beyond words that she too had lost Londonderry's confidence.

Writing to Metternich she said: " Why on earth has Londonderry contracted these suspicions? It seems to me that I have an honest face. Why cannot he see what is in my heart? Well, I shall leave him to calm down a little; he will soon come to his senses."

She was due to dine with Castlereagh on the day the King was to speak to him of his plans. As she drove to St. James's Square her mind was a little apprehensive, for the King was so capricious that he changed his mind with the wind. Castlereagh received her warmly, and she waited for him to speak about the journey, watching him narrowly and trying to read on his face the result of the interview. But his face never betrayed anything he did not wish to convey, and they sat down to dinner without his having spoken a word.

At table he seemed radiant, and she brightened. She knew he enjoyed teasing her, so asked him no questions but began speaking about Metternich instead. She told him that Metternich had sent him a message, and she asked him to give her a message for him in return. He did not comply, but she persisted, and after failing a score of times, which did not discourage her, she managed at length to extract the following: " Tell him that I am hoping to see him soon." The journey then was fixed.

After dinner Charles came up to her and said: " I congratulate you; you must be proud of yourself; you have made the King obey you on every point. My brother found him as prepared as if he were under orders; everything you wish is done, and we must all run at your bidding."

A few days later, however, all the plans were changed. When Countess Lieven called on Lady Conyngham she found her with a tear-stained face and swollen eyes. The King had just written to her to say that he had decided not to go to the Continent after all. He was going to Scotland instead, and had sent for his Ministers to tell them so. He was in fact, at that very moment, communicating to them the intelligence that he had dispatched couriers to give notice of his arrival in Edinburgh, where he was proceeding instead of to Vienna.

The King regretted this decision almost as soon as it was given, but he did not retract. All these repercussions had their effect on the Foreign Minister. Meeting Lord Tavistock he said: " I am sick of the concern and if I could well get out of it, would never get into it again."

The Parliamentary Session of 1822 did not end till 6 August. It was a most arduous and uncomfortable session. When Castlereagh, sinking beneath the weight and the torments of it, was congratulated on its approaching close, he said: "Yes, it had to end, or I should end." To Mrs. Arbuthnot he confessed that he was tired of office, and wished he could slip his neck out of the yoke.

3

It was not only the King's whims and fancies, the favourite's caprices, and his wife's impertinences that were disturbing Castlereagh. He was beginning to show signs at this time of severe mental stress; strange delusions were attacking his mind.

The Rev. J. Richardson in his Recollections gives a curious story, which Castlereagh apparently related himself " to a nobleman." One night, Richardson asserts, when Castlereagh was returning home from the House of Commons he was accosted by a woman, whom he accompanied to a house of ill-fame. There he was shown into an apartment where he soon discovered that his companion was a youth in female attire.

At the same moment the door of the room was forced open, and two men rushed in and accused him of being about to commit a very serious offence. In the horror of the moment Castlereagh lost his presence of mind and allowed himself to be blackmailed into giving them all the money he had with him. The money merely whetted their appetites, and day after day they stationed themselves opposite the windows of his house in St. James's Square, and by signs and motions gave him to understand that unless they received further reimbursements they would disclose the incident.[1]

On 19 July 1822, the Bishop of Clogher, son of the Earl of Roden, had been arrested on a charge of having committed an act of criminal association with a private soldier in a common ale-house in Westminster.[2] Castlereagh was later to mention to the King that he was

[1] Recollections, Political, Literary, Dramatic and Miscellaneous of the Last Half-Century by The Rev. J. Richardson, LL.B.

[2] Annual Register, 1822. *Gentleman's Magazine*, Vol. 21.

accused of the same crime. Nobody, in fact, as far as we know, had accused him of the crime, and Richardson's story seems to have emanated from Castlereagh, himself, for he was now obviously suffering from Melancholia, of which self-abasement is a prominent symptom.

It is a disease in which, as William McDougall asserts,[1] " the patient takes a low and depressed view of himself, and declares that he is a miserable sinner, a wretched creature, that he has committed dreadful crimes, and expects corresponding treatment in this world and the next, that he is incapable of coping with the world by reason of moral and physical deficiencies of the most varied kinds."

About this time Castlereagh began to utter darkly that he would face death rather than disgrace. On 10 June 1822, Countess Lieven had written to Metternich, saying: " Londonderry looks ghastly. He has aged five years in the last week; one can see he is a broken man."

In spite of his condition Castlereagh went on with his work, none of his colleagues noticing apparently the mental stress from which he was suffering.

On the 15 August 1822, he was to set out for the Congress, which was ultimately held at Verona. He had already arranged with Metternich a complete plan of campaign. Britain and Austria were to use their combined influence to dissuade the Czar from sending an army against the Turks; they were also to influence the Turks to accept the Four Points which Russia demanded. These points included the restoration of the Greek churches, and the protection of the Greek religion.

Castlereagh was determined to prevent another war in Europe; he was also desirous of deflecting Russia from her age-old ambition to reach the Dardanelles and the Mediterranean.

His plans were very nearly upset by the Turkish massacre of the Greek population of Scio on the very eve of the Congress. Castlereagh sent a vigorous protest to Turkey in the strongest possible language. The British Ambassador, Strangford, delivering this protest, wrote back to the Government at home, saying:

" I hope I may be permitted to avow the pride which I feel in reflecting that the only Government which has hitherto branded the

[1] William McDougall: *An Outline of Abnormal Psychology.*

transactions at Scio with the indignant and fearless expression of its abhorrence is that of Great Britain."

Strangford at the same time reported his success in having obtained the Four Points from the Porte, which Russia had demanded.

Castlereagh was now engaged in drawing up his own instructions for the approaching conference. On the 8 August 1822 he attended a meeting of the Cabinet to submit these instructions for its approval. His main objects were: to prevent a rupture between Russia and the Porte, to soften as far as possible the rigours of war between the Turks and the Greeks, and to observe in the contest a strict neutrality. There were other questions under consideration. There was the very serious problem of Spain. To the idea of applying force to bring back the revolted colonies of Spain under the dominion of a decadent monarchy he was entirely opposed. Humanity and expediency required, he said, that the personal safety of the Spanish royal family should be assured, but there must be a rigid abstention from any interference in the internal affairs of an independent state. Above all Spain must sign a treaty satisfactory to Great Britain for the abolition of the slave trade. The instructions were fully approved by his colleagues, every member present admiring the justness of his views. These instructions foreshadowed the policy afterwards carried out by Canning, who did not deviate in any way from the line laid down by Castlereagh.

4

At this final Cabinet meeting he seemed fully composed, yet he must have been suffering from the severest mental stress. His resistance had been sapped by the strain under which he was living ; physically and mentally he was exhausted. Strange fears had begun to dominate his mind, a natural outcome or a complication of the Melancholia from which he was now suffering. His mind, which had always been so clear and logical, was full of delusions, his brain seemed on fire, he was tangled up with hideous shadows that seemed more real and insistent than life itself.

It must have needed an almost superhuman effort to preside over Cabinet meetings, and yet he accomplished this task with the same cool manner that had always marked his demeanour. This is no unusual phase in the disease which was attacking him.

"In simple Melancholia," Dr. Yellowlees[1] informs us, "the symptoms are mild, and the patient is not infrequently able to make a fairly good show before strangers, and even to make an attempt or a pretence of doing his ordinary work. As a rule the prominent feature is a general retardation and a dull loss of interest. The patient's consciousness is perfectly clear, and he rarely expresses any delusions, being usually able to rationalise his depression by exaggerating trivialities in his past life." Dr. Yellowlees goes on to say that "in spite of the apparent mildness of the disorder the patient may be acutely suicidal."

It is not remarkable that his colleagues, who thought he looked tired and worn, did not suspect that there was anything amiss, but it is surprising that his wife, who was with him all the time, and who must have known of the delusions and the fears that were beginning to attack his mind, should have allowed him to go on with his plans. But she was desirous above all things of accompanying him to the Congress, and now that the King, who still refused to have her near him, was going to Scotland there seemed nothing to prevent her from going to Vienna, where it was first proposed that the Congress should be held.

Castlereagh, who had never feared anything in his life, began now to fear the Congress. He would have liked a short rest he said, either at Bath or at Cheltenham, but could not take it.

One day, when he was alone with his secretary, Lord George Seymour, he put his hand to his forehead and said pathetically: "My mind is, as it were, gone." Seymour was disturbed, but put it down to the strain under which he was living.

After the Cabinet meeting at which his instructions had been approved, Castlereagh returned to Cray. In the afternoon Seymour saw him walking towards the river at the foot of the garden, looking so melancholy and dejected that he followed him. When he caught up with him he found Castlereagh so completely absorbed that he hardly noticed he was there. He tried to converse with him, and draw him out of his gloomy abstraction, but his attempts to interest him failed.

[1] Dr. Henry Yellowlees. *Clinical Lectures on Psychological Medicine.*

He tried the subject of Castlereagh's approaching journey. He hoped, he said, that his lordship was looking forward with pleasure to their continental trip; he would have the satisfaction of renewing several of his former diplomatic acquaintances.

Castlereagh paused a moment, then said very slowly: " At any other time I should have liked it very much, but I am quite worn out *here*,"—he tapped his forehead—" quite worn out, and this fresh load of responsibility now put upon me is more than I can bear."

The mournful tone in which the words were uttered, as well as the confession itself, were so unlike Castlereagh that Seymour began to be alarmed, fearing that there was something very wrong. He spoke to Lady Londonderry about it later, but she declared that he was merely tired, and would be better after he had rested.

The following day, the 9 August, Castlereagh drove up to town to take his leave of the King. His wife accompanied him in his carriage as far as the gates of the Palace, where she put him down, hoping doubtless that his condition would not be remarked.

Castlereagh showed the King the instructions he had drawn up for himself. George was reading the manuscript aloud, when he noticed that Castlereagh was paying no attention to him. His eyes were circling round the ceiling in a very queer manner.

" What's the matter, my lord ? " asked the King.

" It's that insufferable John, Sir, who is at the door," he replied. " He will not go away, though I am always telling him to." John was his groom, and was certainly not in evidence anywhere.

The King in astonishment folded up the manuscript and said:

" You are ill, my lord. Go home and have yourself bled."

Castlereagh looked at him with terror in his eyes, and said:

" Have you heard the news ? The terrible news ? I am a fugitive from justice. I am accused of the same crime as the Bishop of Clogher."

The King laughed. " What madness," he replied. " You're raving."

But Castlereagh went on in a state of great agitation.

" Indeed I am not," he said. " A warrant has been issued for my arrest, and they are looking for me. I have ordered my horses, and am going to fly to Portsmouth, and there embark for France. I shall leave by the little gate in your garden."

" My lord," said the King with great dignity, " you forget yourself. This pleasantry is misplaced—entirely misplaced."

Castlereagh laughed sardonically.

" I know well that you also are my enemy," he replied. " Everyone hates me and shuns me. When I walk down the streets people take the opposite side to avoid meeting me."

The King, now seriously alarmed, took him by both hands, and begged him to compose himself.

" Do you think you have a better friend than I? " he said. " You have a fever. Have yourself bled and chase away your fit of blue devils."

But Castlereagh's strange mood continued. He accused himself of every crime. He threw out dark hints that he was being blackmailed. He even showed the King two anonymous letters which he had received the day before, threatening to expose his irregular conduct to his wife.[1]

The King dismissed the anonymous letters as nonsense, and informed him again that he had a fever, but Castlereagh buried his head in his hands and said:

" I am mad. I know I am mad. I have known it for some time." He looked up at the King with tortured eyes. " Promise me to keep it secret," he implored, " and above all, swear to me that you will say nothing of it to my colleagues."

The King tried to calm him. Immediately after he had gone he spoke to Wellington, urging him to get Castlereagh's doctor over to him. He also wrote a most affectionate letter to Castlereagh begging him to get medical attention. He then wrote to Liverpool who was at Coombe, informing him that he was nervous about Castlereagh's mental health, and requesting him to come at once.

After his interview with the King, Castlereagh was overtaken by Wellington, who found him still suffering from delusions. He informed the Duke that his horses had followed him to the Palace without his orders, and that a man had told him they were there to enable him to make his escape from the country. but that he was determined to do his duty, and would remain where he was. He insisted that there was a conspiracy against him, and turning to Wellington, asked if he too had not something to say against him. The Duke tried to persuade him that he was under a delusion about

[1] Cp. Appendix II : Mrs. Arbuthnot's Journal.

all these things, that there was no conspiracy, and there were no horses.

But Castlereagh said he would prove he was under no delusion. By this time they had arrived at his house in St. James's Square, and were in the drawing-room. Castlereagh rang the bell. When his man entered, he asked him sharply why his horses had followed him without orders. The man replied that his horses were at Cray. A look of dismay passed over Castlereagh's face, and he said no more. When the servant withdrew the Duke implored him to dismiss these delusions from his mind, and begged him to send for advice. As Castlereagh did not reply he looked him in the face and said with brutal frankness:

"From what you have said I am bound to warn you that you cannot be in your right mind."

Castlereagh's eyes filled with tears. He threw himself down on the couch, and sobbed bitterly.

"Since you say so," he said, "I fear it must be so. I have an oppression at the head, which distresses me perpetually, and makes me fear that my ideas are indeed in disorder." His tortured face was white with terror. Wellington was greatly disturbed, and offered to stay with him, but Castlereagh feared that it would only make his illness the more marked.

As soon as he left, Wellington went to Castlereagh's physician, Dr. Bankhead. Finding he was not at home he sat down and wrote him a note, which was later used as evidence of Castlereagh's insanity. It was the only evidence ever produced.

"I called upon you," Wellington wrote, "with the intention of talking to you on the subject of the health of Lord Londonderry, and to request of you that you would call on him. I told his lordship that he was unwell, and particularly requested him to send for you; but lest he should not, I sincerely hope that you will contrive, by some pretence, to go down to his lordship. I have no doubt he is very unwell; he appears to me to have been exceedingly harassed, much fatigued, and overworked during the late session of Parliament; and I have no doubt he labours under mental delirium; at least this is my impression. I beg you will never mention to anybody what I have told you respecting his lordship."

Bankhead called on Castlereagh the same afternoon, and found him looking pale and distressed. He complained of a severe headache and of confusion in his mind. He had scarcely eaten the whole day and was very weak. It was obvious to Bankhead that he was labouring under a strong mental delusion accompanied by fever.

He administered the great remedy of the eighteenth century and cupped him, taking six ounces of blood from the back of his neck. The operation left Castlereagh weaker than before, and Dr. Bankhead persuaded him to go down to Cray. Castlereagh said he would do so, and that he expected Dr. Bankhead to come down too and stay Saturday night, and if possible Sunday as well, as he seemed to be very ill.

In spite of the condition he was in, he saw Count Lieven before he left for Cray, and talked to him of the journey abroad. He told him that he was not feeling very well, that his mind was somewhat disturbed, and he invited him and Countess Lieven to dine with him at Cray, so that they could have a long talk together.

On the way down to Cray he seemed deeply dejected, but he carried on with his work in the carriage. Seymour, who accompanied him, read him some letters which required attention, and Castlereagh gave him his orders regarding them with his usual precision. The only difference in his manner, Seymour thought, was a greater humility than was habitual to him. He seemed to have lost confidence in his own powers, and accepted the suggestions Seymour made, showing more deference for his opinions.

When he arrived at Cray he was very feverish, but he said he felt much better and stayed up to dinner. The following day, the 10 August 1822, his mind began to wander and he talked darkly of plots against him. He was uneasy and restless, and noticed that he was being watched, which he resented bitterly. But it was necessary that he should be watched, for he had talked more than once of suicide, and had asked his wife for the key of his pistol case. " If you go on talking in this manner," she replied, " I will go away and send Dr. Bankhead to you." He did not repeat his request, but sat silent for a while, and then retired to bed.

Emily continued to treat the matter as unimportant. And yet she allowed none of his intimate friends to see him, and even sent off his secretaries for a few days. On this very day, Saturday, the 10 August 1822, two days before his death, she was writing to Lord Liverpool:

"DEAR LORD LIVERPOOL,

Lord Londonderry desires me to thank you for your communication. He is anxious to meet you in town on Monday, but he has been very unwell for some days, and Dr. Bankhead (who is now here) says he must nurse himself up if he means to be ready to start for the Continent at the time settled.

I will trust to your good nature to forgive my asking you as a great favour to myself to come here either on Monday or Tuesday, for I fear a journey to London would quite counteract the quiet nursing of this place. We can dine either day at any hour you please, and shall be most happy if you will take a bed here. I again exhort you to forgive.

> Believe me,
> Yours very sincerely,
> E. A. LONDONDERRY "

It is one of the very few of Emily's letters that survive.

The following day was Sunday, and Emily and the rest of the house went to church, Castlereagh remaining alone with his doctor. He talked about public opinion, asking Bankhead what people thought of him, and whether they accused him of any crime. The doctor begged him to compose himself and not to imagine such things, but he continued to harp on the same subject. He said he could not go to the Continent as long as he allowed the suspicion of a crime to rest on him.

During the night he got up and went into his dressing-room, telling Emily he wanted to wash his face; an hour later he got up and went again to his dressing-room, saying he wanted to clean his teeth. He was searching for a little knife which he knew to be somewhere in the room. At three o'clock in the morning he asked Emily to bring him one of the red boxes out of the drawing-room below as there were papers in it on which his life depended. She found him the box, but it only contained one or two papers, and they did not appear to be of any importance.

In the morning he asked for his razors, saying he wished to shave. This alarmed his wife, and she locked the razors away. It was the 12 August 1822. He did not get up, but lay in bed talking incessantly, wandering a good deal, harping always on plots. At seven o'clock he rang for his breakfast; but when it was brought to him he found fault with it in a voice so sharp and severe that it surprised the maid; his manner had always been so mild and gentle. At half-past seven he rang again, and asked for Dr. Bankhead. As the maid turned to go, Emily, who was in the room, went to the door and spoke to her. Castlereagh's eyes followed his wife, and seeing her whispering to the maid, he said: " A conspiracy is laid against me."

The maid went away, and after informing Dr. Bankhead that his lordship wished to see him, returned to find Castlereagh sitting up in bed, and Lady Londonderry hurriedly retiring to her boudoir. A moment later Castlereagh was rushing past her into his dressing-room. The maid again called Dr. Bankhead, and he came immediately, but it was too late. When he got to the door of the dressing-room he found Castlereagh standing with his back to him, one hand upraised; from a gash below the ear blood was spurting.

With a cry of " My God," Bankhead ran to him and caught him in his arms. " Oh, Bankhead, it is all over," Castlereagh murmured. In his hand was a small knife with a blade two inches long. Blood was streaming from him; it soaked Bankhead's arm, and he let him fall, and left him lying there with his face to the ground.

5

" Well! " wrote Henry Brougham to Creevey, " this is really a considerable event in point of size. Put all their other men together in one scale, and poor Castlereagh in the other—single, he plainly weighed them down. . . . One can't help feeling a little for him, after being pitted against him for several years pretty regularly. It is like losing a connection suddenly. Also, he was a gentleman, and the only one amongst them."

The King was on his way to Edinburgh. On 13 August 1822, the day after Castlereagh's death, he wrote to him from the *Royal George Yacht*:[1]

" DEAR LORD LONDONDERRY,

A violent gale of wind quite in our teeth obliged us to take

[1] Londonderry Papers.

shelter in this Bay; under these circumstances I have the opportunity of inquiring for your health, which I hope is satisfactorily amended since we parted.

Let me entreat you not to hurry your continental journey until you feel yourself quite equal to it. Remember of what importance your health is to the country, but above all things to me. I am tolerable, not very well.

Believe me, always,

Your sincere friend,

G.R."

This letter of affection from a monarch who had used him so ill Castlereagh was never to receive. On August 20, 1822, he was buried at Westminster beside the grave of Pitt. When his coffin was being carried into the Abbey, some fifteen men, gathered there to create a disturbance, raised a cry of joy, but the indignation of the crowd suppressed it, and the cry was hushed.[1]

---

[1] Cp. Appendix I.

APPENDIX I

LETTERS ON THE DEATH OF LORD CASTLEREAGH
LONDONDERRY PAPERS

From Lord Clancarty to Charles Stewart
London, August 21, 1822

" . . . Some timid people indeed were apprehensive of riot on the occasion, but the good feeling of the more powerful, the sense of gratitude due to his Memory by the whole world, and especially by this empire, prevailed, and his remains have been deposited in the only spot worthy of them, immediately along side of those of Pitt. The terrors of the timid were not justified by any thing which occurred during the procession or Ceremony, on the Contrary, tho the concourse of people was immense, as well about the house in St. James's Square, as along the whole route to the Abbey, and in front of the Abbey so much crowded that the heads of the people might have been walked on, to the credit of the populace be it said, that never was greater decency marked, nay even feeling evinced on any similar occasion. Many were in tears in the streets and windows, and all observed becoming silence and the decorum most eloquent on such ceremonies. It is true that at the gates of the Abbey, a knot of fellows some 12 to 20, evidently paid and collected for the purpose, endeavoured by throwing up their hats, and shouts to excite disturbance; but this attempt was received with such indignation on the part of the mob— that the exciting parties were not induced to renew their efforts. Never did I witness a more general sensation of sincere grief, and sense of public loss, not even at the death of Pitt, than has been generally shown by all classes upon this occasion."

Appendix I

From Lord Camden to Charles Stewart
Arlington Street, August 20, 1822

". . . Your son has been with me at Bayham for a few Days as I was desirous of removing him from the Scene at Cray, and He came to Town to attend as Chief Mourner today, and you will have as much satisfaction as you are capable of having in any Event at present on hearing that the awful solemnity of this day at Westminster Abbey was gone thro, within the walls and in the approach to the Abbey, in the manner every one could wish—a Deep Feeling of grief amongst all descriptions of Persons, his Memory is already beginning to be cherished by those, who even opposed his measures."

From Lord Ellenborough to Charles Stewart
Roehampton, August 20, 1822

"MY DEAR CHARLES,

I am sure it will be satisfactory to you to hear that the crowd which lined the Streets from St. James's Square to the Abbey saw the Funeral pass in perfect silence and with strong marks of respect and grief. There was not a single circumstance or a single expression that would have given pain to Lady Londonderry herself. In the Abbey nothing could be more solemn. All seemed deeply affected, and many very much so, who, one would have imagined, had not had that sort of intercourse with Him which could lead to feelings of that nature. Of course the newspapers will give you the names of those who attended and all the particulars. I was glad to see Mr. Spring there who is a very decided Oppositionist and will be a very considerable Man, and there were several County Members; but it was not known that those who were not personally connected with him would be admitted or there would, I understand, have been a much larger number of Members of Parliament. Ld —— came from Ireland,

and Ld Clive from Wales. Frederick was Chief Mourner, as your Representative, and seemed much distressed. The Bishop of London was there, which I was very glad of, for Lady L. particularly wished it and his name is valuable. The object of a funeral in Westminster Abbey was fully attained. It is proved that the manner of Ld. L's Death has made no difference whatever in the estimate formed of his Character or in the respect entertained for his Memory. It will so stand in History—Lady L. said very nobly that she would rather die than that anyone should be able to say she stole a grave for Him and the decision that the Funeral should take place in Westminster Abbey has been completely justified by the event."

From Colonel Wood to Charles Stewart
Littleton, August, 21, 1822

". . . The crowd was immense the Streets quite occupied from St. James's Square to the Abbey and But that mournful and respectful silence prevailed all seemed impressed with the loss the Country has sustained and His bitterest enemies now begin to do Him justice."

APPENDIX II

THE ANONYMOUS LETTERS

From the Journal of Mrs. Arbuthnot, 1820-1832

August 29, 1822. Mr. Arbuthnot had been for some time receiving threatening letters from a man of the name of Jennings saying that if he did not get an office, he would tell things he knew that would ruin many persons in office; in short, common anonymous letters, though he knew the handwriting to be this man's. A positive refusal of employment was sent to him and, on the 3rd August, Mr. A. received a vulgar placard, evidently printed for the purpose, threatening to accuse *me* of a *love affair with the Duke of Wellington*! This naturally annoyed us both most excessively, and we agreed to consult Lord Londonderry what steps to take. . . .

I had heard in the morning from Mr. A. that Lord Londonderry had taken it into his head that these threatening letters were all aimed at him; and we had thought it very odd, knowing the contempt he usually had for anonymous attacks. On this day, however, as soon as he came into the room he took my hand and entreated me in the most earnest manner to tell him whether I had ever heard anything against him, said he considered me as one of his greatest friends and thought I should have no false delicacy in telling him if I had ever heard anything against his honour or his character. I was excessively astonished and quite laughed at the idea of anything dishonourable against him. I told him I had often heard he was a great flirt and very fond of ladies, but I did not suppose he would consider that as a great crime. He seemed pleased at what I said, and told me that about three years before he had had an anonymous letter threatening to tell of his having been seen go into an improper house. . . .

367

Appendix II

It appears that three years ago he did go with a woman to an improper house from which he was watched by a man, who the next morning wrote to tell him so and asked for a place. However, at that time he thought not of it. So strongly had business and fatigue upset his usually calm mind that he actually fancied the purport of the letter was to accuse him of a crime not to be named, and this notion could not be put out of his head.

August 15, 1823. The Duke told me that when Bankhead found that the whole world abused him for his neglect of Lord Londonderry, he immediately determined to endeavour to justify himself by saying that Lord Londonderry was not mad, and that the crime of which he accused himself he had actually committed. He came to the Duke and told him a long story of what Lord Londonderry had himself told him and stated to him *two facts*, and told it all so plausibly that he actually made the Duke believe there was some truth in what he said However, luckily, the Duke ascertained *beyond a doubt* that *the facts were both positively false*; and he told me he had not a shadow of doubt of the falsehood of all Bankhead's story, which he says he is perfectly certain was made up for his own purpose; and that, finding how much he was abused, he had had the baseness to seize upon the delusion of a mind broke down with the pressure of business to sully the character of the noblest, most high-minded creature that ever existed, for the purpose of saving his own miserable credit.

BIBLIOGRAPHY

Unpublished Papers

CAMDEN PAPERS (*Bayham Abbey*).

INQUEST ON CASTLEREAGH (*British Museum*).

LIEVEN MSS (*British Museum*).

LONDONDERRY PAPERS (*Mount Stewart*).

LONDONDERRY ESTATE OFFICE ARCHIVES (*Newtownards*).

PELHAM MSS (*British Museum*).

PITT MSS (*Public Record Office*).

Other Works Consulted

ADAMS, HENRY, *History of the United States*, 9 vols., Charles Scribner, 1931.

(*Abridged*) *The Formative Years*, Edited by Herbert Agar, 2 vols., Collins.

ALISON, SIR A., *Lives of Lord Castlereagh and Sir Charles Stewart*, 3 vols., Blackwood, 1861.

ARBUTHNOT, MRS., *Journal of*, 1820–1832, Macmillan & Co., Ltd., 1950.

BAGOT, J., *George Canning and His Friends*, John Murray, 1909.

BARRINGTON, SIR J., *Personal Sketches of His Own Times*, Henry Colburn, 1827.

BESSBOROUGH, EARL OF, *Lady Bessborough and Her Circle*, John Murray, 1940.

BOIGNE, COMTESSE DE, *Memoirs*, 3 vols., Edited by M. Charles Nicoullaud, William Heinemann, 1907.

BROUGHAM, LORD, *Historical Sketches of Statesmen of the Reign of George III*, London, 1839.

C 2A

Bibliography

BROWN, PHILIP ANTHONY, *The French Revolution in English History*, George Allen and Unwin, 1918.

BROWNLOW, LADY, *Slight Reminiscences of a Septuagenarian*, Murray, 1867.

BRYANT, ARTHUR, *Years of Endurance*, Collins, 1942. *Years of Victory*, Collins 1944.

BUCKINGHAM AND CHANDOS, DUKE OF, *Memoirs of the Courts and Cabinets of George III*, 4 vols., London, 1853.

BURGHERSH, LADY, *Correspondence*, Edited by Rachel Weigall, John Murray, 1912.

CAMBRIDGE HISTORY OF BRITISH FOREIGN POLICY, 3 vols., Cambridge, 1922.

CAMBRIDGE MODERN HISTORY, Cambridge University Press.

CASTLEREAGH, VISCOUNT, *Letters and Dispatches*, 12 vols., John Murray, 1853.

CASTLEREAGH CORRESPONDENCE, Edited by his brother, Charles Stewart, Marquess of Londonderry, 4 vols., London, 1848.

CASTLEREAGH, RT. HON. LORD VISCOUNT, *Report from the Committee of Secrecy Appointed to take into Consideration the Treasonable Papers Presented to the House of Commons of Ireland*, John Stockdale, 1798.

CECIL, ALGERNON, *Metternich*, Eyre and Spottiswoode, 1932.

CHAMBONAS, COMTE A. DE LA GARDE, *Souvenirs du Congrès de Vienne*, Paris, 1901.

CHARLEMONT CORRESPONDENCE, *Manuscripts and Correspondence of James 1st, Earl of Charlemont*, Edited by Sir J. T. Gilbert, 2 vols., London, 1891 (*Historical Manuscripts Commission*).

COBBETT, WILLIAM, *Political Register*, London, 1835.

COLCHESTER CORRESPONDENCE, *Diary and Correspondence of Charles Abbot, Lord Colchester*. London, 1861.

COOPER, RT. HON. DUFF, *Talleyrand*, Jonathan Cape, 1932.

CORNWALLIS CORRESPONDENCE, *Correspondence of Charles, first Marquess Cornwallis*. Edited by Sir Charles Ross, 3 vols., 2nd edition, London, 1859.

CREEVEY PAPERS, THE, Edited by Sir H. Maxwell, John Murray, 1903.

CROKER PAPERS, THE, 3 vols., John Murray, 1884.

DAVIES, J. D. GRIFFITH, *George III*, Ivor Nicholson and Watson, 1936.

Bibliography

DRENNAN LETTERS, *Correspondence of William Drennan, Edited by D. A. Chart, Belfast,* 1931.

DROPMORE PAPERS, *Correspondence of William Wyndham Grenville, London,* 1892 *(Historical Manuscripts Commission).*

DUDLEY, FIRST EARL OF, *Letters to Ivy, Edited by S. H. Romilly. Longmans Green,* 1905.

EELES, H. S., *Lord Chancellor Camden and his family, Philip Allan,* 1934.

FALKINER, C. L., *Studies in Irish History and Biography,* 1902.

FARINGTON, DIARIES OF JOSEPH, *Hutchinson.*

FERRERO, GUGLIELMO, *Reconstruction of Europe, Putnam,* 1941.

FESTING, GABRIELLE, *John Hookham Frere, Nisbet,* 1899.

FITZGERALD, T. P., *The Political and Private Life of the Marquess of Londonderry, Dublin,* 1822.

FITZPATRICK, W. J., *Secret Service under Pitt, London,* 1892.

FORTESCUE, J. W., *British Statesmen of the Great War,* 1793-1814, *London,* 1911.

FOSTER, VERE, *The Two Duchesses, Blackie and Son,* 1898.

FOUCHÉ, JOSEPH, *Memoirs, William W. Gibbings,* 1892.

FULFORD, R. T. B., *George IV, London,* 1935.

GENTZ, F. VON, *Briefe an Pilat, Leipzig, Vogel Verlag,* 1868.

GENTZ, F. VON, *Dépêches inédites, Paris,* 1876.

GLENBERVIE, SYLVESTER DOUGLAS, LORD, *The Diaries of, Edited by F. Bickley, Constable, London,* 1928.

GRATTAN, H., *Memoirs of the Life and Times of Henry Grattan,* 5 *vols., London,* 1839.

GRANVILLE, HARRIET, COUNTESS, *Letters of, Longmans Green,* 1894.

GREVILLE, CHARLES, *Journal of the Reigns of King George IV and King William IV, Edited by Lytton Strachey and Fulford, Heinemann,* 1937.

GRONOW, CAPTAIN NIMMO, *Recollections of,* 1892.

GUEDALLA, PHILIP, *The Duke, Hodder and Stoughton,* 1937.

HAMWOOD PAPERS, *The Hamwood Papers of the Ladies of Llangollen and Lady Caroline Hamilton, Edited by G. H. Bell, London,* 1931.

HARDY, F., *Memoirs of the Earl of Charlemont, London,* 1810.

HASSALL, A., *Viscount Castlereagh, London,* 1906.

Bibliography

HOLLAND, LADY, *The Journals of,* Edited by the Earl of Ilchester, Longmans, 1908.

HOLLAND, LADY, *Letters to her Son* (1821-1845), *Edited by the Earl of* Ilchester, John Murray, 1946.

HYDE, H. M., *The Rise of Castlereagh,* Macmillan, 1933.

JACKSON, SIR GEORGE, *Diaries and Letters,* Richard Bentley, 1872.

LAS CASES, COMTE DE, *Mémorial de Sainte Hélène,* 4 *vols,* Paris.

LAWRENCE, SIR THOMAS, *Letter-bag,* Edited by George Somes Layard, George Allan, 1906.

LENNOX, LADY SARAH, *Life and Letters of,* Edited by the Countess of Ilchester, 1901.

LIEVEN, PRINCESS, *Private Letters of,* Edited by Peter Quennell, John Murray, 1937.

LONDONDERRY, THERESA, MARCHIONESS OF, *Robert Stewart, Viscount Castlereagh,* London, 1904.

LYTTLETON, SARAH, LADY, *Correspondence of,* Edited by the Hon. Mrs. Hugh Wyndham, John Murray, 1912.

MADDEN, R., *The United Irishmen,* London, 1860.

MALMESBURY, FIRST EARL OF, *Diaries and Correspondence,* London, 1845.

MARRIOTT, SIR JOHN, *Castlereagh,* Methuen, 1936.

MARTINEAU, HARRIET, *History of the Thirty Years' Peace,* John Bell, 1846.

METTERNICH, PRINCE DE, *Mémoires, Plon,* 1880.

MITCHEL, *History of Ireland,* Washbourne, Dublin, 1869.

MOORE, T., *Life and Times of Lord Edward Fitzgerald,* 2 *vols,* London, 1831.

NEUMANN, PHILIP VON, *Diaries of,* P. Allan, 1928.

NICOLSON, HAROLD, *The Congress of Vienna,* Constable, 1946.

NIGHTINGALE, J., *Calm and Dispassionate View of the Life and Administration of the Marquess of Londonderry,* London, 1822.

O'MEARA, BARRY EDWARD, *Napoleon at St. Helena.*

PETRIE, SIR CHARLES, *Life of George Canning,* Eyre and Spottiswoode, 1930.

PETRIE, SIR CHARLES, *The Four Georges,* Eyre and Spottiswoode.

PHILIPS, W. ALISON, *The Confederation of Europe,* London, 1914.

PLOWDEN, F., *History of Ireland to the Union,* London, 1809.

Bibliography

REEDE, F., *The Private Life and Character of the Marquess of Londonderry*, London, 1822.

ROSE, J. H., *William Pitt and the Great War*, London, 1911.

ROSEBERY, LORD, *Pitt*, London, 1891.

ROSEBERY, LORD, *Napoleon; the Last Phase*, London, 1900.

RUSH, RICHARD, *The Court of London*, 1819-1825, Bentley, 1873.

RUSSELL, LORD JOHN, *Recollections*, London, 1875.

SALISBURY, MARQUESS OF, *Biographical Essays*, London, 1905.

SHELLEY, FRANCES, LADY, *Dairy of*, John Murray, 1912.

SOREL, A., *L'Europe et la Révolution Française*, Paris, 1904.

STANHOPE, EARL, *Life of William Pitt*, London, 1862.

STAPLETON, *Political Life of Canning*, London, 1831.

SRBIK, HEINRICH, *Metternich*, F. Bruckmann, München, 1925.

TALLEYRAND, *Memoirs*, Griffith Farren, 1891.

TEELING, C. H., *Personal Narrative of the Rebellion of* 1798, London, 1828.

TEIGNMOUTH, *Reminiscences of Many Years*, David Douglas, 1878.

TEMPERLEY, H. W. V., *Foreign Policy of Canning*, G. Bell, 1925.

THIERS, L. A., *Consulat et l'Empire*, Paris, 1893.

TOYNBEE, ARNOLD, *Glimpses of the Twenties*, Constable, 1909.

TWISS, *Life of Eldon*, John Murray, 1844.

VITROLLES, BARON DE, *Mémoires*, Paris, Charpentier, 1884.

WALPOLE, SPENCER, *Life of Spencer Perceval*, Hurst and Blackett, 1784.

WARD, ROBERT PLUMER, *Mémoirs of the Political and Literary Life of*, Edited by the Hon. Edmund Phipps, John Murray, 1850.

WEBSTER, DR. C. K., *The Foreign Policy of Castlereagh*, G. Bell, 1931.

WEBSTER, DR. C. K., *The Congress of Vienna*, G. Bell, 1937.

WEIL, COMMANDANT, *Les dessous du Congrès de Vienne*, Payot, 1917.

WELLINGTON, DUKE OF, *Despatches*, London, 1847.

WELLINGTON, DUKE OF, *Supplementary Despatches*, London, 1860.

INDEX

Abbott, Charles, 158

Abercromby, Sir Ralph, 95-6, 101, 121-2, 142

Aberdeen, Lord, 257, 260

Addington, Henry, 134, 137, 141-2, 146, 148, 152, 154, 156, 220, 238-9, 242, 339

Aix-la-Chapelle, Congress of, 325-6

Amelia, Princess, 222, 228

America: *Chesapeake* incident, 180-1, 217; at war with England, 247, 250, 258-9, 290-1

Amiens, Treaty of, 147

Ards Independents, 20

Auckland, Lord, 136

Austria : Peace treaty with France, 136

Bagot, Sir Charles, 193

Baltic League, 142

Bankhead, Dr., 358-60, 362

Barclay, Admiral, 180, 217

Barrington, Sir Jonah, 150

Bayham, Lord, 27, 47, 54, 68

Beauharnais, Josephene de, *see* Josephene, Marie Rose

Bellingham, John, 242

Bentinck, Lord William, 306

Beresford, 101, 234

Bernadotte, General, 175, 251, 255-6, 266, 273-4

Bessborough, Lady, 177

Blücher, 268, 272, 274, 311

Boigne, Countess of, 223-4, 282

Bond, Oliver, 76, 97, 102

Borgo, Count Pozzo di, 260

Britain's Maritime Rights, 257, 262, 266, 268

Brougham, Lord, 12, 322

Buonaparte, Joseph, 192

Buonaparte, Napoleon, *see* Napoleon

Burghersh, Lady, 272, 277, 282

Burke, Edmund, 42-4, 46

Burrard, Sir Harry, 185-7, 194

Byrne, Michael, 102

Byron, Lord, 14

Camden, Lord (Father of Castlereagh's stepmother), 16, 17, 19; appointed President of the Council and created an earl, 20; his friendship with and high opinion of his daughter's stepson, 21, 26-9, 31; advice to him on entering Parliament, 31-2; complaint from Lord Lieutenant of Ireland, 35; fears for Ireland, 38; illness and death, 53-4, 56

Camden, Lord (Lord Bayham), appointed Lord Lieutenant of Ireland, 68-9; his reliance upon Castlereagh, 95-6; recalls Castlereagh from his regiment to become Acting Chief Secretary of Ireland, 98, 100; resigns Lord Lieutenancy of Ireland, 105; succeeded at War Office by Castlereagh and becomes President of the Council, 165; connivance in plot against Castlereagh, 211, 214-16; reconciliation with Castlereagh, 229-30; letter to Charles Stewart on Castlereagh's death, 365

Canning, George, Under-Secretary at Foreign Office, 73; his love of intrigue, 94-5; enthusiasm for union with Ireland, 124; comment on Pitt's Peace overtures, 133; his craving for office,

375

Canning, George—*contd.*

152-3; his jealousy and unpopularity, 166-7; tribute to Pitt, 172; as Foreign Minister, 178; relations with America, 180-1, 217; disagreement with Castlereagh, 182; antagonism to Sir John Moore, 185, 191; his claims regarding Peninsular War, 193-4; fear of Castlereagh's rivalry for Premiership, 195-6; intrigues behind Castlereagh's back, 201; desire to direct Peninsular campaign, 202; calls for Castlereagh's removal from office, 209; efforts to obtain Premiership, 210; Castlereagh learns of his intrigues, 211; duel with Castlereagh, 212-14; loss of friends through quarrels and intrigues, 219-21; readiness to join Cabinet under Perceval, 227-8; prepared to serve under Lord Wellesley, 243; reconciled with Castlereagh but unwilling to serve under him, 245-6; approval of Castlereagh's Peace Treaty, 286; supports Castlereagh on his Irish Administration, 322; his defence of the Six Acts, 327-8

Carlisle, Lord, 227

Caroline, Princess, 232-3, 237, 287, 289, 323-5, 328, 333-5, 339-40

" Castlebar Races," 109

Castlereagh, Lady, 55-6, 103, 127, 130, 176-7, 223-4, 240-1, 262-4, 277, 280-3, 293, 310-11, 326, 329, 340-1, 347, 360-1

Castlereagh, Lord: character and appearance, 11; veneration for his mother, 14; his birth, 15; his mother's death, 15; his education, 18-19; musical abilities, 21; escapes from drowning, 21, 167; described by Lord Hertford as a prodigy, 22; his affection for Lady Elizabeth Pratt, 22-5, 27; at Cambridge University, 23; holiday in

Castlereagh, Lord—*contd.*

Ireland, 25; duel with Lord Charles Fitzgerald, 25; indicision about a career, 26; Lord Camden's appreciation of his talents, 28; his passion for Mrs. Jordan, 28; elected to Irish Parliament as member for County Down, 29-30; seeks Lord Camden's advice, 31; his praise of Pitt in maiden speech, 32; ghostly experience in Irish country house, 32-3; his affaire with Nelly Stoal, 34; concern at conditions in Ireland, 35; opposed to England's government of his country, 35; Lord Lieutenant's complaint against him, 36; his conviction of the wisdom of unity with England, 36; visit to Paris and a call on Madame de Stael, 37; received by French King and Queen, 38; supports Government on disbandment of Irish volunteers, 48; supports Irish Militia Bill and applies for a commission, 49; his views on the war with France, 52-3; engagement to Lady Amelia Hobart, 56; joins English Parliament as member for a Cornish constituency, 57; marriage to Lady Amelia Hobart, 62; takes charge of his regimental band in Ireland, 63; recalled to England by Pitt, 64-7; letters to his wife, 65-6, 80, 84, 92-3, 130-2, 269, 277-8, 343; supports Government and resigns from Whig party, 69; maiden speech in House of Commons, 70; elected member for Orford, 72; investigates treasonable activities in Northern Ireland, 74; his " political delinquency" and growing unpopularity in Ireland, 75; task of rounding up traitors, 75-80; appointed Keeper of the King's Signet, 87; his part in suppressing Irish rebellion, 89; acquiesence in methods of suppressing

Index

Shelley, Percy Bysshe, 13
Sheridan, Richard Brinsley, 44, 218
Sidmouth, Lord, *see* Addington, Henry
Sinclair, Rev. William, 80
Sirr, Major, 102, 155
Smith, Sydney, 173
Soult, 190-1, 202
Spain, relations with England, 183-5
Stael, Madame de, 37
Stapleton, Mr., 185n, 193
Stewart, Alec., 131
Stewart, Alexander (Castlereagh's grand-father), 15, 16, 19
Stewart, Catherine (first wife of Charles Stewart), 240
Stewart, Charles (Castlereagh's half-brother), 53, 195-6, 208, 223-4, 257, 260, 264, 268-9, 275-6, 278, 282-3, 306, 313, 315, 317, 333, 349-52; wounded in action, 62; accompanies Sir Ralph Abercromby on expedition to Holland, 121; with Sir John Moore in Spain, 189; Adjutant-General to Sir Arthur Wellesley, 226; letters to *Morning Chronicle* on Peninsular War, 235-6; death of his wife, 240-1; Britain's representative at Prussian Headquarters, 252; stormy interview with Berna-dotte, 256; created a peer, 286; vanities and indiscretions at Vienna, 292-3; marriage to Frances Anne Vane Tempest, 316; reported chal-lenge to Prince Metternich, 336; letters received by him on Castle-reagh's death, 364-8
Stewart, Fred (Castlereagh's nephew), 240-1
Stewart, Hon. Frances (Castlereagh's stepmother), 16, 17
Stewart, Lady Robert (Castlereagh's mother), 14 15
Stewart, Robert (Castlereagh's father), 14; marriage to Frances Pratt, daughter

Stewart, Robert—*contd.*
of Lord Camden, 16; returned M.P. for County Down, 17; ambitions for peerage, 20; created a baron, 29; mortgages estate to raise funds for son's parliamentary candidature, 30; created first Earl of Londonderry, 74; Mount Stewart invaded by rebels, 93; created a marquess, 286; death, 338
Stewart, Thomas, 241n
Stoal, Nelly, 34, 144
Storrock, Rev. Mr., 19
Strahan, Sir Richard, 199-201, 204, 206, 221
Sussex, Duke of, 289
Swan, Major, 102
Sweden, Relations with England, 181-2

Talleyrand, 38, 133, 248, 278, 284, 295-7, 300-2, 305, 308, 310
Tandy, Napper, 76, 109-10
Teeling, George, 77
Tempest, Frances Anne Vane, 316
Tempest, Sir Harry Vane, 316n
Thiers, 265
Thistlewood, Arthur, 330-1
Tierney, George, 108
Tilsit, Treaty of, 178, 248
Tone, Wolfe, 75, 76, 79, 89, 110
Turkey, 248

United Irishmen, The, 76-5, 89, 91

Vienna Congress, 291 *et seq.*

Walcheren Expedition, 197, 200-1, 203-6, 209, 216-7, 220-1
Wales, Prince of, 42, 174, 218, 228, 236-7, 239, 241, 317; becomes Prince Regent, 229; decides not to change Ministers, 231; his treatment of Princess Caroline, 232-3; impressed by Castlereagh's dignity of character,